THE 1990s SLUMP

CENTRAL ISSUES IN CONTEMPORARY ECONOMIC THEORY AND POLICY

General Editor: **Mario Baldassarri**, *Professor of Economics, University 'La Sapienza', Rome, Italy*

Published titles

Mario Baldassarri (*editor*)
INDUSTRIAL POLICY IN ITALY, 1945-90

Mario Baldassarri (*editor*)
KEYNES AND THE ECONOMIC POLICIES OF THE 1980s

Mario Baldassarri (*editor*)
THE ITALIAN ECONOMY: HEAVEN OR HELL?

Mario Baldassarri and Paolo Annunziato (*editors*)
IS THE ECONOMIC CYCLE STILL ALIVE?: THEORY, EVIDENCE AND POLICIES

Mario Baldassarri, Massimo Di Matteo and Robert Mundell (*editors*)
INTERNATIONAL PROBLEMS OF ECONOMIC INTERDEPENDENCE

Mario Baldassarri, Cesare Imbriani and Dominick Salvatore (*editors*)
THE INTERNATIONAL SYSTEM BETWEEN NEW INTEGRATION AND NEO-PROTECTIONISM

Mario Baldassarri, John McCallum and Robert Mundell (*editors*)
DEBT, DEFICIT AND ECONOMIC PERFORMANCE

Mario Baldassarri, John McCallum and Robert Mundell (*editors*)
GLOBAL DISEQUILIBRIUM IN THE WORLD ECONOMY

Mario Baldassarri and Robert Mundell (*editors*)
BUILDING THE NEW EUROPE
Volume 1: The Single Market and Monetary Unification
Volume 2: Eastern Europe's Transition to a Market Economy

Mario Baldassarri, Luigi Paganetto and Edmund S. Phelps (*editors*)
EQUITY, EFFICIENCY AND GROWTH: THE FUTURE OF THE WELFARE STATE

Mario Baldassarri, Luigi Paganetto and Edmund S. Phelps (*editors*)
INTERNATIONAL ECONOMIC INTERDEPENDENCE, PATTERNS OF TRADE BALANCES AND ECONOMIC POLICY COORDINATION

Mario Baldassarri, Luigi Paganetto and Edmund S. Phelps (*editors*)
PRIVATIZATION PROCESSES IN EASTERN EUROPE: THEORETICAL FOUNDATIONS AND EMPIRICAL RESULTS

Mario Baldassarri, Luigi Paganetto and Edmund S. Phelps (*editors*)
THE 1990s SLUMP: CAUSES AND CURES

Mario Baldassarri, Luigi Paganetto and Edmund S. Phelps (*editors*)
WORLD SAVING, PROSPERITY AND GROWTH

Mario Baldassarri, Luigi Paganetto and Edmund S. Phelps (*editors*)
INTERNATIONAL DIFFERENCES IN GROWTH RATES: Market Globalization and Economic Areas

Mario Baldassarri and Paolo Roberti (*editors*)
FISCAL PROBLEMS IN THE SINGLE-MARKET EUROPE

The 1990s Slump

Causes and Cures

Edited by

Mario Baldassarri
Professor of Economics
University 'La Sapienza', Rome

Luigi Paganetto
Professor of Economics
Dean of the Faculty of Economics and Business Administration
University 'Tor Vergata', Rome

and

Edmund S. Phelps
McVickar Professor of Political Economy
Columbia University
New York

in association with
Rivista di Politica Economica, SIPI, Rome
and
CEIS, University 'Tor Vergata', Rome

First published in Great Britain 1996 by
MACMILLAN PRESS LTD
Houndmills, Basingstoke, Hampshire RG21 6XS
and London
Companies and representatives
throughout the world

A catalogue record for this book is available
from the British Library.

ISBN 0–333–66193–1

First published in the United States of America 1996 by
ST. MARTIN'S PRESS, INC.,
Scholarly and Reference Division,
175 Fifth Avenue,
New York, N.Y. 10010

ISBN 0–312–16012–7

Library of Congress Cataloging-in-Publication Data
The 1990s slump : causes and cures / edited by Mario Baldassarri,
Luigi Paganetto, Edmund S. Phelps.
p. cm. — (Central issues in contemporary economic theory and
policy)
Includes bibliographical references and index.
ISBN 0–312–16012–7 (cloth)
1. Economic history—1990– 2. Business cycles. I. Baldassarri,
Mario, 1946– . II. Paganetto, Luigi. III. Phelps, Edmund S.
IV. Series.
HC59.15.A13 1996
330.9'049—dc20 95–53120
CIP

10 9 8 7 6 5 4 3 2 1
05 04 03 02 01 00 99 98 97 96

Printed in Great Britain by
Ipswich Book Co Ltd, Ipswich, Suffolk

Contents

I - UNDERSTANDING DISPARITIES IN NATIONAL EXPERIENCE

Employment and Unemployment*

John Llewellyn
OECD, Paris

Introduction

In creating the Organisation for Economic Co-operation and Development in 1960 as the successor to the Organisation for European Economic Co-operation, the (then) twenty signatory countries to the OECD convention "established their basic aims as the promoting of policies designed: *a)* to achieve the highest sustainable economic growth and employment and a rising standard of living in Member countries, while maintaining financial stability, and thus to contribute to the development of the world economy; *b)* to contribute to sound economic expansion in member as well as non-member countries in the process of economic development; and *c)* to contribute to the expansion of world trade on a multilateral, non-discriminatory basis in accordance with international obligations"[1].

By and large OECD economies have been uncommonly successful in fulfilling these economic ambitions. Output, productivity, and thereby living standards have grown unprecedentedly. But the system has not, at least since the mid-1970s, been successful in maintaining sufficiently rapid employment growth to prevent a steep rise in unemployment.

Over the last three years OECD unemployment has exceeded its

---

* *Source, Employment/Unemployment Study, Interim Report by the Secretary-General,* Paris, OECD, 1993.

[1] Article 1 of the Convention of the OECD, December 1960.

1983 record level of over 30 million, and is projected to reach nearly 36 million by the end of the year. These figures are alarming, yet do not fully reflect the extent of labour market slack and idle or ineffectively used resources. Many workers have withdrawn from the labour market because they regard further job search as futile and/or because they have been encouraged to do so by generous income support, such as early retirement and disability shemes. There is also considerable involuntary part-time work, and many instances of low-wage jobs being held by workers who are overqualified for them.

This situation dates hasically from the surge in inflation in the early 1970s, including the sharp increase in oil prices in 1973-1974, which marked the end of a long period of low unemployment in the OECD area (Graph 1). Unemployment thereafter rose, and was still rather high when, in 1979-1980, oil prices surged again. By 1983, the unemployment rate had increased to a post-war peak of about 8.5%. It then fell during the subsequent recovery but, at just over 6% in 1990, the OECD-area figure was still almost twice that of the 1960s and early 1970s. Thus the job losses resulting from the most recent recession have been superimposed on an already-high starting level.

There have been some important exceptions to this general picture, however. Japan and, until recently, the EFTA countries have experienced very low rates of unemployment. These differences are striking, indicating that over the past two decades at least, labour market adjustments proved much more effective in some countries than in others in coping with major shocks and other sources of structural change.

A modest improvement in employment growth in the second part of the 1980s was followed by a new and severe deterioration of the employment performance of Member countries, and this is giving rise to concern for two principal reasons. First, the problem is serious in its own right, because it brings with it individual hardship, economic loss and threat to the social and political fabric. Second, it increasingly risks provoking precipitate and counter-productive policy action, e.g.: *a)* hasty and possibly ill-conceived macro-economic expansion; *b)* inappropriate reversal of earlier labour market reforms to facilitate structural adjustment; and *c)* further resort to open or (more likely) disguised trade protectionism.

GRAPH 1

UNEMPLOYMENT RATES IN OECD REGIONS, 1960-1994
(% - OECD projections in shaded area)

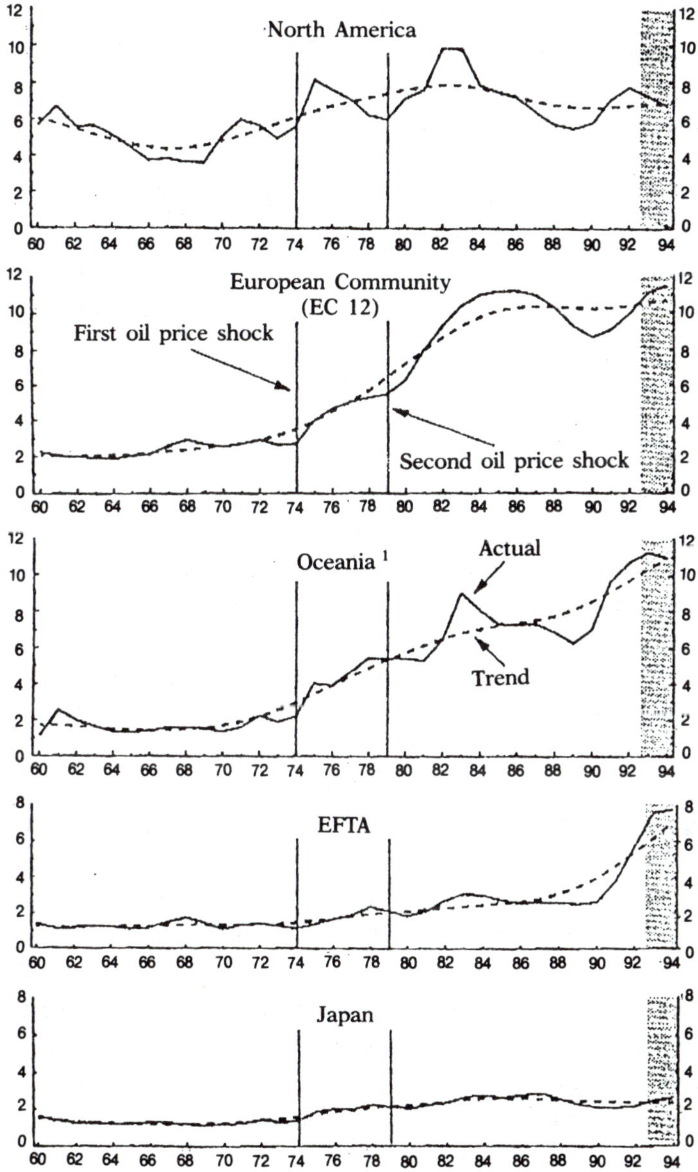

[1] For all charts, Oceania refers to Australia and New Zealand.
Source, OECD.

1. - Employment and Unemployment: Key Facts

1.1 *Labour Market Performance Over the Past Three Decades*

The years following the 1973-1974 surge in inflation saw both nominal and real wage inflation in most countries remaining high. Wage shares increased, contributing importantly to the sharp rise in unemployment. But the 1979-1980 surge in oil prices was fairly generally followed — in an environment of tight macroeconomic policies to contain inflation — by considerable wage moderation, with price inflation abating over the 1980s to rates not seen since the 1960s. Wage shares generally fell back to, or even below, their early 1970s levels. However, the ensuing improvement of the profit situation did not spur a markedly better investment climate and sufficient job growth to reduce unemployment significantly.

Despite the decline in wage shares over the 1980s, job growth picked up only modestly in the European Community, compared with much more rapid growth elsewhere (Graph 2). Thus recent years have seen a continuation of the trend of the previous three decades: rapid employment growth but slow productivity growth in North America and Oceania; the opposite in the European Community. In Japan and the EFTA countries, employment also rose steadily, albeit at a somewhat slower pace than in North America and Oceania.

Job growth in the United States and in Japan has taken place largely in the private sector. Employment growth in the European Community and the EFTA countries since the early 1970s, however, has mainly been in the non-commercial public sector (Graph 3). Indeed, up to the mid-1980s, more than all of the growth in total employment in the European Community took place in the non-commercial public sector. More recently, however, the pace of public sector job growth has slowed considerably, with some pick-up of private sector employment, most notably in Germany, the Netherlands and the United Kingdom. Oceania has seen an actual contraction of public employment from the late 1980s.

The share of part-time employment in total employment rose in most countries over the 1980s, particularly in Australia, Belgium, Canada, France and the United Kingdom. In France and Spain,

GRAPH 2

EMPLOYMENT GROWTH IN OECD REGIONS, 1960-1994
(index 1960 = 100)
(OECD projections in shaded area)

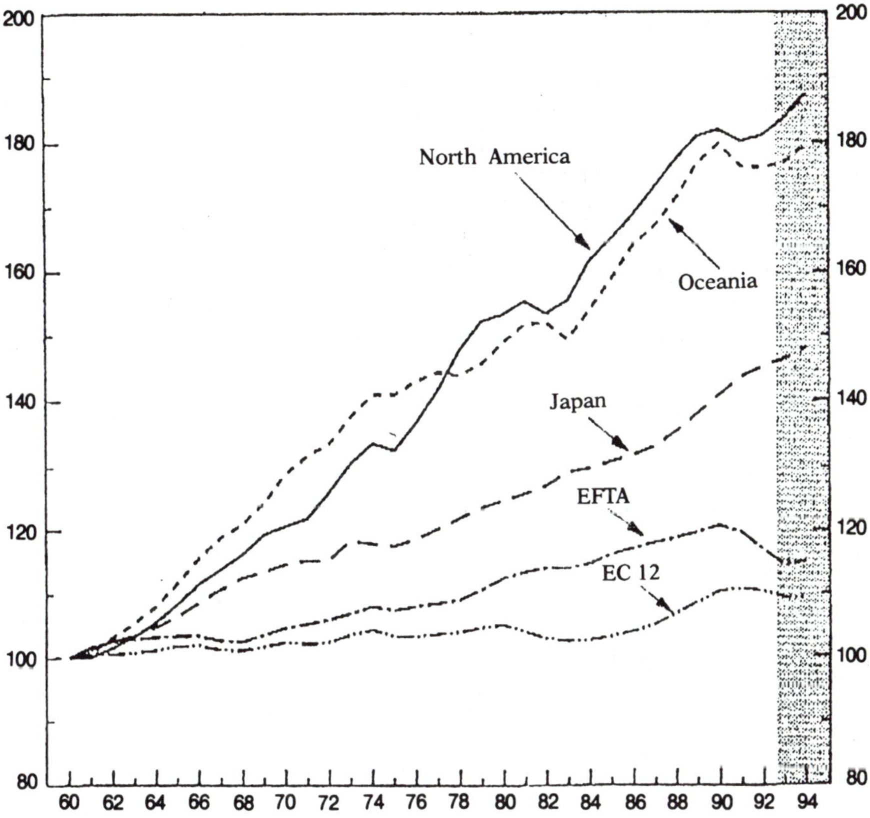

Source, OECD.

employment under temporary contracts increased significantly following changes in legislation. Women, in the services sector, have accounted for much of the general rise in part-time or temporary employment.

A long-term shift in the composition of employment, from manufacturing to services, has occurred in all OECD countries. By the end of the 1980s only 1 worker in 5 was employed in manufacturing, compared with 1 in 4 in 1960; and almost as many workers are now

GRAPH 3

CUMULATIVE EMPLOYMENT GROWTH IN THE PUBLIC AND PRIVATE SECTORS
(change in thousands since 1973)

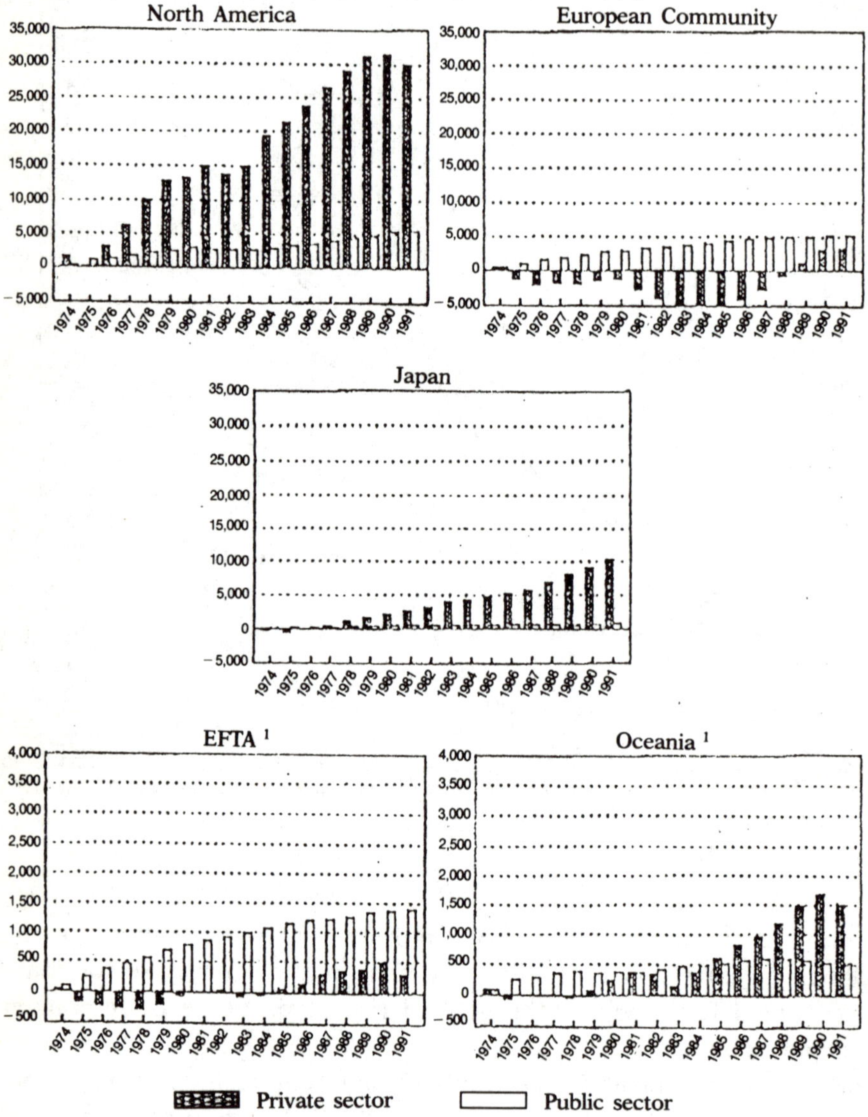

[1] The scale for EFTA and Oceania is higher than that for North America, the European Community and Japan by a factor of 10.

Source, OECD.

employed in wholesale and retail trade as in manufacturing. Within services, the fastest growth has occurred in finance, insurance and business services, and in community and personal services. At the same time, however, *sectoral employment shifts* during the 1980s were in general no more rapid than in previous decades.

While these sectoral employment shifts during the 1980s were in general no more rapid than in previous decades, they were accompained by a widening of wage differentials between high- and low-paid workers in a number of countries — Australia, Canada, Japan, Sweden and the United Kingdom — although all groups in these countries experienced increasing real wages. In the United States, however, where differentials increased particularly markedly, real hourly wages of low-skilled young men actually fell — by around 20% over the past ten years. Differentials have increased modestly in France and the Netherlands, while in Italy and Germany since the mid-1980s they have been stable or have declined.

Typically, although with some variation from country to country, around 10% of all jobs have disappeared each year, in establishments that contract or go out of business, while a broadly similar number of new jobs have traditionally been created, whether through the expansion of existing establishments or the birth of new ones. In the United States, more job creation and more job destruction is accounted for by firms being born or dying than by existing firms expanding or contracting (Graph 4). The reverse would appear to be the case for Canada, Germany, and Italy. The United Kingdom is in an intermediate position, with more job creation coming from expansion of existing firms than from births of new firms, and more job destruction coming from the death of firms than from contractions[2].

Participation rates in the labour force have generally been rising for women and falling for men. In Australia, the rise in women's participation rates was particularly rapid over the 1980s, and hence notwithstanding substantial employment growth, unemployment rates declined only relatively slowly. However, women's activity rates in a number of EC countries — Ireland, Italy and Spain — are still

[2] These country differences in the composition of job creation and job losses need to be interpreted with caution given (unavoidable) differences in methods used to estimate job flows.

Graph 4

JOB CREATION AND JOB DESTRUCTION
(percentage contributions to growth in total employment)

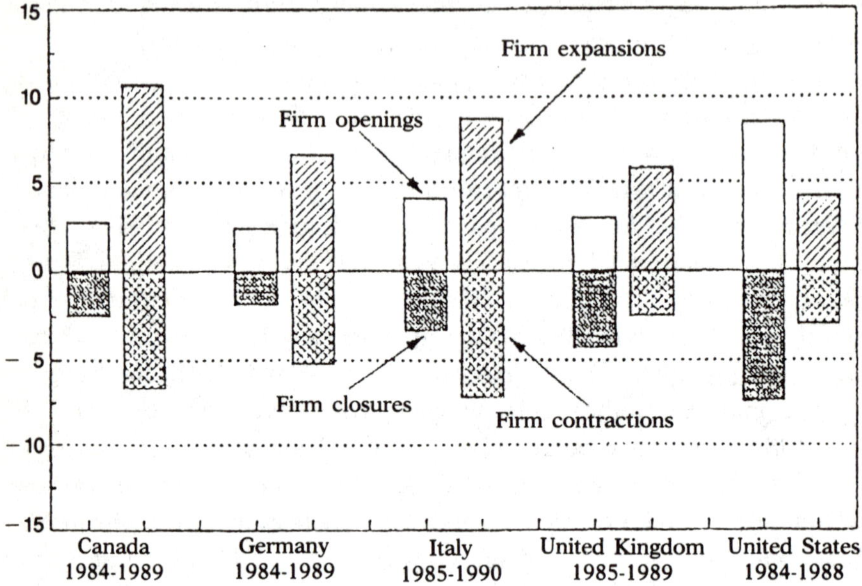

Source,

Canada, *Statistics Canada; Small Business and Special Surveys.*

Germany, Boeri T. - Cramer U., *Employment Growth, Incumbants and entrants; Evidence from Germany*, «International Journal of Industrial Organization», vol. 10, 1992, pp. 545-85.

Italy, National Institute for Social Security (Inps).

United Kingdom, Gallagher C. - Daly M. - Thompson J., *The Growth of UK Companies 1985-1987 and their Contribution to Job Generation*, University of Newcastle, Department of Accounting and Management (mimeo); and Daly M. - Campell M. - Robson G. - Gallagher C., *Job Creation 1987-1989; The Contributions of Small and Large Firms*, «Employment Gazette», November, 1991.

United States, US Small Business Administration, Office of Advocacy: United States Establishment and Enterprise Microdata (Uslem) and United States Establishment Longitudinal Microdata (Uslem) files.

much lower than elsewhere. Participation rates for young men generally declined over the 1980s, partly reflecting higher enrolment and retention rates in schooling. And large numbers of older workers withdrew from the work force, in part induced to do so by early retirement schemes and disability pensions.

The upshot of these diverse trends in employment, labour force, and wages has been an upward drift in unemployment in most OECD countries, strongly suggestive of a growing "structural" component. Structural unemployment — that which is not reversed by subsequent economic upturn — can be estimated only indirectly. But recent Secretariat work using a variety of measures[3] suggests, as shown in Graph 1, that it has risen broadly in line with trend unemployment. The largest trend rise of unemployment has occurred in the European Community, followed by Oceania, with the levels starting to become high by the mid-1970s. In North America, the average unemployment rate has been relatively high, but trend movements have been relatively modest, with large cyclical fluctuations. In Japan, and the EFTA countries unemployment has until recently been generally low. Structural unemployment apparently reached a historical peak in the OECD area in the mid-1980s, the European Community having the highest rate and Japan and the EFTA countries the lowest.

Today's unemployment is characterised by very uneven incidence across labour-force groups, and a high share of long-term unemployment in the total. Young and low-skilled workers have unemployment rates generally well above the national average (Table 1) but in Austria and Germany the rate of youth unemployment is equal to or slightly below the average, a strong apprenticeship system facilitating the transition from school to work. In the European Community, a particular problem for all age groups is long-term unemployment: nearly 50% of all unemployed job seekers in the EC were out of work for 12 months or more in 1991, compared with around 6% in North America. In some countries, particularly Italy, Spain and, more recently, Germany, the geographical distribution of unemployment also is very uneven.

1.2 *The Recent Recession in Historical Perspective*

In terms of overall employment losses, the most recent recession has, to date at least, been less severe for the OECD area as a whole

---

[3] The different estimates of structural unemployment included: the non-accelerating wage rate of unemployment (NAWRU); the unemployment rate associated with a normal vacancy rate (derived from the Beveridge curve); and the full-capacity utilisation rate of unemployment (derived from the Okun curve). Each estimate has its drawbacks as a measure of structural unemployment, but nevertheless all show the same broad pattern for each country, alberit with some small differences in levels.

TABLE 1

THE PROFILE OF CURRENT UNEMPLOYMENT (1992)

	Unemployment rates				Ratio of lower secondary education unem-ployment rate to total rate [2]	Long-term unemployed as a share of total unem-ployment (%)[3]
	total (standardised definition)	total [1]	youth	women		
North America	*7.7*	*7.8*	*14.6*	*7.3*	–	*6.4*
Canada	11.2	11.3	17.8	10.4	1.5	7.2
United States	7.3	7.4	14.2	6.9	2.3	6.3
Japan	2.2	2.2	4.5	2.2	2.7	17.9
Oceania	10.6	10.7	19.5	9.9	–	24.3
Australia	10.7	10.8	19.7	10.0	1.6	24.9
New Zealand	10.3	10.2	18.5	9.5	–	21.3
European Community	*9.4*	*9.5*	*18.4*	*11.5*	–	*45.8*
Belgium	7.8	8.2	17.6	12.2	1.3	61.6
Denmark	–	9.5	11.4	10.8	1.7	31.2
France	10.2	10.0	21.8	12.5	1.3	38.7
Germany	4.8	4.5	4.0	5.1	2.0	45.5
Greece	–	9.2	–	15.4	–	47.0
Ireland	16.1	17.8	27.6	19.4	1.1	60.3
Italy	10.5	10.1	27.9	15.7	0.9	67.1
Luxembourg	–	1.9	3.8	2.8	–	28.3
Netherlands	6.7	6.7	10.6	8.7	1.0	43.0
Portugal	4.1	4.8	10.3	6.5	1.7	38.3
Spain	18.1	18.0	32.5	25.5	1.2	49.1
United Kingdom	10.0	10.8	17.0	9.2	1.8	28.1
EFTA	–	*5.5*	*9.3*	*5.0*	–	*12.9*
Austria [4]	–	3.6	3.6[5]	3.8	–	15.2
Finland	13.0	13.1	23.5	10.7	1.4	9.1
Norway	5.9	5.9	13.9	5.2	1.1	20.6
Sweden	4.8	4.8	10.8	3.8	1.4	4.4
Switzerland [6]	–	2.7	4.7	3.4	–	19.8
Turkey [7]	–	7.8	15.2	7.2	1.5	39.2

[1] Comparable unemployment rates for the EC countries and national estimates for the other countries.

[2] For adults aged 25-64. Data refer to 1989 for all countries; except Japan, 1987, Denmark, 1988, the Netherlands, 1990 and Turkey, April 1990.

[3] Long-term unemployed refers to all persons unemployed in 1991 for 12 months or more.

[4] Unemployment rates refer to the first half of 1992.

[5] Estimated.

[6] All data refer to the second quarter of 1992.

[7] Unemployment rates refer to October 1992.

Source, OECD, *Employment Outlook 1992*; OECD, *Education at a Glance*; OECD, *Labour Force Statistics*; OECD, *Quarterly Labour Force Statistics*; EUROSTAT, *Labour Force Survey 1991*; EUROSTAT, *Unemployment*; AUSTRIAN MICROCENSUS; SWISS, *Labour Force Survey* and TURKISH, *Household Labour Force Survey Results.*

than were the two preceding ones. But it has been more protracted (Graph 5). Given, however, that unemployment had been reduced only modestly in many countries during the growth period of the second half of the 1980s, these job losses have been sufficient to take OECD unemployment to record levels. Further, in some countries — Australia, Finland, Sweden and the United Kingdom — employment losses have been larger than in earlier recessions.

In previous recessions, job losses in the services sector were typically relatively limited. But in the recent recession a number of countries experienced an unprecedented shake-out of white-collar employment, notably in finance, insurance and business services. Manufacturing and construction generally continued to bear the brunt, however, with particularly large employment losses (over 25%) occurring in Finland and Sweden in chemicals, non-metallic mineral products, textiles, and wood and wood products.

Regional differences in unemployment rates typically increase during economic downturns; yet in a number of countries during the recent recession these differentials have either narrowed or at least have not risen as much as previously. In part this may reflect greater job losses in some service sectors, such as finance and business services, in combination with a higher concentration of these sectors in regions which previously had below-average unemployment. In the United Kingdom, in particular, there has been a striking compression of regional differences in unemployment rates.

1.3 *The Seriousness of the Present Situation*

There are thus a number of disturbing, perhaps alarming, aspects of the current situation:

a) in EFTA and in the European Community until relatively recently almost no job growth occurred in the private sector, virtually all taking place in the non-commercial public sector. So far, significant reversal of this trend has been seen only in (the western part of) Germany, the Netherlands and the United Kingdom;

b) the present recession-induced increase in unemployment comes on top of already-high inherited structural unemployment. In

GRAPH 5

CYCLICAL BEHAVIOUR OF EMPLOYMENT IN OECD REGIONS: THE LAST THREE DOWNTURNS

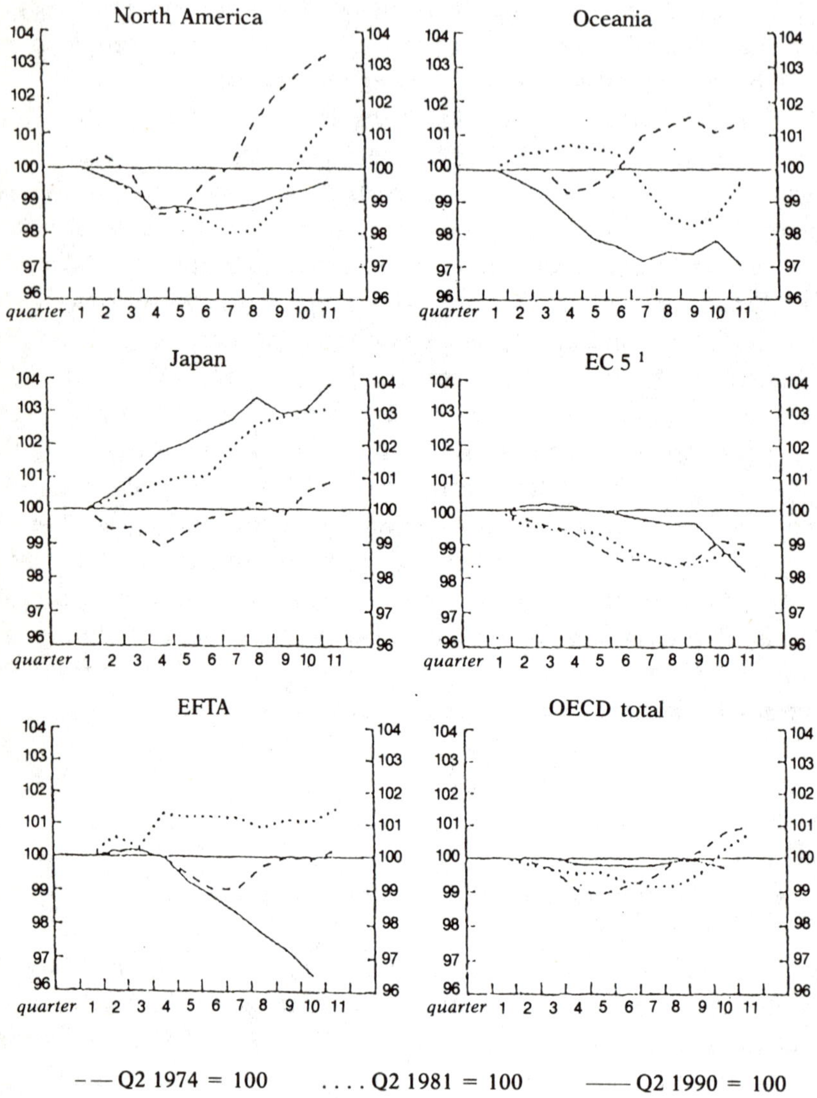

---

[1] France, Germany, Italy, Spain and United Kingdom.
Source, OECD, *Quarterly labour force statistics.*

the European Community, unemployment appears to be "ratcheting up" from each cyclical trough to the next. As a result, almost half of the unemployed have been out of work for 12 months or more;

c) in the United States unemployment has been more cyclical. Longer-term structural problems have nevertheless manifested themselves, both in a secular fall of real wages below a (normatively set) poverty threshold for *low-skilled workers*, and in the withdrawal of significant numbers of prime-age male workers from the labour force;

d) the EFTA countries, which hitherto had been successful in maintaining full employment, are now experiencing drops in employment and rises in unemployment, in some cases dramatically so;

e) during the recent recession job losses for low-skilled workers have occurred not only in manufacturing but also in the service sectors;

f) youth unemployment remains stubbornly high in many countries, notwithstanding significant youth programmes and the receding effects of the baby boom;

g) last, this poor labour market situation is rendering the effective integration of legally admitted immigrants more difficult, adding to social tensions.

2. - Towards a Strategy for Boosting Employment and Reducing Unemployment

2.1 *Overview*

Achieving a sound understanding of the present situation is a complicated task. Much of the development of employment and unemployment has been conditioned by a complex interaction between economic forces, both macro and micro, on the one hand and customs, institutions, laws and policies on the other. This is reflected in the wide diversity of experience, both across countries and over time. Deriving satisfactory policy responses is equally complex.

Analysis of a series of country experiences, however, suggests that a range of conditions, some macroeconomic, others structural, all have to be at least broadly met if employment and hence unemployment performance is to be reasonably satisfactory. Taken together these could contribute to a strategy for boosting employment and reducing unemployment, without exacerbating inflation performance - one that OECD governments could consider, endorse, begin to implement or, in some instances, implement more effectively. Such a strategy would focus on: 1) macroeconomic policy, and in particular its role in providing a stable framework for private sector decision making; 2) development and diffusion of technological change, as the principal source of the new skill-intensive jobs; 3) competition, both national and international, as a main mechanism impelling the development, introduction and diffusion of new technologies; 4) wage and price flexibility as a means of widening job opportunities; 5) human resource development, as an important way to strengthen the growth of economic potential; and to equip people to fill high-productivity, high-wage jobs; 6) active labour market policies to facilitate the adjustment process; 7) the encouragement of enterprise, in particular the creation of new firms or the transformation of existing ones, so as to benefit from new technological opportunities and provide jobs for those displaced from out-dated activities; 8) solidarity and policy coherence, so as to reconcile efficiency and equity in the adjustment process.

Before considering each of these elements in turn, four general points are made.

First, the various elements outlined above are not wateright compartments. Indeed, there are several sorts of synergy among them that need to be exploited for such a strategy to be successful. The most obvious is between macroeconomic and structural policies. Macroeconomic policy to support a desired level of aggregate demand for output and employment for a sustained period has a better chance of succeeding if appropriate micro policies are in place to ease structural rigidities. Similarly the effectiveness of structural policies will he enhanced if the macroeconomic conditions permit. *The price of not exploiting this virtuous relationship is a vicious circle.* Once structural adjustment, and in particular labour market adjustment, slows down for whatever reason, rising unemployment usually involves rising long-term unemployment; and the deterioration of human capital which this entails in turn makes adjustment more difficult.

A second type of synergy exists between specific labour-market and other structural policies. The effects from any *single* cause or policy action often tend to be small. But substantial results may flow over time from the cumulation of a range of actions, tailored appropriately for each individual country.

Third, correcting for the effects of past policy mistakes will in some cases require careful examination to avoid the risk of compounding them. For example, some of the current problems of unemployment reflect macroeconomic policy settings that, through errors of judgement, had allowed substantial disequilibria or imbalances to build up. Striking examples are rising inflation through the 1970s; unsustainable public debt positions in the second half of the 1970s and the 1980s; and unsustainable private debt positions more recently. However, the adverse effects of this lack of macroeconomic rigour in the past cannot be reversed by a unduly easy setting of macroeconomic policies in the future. Likewise, insufficient structural reforms, which opened the door to a build-up of rigidities and poor employment performances in many countries, cannot be offset by introducing new rigidities.

Finally it is imperative in any strategy for boosting employment to ensure that policy changes are addressed to basic causes rather than to symptoms. In part, this involves ensuring that any policy action to affect employment in the short term should not at the same time prejudice the achievement of higher employment in the medium to longer term, for example through jeopardizing inflation performance or international competitiveness.

2.2 *Broad Lines for Macroeconomic Policy*

Macroeconomic policy has a key strategic role over the medium to longer term in providing a healthy, stable, and predictable economic environment. This requirement always has a range of conjunctural and country-specific dimensions: for the period ahead these are to have been considered, in the customary way, by the

Economic Policy Committee just prior to the meeting of the Council at Ministerial level. A summary of the Committee's deliberations will be presented to the Ministers by the Chairman.

A fully satisfactory macroeconomic environment would differ from the present situation in a number of key respects: 1) there would be less pre-emption of private-sector saving by public sector deficits; 2) long-term real interest rates, particularly but not only in Europe, would be lower; 3) consumer and business confidence would be higher; 4) investment, particularly private-sector investment, would be stronger; and 5) low inflation would be more widespread, and more firmly established.

It is probably not possible to account fully for the unsatisfactory configuration of macroeconomic conditions in the present situation. And in seeking a better configuration it would be unhelpful to attempt to analyse — let alone try to target through policy — the various components separately: they are highly inter-related. Rather what has to be sought is the right palce to "break in". For policy, probably the only place to "break in" to quantitatively important effect is via a major reduction in structural budget deficits.

If governments were to undertake, credibly, to reduce their longer-term claims on national savings, this would exert downward pressure on long-term interest rates. With the public sector reducing its claims on future output, central banks would thereby be better able to reduce short rates without exacerbating the risk of inflation. Lower interest rates, short and long, would create conditions favourable to higher consumption and investment. Faster growth and stronger investment would increase both job creation and the momentum of structural adjustment.

In parallel with the process of budget consolidation, it would be appropriate to seek to improve, as quickly as possible, the efficiency and effectiveness — i.e. the quality — of public sector spending and taxation. Carrying out the necessary reviews of the main activities of the public sector and implementing desirable changes in the quality of budgests will be a slow task, but the rewards of improving the efficiency of resource use within the public sector are potentially great, given the large size it has reached in OECD countries. Further work is to be undertaken in this area by the Secretariat.

2.3 *Forces for Change*

2.3.1 Technological Progress, Competition and Trade

History has demonstrated amply the extent to which over the long term the growth of output, living standards and, importantly, employment, has depend on the ability continually to develop, absorb, and make effective use of technology. In market economies, the main spur to the introduction and diffusion of technology is competition; and a major part of overall competitive pressure is transmitted through international trade.

2.3.1.1 Technological Change

Technological and organisational changes comes about in essentially two ways: through the development and diffusion of new end products, and through the introduction and diffusion of new production processes. The introduction of new products made possible by technological advances or new ideas leads directly to new employment in these areas. The introduction of new production processes meanwhile can render particular skills obsolete and destroy existing jobs; but it increases productivity in the new jobs and thereby allows real wages to rise.

Over the last decade or two, virtually all sectors of the economy, including services, have been pervaded by new technologies, particularly the new information technologies. These are generating whole new ranges of products; and are leading to the development of many new production processes. So far, the effects on productivity and on employment have not been as great as was expected. However, the process may still be in its relatively early stages. The relative price of the core element of the technology, microelectronics, continues to fall very fast. Evidence is beginning to mount that widespread technological change, even in the most flexible of economies, often requires radically new perceptions and attitudes, and fundamental changes in the processes of design, of production, and of work organisation. On this argument, many of the consequences of the new information technologies are yet to be seen — consequences for the creation of new jobs, the destruction of old ones, and for the general capacity to adjust.

2.3.1.2 Competition in Product Markets

In this general market economy schema, open and efficient product markets provide the underpinning for high employment and high incomes through two basic mechanisms. First, by spurring innovation, competition also encourages the creation of high-productivity and hence high-wage jobs. Second, by restricting monopolistic tendencies, it leads to lower prices and thereby increases output and employment.

2.3.1.3 International Trade

A key role is played by the international trade regime both in allowing economies to reap the advantages of specialisation and in transmitting the forces of competition and hence of innovation. Enterprises or sectors which lead in innovation and diffusion of products and/or processes tend also to lead in export performance. They typically exhibit relatively fast job and employment growth, and pay high wages. Income generated in these sectors spills over into demand for goods and services and thereby stimulates incomes and job growth throughout the economy. At the same time, shifts in the patterns of trade, reflecting changes in patterns of comparative advantage over time, can also contribute to job displacement. One example of this is the growth in OECD imports of some unskilled labour-intensive manufactures such as clothing, footwear and some electrical goods.

An important emerging feature is the increasing ease with which production locations change. This has been facilitated at the regional level by various regional trade agreements. And it was spurred by the wide-spread liberalisation of financial markets and capital controls in the 1980s, which underpinned a substantial increase in foreign direct investment. Large swings in exchange rates also contributed, through substantial, sustained changes in the relative costs of production across OECD countries. Other factors contributing to changing the location of production include the greatly increased capacity to control operations at long distance that is afforded by modern real-time communication, and information systems and the continuing fall in the relative price of transport and communication.

One consequence has been to bring labour in an increasing number of low-wage countries into direct competition with labour in OECD countriers. The effects to date have fallen most on unskilled labour, which is markedly less expensive in non-OECD countriers. This has put downward pressure both on the wages and the employment of unskilled labour in many OECD countriers. On the other hand it has benefitted OECD consumers, through better and cheaper products; and for other workers, higher OECD exports have led to higher wages and better quality of working life.

This process has been reflected since the mid-1970s in the rapid growth of ownership by OECD-based firms of production facilities for relatively labour-intensive manufacturing activities in low labour-cost regions or developing countries. It has contributed to a rapid growth of manufactured exports from those regions or countries; first to the United States and then also to Europe. Asian NIEs were already outward-oriented in the 1970s and their integration with OECD countries — particularly Japan and Oceania has increased through the working of market forces and the realisation of comparative advantage. Beyond the Asian NIEs, many developing countries have also shifted over the last decade from inward-oriented to export-oriented industrialisation strategies. Within the OECD area, shifts in production have mainly occurred in anticipation of the Single European Market. Looking ahead it is certain that the economic prospects in, and implications of, the Eastern European countries will also depend importantly on their export performance and capacity to attract foreign direct investments. These considerations suggest that the innovative abilities of countries and regions, and especially the competences and learning abilities of their workforces, will become even more important in the future.

2.3.2 Implications for Policy

The rapid technological change and enhanced competition that characterises much of today's world bodes well for output, real wages and employment in industries that successfully embrace new technologies. But technological change also destroys out-of-date, low productivity and low wage jobs. Hence for technology and competition to bode well for society as a whole, all its members must be appropriately equipped to adapt to, and thereby benefit from, structural change. What is called for is two simultaneous policy thrusts: one toward strengthening the forces of competition and trade that lead to the creation of new products, new jobs, and high wages; and at the same time a marked strengthening of the processes of adaptation and the ability of all workers to benefit from them.

In neither respect has performance been fully satisfactory in recent years. On the first aspect the OECD *Technology/Economy Programme (TEP)* concluded that national science and technology programmes should be better designed so that the risk of creating international friction is minimised and that the opportunities for international co-operation in major science and technology areas are fully exploited. In the trade area significant liberalising steps have been taken in the context of regional trading arrangements, but these moves probably do not counterbalance the continued deterioration in the multilateral trading system. Recent increases in recourse to trade protection, almost always applied on a basis inconsistent with the letter and spirit of the *GATT* and in a manner that imposes large economic costs, have been well rehearsed in many fora, as has the need to check and reverse these trends.

Most importantly, perhaps, adjustment policies have not proved adequate to their task over the last decade or more, leading to the build up of structural unemployment. Policies to assist structural adjustment are considered in the next section.

2.4 *Adjusting to and Benefiting from Structural Change*

There are a number of areas where adjustment mechanisms can be improved and where new approaches need to be explored. Not all are in the labour market area, and not all concern workers. Price adjustment in product and other factor markets, for instance, is also important, as are management styles and hierarchical structures within enterprises, professional cartels or restrictions on enterprise creation, tax structures, and discrimination against certain categories of workers. This interim report explores only some areas, but perhaps the most important ones, where in many countries progress seems both necessary and possible. It is important to view these policies and institutional reforms as "investments in adaptive capacity" and to recognise their instrumental role in coping with and benefiting from the future pressures of structural change.

2.4.1 Wage Structures

Wage structures in some countries have moved out of line with the structure of employment opportunities: employers are unable to offer some types of jobs and remain profitable. In periods of high employment, low-productivity, low-wage jobs tend to become obsolete as part of the process of economic progress. But in periods of chronic unemployment this may be a sign of imbalance. Those most likely to be hit by technological change, shifts in trade and dislocations of production are the least skilled, or those whose skills are too narrow. The natural tendency, in the absence of any countervailing policy, social force, or institution, is for wage differentials to reflect the decreasing demand for unskilled labour, and the increasing demand for skilled labour. Such a development — as has happened in the United States — slows the process of job loss for unskilled workers. But this achieved at the risk of creating a larger class of the "working poor" and, at the limit, of significant withdrawal from the labour force.

In an attempt to avoid the creation of a significant and possibly increasing number of low wage jobs, the policy response in a number of countries, especially in Europe, has been to seek to disallow the problem by setting a mininum wage — whether by law or through collective bargaining — which is relatively close to the average wage and indexed over time to prices and/or earnings. But truncating the wage scale at a level above that consistent with the productivity of unskilled workers serves only to manifest the problem in a different form: instead of being working poor, unskilled workers are unemployed.

A third policy response that has been adopted in a number of economies, particularly in Nordic countries, has been to seek to compress wage differentials, on the argument that this tends to squeeze out inefficient firms more rapidly and thereby improve productivity performance and employment growth over the longer term. However under present circumstances the adjustment pressures stemming from technological change and international competition are already considerable, so that there does not seem any strong reason at present to seek to put further pressure on jobs through this mechanism.

An effective general approach, therefore, starts from the recognition that low-productivity jobs warrant the payment of only a low wage. Accordingly it sees the route to better remunerated employment as being achieved through higher-productivity jobs filled by workers with higher skills. Low-wage jobs may perform a useful role in some respects, for example in introducing young people to work. They are also essential for the successful integration of many immigrant workers and their families who need a "port of entry" to the labour market. But the overall strategy must be that people not become trapped in them, and that low-paid jobs should not become widespread.

Accordingly a balanced policy would allow greater wage flexibility than has characterised behaviour in some countries, whether in respect of industries, occupations, qualifications, or regions; yet buttress this with a comprehensive policy which would include education, the school-to-work transition, training, and retraining.

Quite different bargaining regimes are capable of producing reasonably satisfactory results on wage outcomes; there is no one regime that is suited to the needs and circumstances of all countries. Centralised and decentralised regimes both have the potential to deliver satisfactory wage flexibility and responsiveness, through the forces of co-ordination in the former case, and competition in the latter. On the other hand, difficulties may arise in sytems with inadequate degrees of co-ordination or competition, in the form, for example, of wage relativities which adjust very slowly, or bargaining geared just to the interests of employed "insiders" and employers. It is also possible that the desirable form of bargaining regime will differ across sectors within the economy, depending in part on the degree of competitive pressure, from internal and external sources, faced by these sectors.

The next section outlines a range of policies to support the capacity of people to fill high-productivity, high-wage jobs.

2.4.2 Investment in Human Capital

Comprehensive human resource development policies will have to play a major part in any strategy to boost employment and reduce unemployment. Only a well trained and highly adaptable labour force can provide the capacity to adjust to structural change and seize new employment opportunities created by technological progress. Achieving this will in many cases entail a re-examination, perhaps radical, of the economic treatment of human resources and education.

Sound initial education is the essential base for acquiring higher order skills. Problems in literacy and numeracy, and the absence of qualifications, are condemning too many young adults to unemployment and poor career prospects. Policies must aim at raising the level of student performance, eliminating early school leaving, and improving the performance of under-achievers. Sustained reforms are needed in teaching, curriculum, and "education technologies" to cater for the full spectrum of learning needs of the school-age population.

Next, the link between academic and vocational studies needs to be strengthened further. Academic studies need to be oriented towards work and working life; some have started embracing basic "tool skills" of advanced technologies that pervade the workplace and everyday life. Greater emphasis must in turn be given to acquiring general skills and competences to supplement more specific vocational qualifications. This will provide the essential basis for further learning on the job, and during adult life.

The flow of information and expertise between schools and work, and the exchange of information and ideas, also needs to be improved. In some countries this articulation between schools and the world of work is achieved particularly successfully through apprenticeship schemes. In others, partnerships and other forms of linkage between schools and employers are showing promise, but need to be developed and strengthened further.

As post-secondary education continues to develop as a mass phenomenon, it is essential to address the increasing demand for mid-level qualifications. This involves not only the extension of past arrangements but, more importantly, the continuing consolidation of universities with the broad range of vocational, technical, and professional education and training institutions that follow secondary education. This trend will be encouraged by establishing financing and incentive structures in tertiary education that reward institutions for ensuring better "occupational relevance", for workers and employers alike.

The extent to which enterprises provide further training varies widely by enterprise and by country. In some firms the training process seems to have been highly successful; in others the hoped-for productivity gains are not appearing. Reasons include: insufficient changes in work organisation; and shortcomings in human resource management strategies. These problems derive in part from the limited capacity of education and training institutions to provide appropriate and cost-effective training and in part because these institutions often have gaps in the expertise necessary to adapt training precisely to work requirements, or to advise more generally on how to improve productivity of more qualified workers. These problems affect particularly smaller enterprises.

Adult training outside the world of work is generally poorly developed, except for cetain programmes for the unemployed. Where training is provided, it rarely benefits from the systematic consulation and decision making arrangements or joint action of the kind found in successful youth apprenticeship systems. Such arrangements would ensure that such publicly-provided training is well adapted to the needs of industry.

Part of the overall problem of insufficient or inadequate provision of skills comes from unhelpful economic incentive structures. The bulk of further training will in general have to be paid for by employers and employees; but to encourage this it is necessary to improve their likelihood of reaping at least some of the benefits. To achieve this a number of actions are necessary: the establishment of frameworks for the assessment and recognition of acquired qualifications; and the creation of mechanisms for ensuring that the economic value of qualifications and the investment nature of training are reflected in wages and company accounts, so that the resulting accrual of qualifications is reflected better as assets for enterprises and possibly individuals.

2.4.3 Active Labour Market Policies

Education and enterprise training to equip the labour force with the skills and competences that will enable it to benefit from structural change, while highly necessary, is, however, not sufficient: in many areas there is a need also for a range of active labour market policies (ALMPs) to facilitate the adjustment process in various ways. The main function of ALMPs is to shorten the time spent on job search and thereby the length of unemployment spells and vacancy duration, while also making job matches more efficient. The principal policy instruments are: training and retraining programmes to raise the employability of the unemployed; improving information flows between job seekers and employers; and assisting job seekers and employers through counselling, job search techniques, screening and placement services. Job creation measures (either through subsidies to the private sector or in the public sector) are intended to create demand for categories of workers in strong excess supply or for which prolonged idleness appears particularly harmful (e.g. long-term unemployed youth).

A corner-stone of successful ALMPs is an effective Public Employment Service (PES). The task of the PES is greatly facilitated by computer information systems, allowing for as full a dissemination as possible of information about job seekers, vacancies, and other services. This information system needs to be combined with the control of benefit entitlements and the allocation of job-seekers to labour-market programmes. To avoid the drift into long-term unemployment, regular contact between benefit claimants and PES officers is needed so that the possibility of placing claimants into jobs or labour market programmes can be carefully assessed.

Although in most OECD countries the PES plays the major role (apart from private advertising and personal contacts) in matching job-seekers to vacancies, appropriately regulated private placement agencies and temporary work agencies can play a useful complementary (and sometimes even dominant) role.

The design and management of ALMPs risk becoming distorted during periods of high and persistent unemployment, especially when they are expected to contribute substantially to the reduction of unemployment. The focus then tends to be on direct job creation, with less emphasis on supply-enhancing programmes. Job creation programmes can suffer from deadweight and displacement effects and artificial work environments, while subsidised jobs risk never becoming self-sustaining. Training programmes may be far removed from the discipline of a full-time work schedule, may put unemployed people into a classroom enviroment which they find hostile, *or teach skills that in fact are not in short supply*. In some cases, they have no measurable impact or later job-finding chances. Such disappointing results have sometimes, unjustly, discredited ALMPs as a whole. It is important therefore to adjust ALMPs to changing economic circumstances and to focus on the longer-term supply enhancing aspects. These were spelt out in the *New Framework for Labour Market Policies* and endorsed by OECD Ministers of Labour in 1992. The main message remains valid: to improve the longer term performance of the labour market it is essential to mobilise and strengthen all dimensions of labour supply i.e. labour force participation, talent and qualifications as well as flexibility and adaptability.

Continual review and evaluation is needed to ensure that public resources are spent in the most cost-effective way, and that the design of these programmes adapts to changing conditions and circumstances. These policies are condiered in detail in the Employment, Labour and Social Affairs Committee, including by comparative country reviews.

2.4.4 Encouraging Enterprise

Education and training policies, together with a range of active labour market policies and flexible wage-setting policies, seek to equip people for employment and to help them find it, but ultimate success depends upon there being a satisfactory number of jobs available. In part some of these jobs will result from the expansion of existing enterprises; but today many large firms are in fact downsizing under competitive presure, so that in practice very many of the new jobs will have to come through the creation of new firms and quite probably an increase in self-employment. The factors determining net job creation rates are complex and vary in importance between countries, regions and localities. Macroeconomic conditions are likely to have an important influence on the rate of net enterprise creation, and hence the importance of the "framework-setting" role for macroeconomic policy considered above. A range of microeconomic conditions are also important.

One fundamental prerequisite is the existence of an entrepreneurial culture. There are strong differences between OECD countries in the rate of firm births, as well as deaths, yet there are no obvious reasons why entrepreneurial talent should be so unevenly distributed. Differences in social attitudes and traditions as well as institutional impediments towards risk-taking and entrepreneurship may provide some answers. Recent experience in some member countries suggests that attitudes towards entrepreneurship can be influenced, perhaps significantly, by appropriate public relations strategies of governments and other public and semi-public bodies.

Access to start-up capital and, even more so, to long-term capital during the early expansion period is often very important. Removal of imperfections in capital markets and the development and spreading of well-functioning markets for risk and venture capital are appropriate policy responses. Banks, used to lending against the collateral of fixed assets, will increasingly have to learn how to evaluate the potential of, and how to lend to, knowledge-intensive firms whose principal asset is the intellectual and knowledge base of its (mobile) individuals.

Many non-financial barriers also impinge on new firm creation.

Most countries impose a host of paperwork-intensive regulations both on the setting up and the running of a new company. These regulations constitute fixed costs, whose burden falls disproportionately heavily on smaller companies. The openness of the tertiary education system to business development and the strategic role played by local and regional governments also appear to be important. Thus, it is important for governments to review rules and regulations in a wide range of areas which directly and indirectly affect business organisation, to ensure that small firms are not inadvertently disadvantaged.

2.5 *Solidarity, Equity and Efficiency*

No matter how successful society may be in designing and carrying out the range of policies outlined above, there will always be some people who will be unable to earn a satisfactory income, whether for short periods or longer. All modern societies ensure at least a minimum level of income and social protection. The current and foreseeable pressures of competition and technological progress, outlined above, call for increased efforts of adjustment and flexibility. Social cohesion and a certain degree of solidarity, with the "winners" from structural change accepting an obligation to assist the "losers", will facilitate the process of adjustment. Solidarity, in turn, depends importantly on the effectiveness and cohesion of policies — basically labour market and social policies — which are aimed at achieving prompt but equitable adjustments to change. Without such policy coherence there is a danger of growing income dependency, lack of motivation, decaying skills and, eventually, of tax resistance from those who have to pay for a rising number of people who are perceived as being no longer employable.

Labour market and social policies have often been seen as intrinsically separate areas. Labour market policies have been designed primarily to help integration or re-integration into the labour market, while social policies seek to help those who have insufficient income. But experience in a number of countries shows this to be a false, and even a counterproductive, dichotomy. In practice, many labour market programmes have at least some social component in them. And virtually all social programmes impinge, in one way or another, on the incentive structure of the labour market.

The most effective policies ensure that social provisions and labour market incentives reinforce one another, rather than the reverse. It is particularly important to avoid circumstances in which social policies impart unnecessary rigidities to labour markets, while not in practice achieving their basic objectives sufficiently well to justify the efficiency losses. As a guiding principle, the labour market and social policies which work best are those which jointly enhance and encourage labour force participation and thereby ensure that incomes are sufficient, even though in some cases temporary or permanent subsidies (for example for the handicapped) may be necessary in order to achieve this.

Unemployment benefits are a particular case. Most unemployment benefit systems were originally established on an insurance basis: to provide people and their families with income support while they re-established themselves in the labour market. They were originally inspired by the realisation that vagrancy was not the result of moral failure by individuals, but rather a social state which follows from casualisation and turbulence in the labour market.

However, the growth and persistence of unemployment has meant that in many countries unemployment benefits have become also a means for longer term income support. This is ultimately a destructive development, for it means — indeed in many it requires — that time out of work is wasted. A more positive approach is one which ensures that those out of work for more than a given time are guaranteed the opportunity to engage in activity which re-integrates them into the labour force. Japan, for example, re-titled its scheme «employment insurance» in the 1970s to emphasise this goal, and has built into the scheme a number of features designed to discourage recipients of income support payments from relying on benefit payments for too long.

The bulk of social expenditures — for example those which ensure access to health care, provide additional support for families, and ensure income support in old age — have purposes other than labour market integration, but can nonetheless have labour market impacts. Tax and social transfer systems in many countries often interact so as to create «dependency traps», i.e. situations in which additional work effort leads to little or no increase in net income because incremental gross earnings are largely or fully offset by marginal income taxes and the reduction, or loss, of benefit payments.

Many social expenditures are financed by social security contributions (payroll taxes) paid both by employers and by employees: in the OECD area as a whole, these contributions raise a quarter of all tax revenue. This has given rise to concern that, by taxing the use of labour, these contributions may thereby reduce employment and raise unemployment. The empirical evidence is mixed as to whether or not these taxes raise structural unemployment in the long run, but there is better evidence that they do raise it over the short to medium run. Accordingly it is important to investigate the scope for switching the financing of social expenditures away from payroll taxes to other taxes which may have a less unfavourable impact on employment.

Some policies — particularly some forms of employment protection legislation — seek to ensure that conditions of employment are of a satisfactory standard. Some, such as health and safety provisions and training requirements, can involve an investment in longer term productivity and welfare which has to be balanced against the higher immediate costs involved. Others, such as minimum wages and other provisions which prescribe minimum employment standards, do increase labour costs and will in most circumstances result in a lower employment level than would otherwise be the case. These need to be examined to ascertain whether their distributional goals can be achieved in other ways which minimise negative effects on employment. For example, wage subsidies directed at families with low overall income will be more cost effective than minimum wages in alleviating poverty amongst households with employed members.

These considerations underline the importance of achieving fundamental objectives of equity and social protection with policies that do not, at the same time, have counterproductive effects on the functioning of labour markets.

Following the meeting of Ministers of Social Affairs in December 1992, the Secretariat is proceeding with the development of a set of *New Orientations for Social Policy*. These will seek to set the framework for a more integrated approach to labour-market, social, and education policies, as well as a set of indicators to provide the basis for reviewing social policy developments in OECD countries.

3. - Broad Lines for Action: a Summary

This paper is an interim report, which highlights only some of the work that will be presented in the final report to Ministers next year. It starts from the observation that present-day unemployment is part cyclical, and in larger part structural. The two elements are closely inter-related, because in a world of continual change unemployment which starts off being cyclical soon becomes structural. Dealing with this problem, and preventing its recurrence, requires action in a number of closely interrelated areas, of which to date three seem particularly important:

1) macroeconomic policy always needs to aim at achieving a sound, stable, predictable economic environment. A credible macroeconomic policy framework will strengthen the willingness of economic agents to accept structural change and to exploit new economic opportunities. Conversely, appropriate structural policies will increase the scope and effectiveness of macroeconomic policies in fostering non-inflationary growth of income and employment. Given the economic interdependence of OECD economies there is a compelling need for enhanced co-operation between OECD countries in macroeconomic management;

2) structural policy needs to support the process of adjustment to change and the transition to higher productivity and more skill-intensive economies. In some economies, greater flexibility appears warranted in the wage-setting process. A comprehensive approach to human resource development is required, involving the improvement and expansion of education and training and retraining for all age groups. This would also be the most effective insurance against the emergence of low-wage jobs. A range of active labour market policies can improve allocative efficiency while providing job finding assistance to those in need, especially the long-term unemployed. Entrepreneurship and the processes of enterprise creation and job creation need to receive considerably more attention, particularly in those

countries where virtually all of the employment creation in recent decades has been in the public sector. Structural policies which are economically sound and socially equitable will be the best guarantee for OECD countries to profit from new technologies and shifts in trade;

3) success with structural adjustment in a competitive world can be achieved only on the basis of a degree of social solidarity to pay for the costs of these adjustment policies, and support those who nevertheless fall permanently behind. Systems of compensation and protection now in place are ill-adapted to cope with the new inequalities and erosion of social cohesion engendered by high and persistent unemployment. Policies to effect adjustment and support can be better, and more coherently, designed so as to continue to achieve equity objectives while contributing more effectively to labour-market efficiency, and thereby to higher employment with higher living standards over the longer term.

Explaining Disparities in Unemployment Dynamics

Marika Karanassou - Dennis J. Snower *
Birkbeck College, University of London

1. - Introduction

It is difficult, if not impossible, for the standard Keynesian and neoclassical macroeconomic models to explain the vastly different unemployment experiences of OECD countries over the past two decades. The dominant macro theories have failed us in this regard, and it is important to be aware of how far-reaching this failure has been.

From the traditional Keynesian perspective, the source of unemployment lies in the product market. A fall in product demand leads to a fall in labor demand via an intermarket spillover that arises when wages and prices are sticky. Alternatively, when prices are more flexible than wages, a fall in product demand leads to a fall in the price level relative to the wage level, and the resulting rise in the real wage leads to a fall in labor demand. In either case the product and labor market activities are firmly coupled to one another. This vision is starkly at variance with what happened in the 1980s. In most European countries, the recession of the early 1980s lasted much

---

* We are deeply indebted to David Begg, David Blake, and Ron Smith for their insightful comments.

This research was carried out as part of the *Labour Market Imperfections Programme*, funded by the Department of Employment and organized by the CEPR. The views expressed in this paper are those of the authors and do not necessarily reflect those of the Department or the CEPR.

N.B.: the numbers in square brackets refer to the Bibliography at the end of the paper.

longer in labor than in product markets. Product demand grew at robust rates throughout much of Europe after 1982, but many European labor markets continued to stagnate for four to six years later. In short, Europe experienced a "decoupling" of product and labor markets, quite at variance with Keynesian thinking. This decoupling was far more pronounced in the EC countries than in the EFTA or the US. Whereas the Keynesian theory would lead us to expect that the close relation between product demand and unemployment would be most pronounced in countries with particularly sluggish wages and prices, it is impossible to argue that the EFTA and the US economies are characterized by far more wage-price inertia than the EC.

From the *New Classical Macro* perspective, variations in unemployment can be attributed to: *(i)* variations in the natural rate of unemployment due to, say, demographic changes, changes in minimum wages, and supply-side impediments to labor market activity, or *(ii)* deviations of unemployment from its natural rate due to errors in price expectations or intertemporal substitution. This approach looked quite plausible in the late 1960s and the 1970s, when the rising unemployment seemed closely related to the influx of women into the labor force, the rise in union militancy, the increasing stringency of job security legislation, and the surge of state involvement in product markets. The appearance of sustained, high inflation in the aftermath of the Vietnam war — an unprecedented occurrence in much of the postwar OECD — could also perhaps be identified as a source of expectational errors and intertemporal substitution.

This however ceased to be a compelling diagnosis in the 1980s. After the oil price shock of 1979 and the contractionary fiscal and monetary policies of the early 1980s, inflation declined and then stabilized over much of the rest of the decade, leaving precious little latitude for mistaken inflationary expectations or intertemporal substitution. Thus it was difficult to argue that the rising unemployment of the 1980s was due to a substantial increase in unemployment over its natural rate. Nor could it be blamed on a sustained rise in the natural rate itself. For, with the Conservative Revolution of this period came a break-up of supply-side impediments in labor and product markets; deregulation, privatization, and retrenchment in job security legislation were common in many European countries. Union density was no longer on the rise and the demographic changes of the 1960s and 1970s were no longer strongly in evidence. Thus it was hard to see where the rise in the natural rate should have come from.

Out of the consequent dissatisfaction with the Keynesian and classical explanations of unemployment has grown a renewed interest in the way lags in the process of employment determination, wage setting, and labor force participation allow labor market shocks to have a prolonged effect on unemployment. The underlying hypothesis is that an important part of the differences in the unemployment experiences among OECD countries over the past two decades is attributable to differences in lag structures. Specifically, countries that differ in terms of the labor turnover costs are likely to differ in terms of the way lagged employment affects current employment and current wages. Differences in union membership rules may be expected to result in differences in the way past union membership affects current wages. Differences in wage bargaining procedures may give rise to significant differences in the degree of wage staggering and thereby influence the way lagged wages affect current wage determination. Differences in unemployment benefit systems are bound to affect the search intensities of the long-term unemployed and thereby influence the way lagged unemployment affects current wages. Differences in other welfare state provisions will influence people's propensity to drop out of the labor force and their eagerness to reenter and thereby influence the way in which the lagged labor force affects the current participation rate. Clearly, this list could be extended considerably.

The upshot of this line of thinking is that if there are important inter-country differences in these lagged effects and if these effects play a significant role in explaining a country's unemployment dynamics, then they may also have an important role in explaining why different countries, facing similar labor market shocks in the course of a global recession, should have such different unemployment experiences. This is the issue that motivates this paper: *a)* why temporary labor market shocks (such as the supply-side shocks of the mid-1970s and early 1980s) had such prolonged effects on unemployment and *b)* why longer-term labor market shocks (such as the disinflationary macro policies of the early 1980s and possibly also the early 1990s) have such delayed effects on unemployment.

Thus far, the prolonged effects of temporary labor market shocks have received much more attention in the macro literature than the delayed effects of permanent shocks. Many economists, following Blanchard and Summers [3], have argued that European labor markets are characterized by hysteresis, whereby temporary shocks have *permanent* unemployment effects, so that the unemployment tends to get stuck at whatever it happens to be at the moment. This view, however, flies in the face of a widely recognized empirical phenomenon: although unemployment rates may be high (say, over 15%) for limited periods of time, they tend to return within a narrow band, lying between 2% and 8% in most OECD countries. In the presence of hysteresis and random labor market shocks there could be no such tendency. For this reason, models in which temporary shocks have *prolonged* effects appear more plausible than those in which they have permanent effects.

There is certainly no reason to believe, however, that all the significant labor market shocks experienced in the OECD over the past two decades have been temporary (lasting, say, a year). Longer-term shocks, particularly those associated with demand management and supply-side policy swings, have no doubt played an important role as well. The interesting issue regarding permanent shocks is not whether they have permanent effects on unemployment — for permanent supply-side shocks, such as deregulation or changes in union legislation, generally do have such effects — but rather why these effects take such a long time to manifest themselves. This phenomenon could take two different forms: On the one hand, unemployment may be said to display "inertia" when a permanent shock has a smaller effect on unemployment in the short run than in the long run (so that, in the aftermath of a permanent shock that raises the long-run unemployment rate, the short-run unemployment rate remains beneath the long-run one in the transition period). On the other hand, there is unemployment "over-shooting" when the short-run effect is greater than the long-run one.

In this paper we attempt to capture these various features of unemployment dynamics, through two concepts: 1) *unemployment persistence* occurs when a temporary labor demand shock has prolonged effects on unemployment and 2) *imperfect unemployment responsiveness* occurs when a permanent labor demand shock has delayed effects on unemployment.

Positive unemployment pesistence arises when a temporary drop in labor demand continues to raise unemployment after the shock has disappeared. Unemployment is "under-responsive" when there is inertia and "over-responsive" when there is over-shooting.

Clearly, however, the dynamic unemployment responses to temporary and permanent shocks leave a dramatic feature of the unemployment experience of many OECD countries over the past two decades unexplained, namely, the rapid rise in unemployment in the onset of global recessions. Many economists have observed that a moderate drop in labor demand often has a large impact on unemployment in the short run. Let us refer to this feature as the *"fragility"* of the short-run unemployment equilibrium. The greater the effect of a labor demand shock in period *t* on equilibrium unemployment in that period, the more fragile is equilibrium unemployment. This concept is closely related to its namesake in Blanchard and Summers [2][1].

The degree of unemployment fragility obviously affects the unemployment dynamics. The greater is the degree of unemployment fragility, the more a current drop in labor demand reduces current employment and increases current unemployment. But since current employment and unemployment affect future employment and real wages via the lagged effect mentioned above, the degree of fragility also has a clear bearing on the degree of unemployment persistence and imperfect responsiveness.

This paper takes a first step toward tracing the interrelations among the fragility, persistence, and imperfect responsiveness of unemployment and provides empirical measures of these phenomena.

---

[1] In BLANCHARD O. - SUMMERS L. [2] the equilibrium is fragile in the sense that once the labor market has been perturbed from such an equilibrium, it has little — if any — tendency to return to it. Under various well-known specifications of labor market dynamics, the more sensitive the equilibrium to labor demand shocks, the longer it takes the labor market to reach its equilibrium after such shocks. See, for example, the analysis in the next section.

Section 2 sets out a simple analytical framework for studying these phenomena. Section 3 presents general measures of unemployment persistence and imperfect responsiveness. Section 4 contains an empirical analysis of fragility, persistence, and imperfect responsiveness in Germany, the UK, and the US. Section 5 concludes.

2. - Some Simple Analytics

The simplest way to represent unemployment fragility is to consider the following labor market system:

labor demand equation:

$$n_t = a_0 + a_1 w_t \tag{1a}$$

wage setting equation:

$$w_t = b_0 + b_1 n_t \tag{1b}$$

labor force equation:

$$l_t = l \tag{1c}$$

where n_t is aggregate employment, w_t is the real wage, and l_t is the aggregate labor force (all in logs). Let equation *(1a)* be the short-run labor demand curve, representing the condition that the real marginal revenue product of labor is equal to the real wage. The curve is downward-sloping under full capacity and diminishing returns to labor, but it may be flat or even upward-sloping under excess capital capacity[2]. Equation *(1b)* could be interpreted as the real wage that emerges from an implicit or explicit nominal wage bargain between employers and their employees, at any given level of employment, taking employers' price responses to the negotiated wages into account. The equilibrium real wage and employment is given by the

[2] See LINDBECK A. - SNOWER D.J. [9] and KARANASSOU M. - SNOWER D.J. [6].

intersection of these labor demand and wage setting curves. The difference between the labor force and employment at the equilibrium real wage is the short-run equilibrium level of unemployment. Approximating the level of unemployment by $U_t \approx l_t - n_t$, equilibrium unemployment is:

$$U_t = l - \frac{a_0 + a_1 b_0}{1 - a_1 b_1} \qquad (2)$$

We define the fragility unemployment in terms of the effect of an exogenous shift in the labor demand curve on equilibrium unemployment:

$$\rho = - \frac{\partial U_t}{\partial a_0} = \frac{1}{1 - a_1 b_1} \qquad (3)$$

The larger is ρ, the more fragile is the unemployment equilibrium.

To explore the relation of unemployment fragility to the persistence and responsiveness of unemployment, we need to introduce lagged endogenous variables into the equation system *(1a)-(1c)*. For brevity, we do not consider the microeconomic foundations for these lags; this has been done in detail elsewhere in the literature[3], which has highlighted a number of particularly important lags operating on the labor demand, wage setting, and labor force participation decisions. Our next step, rather, is to examine how each of these lags — considered in isolation — interacts with the degree of labor market fragility to produce unemployment persistence and responsiveness.

For expositional simplicity, we will give names to the various sets of lags, suggesting some underlying rationales:

1) lagged employment terms in the labor demand equation will be called the "*employment adjustment effect*", since firms' employment adjustment costs often make current labor demand depend on past employment[4];

---

[3] References are given below.

[4] See, for example, NICKELL S. [13].

2) lagged employment terms in the wage setting equation will be called the "*insider membership effect*", since the size of firms' insider workforces may influence the insiders' objectives in the wage setting process;

3) lagged real wage terms in the wage setting equation will be called the "*wage staggering effect*", since staggered wage setting makes current real wages depend on their past values[5];

4) lagged unemployment terms in the wage setting equation will be called the "*long-term unemployment effect*", since the long-term unemployment may search less intensively for jobs and thus have less influence on the wage setting process than the short-term unemployed[6];

5) lagged labor force terms in the labor force equation will be called the "*labor force adjustment effect*", since costs of entry to and exit from the labor force often make the current labor force depend on its past magnitudes.

Clearly, there is no presumption that these rationales provide a comprehensive explanation of the associated lags; to the contrary, it is not difficult to think of other, perhaps equally important, explanations for each of the lags. Our nomenclature is no more than an expositional device. Furthermore, these are not of course the only lags that occur in the labor demand, wage setting, and labor force equations, but they are particularly important both in the empirical and theoretical literature, so that it makes sense to focus our attention on them.

The simplest way of illustrating the *employment adjustment effect* is to include lagged employment in the labor demand equation *(1a)*:

$$n_t = a_0 + a_1 w_t + a_2 n_{t-1} \tag{4}$$

Solving the system *(4)*, *(1b)* and *(1c)*, we obtain the following unemployment dynamics equation:

$$u_t = A_0 + A_1 u_{t-1} \tag{5}$$

---

[5] See, for example, TAYLOR J.B. [14]. If there is staggered price setting as well, the lag structure can no longer be explained exclusively in terms of lagged *real* wages. See BLANCHARD [4].

[6] See, for example, BEAN C. - LAYARD R. [1].

where:

(5a) $A_0 = [(1 - a_1 b_1 - a_2) l - a_0 - a_1 b_0]$ and $A_1 = a_2 \rho$

To ensure stability, we assume that $0 \leq A_1 \leq 1$.

In this first-order difference equation, the coefficient A_1 determines the degree of unemployment persistence as well as the degree of imperfect responsiveness. Consider a temporary negative labor demand shock occurring only in period $t = 0$, $d\,a_0 < 0$, which corresponds to a temporary positive shock to the unemployment dynamics equation: $dA_0 > 0$ in $t = 0$. Clcarly, in the initial period, $du_0 = dA_0$, and since the shock disappears thereafter, $du_1 = A_1\, dA_0$, $du_2 = A_1^2\, dA_0$, and so on. In general, the effect of the temporary shock on uneployment is $du_t = A_1^t\, dA_0$. Thus, the greater the coefficient A_1, the greater is the degree to which the temporary shock persists.

Now consider a permanent shock: $dA_0 > 0$ for $t \geq 0$. The long-run unemployment level before the shock is $\bar{u}_t = \bar{u} = A_0 / (1 - A_1)$. In the first period after the shock, $du_1 = dA_0$, and since the shock is permanent, $du_2 = dA_0 + A_1 du_1 = (1 + A_1)\, dA_0, du_3 = dA_0 + A_1\, du_2 = (1 + A_1 + A_1^2)\, dA_0$ and so on. In general, the effect of the permanent shock on unemployment is

$$du_t = [(1 - A_1^{t-1}) / (1 - A_1)]\, dA_0$$

The effect on the long-run unemployment level is:

$$d\bar{u} = [1 / (1 - A_1)]\, dA_0$$

If unemployment were perfectly responsive, the full effects of the permanent shock would manifest themselves immediately so that $d\bar{u}_1 = d\bar{u}$. When $A_1 > 0$, however, the full effects are delayed, so that:

$$du_1 - d\bar{u} = - A_1^{t-1} / (1 - A_1)\, dA_0 < 0$$

Here unemployment is "under-responsive" in the sense that unemployment displays inertia in response to the permanent shock. The greater the coefficient A_1, the greater is the degree of under-responsiveness.

Proposition 1: For the first-order unemployment dynamics equation *(5)*, unemployment persistence and imperfect responsiveness are firmly related: the more persistent are the unemployment effects of a temporary shock, the more under-responsive is unemployment to a permanent shock.

Equation *(5a)* shows that when the employment adjustment effect above is responsible for the unemployment dynamics, then the fragility of the unemployment equilibrium gives leverage to the degree of unemployment persistence and under-responsiveness. The reason is straightforward. The greater the fragility coefficient ρ, the greater is the effect of a current positive labor demand shock on current employment. Due to the employment adjustment effect, the greater the rise in current employment, the greater will be resulting rise in future employment. Thus, if the shock is temporary, the more persistent will be its effect on employment and (since the labor force is constant) also on unemployment. If the shock is permanent, the longer it will take for the entire long-term effect to appear.

Along the same lines, it is easy to examine the effect of fragility on persistence and imperfect responsiveness with respect to the other major sources of unemployment dynamics. Turning to the *insider membership effect*, this may be positive or negative, depending on the relative strength of two counterveiling influences: *(i)* For any given distribution of labor demand shocks, the smaller is the insider workforce of a firm, the greater will be the insiders' job security at any given real wage, and consequently the higher the negotiated wage will be[7], *(ii)* The smaller is the insider workforce, the smaller will be the bargaining power of the insiders (because, for example, the weaker are the threats that the insiders make to the firms in case of bargaining disagreement), and therefore the lower the negotiated wage will be[8]. If the size of the current insider workforce depends on past employment, the negotiated wage will depend on past employment as well[9]. The simplest way of illustrating the insider membership

[7] See, for example, BLANCHARD O. - SUMMERS L. [3] and LINDBECK - SNOWER [10].

[8] See, for example, LINDBECK A. - SNOWER D.J. [11].

[9] This is of course not the only reason why the negotiated wage may depend on past employment. Employment adjustment costs may be responsible as well, since firms' objectives in wage negotiations will then depend on their past employment levels.

effect is to include lagged employment in the wage setting equation *(1b)*:

(6) $$w_t = b_0 + b_1\, n_t + b_2\, n_{t-1}$$

Solving the system *(1a)*, *(6)* and *(1c)* again yields an unemployment dynamics equation of the form *(5)* with slope:

(6a) $$A_1 = a_1\, b_2\, \rho$$

where both a_1 and b_2 could be either positive or negative. If the job security effect dominates ($b_2 < 0$) and the labor demand curve is downward-sloping ($a < 0$), or if the bargaining power effect dominates ($b_2 > 0$) and the labor demand curve is upward-sloping, then current unemployment depends positively on lagged unemployment. Here, as in the previous case, unemployment displays positive persistence and under-responsiveness. On the other hand, if the bargaining power effect dominates ($b_2 > 0$) and the labor demand curve is downward-sloping ($a < 0$), or if the job security effect dominates ($b_2 < 0$) and the labor demand curve is upward-sloping ($a > 0$), then there is negative unemployment persistence and over-responsiveness. In either case, however, the more fragile is the unemployment equilibrium, the more leverage the insider membership effect has on the degree of unemployment persistence and imperfect responsiveness.

To illustrate the isolated influence of the *wage staggering effect* on unemployment persitence and imperfect unemployment responsiveness, we include a lagged wage term in the wage setting equation *(1b)*:

(7) $$w_t = b_0 + b_1\, n_t + b_3\, w_{t-1}$$

By *(1a)*, *(8)* and *(1c)*, we then obtain an unemployment dynamics equation with slope:

(7a) $$A_1 = b_3\, \rho$$

Here, once again, the fragility of the unemployment equilibrium gives leverage to the persistence and under-responsiveness of unemployment arising from this wage staggering effect.

The simplest way of viewing the *long-term unemployment effect* is to suppose that the greater is last period's unemployment, *ceteris paribus*, the larger is the pool of the long-term unemployed, and the smaller is the number of workers competing for the vacant jobs, and consequently the higher will be the negotiated real wage. The isolated influence of this effect on unemployment persistence and imperfect responsiveness may be illustrated by transforming the wage setting equation *(1b)* as follows[10]:

$$w_t = b_0 + b_1 n_t + b_4 (u_{t-1} - l) \tag{8}$$

and, by *(1a)*, *(8)* and *(1c)*, deriving the slope of the corresponding unemployment dynamics equation:

$$A_1 = -a_1 b_4 \rho \tag{8a}$$

How the long-term unemployment effect influences unemployment persistence and imperfect responsiveness depends on the slope of the labor demand curve and the degree of fragility of the unemployment equilibrium. When the labor demand curve is downward-sloping, there is positive persistence and under-responsiveness; when it is upward sloping, there is negative persistence and over-responsiveness. The degree of fragility amplifies this effect, whichever direction it goes.

Finally, the simplest from of the *labor force adjustment effect* is described by the following modification of the labor force equation *(1c)*:

$$l_t = c_0 + c_1 l_{t-1} \tag{9}$$

---

[10] To motivate this wage setting equation, supose that $\theta (U_t/L)$ is the probability of finding a job in the current period, where U_t is the level of unemployment (not in logs), L is the labor force (also not in logs), and θ is a constant ($0 < \theta \leq 1$). Then the number of long-term unemployed is $U_t^{LT} = \hat{\theta} (U_t / L) U_{t-1}$, and in logs $u_t^{LT} = \theta + u_t - l + u_{t-1}$. If the wage setting function takes the form $w_t = \hat{b} + b_1 n_t - b_4 (u_{t-1} - u_t)$, it may be rewritten in the form $w_t = b_0 + b_1 n_t - b_4 (u_{t-1} - l)$, with $b_0 = b + b_4 \theta$.

By *(1a)*, *(1b)* and *(9)*, the slove of the resulting unemployment dynamics equation is:

$$(9a) \qquad A_1 = c_1$$

which is clearly independent of the degree of labor market fragility.

In short, the way in which the degree of fragility affects the strength of each source of unemployment persistence and imperfect responsiveness may be summarized as follows.

Proposition 2: The greater the degree of labor market fragility (ρ), *ceteris paribus*, thc greater is the leverage of: 1) the employment adjustment cost effect (a_2); 2) the insider membership effect (b_2); 3) the staggered wage setting effect (b_3), and 4) the long-term unemployment effect (b_4), each considered in isolation, on unemployment persistence and responsiveness.

3. - Measuring Persistence and Imperfect Responsiveness of Unemployment

In the previous section we have seen that, when the dynamics of unemployment can be represented by a first-order difference equation, such as equation *(5)*, the coefficicnt $A_1 = (\partial U_t / \partial U_{t-1})$ can serve as measure of both unemployment persistence and imperfect responsiveness. But this is a special case. When more than one of the lags in the determination of employment, wages, and labor force participation are operative at the same time, the resulting unemployment dynamics will be of higher order and will require more general measures of unemployment persistence and imperfect responsiveness. We now proceed to present such measures.

If we extend our system of labor market equations to include all the lags discussed in the previus section, we obtain:

$$(10a) \qquad n_t = a_0 + a_1\, w_t + a_2\, n_{t-1}$$

$$(10b) \qquad w_t = b_0 + b_1\, n_t + b_2\, n_{t-1} + b_3\, w_{t-1} + b_4\,(u_{t-1} - l)$$

$$(10c) \qquad l_t = c_0 + c_1\, l_{t-1}$$

Approximating the unemployment rate by $U_t \approx l_t - n_t$, equations *(10a)-(10c)* may be used to derive a higher-order unemployment dynamics equation. While it is not difficult to think of other lags and variables to include in this system, the ones above are ample to illustrate the general problem of measuring unemployment persistence and imperfect responsiveness. As we will see, the associated unemployment dynamics equation may display complex cyclical patterns for which the degree of unemployment persistence and imperfect responsiveness need not invariably be inversely related.

3.1 *Measures of Unemployment Persistence*

Since unemployment persistence arises only when a temporary labor demand shock continues to affect unemployment after the shock has disappeared, it appears natural to measure it in terms of either: *(i)* the discounted sum of the differences through time ($t \geq 1$) between unemployment in the presence and absence of the shock (occurring at $t=0$), normalized by the size of the shock or *(ii)* the number of periods after the shock has occurred that it takes unemployment to return to an ε-neighborhood of the time path it would have followed in the absence of the shock. We denote these two measures by π_1 and π_2, respectively.

Specifically, consider a temporary drop in labor demand whereby the coefficient a_0 in equation *(1a)* falls in period $t=0$ ($\Delta a_0 < 0$) and then returns to its original value. Now, for all the periods after the shock ($t>0$), compute the comparative dynamic term Δu_1, representing the difference between unemployment in the presence and the absence of the shock. Then the first measure of unemployment persistence may be expressed as:

$$\pi_1 = \sum_{t=1}^{\infty} \delta^t \frac{\Delta u_t}{\Delta a_0} \qquad (11a)$$

where δ ($0 \leq \delta \leq 1$) is the time discount factor. When $\pi_1 = 0$, there is no persistence; when $\pi_1 > 0$ (so that a temporary drop in labor demand causes the discounted stream of subsequent unemployment levels to be positive) there is "positive persistence"; and when $\pi_1 < 0$, there is "negative persistence". For $\delta = 1$, an infinite π_1 characterizes the special case of "hysteresis".

The second measure of unemployment persistence may be specified as:

$$\pi_2 = \underset{t}{\operatorname{argmax}} \left(\frac{\Delta\, u_t}{\Delta\, a_0} > \varepsilon \right) \tag{11b}$$

for some small positive constant ε. In other words, this measure represents the maximum number of time periods over which the effect of the temporary shock on unemployment exceeds some small positive value. Here we are not able to distinguish between positive and negative persistence. In a dynamically stable system, where the unemployment effects of a temporary labor demand shock eventually decline toward zero, this measure is positive and finite. When there is no persistence, $\pi_2 = 1$; at the oppositive extreme of hysteresis, π_2 is infinite.

Although these measures can clearly be applied to *any* stable system of labor market equations determining the unemployment rate, we can get a better intuitive grasp of what these measures mean by applying them to the first-order equation *(5)*. As shown in Section 2, when a temporary shock dA_0 occurs in time period $t = 0$, the difference between unemployment in the presence and absence of the shock in all subsequent time periods $t >$ is $du_t = A_1^t\, dA_0$. The discounted sum of these differences yields our first measure of unemployment persistence:

$$\pi_1 = \frac{\delta\, A_1}{1 - \delta\, A_1} \tag{12a}$$

and second measure is:

$$\pi_2 = \underset{t}{\operatorname{argmax}}\, [A_1^t > \varepsilon] \tag{12b}$$

Observe that, in line with our discussion in the previous section, both measures do indeed depend positively on the slope A_1 of the unemployment dynamics equation.

3.2 *Measures of Unemployment Responsiveness*

Since unemployment is imperfectly responsive when the long-term effects of an permanent shock are delayed, it appears natural to measure it in terms of either *(i)* the discounted sum of the differences through time between the actual unemployment effect of the permanent shock and the long-run effect, or *(ii)* the number of periods after the shock has occurred that it takes unemployment to reach an ε-neighborhood of its long-run level in the presence of the shock. We denote these two measures by σ_1 and σ_2, respectively.

In particular, let Δu_t be the difference between unemployment level in the presence and absence of a permanent shock, Δa_0, occurring in time period $t = 0$. Let $\Delta \bar{u}_t$ be the difference between the corresponding long-run levels in the presence and absence of the shock. If unemployment were perfectly responsive in a stable dynamic system, Δu_t would be equal to $\Delta \bar{u}_t$ in every time period t. The difference $(\Delta u_t - \Delta \bar{u}_t)$ may then be attributed to imperfect unemployment responsiveness. Thus our first measure of unemployment responsiveness may be expressed as:

$$\sigma_1 = \sum_{t=1}^{\infty} \delta^{t-1} \frac{\Delta u_t - \Delta \bar{u}_t}{\Delta a_0} \qquad (13a)$$

When $\sigma_1 < 0$, there is "under-responsiveness" of unemployment, in the sense that the permanent shock leads to a smaller discounted stream of actual unemployment increments than long-run unemployment increments, i.e. unemployment displays "inertia". When $\sigma_1 > 0$, there is "over-responsiveness" of unemploymnent, in that the discounted stream of actual unemployment increments exceed that of long-run unemployment increments; this can happen when unemployment "overshoots" its long-run equilibrium.

Our second measure of unemployment responsiveness is:

$$(13b) \qquad \sigma_2 = \underset{t}{\operatorname{argmax}} \left[\left| \frac{\Delta\, u_t - \Delta\, \bar{u}_t}{\Delta\, a_0} \right| > \varepsilon \right]$$

This measure, in other words, represents the maximum number of time periods over which the absolute value of the difference between the actual and the long-run effect of the permanent shock on unemployment exceeds some small, positive value. Once again, this measure does not permit us to distinguish between under-and over-responsiveness of unemployment. When unemployment is perfectly responsive, $\pi_2 = 1$; at the oppositive extreme of hysteresis, π_2 is infinite.

For the first-order unemployment dynamics equation *(5)*, stability implies that $0 \leq A_1 \leq 1$, and then the long-run unemployment level is $\bar{u}_t = \bar{u} = A_0 \;/(1 - A_1) > 0$. The actual unemployment effect of a permanent shock dA_0 is $du_t = [(1 - A_1^t) \;/\; (1 - A_1)]\; dA_0$; the long-run effect is $d\bar{u} = dA_0 \;/\; (1 - A_1)$. The discounted sum of the difference between these two effects over all periods yields our first measure of imperfect responsiveness:

$$(14a) \qquad \sigma_1 = - \frac{A_1}{(1 - A_1)\,(1 - \delta\, A_1)}$$

and our second measure becomes:

$$(14b) \qquad \sigma_2 = \underset{t}{\operatorname{argmax}} \left(\left| \frac{A_1^t}{1 - A_1} \right| > \varepsilon \right)$$

Once again, note that both measures depend positively on the slope A_1 of the unemployment dynamics equation.

It is easy to show that our measures of unemployment persistence and imperfect rsponsiveness do not depend on whether unemployment in the initial time period ($t = 0$) is at its long-run equilibrium value.

4. - Empirical Analysis of Unemployment Persistence and Imperfect Responsiveness

We now construct an empirical framework for assessing the decree of labor market fragility and measuring the persistence and imperfect responsiveness of unemployment. We focus attention on four countries — Germany, Spain, the UK and the US — over the postwar period. The empirical analysis should be seen as illustrating our methodology for analyzing fragility, persistence and imperfect responsiveness, rather than providing definitive measures of these magnitudes. With this in mind, our primary concern in constructing the empirical model has been to keep it sufficiently simple to identify the sources of persistence and unemployment responsiveness with ease. This explains why we have chosen not to disaggregate the model by sector (it is a one-sector model) or by time period (the model is annual).

In estimating a system of labor market equations for each of the three countries, we followed a three-step procedure: First, we estimated an employment equation, a wage setting equation, and a labor force equation independently by *OLS*, conducting a full range of misspecification tests. Second, we estimated the preferred specifications of these equations as a system, using 3*SLS*. And finally, we performed the simulation exercises necessary to yield our measures of the persistence and imperfect responsiveness of unemployment. Details of the estimation procedure and results of the econometric tests are described in detail in Karanassou and Snower [6]. For our purposes here it is sufficient to summarize the system of equations that we ultimately settled on for each of the countries[11].

The German system[12]:

$$n = \underset{(2.49)}{1.58} + \underset{(8.84)}{1.24}\, n_{-1} - \underset{(-2.93)}{0.40}\, n_{-2} - \underset{(-1.79)}{0.06}\, w - \underset{(-2.94)}{0.05}\, r + \underset{(1.55)}{0.001}\, t$$

[11] The estimations are based on OECD data for the period 1952-1988. The equations pass the tests for misspecification and structural stability.

[12] The following are the definitions of the variables used: r = competitiveness $(P_M - P)$, P_M = deflator for imported goods and services, P = GNP deflator, t = time, τ_2 = average income tax rate. (All variables are in logs). The *t*-rations are in parentheses. The instruments-are n_{-1}, n_{-2}, r, t, w_{-1}, τ_2, l_{-1}, l_{-2}, and GNP.

$$w = \underset{(-0.71)}{-0.05} + \underset{(12.38)}{0.73\, w_{-1}} - \underset{(-5.21)}{1.05\, u} + \underset{(3.57)}{0.008\, t} + \underset{(2.51)}{0.10\, \tau_2}$$

$$l = \underset{(1.25)}{0.99} + \underset{(8.14)}{1.59\, l_{-1}} - \underset{(-3.80)}{0.70\, l_{-2}} + \underset{(0.96)}{0.08\, u} + \underset{(0.90)}{0.0003\, t}$$

The Spanish system[13]:

$$n = \underset{(4.92)}{1.91} + \underset{(9.86)}{1.33\, n_{-1}} - \underset{(-4.37)}{0.53\, n_{-2}} - \underset{(-3.10)}{0.02\, w} + \underset{(-3.93)}{0.07\, r}$$

$$w = \underset{(1.91)}{8.40} + \underset{(7.38)}{0.73\, w_{-1}} - \underset{(-3.02)}{1.75\, u_{-1}} + \underset{(3.13)}{0.03\, t} - \underset{(-2.00)}{0.96\, n_{-1}}$$

$$l = \underset{(3.56)}{2.64} + \underset{(9.91)}{1.29\, l_{-1}} - \underset{(-3.42)}{0.50\, u} + \underset{(3.77)}{0.54\, u_{-1}} - \underset{(-4.00)}{0.56\, l_{-2}} + \underset{(3.44)}{0.03\, w}$$

The UK system[14]:

$$n = \underset{(4.04)}{3.72} + \underset{(9.83)}{1.07\, n_{-1}} - \underset{(-3.30)}{0.33\, n_{-2}} + \underset{(2.77)}{0.10\, w} - \underset{(-2.77)}{0.08\, k}$$

$$w = \underset{(4.03)}{8.06} + \underset{(5.47)}{0.51\, w_{-1}} - \underset{(-5.92)}{1.51\, u} + \underset{(7.10)}{0.02\, t} - \underset{(3.37)}{0.11\, \tau_1} - \underset{(-4.36)}{0.87\, n_{-1}}$$

$$l = \underset{(-2.61)}{-0.96} + \underset{(9.70)}{1.16\, l_{-1}} - \underset{(-3.78)}{0.45\, l_{-2}} + \underset{(-4.20)}{0.37\, z}$$

---

13 The instruments are n_{-1}, n_{-2}, r, w_{-1}, t, τ_2, l_{-1} and l_{-2}.

14 k = capital stock (from *IQ*, 3% annual depreciation), τ_1 = employment tax rate, and z = population. The instruments are n_{-1}, n_{-2}, r, t, w_{-1}, τ_1, l_{-1}, l_{-2}, z and k. We have not felt it necesary to exclude ex ante the possibility that labor demand may be positively associated with the real wage. A number of recent theories, such as increasing returns to job matching (as in HOWITT - MCAFEE [5]) and increasing returns under excess capital capacity (as in KARANASSOU - SNOWER [7]) explain how this may arise. See also BLANCHARD - SUMMERS [2].

The US system [15]:

$$n = \underset{(0.28)}{0.09} + \underset{(4.66)}{0.60\,n_{-1}} - \underset{(-2.49)}{0.27\,w} + \underset{(3.09)}{0.28\,k}$$

$$w = \underset{(1.82)}{0.61} + \underset{(27.70)}{0.90\,w_{-1}} - \underset{(-2.96)}{0.48\,\Delta u} + \underset{(1.98)}{0.07\,\tau_2} - \underset{(-1.70)}{0.04\,n_{-1}}$$

$$l = \underset{(-3.16)}{-1.83} + \underset{(24.57)}{0.86\,l_{-1}} + \underset{(4.59)}{0.29\,z} - \underset{(1.34)}{0.11\,u} - \underset{(1.94)}{0.001\,t}$$

To derive our measures of unemployment persistence, we conduct simulation exercises on each of the systems above, together with an identity defining the unemployment rate. To preserve the linearity of the system, we use the approximation $u_t \approx l_t - n_t$, with l_t and n_t in logs. To generate the base runs, each system is solved from 1988 up to the period in which the system reaches its long-run equilibrium, using the 1988 values of all exogenous variables. The associated unemployment time series we call u_t "base unemployment". Next, a temporary labor demand shock is imposed: the constant term in the employment equation was reduced by 0.01005 in year 1988 only; this is equivalent to a 1% reduction in the constant term of the corresponding equation expressed in absolute terms, rather than logs. Let the resulting unemployment time series be u'_t, "post-shock unemployment". The difference between base unemployment and post-shock unemployment is the time series of unemployment increments $\Delta u_t = u'_t - u_t$.

To derive our measure of unemployment fragility, we convert the first element (Δu_{1965}) of this time series of incremental unemployment rates into an incremental unemployment level (ΔU_{1965}) and divide it by the temporary employment shock, to yield the effect of the shock on the short-run unemployment level. The results are given in Table 1. By our calculations, the UK unemployment equilibrium is more fragile than that of Germany (i.e. a given labor demand shock has a larger effect on the short-run equilibrium unemployment rate in

---

15 The instruments are n_{-1}, r, t, w_{-1}, τ_1, τ_2, l_{-1}, z and $(P_c - P)$, where P_c is the consumption deflator.

the UK than in Germany); and the German unemployment equilibrium, in turn, is more fragile than that of the US, which is followed by Spain.

Normalizing the time series Δu_t by the size temporary shock (in logs) yields the series $(\Delta u_t / \Delta a_0)$, and the discounted sum of the elements of this series, from 1988 until the system reaches its long-run equilibrium, yields our first measure of unemployment persistence, π_1 in Table 1. Our second measure is the number of periods it takes for the post-shock unemployment rate to return to a neighborhood of $\varepsilon = 0.001$ of the base unemployment rate, given by π_2 in Table 1.

Observe that all of the systems exhibit positive persistence, i.e. the discounted sum of the unemployment increments in the aftermath of a temporary shock is positive. By our calculations, Spanish unemployment displays more persistence than that in Germany (i.e. a termporary shock has a more long-lasting effect on unemployment in Spain than in Germany); and Germany, in turn, exhibits more unemployment persistence than the UK, which is followed by the US.

To derive measures of imperfect unemployment responsiveness, we impose a permanent shock whereby the constant term in the employment equation is reduced by 0.01005 (the equivalent of a 1% exogenous reduction in employment) for all years from 1988 until the system achieves its long-run equilibrium, holding all exogenous variables constant at their 1988 values. Let the resulting unemployment time series be u_t''. The effect of the permanent shock on the actual unemployment rate in each time period t may be represented by $(u_t'' - u_t) / \Delta a_0$, where u_t is base unemployment. Next, we compute the long-run unemployment rates in the presence and the absence of the shock: $\bar{u}''$ and $\bar{u}$ respectively. The effect of the shock on the long-run employment rate is $(\bar{u}'' - \bar{u}) / \Delta a_0$. The discounted sum of the differences between these actual and long-run effects yields our first measure of unemployment responsiveness, σ_1 in Table 1.

Note that whereas Germany exhibits *over-responsiveness* (unemployment overshooting), the other three countries all display *under-responsiveness* (unemployment inertia). Moreover, UK unemployment is more under-responsive than US unemployment, followed by that of Germany. The number of periods after the shock that it takes for the unemployment rate to reach a neighborhood of $\varepsilon = 0.001$ of

TABLE 1

FRAGILITY, PERSISTENCE, AND IMPERFECT RESPONSIVENESS OF UNEMPLOYMENT

	ρ	π_1	π_2	σ_1	σ_2
Germany	0.103	2.598	25	5.489	37
Spain	0.059	3.198	15	− 3.881	21
UK.	0.117	1.465	13	−20.567	13
US.	0.080	1.192	3	−13.541	36

its new long-run rate (or, equivalently, the number of periods it takes for the delayed unemployment increments to reach an ε-neighborhood of zero) is given by σ_2 in Table 1. Observe that the full effects of a permanent shock take longest to manifest themselves in Germany, followed by the US, Spain, and the UK.

5. - Concluding Remarks

The analysis above attempts to shed light on the disparities in unemployment dynamics among different OECD countries by examining the fragility, persistence and imperfect responsiveness of unemployment. The *fragility* of the unemployment equilibrium is significant because it indicates how sensitive unemployment is to labor demand shocks in the short run and because, as we have shown, it provides leverage for unemployment persistence and imperfect responsiveness. *Unemployment persistence* has received much attention in the macro literature over the past years, but thus far we have had no sufficiently general measures of it to permit us to compare how labor market systems with different dynamic structures respond to temporary shocks. The analysis above offers two such measures. Although *imperfect responsiveness* of unemployment has received far less attention in the literature, we maintain that it is no less important than unemployment persistence. There is no evidence that labor market shocks are predominantly temporary, rather than permanent, and it is vital to explore the degree to which labor market systems respond differently to temporary and permanent shocks. Once again, our analysis yields two general measures that permit us to compare systems with different dynamic structures.

Being able to compare unemployment persistence and imperfect responsiveness across different dynamic systems is important because, as our empirical estimates suggest, countries differ dramatically in terms of the lag structures characterizing their labor markets. Whereas the labor market experiences of Germany, Spain, and the UK have been superficially similar in the sense that unemployment in all these countries has been slow to recover from the global recessions of the past two decades, our analysis suggests that the lags responsible for the slow recoveries differ substantially from country to country.

This implies that different countries may require quite different unemployment policies to overcome what, on the surface, looks like the same unemployment problem. Through changes in job security legislation, wage subsidies to the long-term unemployed, and so on, policy makers are able to influence the lagged effects operative in the employment, wage setting, and labor force participation decisions. Insofar as the lags underlying unemployment persistence and imperfect responsiveness differ from one country to another, different policy approaches may be needed to improve the resilience of these countries' labor markets. A first step toward identifying the required policy differences would be to measure the degree to which each of the different lagged effects contribute to unemployment persistence and imperfect responsiveness. This is the subject of another paper (Karanassou - Snower [6]).

Beyond that, our empirical results indicate that countries where unemployment responds relatively sluggishly to temporary shocks need not be ones where unemployment also reacts sluggishly to permanent shocks. Our empirical results indicate that whereas Spain, the UK, and the US are characterized by positive persistence and under-responsiveness, Germany features positive persistence and over-responsiveness. Whereas Spain displays more unemployment persistence than the UK, UK unemployment is more under-responsive than Spanish unemployment. In the aftermath of a temporary shock, it takes UK unemployment a shorter time to reach its long-run equilibrium than German unemployment; but in the aftermath of a permanent shock, it is the other way around. A glance at the German and UK unemployment rates over the past two decades reveals that both have recovered slowly from global recessions; our analysis indicates, however, that the reason why each did so may be quite different. This suggests that the relative unemployment performance of different countries depends importantly on the degree to which their labor market shocks are temporary or permanent.

BIBLIOGRAPHY

[1] BEAN C. - LAYARD R., «Why Does Unemployment Persist?» *Department of Economics, London School of Economics, Discussion Paper*, n. 321, August 1988.

[2] BLANCHARD O. - SUMMERS L., «Beyond the Natural Rate Hypothesis», *American Economic Review*, vol. 78, n. 2, May 1988, pp. 182-7.

[3] ————, «Hysteresis and the European Unemployment Problem», *NBER Macroeconomics Annual*, vol. 1, Cambridge, (Mass.), MIT Press, 1986, pp. 15-77.

[4] BLANCHARD O., «The Wage-Price Spiral», *Quarterly Journal of Economics*, vol. 101, n. 3, 1986, pp. 543-65.

[5] HOWITT P. - MCAFEE PRESTON R., «Costly Search and Recruiting», *International Economic Review*, n. 33, February 1987, pp. 89-107.

[6] KARANASSOU M. - SNOWER D.J., *The Sources of Unemployment Persistence and Imperfect Responsiveness*, mimeo, 1993.

[7] LINDBECK A. - SNOWER D.J. - KARANASSOU M. - SNOWER D.J., *Excess Capital Capacity and Unemployment Volatility*, mimeo, 1993.

[8] LAYARD R. - NICKELL S., «The Causes of British Unemployment», *National Institute Economic Review*, n. 111, 1985, pp. 62-85.

[9] LINDBECK A. - SNOWER D.J., «How are Product Demand Changes Transmitted to the Labor Market?», *Economic Journal*, forthcoming, 1993.

[10] ————, «Union Activity, Unemployment Persistence, and Wage-Employment Ratchets», *European Economic Review*, n. 31, February 1987, pp. 157-67.

[11] ————, «Strike and Lock-Out Threats and Fiscal Policy», *Oxford Economic Papers*, n. 39, December 1987.

[12] MCDONALD I.M. - SOLOW R.M., «Wage Bargaining and Employment», *American Economic Review*, n. 71, 1981, pp. 896-908.

[13] NICKELL S., «Fixed Costs, Employment and Labor Demand over the Cycle», *Economica*, 1978.

[14] TAYLOR J.B., «Aggregate Dynamics and Staggered Contracts», *Journal of Political Economy*, n. 88, 1979, pp. 1-23

Structural Unemployment and Labour Policies

Luigi Frey
Università «La Sapienza», Roma

1. - Introduction

The following pages present a synthesis of documentary and analytical material on the situation as it is today, on the prospects facing problems of employment in the European Community and on possible strategies for containing these problems as well as for devising ways and means of solving them, a subject however that is dealt with in much greater length elsewhere [1].

All this material has been collected and elaborated over the last three years, and in particular while collaborating with a small working group set up by the EC's DG5 on the social aspects of European Economic and Monetary Union [2]. From this a conviction is gaining ground that:

a) a feature of employment problems in Europe over the last decade has been an accentuation of the structural components of unemployment, and this feature will become more marked in the near future;

b) the reasons advanced to explain European unemployment, based essentially on explicative variables such as trends in real wages or aggregate demand, do not seem convincing. Neither does it appear convincing to lay emphasis on the wage structure and/or on related prices other than wages. Doubts also arise concerning hypotheses that seek to explain the differences in unemployment between one country

[1] See FREY L. [10].

N.B.: the numbers in square brackets refer to the Bibliography at the end of the paper.

[2] See CALON A. - FREY L. - LINDLEY R. - LYON CAEN A. - MARKMANN M. - SIMITIS S. [3] and [4].

and another by referring to dissimilarity in legislation and control of the labour market. It seems advisable to assume that, for one thing, due weight should be given to factors of labour supply and, for another, that it is important to underline pursuance of technical progress in the broad sense as a decisive factor regarding labour demand and the *mismatches* that occur at professional and territorial levels. The explanatory value of these assumptions is clearer if they are considered together with others for interpreting trends of employment sectorally and territorially;

c) discussion on explicative assumption notably affects hypothetical strategies for containing problems of employment in the European Community and for finding ways of dealing with them.

It appears among other things that though labour policies favour specific groups of workers, with uncertain effects on employment levels for all workers, they are necessary in order to avoid accentuation of the structural components of unemployment. Bearing in mind the features of these structural components, those policies aimed at enhancing the value of the human resources available acquire greater importance, favouring possibilities of workers moving from one job to another and their active inclusion in production undergoing development in specific areas.

First and foremost documentary material will here be presented to support the belief that employment problems in Europe have been characterized by the structural component of unemployment and that this tendency will become stronger in the future.

Explicative hypotheses of European unemployment will then be discussed aiming to clarify why some assumptions do not seem convincing and the essential content of those it is proposed to support.

Finally, conclusions will bed drawn on the significance and content of labour policies as a means for containing and partially solving problems of employment in Europe.

2. - Structural Unemployment in Europe

It is a well-known fact that unemployment in the EC was a great deal higher in the 1980s than in previous decades (Table 1) both in

TABLE 1

BASIC INDICATORS ON EMPLOYMENT AND UNEMPLOYMENT IN THE EC TAKEN AS A WHOLE FROM 1965 TO 1991
(in millions of units)

	Males and females						Of which females were:					
	1965	1975	1985	1988	1990	1991	1965	1975	1985	1988	1990	1991
Total population	293.2	312.4	321.9	324.2	328.0	328.7	151.0	160.2	165.3	166.3	168.1	168.6
Population of working age (15-64 yrs)	188.0	197.9	215.8	218.6	220.7	221.2						
Total employed	122.6	124.3	125.3	130.5	135.0	135.2	39.6	42.5	46.6	50.1	52.5	53.2
% ratio of employed to population of working age	65.2	62.8	58.1	59.7	61.2	61.1						
Total unemployed	2.6	5.3	14.9	13.9	12.1	12.9		2.3	6.9	7.1	6.4	6.6
Rate of unemployment %	2.1	4.1	10.8	9.8	8.3	8.8			12.9	12.6	10.8	11.0
Rate of unemployed young people (below 25 years) %			23.1	19.6	16.6	17.5			25.0	22.2	18.9	19.1
Number employed in agriculture	20.1	13.9	10.4	9.4	8.6	8.4	6.8	4.8	3.6	3.3	3.0	2.9
Number employed in industry	49.5	48.3	41.1	41.5	42.9	42.3	11.5	11.2	9.4	9.7	10.1	10.0
Number employed in services	53.1	62.2	73.8	79.3	83.1	84.2	21.5	26.5	33.4	37.0	39.4	40.3
% composition: agriculture	16.4	11.2	8.3	7.2	6.4	6.2	17.2	11.3	7.7	6.5	5.7	5.5
industry	40.4	38.8	32.8	31.8	31.8	31.3	29.0	26.4	20.2	19.3	19.2	18.8
services	43.3	50.0	58.9	60.7	61.5	62.3	54.2	62.4	71.7	73.9	74.8	75.5

Source, EC COMMISSION ON EMPLOYMENT - INDUSTRIAL RELATIONS AND SOCIAL AFFAIRS, *Unemployment in Europe 1992*, Luxembourg, 1993, p. 40.

Graph 1

TREND OF THE RATE OF UNEMPLOYMENT
IN THE EUROPEAN COMMUNITY

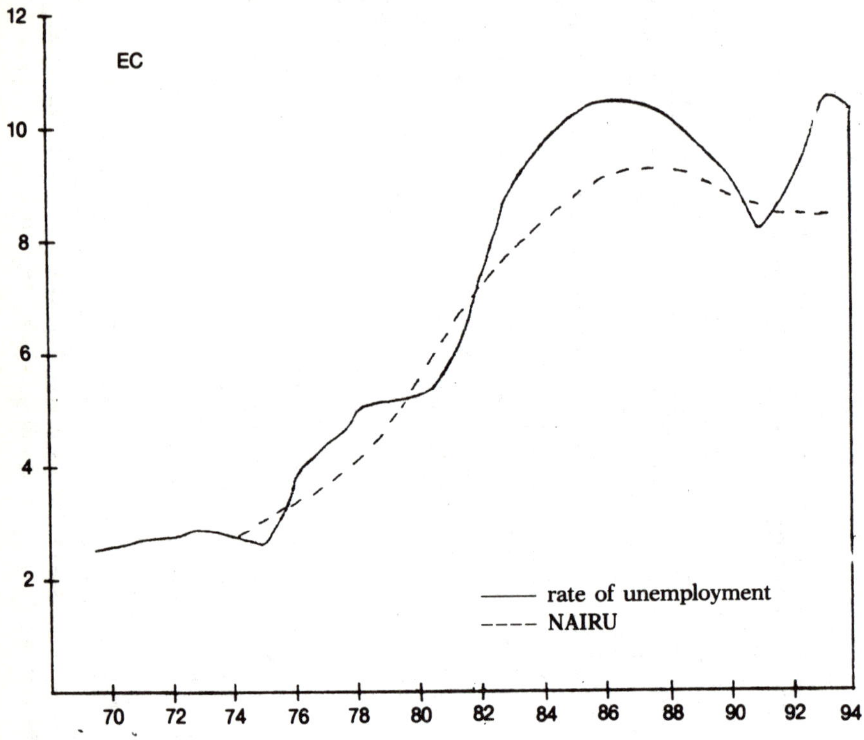

Source, OECD.

absolute terms and in those relating to the European work forces, and also to levels of unemployment in other industrialised countries.

Though discussion could be made of the NAIRU concept (as a particular rate of 'natural' or 'normal' unemployment) and of the way it is used to isolate non-Keynesian components of unemployment, calculations of NAIRU, made for the European Community by OECD [3] experts, appear to indicate the presence of non-Keynesian components (frictional or structural unemployment) which should have a decisive influence on the extent and trend of unemployment in Europe (Graph 1).

[3] See OECD [20], p. 18.

TABLE 2

LONG-TERM UNEMPLOYMENT IN EC COUNTRIES FROM 1983 TO 1991
(percentages of total unemployed)

	Average 1975-1980	1980	1983	1985	1987	1989	1990
Belgium	...	61.9	63.8	57.8	72.7	74.5	65.8
Denmark	...	...	26.8	21.1	22.7	20.7	28.5
W. Germany	...	28.7	36.3	46.1	48.4	47.8	45.1
Greece	...	32.6	32.0	43.1	43.5	49.8	49.2
France	27.1	32.6	38.5	42.8	43.4	42.6	38.6
Ireland	...	38.2	—	61.9	63.6	64.4	63.6
Italy	...	51.2	52.3	63.2	63.4	66.9	67.4
Luxembourg	...	...	31.0	34.6	30.6	30.8	30.9
Holland	...	35.9	46.1	55.0	42.0	43.9	44.3
United Kingdom	...	29.5	44.5	47.6	44.8	37.7	33.2
Portugal	...	...	—	—	53.0	44.4	43.6
Spain	28.4	32.8	—	—	60.4	55.8	50.8
Total for EC	...	...	—	—	51.8	50.8	47.8

Source, EUROSTAT, various publications.

Some experts tend to connect structural unemployment with the long-term kind, defined as an unsuccessful search for work lasting a year or more. It will be seen from Table 2 that, in the second half of the 1980s, structural unemployment in EC countries remained stable at around 50% of total unemployment (with higher peaks in Belgium and Italy), this probably being a higher percentage than that found in the first six months of the 1980s (except for some cases) and above all in the 1970s. Apart from overall figures on long-term employment, the OECD experts press for attention to be given to its composition by sex and age groups (Table 3). Allowing for the differences among the various countries, during the 1980s there was a rise in long-term unemployment that concerned adult workers, including males and also the 25-44 year age groups, alongside long-term unemployment among women that rose in absolute if not in relative terms. The increase in percentage rates of workers of middle age and of women unemployed for long periods in terms of stock during the last ten years will be seen (Table 4) to prevail in EC countries as a whole, a considerable portion relating to an increase among unemployed

TABLE 3

COMPOSITION OF LONG-TERM UNEMPLOYMENT BY SEX AND AGE GROUP IN SOME EC COUNTRIES
(percentages of unemployed for 12 months and more out of respective totals of unemployed)

		Young people below 25 years of age	Adults between 25 and 44	Workers of 45 years and over	Males	Females
France	1981	27.8	45.1	27.1	33.7	66.3
	1983	30.8	45.9	23.2	40.6	59.4
	1985	30.9	50.4	18.7	42.9	57.1
	1988	17.4	60.8	21.8	42.1	57.9
Greece	1983	45.6	39.6	14.8	34.4	65.6
	1985	46.1	41.1	12.8	36.4	63.6
	1988	59.1	29.8	11.1	31.7	68.3
Ireland	1983	33.1	46.3	20.6	77.3	22.7
	1985	35.9	44.8	19.4	71.3	28.7
	1988	29.5	49.4	21.1	70.7	29.3
Holland	1981	28.6	53.6	17.0	65.5	34.5
	1983	29.2	54.2	16.6	70.5	29.5
	1985	28.0	61.5	10.4	67.5	32.5
	1988	18.2	67.2	14.6	68.8	31.2
Portugal	1988	46.4	40.6	13.0	36.7	63.3
United Kingdom	1981	24.4	34.7	40.9	78.2	21.8
	1983	38.5	35.8	25.6	72.8	27.2
	1985	33.9	39.4	26.7	72.2	27.8
	1988	21.6	44.1	34.3	73.6	26.4
Spain	1981	55.7	28.9	15.4	62.3	37.7
	1983	54.2	31.7	14.1	60.3	39.7
	1985	46.9	37.4	15.7	61.8	38.2
	1988	44.6	40.8	14.6	44.8	55.1

Source, OECD, *Employment Outlook*, July 1992, p. 71.

women (especially in the second half of the 1980s and above all compared with the first half of the 1970s).

However, a careful study of information on long-term unemployment leads to serious doubts as to whether this may be the most reliable synthetic indicator of structural components of unemployment as a whole, but it does encourage more attention being given to some components of unemployment that deserve further study.

TABLE 4

MONTHLY FLOWS TO AND FROM UNEMPLOYMENT AND LONG-TERM UNEMPLOYMENT IN EC COUNTRIES
(percentages)

	Years	Inflows on total population of working age	Outflow from total unemployed	Composition of flows in unemployed					Composition of stock of long-term unemployed				
				15-24 yrs	25-44 yrs	45 and over	males	females	15-24 yrs	25-44 yrs	45 and over	males	females
Belgium	1979	0.2	...	...	...	...	43	57	...	...	...	32	68
	1990	0.3	5.1	50	50	...	36	64	17	63	20	36	64
Denmark	1979	0.8	...	...	...	...	47	53	...	...	...	35	65
	1990	0.7	8.3	50	38	12	56	44	10	59	31	44	56
France	1979	0.3	6.1	53	38	9	49	51	28	46	26	37	63
	1991	0.3	5.5	35	58	6	52	48	13	63	24	40	60
W. Germany	1979	0.2	...	...	...	...	54	46	...	...	...	50	50
	1990	0.2	8.0	27	57	16	48	52	8	43	49	51	49
Greece	1979	...	...	...	...	...	...	...	...	...	...	...	...
	1990	0.2	5.6	64	27	9	55	45	43	49	8	31	69
Ireland	1979	0.7	...	...	...	...	52	48	...	...	...	78	22
	1990	0.3	4.2	60	40	...	67	33	24	54	22	70	30
Italy	1979	0.3	...	...	...	...	50	50	...	...	...	50	50
	1990	0.2	3.6	38	51	11	47	53	52	43	5	39	61
Holland	1979	0.3	...	...	...	...	67	33	...	...	...	70	30
	1990	0.1	5.6	53	37	11	41	59	13	64	23	50	50
Portugal	1979	...	...	...	...	...	...	...	...	...	...	...	...
	1990	0.1	3.1	29	57	14	38	63	38	47	15	35	65
United Kingdom	1979	0.6	...	...	...	...	58	42	...	...	...	75	25
	1990	0.6	13.4	43	43	15	48	42	18	43	39	74	26
Spain	1979	0.3	3.7	47	31	22	84	16	57	26	17	60	40
	1990	0.2	2.0	38	45	15	61	39	34	38	28	40	60

Source, OECD, *Employment Outlook*, July 1993, pp. 88-9.

Firstly we have unemployment among women which, apart from the differentiated and variable percentages of long-term unemployment, has shown itself to be, in EC countries, an essential and, to a large extent, a permanent component of overall unemployment (Table 5).

Material available on Europe [4] also indicates that problems of women's employment are not only expressed in terms of increased unemployment compared with that of men (see Table 1 again) and by a percentage of long-term unemployment but are also characterized, in EC countries by particularly low rates of employment (in spite of the considerable growth in the number of women in jobs over the last 15 years), as well as by segregation of work for women within sectors and segments of the labour market (such as part time work) where risks of dismissal due to restructuring are highest. Contrary to widespread belief, rates of employment for men (and therefore the related opportunities for work in terms of stock) are in no way less in the European Community than they are in other industrialised countries, such as the USA or Japan. On the other hand there are fundamental differences as regards the rates of employment for women: at the close of the 1980s — apart from some considerable divergencies between countries of northern and southern Europe — the average percentage of employed women in the EC and the female population over 14 years of age was 36.7% against an analogous 62.9% of employed men. It has been pointed out[5] that, notwithstanding the increased ratio between employed women and the number of those employed of both sexes, of from 33% in 1970 to 39% in 1989 within the EC, it is a ratio that has remained decidedly lower than that found in other industrialised countries where it normally reaches 45%. From the point of view of an analysis of employment problems, it is important to note the concentration of employed women in certain sectors and in part time work particularly as regards employment known as 'involuntary'. DG 5 experts have shown [6] that about one third of the women employed in 1991 in six member countries (Belgium,

---

[4] See for example, Chap. 6 (and especially pp. 133 and foll.) of the report by the DG 5 of the European Community Commission [7].

[5] See European Community Commission [7], pp. 134-5.

[6] See European Community Commission [7], pp. 139-41.

TABLE 5

TREND IN FEMALE UNEMPLOYMENT IN EC COUNTRIES FROM 1973 TO 1992 (in thousands)

	1973	1979	1983	1991	1992	% of women unemployed for 12 months or more on total unemployed women		
						1983	1988	1991
Belgium	43	191	292	232	...	70.9	79.1	64.3
Denmark	11	95	153	135	...	38.6	29.2	34.3
France	369	780	1,085	1,294	...	44.8	46.8	39.0
Germany	124	459	985	792	825	37.7	45.2	42.0
Greece	25	33	154	(1990) 174	...	44.7	54.4	53.7
Ireland	11	22	43	52	...	25.0	57.1	52.1
Italy	700	962	1,202	1,511	1,572	59.9	69.6	68.2
Luxembourg	0	1	1	1	...	31.1	35.7	18.2
Holland	22	102	271	264	...	50.7	44.6	36.7
Portugal	48	222	228	124	99	...	55.3	41.3
United Kingdom	81	346	839	533	617	36.3	29.5	21.1
Spain	96	370	830	1,273	1,405	58.5	67.7	58.8
Total for EC	1,530	3,583	6,073	6,324	...			
% of unemployed MF	43.3	48.0	43.1	48.0	...			

Source, see Table 4, pp. 193 and foll. Our calculations.

Denmark, France, Germany, United Kingdom and Spain) was concentrated in only three sub-sectors (retail trade, health services and education); still in 1991, six sub-sectors out of 58 employed over half the number of working women; 75% of women were working in only 14 sub-sectors, the concentration appearing to have risen during the 1980s. Some of these sectors had shown a high rate of expansion in the preceding decade but then prospects of giving more jobs worsened in the first half of the 1990s (on account of a drop in consumption of goods by families and also in public spending on health) and in the subsequent five-year period (in relation to far-reaching restructuring in production of services as well). With regard to part time work in the EC, there was both an absolute and a relative growth of this in the 1980s of considerable importance and at a steadier pace than that in other Western industrialised countries, such as Sweden, the United States and Japan where the proportion of part time work out of total employment was already high at the end of the 1970s (Table 6). Among those employed part time — mainly women — there appears to be a fair amount of what is called 'involuntary' [7] work, namely that done by people who usually work full time and have had to take part time jobs for economic reasons, or others to do it because they cannot find full time work. This second category of 'involuntary' workers consists mainly of middle-aged women (Table 7) contributing thereby not a little to increasing female employment problems, together with those workers described as being 'discouraged' who are not seeking work because there in none to be had or, in any case, those who do not know where to find it.

On the other hand, among the middle-aged women, the ones who represented the greater part of the unemployed at the end of the 1980s were those with least education (Table 8). This applies only partly to the younger women (and to young people generally of both sexes) so that we have very high rates of unemployment for those who have completed secondary school or have graduated.

Particularly as regards long-term unemployment of adult workers, however, a greater and growing set of problems came to

---

[7] For a definition of involuntary part time work see OECD [16], Chap. 7, pp. 179 and foll.

TABLE 6

PART TIME WORK IN SOME INDUSTRIALIZED COUNTRIES FROM 1973 TO 1991
(percentages)

	Ratio of part time employment to full time for both sexes				Ratio F/MF			
	1973	1979	1983	1991	1973	1979	1983	1991
Belgium	3.8	6.0	8.1	11.8	82.4	88.9	84.0	89.3
Denmark	...	22.7	23.8	23.1	...	86.9	84.7	75.5
France	5.9	8.2	9.7	12.0	82.3	82.2	84.4	83.7
Germany	10.1	11.4	12.6	15.5	89.0	91.6	91.9	89.6
Japan	13.9	15.4	16.2	20.0	70.0	70.1	72.9	69.9
Greece	...	...	6.5	3.9	...	...	61.2	62.9
Ireland	...	5.1	6.6	8.4	...	71.2	71.6	71.6
Italy	6.4	5.3	4.6	5.5	58.3	61.4	64.8	65.4
Luxembourg	5.8	5.8	6.3	7.5	87.5	87.5	88.9	83.3
Holland	...	16.6	21.4	34.3	...	76.4	77.3	70.1
Portugal	...	7.8	...	6.8	...	80.4	...	66.7
United Kingdom	16.0	16.4	19.4	22.2	90.9	92.8	89.8	86.1
Spain	...	...	...	4.6	...	...	...	78.0
United States	15.6	16.4	18.4	17.4	66.0	68.0	66.8	67.2
Sweden	...	23.6	24.8	23.7	...	87.5	86.6	83.4

Source, see also for explanatory notes Table 4, pp. 188-9.

light during the 1980s for those who had only completed secondary school and for others with relatively low qualifications.

Secondly, apart from the level of education, an important problem emerges relating to what is termed 'skills mismatch', namely the divergence between the qualitative structure of the demand for workers and that of the supply which can lead to long-term unemployment even of workers (especially if young and inexperienced) possessing a good level of education. It is no easy matter to measure this factor of 'skills mismatch' [8]. Leaving aside problems concerning availability and comparability of data from different countries, it has been shown that any such measurement is affected by the dynamics of unemployment rates and by how those concerned are split up into

[8] See remarks ABRAHAM K.G. [1], pp. 453 and foll.

TABLE 7

DISTRIBUTION OF INVOLUNTARY PART TIME WORK BY SEX AND AGE GROUPS IN 1991

	In thousand		Percentages of workers on part time for economic reasons					Percentages of workers on part time due to impossibility of finding full time work				
	part time for economic reasons, usually on full time	part time due to impossibility of finding full time	males	females				males	females			
				total	15-24 yrs	25-54 yrs	55-64 yrs		total	15-24 yrs	25-54 yrs	55-64 yrs
Belgium	3	119	67.9	32.1	4.5	27.6	0.0	11.3	88.7	19.4	67.8	1.5
Denmark	11	85	75.7	24.3	4.8	18.0	1.5	17.9	82.1	17.3	56.2	8.6
France	77	...	75.8	24.2	5.4	17.8	0.8	...	...	...	...	...
Germany	20	193	76.8	23.2	3.9	16.3	3.0	22.8	87.2	7.9	70.7	8.6
Japan	330	630	39.4	60.6	3.0	42.4	15.2	50.8	49.2	14.0	32.7	2.5
Greece	58	40	65.6	34.4	4.2	21.6	8.6	52.5	47.5	9.7	35.1	4.7
Ireland	7	29	60.7	34.3	15.6	18.3	0.4	50.8	49.2	14.0	32.7	2.5
Italy..........	97	416	60.5	39.5	7.7	30.0	1.8	42.3	57.7	17.3	38.1	2.3
Holland	14	363	74.6	25.4	18.0	7.4	0.0	22.5	77.5	14.5	58.1	4.9
Portugal	6	66	61.1	38.9	8.4	28.4	2.1	17.3	82.7	13.2	58.6	10.9
United Kingdom	177	446	82.0	18.0	7.0	10.3	1.7	26.6	73.4	15.2	47.9	10.3
Spain	38	128	60.6	39.4	9.1	26.0	4.3	20.5	79.5	19.8	52.1	7.6
United States	2,026	2,867	62.3	37.7	7.4	26.7	3.6	61.5	38.5	16.4	18.8	3.3
Sweden	27	...	30.8	69.2	15.7	48.1	5.4	...	...	...	...	...

Source, see Table 4, p. 16.

TABLE 8

UNEMPLOYMENT RATES IN SOME EC COUNTRIES FOR 1938 ACCORDING TO EDUCATIONAL LEVEL
(percentages)

	Level	Males						Females					
		all ages	20-24 yrs	25-34 yrs	35-44 yrs	45-54 yrs	55 yrs and over	all ages	20-24 yrs	25-34 yrs	35-44 yrs	45-54 yrs	55 yrs and over
Belgium	total	6.9	15.3	6.6	5.9	5.0	5.3	17.4	25.8	19.9	13.6	11.1	6.5
	A	9.0	15.9	9.6	8.7	6.7	6.5	22.4	32.1	28.3	18.7	14.8	8.9
	B	4.6	12.6	3.4	2.7	3.2	4.3	15.9	25.8	16.1	10.8	8.8	—
	E	3.2	16.1	3.2	1.6	1.2	2.3	7.7	14.8	8.6	4.5	0.0	—
Germany	total	6.9	10.3	7.8	5.6	5.6	7.3	9.4	9.6	11.1	8.6	7.8	9.1
	A	14.4	17.5	19.8	13.9	11.4	11.4	12.9	17.6	18.0	12.7	9.4	10.0
	B	5.5	9.2	9.1	3.4	2.2	2.1	8.1	8.0	12.8	4.5	3.9	7.9
	C	5.9	8.1	5.9	5.0	4.9	7.6	8.2	7.4	9.1	8.1	7.4	9.1
	D	3.0	8.3	3.6	3.0	2.0	4.0	8.8	8.7	10.5	8.3	7.4	—
	E	3.0	2.0	5.2	2.6	1.7	1.2	6.9	16.7	11.1	4.6	3.6	2.3
Greece	total	4.8	18.8	6.1	3.1	2.8	2.0	9.9	31.3	12.7	6.4	4.0	1.0
	A	3.9	14.0	5.5	3.2	2.9	2.1	6.2	18.0	11.2	6.8	3.9	1.1
	B	7.3	24.6	6.3	2.7	3.7	2.9	18.7	36.8	15.5	8.2	9.1	—
	D	8.1	23.1	8.2	5.1	—	—	14.1	29.4	11.8	6.3	—	—
	E	4.2	33.3	7.1	2.2	0.0	16.1	12.7	41.7	11.8	2.2	—	—
Italy	total	6.7	25.9	12.0	3.9	2.4	2.7	16.3	38.1	23.7	11.9	7.4	4.4
	A	6.2	21.4	10.6	4.5	2.9	3.0	15.3	33.6	23.1	14.4	9.1	5.1
	B	9.2	36.3	13.0	2.9	0.8	1.3	20.0	43.4	22.9	9.6	3.4	1.8
	E	3.3	25.0	22.2	2.8	—	—	9.3	60.0	32.2	5.9	0.8	—
Holland	total	7.5	10.4	7.3	5.6	6.1	13.1	13.2	12.6	13.6	14.3	11.6	12.8
	A	10.9	11.8	10.7	9.0	9.2	18.1	16.5	16.9	19.3	16.8	12.8	14.7
	B	4.8	8.1	4.3	3.3	3.7	9.1	10.3	8.7	9.9	12.7	10.9	6.9
	D	4.3	12.0	5.2	2.6	2.9	9.3	10.7	15.0	9.4	10.6	9.5	20.0
	E	4.4	—	7.6	3.0	2.3	4.2	11.4	—	15.2	8.0	14.3	—
United Kingdom	total	10.4	15.3	11.5	7.8	8.8	11.2	9.7	13.9	12.9	7.7	6.7	7.4
	A	14.8	19.9	17.9	11.6	12.1	11.8	11.3	16.8	15.9	8.1	7.5	7.0
	B	7.7	11.8	5.8	5.3	—	—	7.0	7.2	8.4	—	—	—
	C	8.1	8.4	8.7	6.4	7.9	12.1	10.1	11.8	12.3	13.3	—	—
	E	3.7	5.4	2.5	1.5	—	4.6	4.7	—	6.0	4.7	—	—
Spain	total	15.5	35.4	17.7	9.7	10.5	10.5	24.4	46.8	27.0	16.2	10.6	5.9
	A	14.7	37.1	19.8	11.9	11.7	11.6	17.9	41.7	27.1	18.2	11.2	6.2
	B	18.8	34.6	15.7	5.4	6.6	6.7	33.7	46.8	27.5	15.6	12.1	6.7
	D	11.3	39.1	16.8	5.6	3.0	5.1	21.8	52.9	23.4	6.2	2.8	3.8
	E	9.9	42.9	17.5	3.4	1.7	2.6	27.4	65.4	29.4	11.4	—	—

Legend, Level A = higher secondary school uncompleted;
Level B = higher secondary school completed;
Level C = level 1 professional training completed;
Level D = post-secondary training completed without university degree;
Level E = at least one university degree obtained.

Source, OECD, *Employment Outlook*, July. 1989, pp. 85-6.

professional groupings. However, the surveys, even if partial, made in EC countries, emphasise both the growing lack of work with the professional qualifications considered necessary (see results of EC surveys on manufacturing firms), and the increasing unemployment among workers whose qualifications employers consider inadequate (for the younger workers) or no longer adequate (for adults who are already employed). A comparison between the professional structure of the demand and that of the supply shows up growing contradictions and this induces a consideration of the distinct groups of labour markets, according to the professional qualifications of the workers, to be made.

A first group of markets concerns poorly qualified workers. In EC countries, in past decades and still in the 1980s, there was a marked lack of workers who could do jobs in manufacturing and in services (in addition to agriculture) who were considered of low quality from the labour demand aspect (as well as from economic and social standpoints generally) and who would therefore accept work at relatively low levels of wages and conditions. This led to mass immigration first from southern Europe towards central and north European countries, later increasingly from Asian countries (particularly from Turkey and the Far East) as well as from Africa and Eastern Europe. From the second half of the 1980s onwards, immigration from African, Asiatic and East European countries became established in Southern Europe as well, particularly in Italy and Spain[9], bringing out a contradiction which in recent years has become a subject of urgent study, latterly in Germany too. This is coexistence of a lack of workers prepared to accept work at poor conditions, probably willing to undertake low quality jobs, alongside growing unemployment of workers whose qualifications are considered low by a changing system of production. Among other things the powerful migratory potential from East Europe (including the ex-USSR) and from countries on the Mediterranean seaboard is (acccording to available information) greatly increasing the supply of poorly qualified — and often poorly educated — people.

---

[9] See data and comments in FREY L. - LIVRAGHI R. - MOTTURA G. - TAGLIAFERRI T. - VENTURINI A. - CROCE G. - GHIGNONI E. [13] and in FREY L. - CHILOSI A. - MALLE S. [12].

This initial contradiction appears to be associated with another, related to those workers whose level of education and/or of acquired professional experience makes them believe they are well qualified. The contradiction concerns coexistence of a growing number of unemployed persons of relatively good education (possession of a vocational diploma and/or completion of secondary education or who have learned some skills) alongside the problems, previously mentioned, of a lack of qualified labour. This contradiction, according to what we know [10], appears to be caused by the combined presence of a growing supply of better educated workers, whose previous experience has qualified them (making them unwilling to accept what they think are unsatisfactory conditions of work for any length of time), with an unceasingly changing demand for professional qualifications that differ from those presented by the available and constantly varying mass of workers seeking jobs.

Research on labour mobility in Europe [11] has brought to light a third contradiction, one that concerns workers whose professional levels are very high. In Europe the need for highly qualified personnel able to undertake active management and control of innovative processes made possible by the 'new technologies' has led to a demand for such people that tends to exceed the jobs available where they live. This lack has been, and still is, accompanied (especially in Spain, Greece and Italy and particularly among women — refer back to Table 8) by unemployment among university graduates. A normal way of overcoming the lack of highly qualified people is that of territorial mobility, sometimes associated with professional mobility inside the big firms or within multinationals. This leads to processes of selection from among the labour available which favours territorial concentration of the highly qualified unemployed (most of all among young men and women in search of their first job) in certain parts of Europe, such as for example a good deal of southern Italy and the eastern Länder in Germany.

Thirdly, this growing territorial concentration of unemployment in certain regions does not only concern university graduates, it is one

---

[10] See for example the discussion in Chap. 7 of the 1991 report of the DG5 EUROPEAN COMMUNITY COMMISSION [7], pp. 125 and foll.

[11] See MANSDEN D. [15].

of the most important aspects of structural unemployment in the European Community.

The regions whose development of production lags most behind, corresponding to those classified as Objective 1 regions for access to Community structural funding, appear to be particularly hard hit by unemployment. Not only is this true but, between 1985 and 1989 when unemployment in other EC regions fell appreciably (−12%), unemployment in «Objective 1» regions showed a rise both in absolute and in relative terms (+0.5%) [12].

Problems of employment in regions where development has been delayed are even clearer when we look at rates of employment, namely at the relation between employed persons and the population of working age: a good proportion of «Objective 1» regions showed rates of employment below 55% against much higher ones, as high and even higher than 65% in other regions [13]. The rise in unemployment between 1985 and 1989 in underdeveloped regions is associated with an increase of only 1.5% in their employment levels against +3% in other areas of the EC, and such a low rate has not been able to absorb the larger work forces that have been added to the excess of labour supply in those regions.

The higher concentration of employment problems in certain areas is itself a structural aspect of considerable and increasing importance. To accentuate it there is the fact that, in the less developed regions, the other structural components referred to above have particular weight. Mention has already been made of the concentration in those regions of unemployment among university graduates. This also applies to young people with secondary school certificates thus aggravating the growing territorial concentration of problems of finding work for young workers, and this (especially through the underdeveloped regions) continues to form a large component of structural enemployment although it appears to impinge less on the situation prevailing in European countries as a whole. The same applies to the female component shown by the increasing territorial differences among rates of unemployment among women.

---

[12] See DG5's report to EUROPEAN COMMUNITY COMMISSION [7], pp. 73 and foll.
[13] See EUROPEAN COMMUNITY COMMISSION [7], p. 72.

Information available from the EC [14] indicates that, still in 1989, female unemployment stood at 33% in «Objective 1» regions, against 49% in others, the net rise being less in the former than in the latter (from 30% to 33%, instead of from 43 to 49%) in the second half of the 1980s.

A sum of the different structural aspects of employment problems in certain regions makes highly questionable any attempt to analyze and to propose solution for them without a territorial breakdown.

3 - Assumptions for an Explanation of European Unemployment

In discussing the «slump in Europe» of the 1980s, Fitoussi and Phelps resort once more to the «classical» (or rather «neo-classical») of the most frequently used explanations, one that attributes a decisive role to trends in real wages (related to the marginal productivity of labour), and to the Keynesian explanation that attributes this role to a restrictive fiscal policy [15].

Neo-classical are also considered what are termed «Pigouvian» hypotheses which take as their basis a substantial rigidity of real wages in the context of a general non-Walrasian economic balance with rationing [16]. In actual fact the neo-classical origin of these hypotheses appears to be modified by introduction of assumptions on the presence of imperfect competition in determining wages and prices, including implicit and explicit contracts which tie up wages and prices, and of price policies laid down by firms who have to allow for the market demand there is for the products. Not by chance European economists organized in the European Unemployment Program [17] and who (thanks particularly to Drèze) are in some

---

[14] See EUROPEAN COMMUNITY COMMISSION [7], pp. 77-9.

[15] See FITOUSSI J.P. - PHELPS E. [9], pp. 2 and foll.

[16] It is well-known that this explanation refers back to MALINVAUD E. [14].

[17] Their first lecture on *The Rise of Unemployment* was held at Chelwood Gate, Sussex, in May 1985 (see documents published in *Economica*, supplement 1986). Economists supporting the programme decided to meet again in London or at Louvain-la Nueve.

considerable degree aligned with the analyses of non-Walrasian balance with rationing, finally show themselves favourable, though with due caution and reservations, to neo-Keynesian employment policies, including the fiscal measures of deficit-spending (so long as it is applied to productive investments) and to a reduction in the fiscal burden on labour [18].

According to Fitoussi and Phelps the Keynesian explanation, so dear to United States economists, ignores mechanisms to compensate for the effects of fiscal policies on employment. A more complete explanation should take into account the indirect part played, in relation to Europe, of American policies; these policies are thought to have influenced the trend of production and employment in Europe through mechanisms that fix profit margins in consumer goods markets and make wages more or less index-linked, as well as through the costs effects of real interest rates.

This reinforces the analysis since it gives a role, neither necessary nor sufficient for the trend in real wages (or rather in the wage gap between wages and productivity) to explanations of the trends in employment and unemployment and since it adds to neo-Keynesian analysis elements concerning mechanisms for passing on the shock effects from outside open economies.

The proposed explanation obviously departs from that of the more strictly neo-classical economists who consider it necessary for increases in monetary wages (due to a variety of causes) to be associated with rising unemployment, the consequences of this being all the greater the more real wages become rigid. To some extent it also departs from those explanations which, in emphasising the role played by rigidity of real wages, seek to clarify the institutional or contractual causes.

The conclusion in terms of economic policy reached by Fitoussi and Phelps differs little from that of Drèze and Bean: an expanding fiscal policy could have had a positive effect on the trend of employment in Europe within a context of international relations between 'Europe' and 'America' of the type analyzed, if it had favoured expansion of spending on capital goods, both by offering taxation

[18] See preface by DREZÈ J.H. - BEAN C.R. [8].

incentives to private investments and by increasing public investments.

Seen thus, the growing structural unemployment in Europe should be due mainly to inadequate constitution of capital. At this point however something is added (suggested by further thought on empirical research carried out in various countries) by economists engaged on the European Unemployment Program: apart from conflicting indications concerning a possible increase in mismatches between labour demand and supply in Europe during the '80s [19], it is emphasised that, to lower tension in the labour market, it is important to increase the supply possessing specific qualitative characteristics for which there is an excess in the demand, both by adoption of strategies for training and by others that concern wage differentials [20]. We therefore have assumptions explaining structural unemployment that, in line with the road opened by Keynesian economists as long ago as the 1920s [21], refer to the lack of mobility between one labour market and another as being a cause of long-term unemployment; among the factors presumed to influence mobility emphasis is laid on those regarding human capital that can be accumulated through training and the existence of inacceptable wage differentials.

Information available on the growing contradictions prevailing in European labour markets, with regard to mismatches between the professional structures of demand and supply, suggests that the latest explanatory assumptions, though useful, cannot satisfactorily clarify the reasons for an increase in components of structural unemployment among workers whose qualifications are inadequate from the standpoint of segments of labour demand where vacancies exist. Apart from problems of corresponding quality between the results of training done by workers and expectations of qualification/productivity by employers, it is clear how inadequate are the hypotheses of behaviour by the supply that continues to consider wages (even giving due importance to the specific role of wage differentials) as being the only and determining factor. It is of course true that consideration of

---

[19] See comparison between different countries and different aspects of mismatches as given in PADOA-SCHIOPPA F. [21].

[20] See the preface by DREZÈ J.H. - BEAN C.R. [8], p. 60.

[21] See the short summary in FREY L. [11], pp. 59 and foll.

TABLE 9

LACK OF WORKERS WITH GIVEN QUALIFICATIONS IN MANUFACTURING FIRMS IN EC COUNTRIES, ACCORDING TO HARMONIZED SURVEYS ON THESE FIRMS

	An important or very important reason for not employing more labour is the lack of any suitably qualified (% of firms interviewed)			
	1985-1986 all sizes	1989		
		all sizes	less than 200 employess	1000 and more employees
Belgium	51	63	64	61
Denmark	...	...	...	...
France	36	53	61	44
Germany	53	66	65	66
Greece	35	50	53	67
Ireland	20	28	30	...
Italy	42	75	59	88
Luxembourg	43	...	...	...
Holland	44	70	68	82
Portugal	...	67	...	...
United Kingdom	37	62	76	48
Spain	...	37	37	42
Total	43	62	62	59

Source, Ec, data processed and published by OECD, *Employment Outlook*, July 1992, p. 27.

wage differentials opens the way to explanatary hypotheses of behaviour by those in search of work that emphasise the value of job search schemes; it is also true that inclusion of elements of theory on contracts (implicit or explicit) as part of neo-Keynesian explanation, just referred to above, further paves the way for closer integration between microeconomic hypotheses on behaviour by the labour supply and demand, and for an explanation, by macroeconomic break down, of structural unemployment in Europe. However, recent developments in microeconomic analysis of labour markets and the interesting attempts to include macroeconomic schemes of balance or imbalance, press for much further study.

More thorough microeconomic analysis of behaviour by the labour supply, making use among other things of some recent developments in family economy [22], is most certainly necessary to enable us to find an adequate explanation of the greater number of unemployed women in Europe. Information available in fact shows that figures of unemployment among women in the EC have often been higher in spite of there being considerably more women in employment and also where activity by women has greatly increased.

It seems essential that a more thorough microeconomic analysis be made of behaviour by the labour supply (partly to make the most of developments in proposed dynamic analysis of employment and unemployment) also to find a satisfactory explanation of the growing concentration of unemployment, including that of young people, in those areas of Europe where development has lagged behind. In this case too, increases in overall employment are not, and will not be sufficient to prevent growing unemployment especially of its structural components.

An explanation of the tendency to increase territorial concentration of unemployment does however also require further analysis of the labour demand. We first of all need more convincing assumptions on behaviour of firms in relation to territorial localization. Table 10, drawn up on the basis of a survey carried out on a number of European companies, shows that, alongside costs of production (of which labour costs — including components other than wages — form a part) the institutional basis on which companies operate (political and social atmosphere, economic regulation, economic dynamism and potential market) and the technico-economic infrastructures (availability in quantity and quality and cost of these economic and technical infrastructures) are of considerable and even of greater importance; in the same way as much importance is attached to qualification levels of workers available. Adequate consideration of territorial imbalance in labour demand inevitably imposes an analysis broken down sector by sector [23]. On this point it is important that due consideration be given to the different technical

[22] Ref. some aspects that emerged at the Seminar held in memory of E. Tarantelli, in Rome, May 1993, See VARIOUS AUTHORS [26].

[23] This has forcefully appeared in relation to analyses of employment problems in the southern regions of Italy. See for example the contributions contained in CAZZOLA C. - PERRUCCI A. [5].

TABLE 10

COMPARISON OF PRINCIPLE FACTORS IN LOCALIZATION OF FIRMS IN THE EC

	Factors of localization			
	qualifications of workers	costs of production	institutional framework (1)	technical and economic infrastructures (2)
Importance attributed	14%	26%	35%	25%
Belgium	+	+	0	–
Denmark	+	–	–	+ +
France	+	0	+	+ +
Germany	+ + +	– –	+ +	+ +
Greece	– – –	+ + +	– –	– – –
Ireland	+ +	+	0	– – –
Italy	0	0	0	–
Luxemburg	0	0	0	0
Holland	+ +	0	0	+ +
Portugal	– –	+ + +	– –	– –
United Kingdom	0	+	+ +	+ +
Spain	– –	+ + +	0	– –

Legend,
(1) Political and social atmosphere, economic regulations, economic dynamism and potential market.
(2) Availability of economic and technical infrastructures in terms of quantity, quality and cost.
Source, Prognos AG, IAB, Nuremberg.

coefficients concerning input of labour in the various sectors and to how these vary over time. It is therefore believed essential for a full analysis and break-down to be made of employment bearing in mind the effects of technical progress on production and thus on the quantitative and qualitative structures of employment.

Although widely recognised that unemployment in Europe during the 1980s, and in the first half of the 1990s, is to some considerable extent due to restructuring, explanations offered that pay proper attention to the role of technical progress are almost non-existent. It is assumed that the trend of real wages in relation to productivity, namely the wage gap, has brought about labour-saving restructuring of production and so has done something to create unemployment especially of persons already working. It is often ignored, however, that decisions on technological and organizational changes are not influenced by the cost of labour but rather by other components of production costs and, even more, by changes taking place in the demand for products. Macroeconomists who seek to explain the reasons for unemployment in Europe usually ignore the fact that innovations in processes are only a part (and, for that matter, one that is lessening in importance as little by little the new technologies become more widely used) of new technology and new organization; there are in fact product innovations which may have an important effect on the qualitative structure of labour used but which, quantitatively, may very differently affect the dimensions of overall employment according to sectoral composition of the national or local structures of production.

It is thus clear that a satisfactory explanation of unemployment in Europe over the last ten years, also in view of what appear to be convincing scenarios for the 1990s, will require more precise and complex analyses than those commonly made, analyses that take better account of the improvements achieved by macroeconomic research into behaviour by the labour supply and demand, as well as the role of technical progress as a decisive factor of the production structure and of the demand, and consequently of the quantitative and qualitative structures of employment and unemployment.

A first step in this direction has been made in the monograph from which the material here given has been taken. It will now be advisable to give some brief indications of the consequences this may have on employment policies and on work.

4. - Policies for Employment and Work in Europe

An initial consequence on the employment policies suggested by neo-Keynesian economists appears from a consideration of the importance of the sectoral and territorial structure of production.

It seems clear that merely to stimulate private investments and increase public investments to promote generically job-creating production is not enough, but that careful attention to the quality of sectoral and territorial investments is also necessary. This means that the employment policies adopted must adhere closely to those for industry (in the sense of a policy for sectors of production) as well as to regional policy. As regards public investments, mention has already been made of the importance of technico-economic infrastructures — as far as concerns decisions on where to set up companies — and this leads to a consideration of whether or not it is advisable to make public investments in that direction.

It must be added that, on the question of deciding localization of firms, while the importance of the institutional basis and qualification of labour suggests that the fight against unemployment cannot be separated from broad strategies of economic and social policies, it also contributes to the importance of policies for work.

More generally speaking, a further effect of fuller analysis on structural unemployment, referred to in the preceding paragraph, is that of proposing strategies to contain unemployment (among women, adults with a low level of education and training, young people living in certain areas, immigrants), capable of producing lasting effects on the employment (or rather on the overall streams of labour demand) of groups of workers who are most exposed to risks of losing their jobs where structural changes are in progress or are expected.

Research on these policies [24] has made clear that, apart from problems of defining them, such as possible inclusion of action to regulate and give institutional order to labour markets as well as measures for income transfer that should more correctly be included in social policies, real labour policies should aim at improvement of the weak position of those workers particularly liable to become unemployed.

Among available policies, the system of explicative hypotheses that it is proposed to adopt particularly encourages use of those that:

a) enable the qualitative features (with special reference to professionalism) to be continually and suitably adapted in line with changes in structures of production;

---

[24] See VARIOUS AUTHORS [25] and extensive bibliographical references mentioned and commented on in FREY's preface.

b) facilitate mobility between one job and another and bring the inactive population into employment;

c) channel available resources rather towards creation of permanent jobs, within the framework of developing integrated production in certain areas, than towards guaranteeing incomes to workers exposed to long-term unemployment.

Type *a)* policies would tend to fulfil the imperative need expressed by 'retraining — not redundancy' which has inspired measures of a new kind introduced in Europe during recent years, especially in Germany and in France, to deal with problems raised by industrial restructuring [25]. Experience so gained has turned out to be very interesting since it concerns efforts to retrain and handle mobility inside certain firms: these efforts have prevented further large masses of redundant workers from becoming unemployed, bringing into being responsible participation by the management and by the workers organized to fit in with restructuring processes. This experience has however left open two problems: 1) that of suitable retraining of workers laid off by firms; 2) that of handling mobility so as to permit transfer from one job to another inside or outside a firm, sector and area. These problems appear to be of particular importance when seen against the set of hypotheses adopted for explaining employment problems in Europe. The first type leads to consideration not only of the kind of training structures that might be involved (according to how well qualified the workers to be trained or retrained already are) and of the content of such training, but also of the need for repeated retraining carried out at the right time, namely before workers who risk long-term unemployment actually lose their jobs. The second set of problems invevitably ties up type *a)* labour policies with those of type *b)* (strategies for handling worker mobility). When attempted outside a company, it has been found difficult to do this in all Western industrialised countries, particularly in European countries. Experience in Germany especially has shown how hard it is to reconcile the needs of employed adult workers, made redundant by restructuring, with those of young would-be workers in search of their first jobs. There is a great temptation to 'park' workers on mobility,

---

[25] See Bosch G. [2].

guaranteeing their incomes to some extent (as has been done in Italy with the Cassa Integrazione Guadagni), or to offer early retirement or a similar incentive to the older ones [26]. This temptation once more raises problems — widely discussed in the 1970s and 1980s by labour and welfare economists — of destruction and dispersal of resources in choosing income transfer instead of paid jobs for unemployed workers.

Seen in relation to the explanatory assumptions adopted, strategies for handling mobility can make an effective contribution to solving structural unemployment problems only in so far as — at least at local labour market level — overall streams of demand amply exceed those of new workers, perhaps leaving unsolved problems of mismatches between the qualitative structures of demand and supply to be dealt with by adequate measures. This leads us to relate mobility strategies to those of type *c)* for developing locally integrated systems of production that together can assure an overall labour demand of suitable size, both dependent and independent but forming part of a network of co-ordinated and finalised production interrelations.

The idea of locally integrated system of production comes from experience gained of 'industrial districts', of particular importance in Italy, mainly during the '70s and of which there have been significant examples in other countries as well [27]. Basic features of 'industrial districts' are: *a)* integrated networks of small firms, operating in a single field of production and which, by specialization and decentralization of their activity, divide up among them the manufacture of particular goods; *b)* co-operation among firms, together with specialization, leads to efficiency in terms of economies of scale and economies of scope [28] whether at individual or at district level; *c)* a flexible organization based on entrepreneurial dynamism and co-operation among firms; *d)* cooperation is facilitated not only by localization in areas where there is strong social cohesion and collective awareness but also by supply of services and information by institutions set up

---

[26] See documentary material and comments in OECD [17], pp. 213 and foll.

[27] See PYKE F. - BECATTINI G. - SENGENBERGER W. [23], and in particular the contribution by BRUSCO S.; see also PYKE F. - SENGENBERGER W. [24].

[28] For the concepts of economies of scale and of scope in this context see PYKE F. [22], pp. 2 and foll.

for the purpose; *e)* competition among firms is centered more around products than prices which makes for product differentiation, flexibility over adapting to market changes, keen interest in product innovation; *f)* labour occupies a central position, meaning by this that great importance is attached to availability of suitably trained workers who are adaptable, ready to offer their co-operation and to undertake a variety of functions, even that of entrepreneur.

Starting from this, it is proposed to take the idea further and aim at locally integrated multi-sectoral systems of production. It would be a question of overcoming sectoral specialization by districts and of aiming at economies of scale and economies of scope through local organization of networks of firms (mainly small ones) who co-operate in the pursuit of common objectives in creating more jobs. To do all this would be no easy matter. In the first place there would have to be a local environment favourable to active entrepreneurship and to co-operation among firms. The presence of basic economic and social infrastructures is decisive, just as the possibility of there being suitable incentives to private investments in given areas is also a very important condition. It is also clear that the role of public bodies (especially local) in providing services and information is even more important in this case than in that of the 'industrial districts'. As the role of labour is so crucial, decisive importance is attached to availability of services for use and for training to provide workers possessing the needful professional level, who are adaptable and are prepared to accept change, and whose attitude is one of collaboration. There is obviously a wide field open for labour policies which must necessarily be co-ordinated locally.

Something else that may be achieved by an increase in local entrepreneurial activity is assisting development of independent producers of goods and services, even more than has already been done in Western industrialised countries (Table 11), even consolidating and strengthening the contribution that such work can make towards creating fresh jobs. Labour policies should however assist, orientate and guide independent work to include it within co-ordinated and flexible production initiatives at local level.

Two experimental policies have been planned proposing to ensure supplies of adequate services for general use and for training

TABLE 11

GROWTH OF NON-AGRICULTURAL INDEPENDENT WORK
IN SOME INDUSTRIALISED COUNTRIES FROM 1973 TO 1990

	Thousands				% of civil employment			
	1973	1979	1983	1990	1973	1979	1983	1990
Belgium	394	397	416	469	11.2	11.2	12.3	12.9
Denmark	201	208	188	179	9.3	9.2	8.5	7.2
France	2,111	2,051	2,047	2,109	11.4	10.6	10.5	10.3
Germany	2,259	2,024	1,821	2,076	9.1	8.2	7.4	7.7
Japan	6,400	6,790	6,910	6,670	14.1	14.0	13.3	11.5
Greece	...	732	691	(1989) 745	...	32.0	27.9	(1989) 27.2
Ireland	81	94	99	126	10.1	10.4	10.7	13.3
Italy	3,583	3,234	3,683	4,296	23.1	18.9	20.7	22.3
Luxembourg	154	139	132	130	11.1	9.4	8.8	7.1
Holland	...	400	404	469	...	8.8	8.6	7.8
Portugal	307	323	539	680	12.7	12.1	17.0	17.1
United Kingdom	1,748	1,620	1,949	3,028	7.3	6.6	8.6	11.6
Spain	1,584	1,499	1,525	1,901	16.3	15.7	17.0	17.1
United States	5,451	6,751	7,540	8,710	6.7	7.1	7.7	7.6
Sweden	172	177	190	307	4.8	4.5	4.8	7.0

Source, OECD, *Employment Outlook*, July 1992, Paris p. 158.

purposes aimed at containing and gradually reducing structural unemployment in locally situated systems of production. One of the two experiments concerns a region of Europe where development is low, Calabria, particularly hard hit by high and growing unemployment. Details of this experiment are given in Frey [12]. Results will have to be estimated in the future using an accurate method of evaluating the micro and macroeconomic effects of the specific labour policy measures applied [29]. At the present time, however, it is worth remembering that the experiments so planned have immediately made clear the need to create networks of production that allow for the attempts to define and estimate what is known as human development in the different countries [30]. We should also add that experience gained in Calabria is showing that realization of adequate locally-based integrated production requires active intervention not only by national bodies and the local public organizations, but also by those at European level if economic and social cohesion is to be concretely pursued.

---

[29] See indications on this provided by OECD [19] e [18] Chap. 2, pp. 39 and foll.

[30] See books in the UNITED NATIONS DEVELOPMENT PROGRAMME, *Human Development Report*, Oxford University Press, the last of which was published in New York in 1993.

BIBLIOGRAPHY

[1] Abraham K.G, «Mismatch and Labour Mobility: Some Final Remarks», in Padoa Schioppa F. (ed.), *Mismatch and Labour Mobility,* Cambridge (Mass.), Cambridge University Press, 1991.

[2] Bosch G., *Retraining - Not Redundancy,* International Institute for Labour Studies, Geneva, ILO, 1992.

[3] Calon A. - Frey L. - Lindley R. - Lyon Caen A. - Markmann M. - Simitis S., «The Social Aspect of Economic and Monetary Union», Commission of the European Communities, Directorade-General for Employment, Industrial Relations and Social Affairs, *Social Papers,* April 1992.

[4] ——, «Labour Market, Fundamental Rights and Social Policy in the Community», *Social Papers,* May 1993.

[5] Cazzola C. - Perrucci A. (eds), *Strutture economiche e dinamiche dell'occupazione,* Roma, NIS, 1987.

[6] Commissione delle Comunitá Europee, «Labour Market, Fundamental Rights and Social Policy in the Community», forthcoming in *Social Papers,* May 1993.

[7] ——, *L'occupazione in Europa 1992,* Luxembourg, 1992.

[8] Drezè J.H. - Bean C.R. (eds), *Europe's Unemployment Problem,* Cambridge (Mass.), MIT Press, 1990.

[9] Fitoussi J.P. - Phelps E., *The Slump in Europe,* Oxford, Basil Blackwell, 1988.

[10] Frey L., «Disoccupazione strutturale e politiche del lavoro», *Quaderni di Economia del Lavoro,* n. 49, 1994.

[11] ——, «La disoccupazione in Italia: il punto di vista degli economisti», *Quaderni di Economia del Lavoro,* n. 38, 1989.

[12] Frey L. - Chilosi A. - Malle S., «Mercati del lavoro dell'Europa Centrale ed Orientale e potenziale migratorio», *Quaderni di Economia del Lavoro,* n. 44, 1992.

[13] Frey L. - Livraghi R. - Mottura G. - Tagliaferri T. - Venturini A. - Croce G. - Ghignoni E., «Aspetti economici dell'immigrazione in Italia, *Quaderni di Economia del Lavoro,* n. 43, 1991.

[14] Malinvaud E., *The Theory of Unemployment Reconsidered,* Oxford, Basil Blackwell, 1977.

[15] Mansden D., «Integrazione europea e mobilità del lavoro», Roma, CERES, *Economia del Lavoro,* n. 3-4, 1991.

[16] Ocse, *Employment Outlook,* July 1990.

[17] ——, *Employment Outlook,* July 1992.

[18] ——, *Employment Outlook,* July 1993.

[19] ——, *Evaluating Labour Market and Social Programmes,* Paris, 1991.

[20] ——, *Progress in Structural Reform,* Paris, 1992.

[21] Padoa-Schioppa F. (ed.), *Mismatches and Labour Mobility,* Cambridge (Mass.), MIT Press, 1991.

[22] Pyke E., *Industrial Development Through Small-firm Cooperation,* Geneva, ILO, 1992.

[23] Pyke F. - Becattini G. - Sengenberger W. (eds.), *Industrial Districts and Inter-firm Cooperation in Italy,* Geneva, ILO, 1990.

[24] PYKE F. - SENGENBERGER W. (eds.), *Industrial Districts and Local Economic Regeneration,* Geneva, ILO, 1992.

[25] VARIOUS AUTHORS, «Politiche del lavoro con particolare riguardo all'Italia», *Quaderni di Economia del Lavoro,* n. 46, 1993.

[26] — —, «Economia della famiglia ed economia del lavoro», Seminar held in memory of E. Tarantelli, in Rome, May 1993, of which many of the papers will appear in *Quaderni di Economia del Lavoro,* n. 48, 1993.

II - UNDERSTANDING UNEMPLOYMENT IN EUROPE

Wage Distribution and Unemployment

Jean-Paul Fitoussi - Gylfi Zoega
OFCE, Paris

Introduction

The increase in unemployment in Europe is often traced, at least partially, to the existence of some rigidities in the labor market. It is a common wisdom that wage inflexibility and labor market institutions increase the cost in terms of unemployment of adapting to shocks. In particular, minimum wage legislation is seen to have an important responsibility in countries where such legislation is binding[1]. By preventing relative wages and hence the wage distribution from adjusting, it leads to mounting unemployment among less qualified workers.

At first sight, when one considers the problem of unemployment in the US and Europe in the last two decades, this presumption seems to hold. In Europe unemployment has been quasi-continuously rising and has now reached levels unseen since the great depression whereas in the US, such a trend does not seem to exist. On the other hand, although an increase in income inequality has been observed for the US and many of the countries of Western Europe, the magnitude of this increase seems to have been much higher in the former country than in the latter ones.

---

[1] We acknowledge comments made by members of the International Policy Group of the OFCE.

N.B.: the graphs and tables indicated by a number and the letter *A* are to be found in the Appendix, the references in square brackets in the Bibliography.

In the US, the inequality of earnings increased in the 1980s both between and within industries and groups, defined by age and education. The consequences have been drastic. The combination of increased inequality and stagnant average real wages caused the real wage of the lowest 10% percentile of workers in the wage distribution to fall by around 30% between 1970 and 1989[2].

An increase in earnings inequality has also been observed for countries as diverse as Canada, the UK, the Netherlands, Australia, France and Sweden[3]. The causes of this increase in inequality seem thus to be of a global nature, although it appears that the US economy was most affected.

Two other differences regarding the earning distribution appear between the US and Europe. First, average growth of real wages was lower in the US[4] so the real wage of the lowest income earners declined more in absolute terms. Second, transfers seem to have mitigated some of the effect in many of the European countries, while transfers were reduced in the US[5]. Again, the impact on the lowest income earners is greater in the US.

But simultaneously, there has also been a marked increase in the rate of unemployment among the unskilled workers in the OECD countries. Moreover, the change in the structure of unemployment appears, at first glance, to be roughly comparable across countries. Thus changes in the structure of unemployment seem to have been quite modestly correlated with changes in the wage distribution, as countries with such different experiences with respect to the latter as France and the US, appear to have experienced similar movements in the rate of unemployment among the least skilled.

In this paper we want to focus on labor market institutions and minimum wage legislation and try to explain these evolutions. In particular, we want to look at the possibility that the interaction between the forces affecting the distribution of earnings and labor market institutions has contributed to changes in this distribution, the structure of labor supply and the structure of unemployment.

---

[2] See JUHN C. - MURPHY K.M. - TOPEL R.H. [16].
[3] See GOTTSCHALK P. [10].
[4] See FREEMAN R.B. [9].
[5] See GOTTSCHALK P. [10].

Among the developed countries, considerable variation exists in the institutional structure of labor markets. Belgium, the Netherlands and Luxembourg have mostly non-binding legalized minimum wages. France, Spain, Portugal and Greece have high and constraining minimum wage laws. The US finds itself somewhere in between. In Germany, Denmark and Italy there is no minimum wage legislation but minimum wages are negotiated within each industry. The UK and Ireland are special cases with no apparent effective restrictions on low wages[6].

Because, we want to focus on the role of minimum wages, a comparison of changes in real wages and unemployment rates between France, the US and the UK should be revealing.

In the first section, we will sketch some theoretical arguments which help explain the relationship between earning distribution and unemployment. In the following section, we compare the facts regarding the evolution of the earnings distribution in the three countries considered, and summarize the discussion about the possible causes for changes in this distribution. The third section will be devoted to labor market institutions and their possible effects, focusing on the role of the minimum wage in France. In the fourth section, a quick look at US and UK data on the structure of unemployment will help evaluate the specific effects of the French minimum wage on unemployment in that country. We conclude in the last section by considering the case for employment subsidies both to avoid the unemployment consequences of minimum wages and to alleviate poverty by raising the wage of the poorest workers.

1. - From Earnings Distribution to Unemployment

An increase in the return to skills may lead to a protracted period of low relative wages for the most disadvantaged groups of workers. The fall in real wages received by these workers would then be greater, the lower is the rate of growth of average wages. A period of technological stagnation and increased inequality would thus have a

[6] See GREGORY M. [11].

large effect on poverty. This seems to have been the case in the United States since the early 1970s.

Why would unemployment be higher among the disadvantaged groups? Several possible explanations come to mind. A possible reason is that as jobs become less desirable, workers' propensity to quit increases[7]. Workers who can only hold jobs which carry low monetary and psychological rewards may thus experience voluntary periods of unemployment or even find themselves periodically out of the labor force, provided there is no shortage of low-paying jobs.

A second reason, is that low skilled workers may have relatively higher reservation wages since they may be averse to accepting relatively demeaning employment in view of their low social status and the accompanying low self-esteem. Other reasons for high reservation wages are government transfer policies and possible non-market activities, including crime for the most disadvantaged social groups.

In these two instances one may expect the effect to show up as much in the labor force statistics as in the unemployment statistics.

Additional reasons for unemployment can be found in some form of real wage inflexibility. Labor unions may prevent firms from employing labor which receives a wage equal to some low level of marginal product, at least if those unskilled workers are not members of the unions.

A related explanation is the existence of minimum wage laws. If employment is forbidden at wages below some legalized minimum, the average rate of unemployment will probably be higher. Workers, whose product is valued less than the minimum wage, may become permanently unemployed. Alternatively, they may accept temporary jobs which pay the minimum wage[8] or others which carry nonpecuniary costs which make them less liked than the jobs which are eliminated.

In the last two cases there can arise a trade-off when the demand for unskilled workers falls. The trade-off is between low wages and high employment, on the one hand, and higher wages and lower

---

[7] This and the following point were raised in PHELPS E.S. [30].

[8] MALINVAUD E. [21] documents the increased importance of temporary jobs in the French labor market.

employment, on the other. This trade-off seems to be well grounded in general equilibrium theory.

But the message from *General Equilibrium Theory* is not as clear as one may imagine at first sight. The existence of an equilibrium where wages are above subsistence level is subject to several restrictins. To guarantee such an outcome, Arrow and Debreau have introduced the assumption that initial endowments are distributed in such a way, that, whatever is the prevailing set of prices, no agent is under the level of subsistence. Alternatively, it has been proved that a *competitive equilibrium* without survival exists, and that it has all the properties of the Arrow-Debreau one[9].

To avoid this kind of a solution — absent heroic assumptions on endowments — transfer mechanisms and redistributive schemes have to be devised. Minimum wage cum unemployment benefits and/or minimum income is an example of such a scheme. To investigate its consequences one has to reason inside a general equilibrium model where the labor market is heterogeneous. In the model of Dehez and Fitoussi [8], there exist different categories of labor, each characterized by an inelastic supply and a specific level of productivity. The other assumptions, including wage flexibility, are standard to competitive equilibrium models. The only restriction to perfect flexibility is the existence of a minimum wage.

Two results of the above model are relevant for the present discussion. First, nothing guarantees the uniqueness of the solution in terms of employment and the real wage level, except in particular cases, notably when the different categories of labor are perfect substitutes. This result is intuitively obvious. Suppose strict complementarity. then what matters for labor demand of a profit-maximizing firm, is the cost of each single "bundle" of composite labor. The same cost may be incurred at quite different wage distributions across categories. In that extreme case a relatively high level of the minimum wage may be compensated for by a relatively low wage for the more skilled categories of labor. Hence, if the wage distribution is such that the cost of the "bundle" of composite labor is the same as in the unconstrained general equilibrium solution, full employment may be

[9] See COLES J.L. - HAMMOND P.J. [6].

reached at a quite different relative wage systems. Social norms may thus impose a "fair" distribution of wages, especially in that particular case where individual productivities are not observable. In more general cases where technology exhibits some degree of complementarity between types of labor, the role of social norms is still important for the same reason. Hence, a move towards a greater degree of individualism, where each category tries to strictly maximize the quasi-rent from its human capital, can lead to an increase in unemployment in the low skilled segments of the labor market. In any case, in such a setting, the fact that the minimum wage is binding or not depends also on social conventions. This may explain why the distribution of wages differs across countries, otherwise similar in their technology and human capital.

Second, depending on whether the two types of labor are complements or substitutes, an increase in the minimum wage will lead to a decrease in the real wage of the other category in the first case and an increase in the second. But in both cases it will lead to an increase of unemployment.

The first result may explain why different patterns of wage distribution across countries are consistent with the same evolution in the structure of unemployment. On the basis of the second, one should expect a lesser increase in inequality of wage distribution in countries characterized by a binding system of minimum wage, than in other countries, assuming both types of countries are subject to the same shocks in the structure of the excess demand for labor.

2. - Changes in Earnings Distribution in France, the UK and the US: Facts and Possible Causes

The Appendix contains a summary of studies which compare changes in the wage and income distribution between France, the US and the UK. These studies find that the wage distribution has become more unequal in the US and the UK but only moderately so in France. Furthermore, the wage distribution is more compressed in France than in the other two countries. The small increase in the wage distribution in France has occurred at the top of the distribution but there has been a decline at the bottom.

We will look closer at recent French data since the above studies do not cover the most recent years. The French Statistical Office (INSEE) breaks down real wage indices according to education and age levels. We use this data and the consumer price index to calculate real wages for male workers for the years 1984-1991. Graph 1*A* shows real monthly wages for workers in the 25-49 age category, Graph 2*A* for workers between 15 and 24 and Graph 3*A* for workers over 50. Workers are divided into 7 categories[10] on the basis of educational attainment (Table 1).

TABLE 1

EDUCATION LEVELS

Group	Definition
1 - NDIP	Not reported
2 - CEP	No degree or CEP degree only
3 - BEPC	BEPC degree only
4 - CAP	CAP, BEP or other similar degree
5 - BAC	Baccalauréat or vocational or similar degree
6 - UN1	1st level university degree, BTS, DUT, paramedic degree, etc.
7 - UN2	2nd or 3rd level university degree, degree from important polytechnic, etc.

A small number of workers do not report their educational level. Moreover, this group varies substantially in size between years. It is therefore not clear, what significance should be put into the series. The second category includes workers who have the older CEP degree. The BEPC degree is the lowest degree in the current educational system and corresponds to 9-10 years of schooling. The other important levels are CAP which is vocational school training and the university levels, BAC and one year and more than two years of university education. The number of workers which belonged to each category in 1991 are indicated in Table 2.

[10] For real wages the first two are lumped into one using the labor force as weights.

TABLE 2

NUMBER OF MALE WORKERS
IN DIFFERENT AGE-EDUCATION GROUPS

Group	15-24	25-49	50+
1 - NDIP	82,980	84,833	14,219
2 - CEP	451,696	2,886,299	1,343,056
3 - BEPC	100,702	695,837	114,454
4 - CAP	568,633	3,310,571	545,796
5 - BAC	116,990	982,751	213,852
6 - UN1	62,113	712,760	82,396
7 - UN2	11,356	912,157	261,813

In order to describe changes in income distribution we calculate the ratio of the monthly wage of workers in group 7 to those in group 2. Then in order to detect at which end of the income distribution changes are taking place we also calculate the ratio of the wage of workers in group 7 to those in group 5 and then for workers in group 5 to those in group 2. The results are summarized below for workers between 25 and 49 years of age (Table 3).

The figures (Table 3) confirm the results of the three studies. Overall earnings inequality fell slightly between 1984 and 1988 and has risen a little since then. Inequality has fallen at the bottom of the wage distribution and risen at the top.

Two hypothesis for the different situation in France come to mind. First, France was subject to different demand and supply shifts

TABLE 3

CHANGES IN RELATIVE WAGES, 1984-1991
MALE WORKERS, 25-49 YEARS OF AGE

	7/2	5/2	7/5
1984	2.19	1.47	1.49
1988	2.16	1.40	1.54
1991	2.23	1.41	1.58

than the two other countries in the period[11]. Second, as discussed above, government intervention in the labor market and/or union activity prevented the demand/supply shifts from affecting relative wages. In particular, high and rising minimum wages may account for the reduction in wage dispersion at the bottom of the distribution.

In both cases, the structure of unemployment could be different in France. Before taking a look at the unemployment data, we will review some proposed explanations for changes in relative earnings.

2.1 *Possible Causes for Changes in Earnings Distribution*

The causes of increased inequality have been analyzed extensively in the case of the United States. The consensus appears to be that both supply and demand shifts are needed and that the data is consistent with a steadily increasing demand for skilled workers and fluctuations in relative supply of workers with different skills and educational background. Also the shift in demand occurred both within and between industries and both between and within education-age groups.

2.2 *Supply Explanations*

Changes in labor supply — across skill and age levels — are considered to be an important explanation for the fall in the education premia in the United States in the 1970s and the subsequent rise in the 1980s[12]. Such changes can be caused by public incentives to acquire training and education, immigration, changes in the system of edu-

---

[11] Changes in the experience premium in France (calculated by Davis) provide some evidence against the former hypothesis since changes in both the education and the age premium may be affected by changes in the demand for skills. The ratios of age group mean earnings exhibit an upward trend — indicating a rising age premium — for France and the UK after the mid-1970s, for the US after 1970. This evidence does not become conclusive, though, until one has looked at changes in the supply of labor at various skill and age levels.

[12] The latter applies to college graduates.

cation and increased labor force participation of women, in addition to demographic factors. In the US the baby-boom generation which entered the labor market in the 1970s and the increase in college attendance during the war in Vietnam are the primary suspects.

In France, immigration was important in the 1960s and early 1970s. In addition, some government policies have slowed down the rate of growth of the labor force in France. These include inducements to early retirement and extended schooling for young people who are not employed. Otherwise, the changes in labor supply in France have not been qualitively different from those in other western countries. There has been an increase in labor force participation by women and a post-war baby-boom which lasted until the mid-1960s.

2.3 *Changes in Demand for Final Output*

Some attention has been paid to the possible effect of international trade on goods produced by manufacturing industries. The presumption is that those industries employ a higher proportion of relatively unskilled labor.

A real exchange rate appreciation, which makes exports less competitive in foreign markets, would then reduce the relative wage of unskilled workers in countries which either export or compete with imports of manufacturing goods. The developed countries have traditionally exported such goods. This is related to the idea of 'deindustrialization' which has also been blamed on 'unfair' foreign competition in the current trade policy debates.

A related idea is the effect of changes in public purchases on manufacturing goods, in particular defense related goods. It is, for example, possible that defense related industries may employ relatively more skilled labor[13].

Alternatively it has been shown[14] how increased international competition can reduce both the real average wage and the wage received by workers in export industries. Thus, if a country exports a good in which it has a comparative advantage and this good is now

---

[13] See BEARMAN E. - BOUND J. [2].
[14] See STAFFORD F.P. [30].

produced more efficiently than before in other countries, both average real wages and the relative wage of workers in that industry — assuming imperfect labor mobility between industries — will suffer. This provides a possible explanation for the stagnating real wages in the US after 1973 and in Europe after 1980. Rising levels of productivity in East Asia could have reduced average real wages in the West.

Empirical results[15] suggest that while these hypotheses have some merit, wages have also become more unequal within individual industries.

2.4 *Changes in Demand for Labor within Industries*

Two kinds of explanations have been given for the change in relative wages across age-education groups within industries. The first one involves technological change at home and the latter technological change abroad.

Non-neutral technological progress at home can increase the productivity of those with more skills. A good example is the computer revolution. Studies have found[16] that the ratio of blue collar to white collar employment has a clear downward trend over time which accelerated in the 1980s. Also, the degree of skill-upgrading is correlated with investment in computers and R&D expenditures across industries[17].

The term *outsourcing* refers to the relocation of production to less developed countries following an increase in the productivity of unskilled labor in those countries. Unskilled workers at home lose their jobs as production is moved to less developed countries with lower real wages of unskilled labor. As the workers attempt to find employment in other industries their real wages fall and/or unemployment rises.

An example of this phenomena is the production of computers in East Asia (such as by IBM) which leaves marketing and administration

---

[15] Such as LAWRENCE R. [19] and BLACKBURN MCKINLEY L. - BLOOM D.E. - FREEMAN R.B. [3].

[16] See BERMAN E. - BOUND J. [2].

[17] See MINCER J. [22].

in the country of ownership. Another example is the textile industry[18]. However, this may be important in some industries, e.g. the auto industry and semiconductor production, but less so in others[19].

A possible explanation for changes in both between group and within group inequality is that of Dehez and Fitoussi [8]. This explanation starts from the observation that the productivity of labor cannot be observed and therefore wages are affected by changes in social norms[20] [21].

A related possibility is that wage norms may differ between industries. A change in the industrial mix would benefit groups whose wages were high in expanding industries.

2.5 *Unexplained Issues*

In the case of the US it has been calculated[22] that earnings inequality within groups, defined by education, experience and gender, increased by 30% between 1970 and 1987. This change can be explained in a similar way as between group inequality if it is assumed that unobservable skills are uncorrelated with the education and experience variables.

However, some observers have claimed[23] that the increase in within group inequality in the past 20 years in the US represents the "most important unresolved puzzle" so far.

3. - Labor Market Institutions and their Possible Effect

The three countries have very different labor market institutions. France and the US have a national minimum wage legislation whereas

---

[18] France has lost 50,000 jobs since 1991 in the clothing and design business and expects to lose another 200,000 (*Newsweek*, March 22, 1993).

[19] See Bearman E. - Bound J. [2].

[20] One study (Mitchell D.J.B. [24]), argues that the increased frequency of union wage concessions in the early 1980s, the decline in union membership and the decline in strike activity represented a downward change in wage-norms by unions.

[21] Discrimination may also play a role here.

[22] See Katz L.F. - Murphy K.M. [18].

[23] See Levy F. - Murnane R.J. [20].

Britain does not. Moreover, the policy followed in setting the minimum wage in the past 13 years has been different in the two former countries. The federal minimum wage in the US was raised in 1981 and then kept unchanged in nominal terms until spring 1990[24]. The real minimum wage declined as a result throughout this period. The opposite development has taken place in France[25].

The British labor market has two distinct characteristics. First, there is no national minimum wage. Second, industry-level collective agreements have limited coverage and are not binding on individual employers. An attempt is made to provide protection for those not covered by the collective agreements by 26 Wages Councils but it is also limited in enforceability and coverage[26].

A national minimum wage legislation can have at least two effects. First, it can compress the lower half of the wage distribution by raising the lowest wages and possibly creating unemployment in the process[27]. Second, it can prevent changes in the structure of labor demand from affecting the wages of the lowest paid workers, again possibly affecting the structure of unemployment.

The data above suggests that the French system of minimum wages has had some effect in compressing the distribution at the lower end of the scale. The ratio of the 90-50 to the 50-10 log wage

---

[24] In the US, a universal minimum wage was first put into legislation in 1938 with the passage of the *Fair Standards Act*. The states can decide on a minimum wage which is higher, or extend coverage to workers which are excluded by federal legislation. Because of the recent decline in the real level of the federally imposed wage, it is now lower in proportion to average earnings than in 1960 (50% in 1960 and 36% in 1988).

[25] In France, a universal minimum wage was first put into legislation in 1950. The SMIG did not keep pace with the growth of average real earnings, although it did increase in real terms. It was replaced by the SMIC in 1970. The minimum wage is indexed to inflation and is updated once a year in order to make it rise at the same rate as average wages. The government can also increase the minimum wage whenever it wants at its own discretion. The government used this power to raise minimum wages considerably in 1981-1983.

The minimum wage is universal in that it covers all industries but there are exemptions for young workers, who since recently benefit from schemes which allow employers to claim exemption from social insurance contributions in cases of new hires, and for apprentices and handicapped workers.

[26] See GREGORY M. [11].

[27] An interesting study of the effects of the recent raise in minimum wages in the US (April 1st, 1990) is that of KATZ L.F. - KRUEGER A.B. [17]. They study the effect on wages and employment by surveying fast food restaurants in Texas and find that the effect on employment had been negligible despite a considerable impact on wages.

differential is a measure of the skewness of the earnings distribution. This ratio is much higher in France than in both the US and the UK[28].

The French data also suggests that the second possibility may be true. The wage compression at the lower end of the earnings distribution in France which has taken place simultaneously with the large increase in wage dispersion in the other two countries suggests an important role for minimum wages.

Finally, it has been observed[29] that there is a high incidence of low pay in the UK compared to the other EC countries which may be attributed to the absence of minimum wage legislation or collective agreements at the industry level.

3.1 *Impact of the French Minimum Wage*

Graph 1 on the following page shows the evolution of the minimum wage and the average real wage in France. The ratio of the two increased drastically in the years 1981-1984. The economic consequences of minimum wage legislation should thus be particularly apparent in those years.

The binding minimum wage had several main observable consequences. First, the number of workers receiving the minimum wage rose. Second, as already verified, real wages had remained constant or risen at the bottom of the earnings distribution.

Third, depending on the system of unemployment compensation, labor participation rates among those same groups of workers could remain stable or even increase because of rising real wages. Fourth, unemployment could be more heavily concentrated among the least skilled and in particular among young workers with low skills. A fall in the demand for unskilled workers, in combination with constant minimum wages in real terms, could also have had the same effect.

The first implication is easy to verify. Table A1 has the proportion of workers, both male and female, which received the minimum wage in selected years, 1972-1991. There is a correspondence between the

---

[28] In 1986 this was 0.72 in the US, 1.12 in the UK and 1.67 in France (Davis S., [7]).

[29] See Gregory M. [11].

Graph 1

INDEX OF THE REAL MINIMUM WAGE
AND THE REAL AVERAGE WAGE IN FRANCE, 1977-1991
(January 1977 = 100)

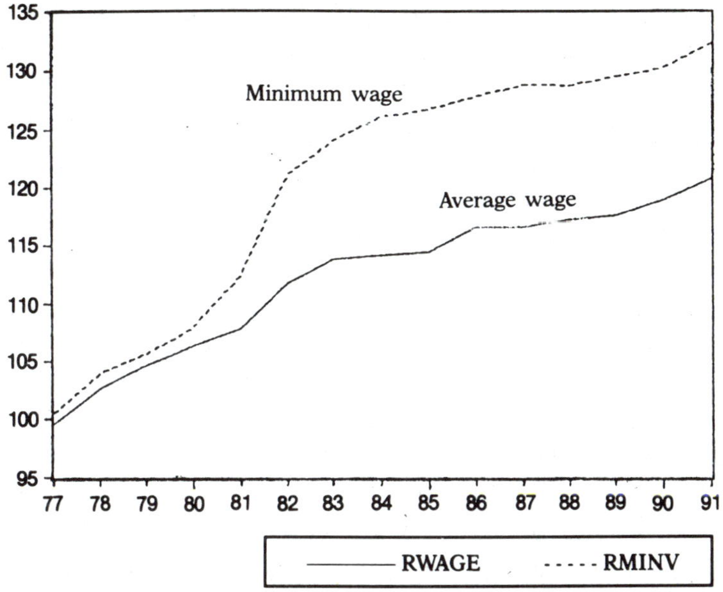

proportion of workers on minimum wages and changes in the minimum wage in real terms. The biggest increases in the minimum wage occurred in 1974 and in 1981-1982. The proportion of workers receiving the minimum wage doubled in both cases.

Between 1974 and 1981 the minimum wage was raised in real terms each year but at a decreasing rate. The same happened after 1982, with the exception of 1986 and 1988 when the value of the real minimum wage fell. The proportion of workers receiving the minimum wage fell in the first interval but rose after 1982 until 1985, was slightly lower in 1987 but then rose again until 1990[30].

[30] The proportion of workers receiving the minimum wage is, as expected, higher among blue collar than white collar workers (5.4% as opposed to 1.7% in 1991 for men) and higher among women than men (10.3% as opposed to 3.6% in 1991). It is highest in certain service industries, such as hotels and restaurants (28% in 1991) and both retail (21%) and wholesale trade in food (10.8%), in addition to the textile industry (16.2%) and the production of furniture (13.1%).

The changes in minimum wages also show up in data on the wages received by the lowest skilled manual workers. Table *A*2 has correlation coefficients for changes in minimum wages and real hourly wages of seven skill groups. The correlation is 0.96 for the lowest skilled workers and 0.80 for the highest skilled. In between, the value of the correlation coefficient is falling. The changes are also shown in Graph 7*A*. This observation is consistent with the hypothesis that changes in minimum wages have an effect on the wage structure. One can imagine more skilled workers also being affected if they care about their relative wages.

The 1982-1983 episode is particularly revealing in this regard since the increase in the minimum wage in those years was almost certainly exogenous, coinciding with the new socialist administration. We can see from Graph 7*A* that the real wage of the least skilled workers responded most and the real wage of the highest skilled workers responded least to this change.

Below (Table 4) are the results from Granger causality tests, using monthly data 1977-1992, which test whether current changes in the real value of the minimum wage carry information about future changes in the real average hourly wage of all workers. Granger causality cannot be rejected at the 5% level of significance in this case using 3 to 30 lags. The reverse hypothesis is also tested. It can be rejected in all cases.

Table 4

GRANGER CAUSALITY TESTS
monthly data, 1977-1992
number of observations: 192

	*F - statistics**				
Number of lags	30	24	12	6	3
d (*rwage*) does not cause *d* (*SMIC*)	1.549	0.911	1.219	1.693	2.172
d (*SMIC*) does not cause *d* (*rwage*)	2.846	2.854	4.571	3.060	7.175

Legend,
rwage = average hourly wage, deflated by the Consumer Price Index.
SMIC = real hourly minimum wage, deseasonalized.

* Bold letters imply rejection of null hypotesis.

We next take a look at labor force participation in the 1980s. Graphs 8*A*-10*A* show data from 1982-1989 for the three age groups and seven education groups.

Labor force participation of older male workers fell in the 1980s for all education groups. There is no apparent difference in the magnitude of this trend across education groups. There is some reduction in participation by prime-aged men with the CEP degree but it is moderate compared to the corresponding rise in the rate of unemployment. The same applies for those who do not report. Most imporantly, no fall in participation is visible for the young workers, not even for the least skilled ones who suffered extremely high rates of unemployment. The participation rates for the latter are consistently high. This contrasts with the experience of the Anglo-Saxon countries.

Turning to the last possible implication, Tables 5-11 and Graphs 4*A*-6*A* give data on unemployment rates among the same age-education groups in 1982-1991[31]. As expected, unemployment is and has been concentrated among the least skilled. More importantly, the ratio of the rates of unemployment of unskilled to skilled workers has been steadily rising over the period. Thus, while the rate of unemployment of the higher categories is about the same in 1991 as in 1982, this is not so for the others. For example, the rate for the CEP group is almost twice as high in 1991 for prime-aged men.

Unemployment has been highest among workers aged 15-24. Most noteworthy, the rate was 34.4% in 1985 for those with the CEP degree and 33.9% for those who did not reveal their degrees, most of which can be expected to be of lower skill levels. This youth unemployment falls after 1985, presumably because of exemptions granted from the minimum wage such as community work schemes, training courses and exemptions from social security contributions in the case of new hires (Bazen - Martin [1]). No comparable reduction in unemployment can be noted for older workers in the same education categories.

Almost all of the increase in overall unemployment between 1982 and 1991 is concentrated among the least skilled.

In order to test more explicitly the impact of minimum wages on

[31] Data was not available for the last four years.

Table 5

UNEMPLOYMENT AMONG WORKERS, 25-49 YEARS OLD

Group	1982	1985	1988	1991
1 - NDIP	5.1	7.2	6.6	8.2
2 - CEP	5.3	8.0	9.9	9.9
3 - BEPC	3.2	4.1	4.2	4.7
4 - CAP	2.6	5.0	4.9	5.3
5 - BAC	2.5	3.9	3.0	3.7
6 - UN1	1.9	2.9	2.7	2.7
7 - UN2	2.5	3.1	2.6	2.6

Table 6

UNEMPLOYMENT AMONG WORKERS, 15-24 YEARS OLD

Group	1982	1985	1988	1991
1 - NDIP	16.9	33.9	19.3	24.6
2 - CEP	20.00	34.4	29.7	26.3
3 - BEPC	17.0	21.2	19.5	15.9
4 - CAP	11.5	20.4	15.2	11.8
5 - BAC	11.3	16.3	11.3	9.8
6 - UN1	5.7	7.2	8.9	5.7
7 - UN2	16.8	12.0	10.6	5.6

Table 7

UNEMPLOYMENT AMONG WORKERS, OVER 50 YEARS OLD

Group	1982	1985	1988	1991
1 - NDIP	3.1	8.6	10.1	5.0
2 - CEP	4.6	6.7	7.8	6.7
3 - BEPC	4.5	4.5	3.8	3.2
4 - CAP	4.6	4.3	5.3	5.3
5 - BAC	3.2	2.9	4.7	3.7
6 - UN1	2.3	2.9	4.1	4.4
7 - UN2	3.8	2.0	2.6	1.9

TABLE 8

UNEMPLOYMENT ELASTICITIES

Group	Males, all	Males, 15-24
1 - NDIP	1.16	1.24
2 - CEP	0.95	1.28
3 - BEPC	0.88	1.09
4 - CAP	1.12	1.29
5 - BAC	0.71	0.90
6 - UNI *	0.47	0.71

* The two university levels are here lumped into one.

unemployment, the elasticity of the rate of unemployment of each skill group with respect to the overall male unemployment rate for the period 1971-1988 can be calculated. One can then check whether the residuals in this estimation correspond to changes in the minimum wage-average wage ratio. Alternatively the sample can be split into two, the first part used to estimate the elasticity and the second for out-of-sample predictions on the basis of total unemployment.

The elasticities, estimated for the whole period, were the following.

A look at the residuals suggests that the first group, all male workers inclusive, may have been affected by the minimum wage. The residuals are rising after 1981. Also, splitting the sample and forecasting for 1982-1988, yields underestimates for those years. The same can be said of the first three groups of young workers. These are more important than the first one, since it is not known which workers belong to the first education group.

4. - A Quick Look at US and UK Data

The fall in demand for skilled labor in the US has been described extensively in one study by Murphy and Topel [26] and another by Juhn, Murphy and Topel [16][32].

[32] They use data from the *Current Population Survey*, 1968-1990.

Table 9 is taken from the first paper and shows unemployment among men in different skill groups. The division according to education level may not correspond exactly to that of France, but the pattern is the same; the relative share of the least skilled, with high school education or less, has increased and those with the best education have not experienced a significant rise in unemployment.

Note that unemployment in the US fell between 1985 and 1988 so use of the same base period as in France would result in smaller increases.

Murphy and Topel claim that relative wage adjustments have been very similar in "high" wage (manufacturing and construction) and "low" wage sectors (retail trade, services). They conclude that nothing in the data suggests that wage rigidities in particular sectors play an important role in rationalizing the trend toward higher aggregate unemployment. This contrasts with the apparent importance of the minimum wage in France.

These results are confirmed in the second study, that by Juhn, Murphy and Topel [16]. A different method is applied to categorize workers. They are now categorized on the basis of their percentile position in the distribution of average hourly wages for each year. Workers who have the same rank in the wage distribution are considered to have the same relative level of marketable skills. Thus if the wages paid to workers in the first decile (Table 10), of the distribution fall, one concludes that the price of their skills has fallen.

TABLE 9

UNEMPLOYMENT IN THE UNITED STATES ACCORDING TO LEVEL OF EDUCATION

Schooling	1977-1979	1980-1982	1980-1985
8-11	7.11	7.64	10.27
12	4.87	5.40	7.45
13-15	3.75	3.66	4.84
16	1.96	1.69	2.18

Source, MURPHY K.M. - TOPEL R.H. [26].

TABLE 10

UNEMPLOYMENT AND LABOR FORCE NON-PARTICIPATION
IN THE UNITED STATES
ACCORDING TO LEVEL OF EDUCATION

Wage percentiles	Change in unemployment %	Change in nonparticipation %
1 - 10	7.08	9.23
11 - 20	5.57	6.59
21 - 40	3.13	3.46
41 - 60	1.45	0.92
61 - 100	0.37	−0.29

Source, JMT, 1991.

Table 10 shows changes in nonemployment by percentiles of the wage distribution between 1967-1969 and 1987-1989. This is the change in the proportion of the year spent in each state between 1967-1969 and 1987-1989.

The same pattern of changes in unemployment emerges as in Table 10. Unemployment rises most among the lowest paid workers. But the increase in non-participation is also of considerable interest. It has the same pattern as the changes in the rate of unemployment. The rise in total nonemployment among the lowest paid workers is over 16%. The comparable magnitude for the highest paid is 0.1%.

Juhn, Murphy and Topel calculate that for workers in the bottom decile of the wage distribution, real wages fell by more than 30% between 1970 and the late 1980s. By contrast, the real wages of persons in the top 40 percentile were stable over the same period.

The main difference between the US and the French data is in changes in real wages and labor force participation. Again, an important role of minimum wage laws may be among the explanations. But the structure of unemployment is similar, suggesting that the rate of unemployment is high among the lowest income earners even in the absence of such laws. The very high rates of unemployment among young unskilled workers in France may though be unmatched by similar groups in the US.

TABLE 11

UNEMPLOYMENT IN BRITAIN ACCORDING TO LEVEL OF EDUCATION FOR MALES (1974-1988) *

Education levels	1974-1980	1981-1985	1986-1988
University degree or equivalent	1.93	4.24	3.56
Intermediate (vocational A or O levels, nursing or clerical)	3.35	8.74	7.72
No qualifications	6.46	17.65	16.40

* Numbers from the *General Household Survey 1974-1988.*
Source, GREGG - MACHIN [12].

Table 11 shows the distribution of unemployment among skill groups in Britain. As in the US we have high rates of unemployment among the unskilled.

5. - Employment Subsidies

The return to human capital should in the long run be equal to the return to other forms of investment. One could on these grounds expect the problem to disappear, at least if average real wages are growing.

However, the relative wages of the poorest workers, when average wages are growing, or their absolute wages, when average wages are constant, may be deemed socially unacceptable. We have seen that minimum wage laws can provide a partial solution, by compressing the wage distribution and make the lowest paid better off in both absolute and relative terms, even in the face of low and falling demand for unskilled workers.

We argued that the cost of the minimum wage may be higher unemployment. Greater equality is attained only at the cost of lower efficiency. The question arises if anything can be done to improve the terms of this trade-off. Presumably, any measure which would change the earnings distribution in such a way as to make minimum wage legislation less important would serve this purpose.

If a transitory increase in the rate of return is caused by higher productivity of skilled workers, more demand for skilled workers or changes in the relative supplies of skilled/unskilled workers, a medium term solution could be subsidies for education and training which increase the ex-ante rate of return and so provides additional incentives to acquire human capital. The transition to equilibrium would be shorter.

This could also be done to affect long run equilibrium. Reducing the private cost of education while the social cost is presumably unchanged would cause larger investment in human capital. This would reduce the education premium and so reduce inequalities but also create inefficiencies in the form of an excessive large stock of human capital.

However, these measures will not help much in the short run. In the short run, the most obvious solution to the wage inequality-unemployment trade-off consists of wage subsidies.

Wage subsidies are also the obvious long term response to changes in wage norms. In that case, the medium to long term responses discussed above would be inappropriate since wages do not reflect accurately the relative productivity of workers. If, however, the demand for skills has increased, the wage subsidies will slow the transition to the new equilibrium and may thus be detrimental in the medium run. This solution may though be better than welfare payments which create incentives for nonemployment.

The government can impose a proportional or progressive tax on wages and use the revenue to subsidize employment of unskilled workers.

There seem to be at least three ways to implement this idea. First, one could give tax credits to the workers themselves to supplement their wage receipts. Second, one could subsidize the employment of unskilled workers by giving firms a tax credit based on wage payments to low-skilled workers. Third, a fixed payment can be made to firms for each employee, independent of the wage paid.

The first system would make the often low earned component visible to the workers and this may affect their morale. Wage subsidies to firms may therefore be preferred. The second option could, however, also run into some practical difficulties. Firms would have

have incentives to label workers as low skilled in order to qualify for the tax credit. The pay received by the worker would be unchanged but the firm's costs would be lower. Also, firms may arise which only engage in the activity of hiring workers and collecting tax credits. This leaves the system of fixed payments per employee.

APPENDIX

Changes in Inequality in France, the UK and the US

A comparison of changes in relative wages across the three countries throws light on important differences. Whereas the situation in the UK and the US appears to be similar, France shows different trends. The results of three independent studies are summarized in Table *A*3.

Davis [7] looks at annual earnings of full time male wage earners who evidence a strong attachment to the work force. This is taken to mean men who work a minimum number of weeks each year. The results are also showed in Graphs 11*A*-13*A*. His observations can be summarized as follows:

1) overall wage inequality for men — measured by the 90-10 log wage differential — was greater in France than in the UK and smaller than in the US for every year in the period 1971-1987;

2) inequality at the top of the wage distribution — measured by the 90-50 log wage differential — was similar in France and the US but lower in the UK;

3) inequality at the bottom of the wage distribution — measured by the 50-10 log wage differential — was similar in France and the UK but much higher in the US;

4) overall wage inequality remained almost constant in France from the late 1960s to late 1980s but rose continuously in the US and in the UK after 1979;

5) inequality at the top of the distribution also rose continuously in the US, increased slightly in France and significantly in the UK after 1977;

6) inequality at the bottom of the distribution rose throughout the two decades in the US, after 1977 in the UK but *declined* in France at least until 1987.

A second study is that of Gottschalk [10]. He uses data from the *Luxembourg Income Study* to compare the distribution of earnings at the beginning of the 1980s and in the mid-1980s. His selection criteria are slightly different (Gottschalk [10]) but the results are very similar. Measured inequality rose substantially in the US and the UK between 1979 and 1986 but moderately in France[33]. A further difference pointed out by Gottschalk is that social policy reduced post-transfer income inequality much more in France and the UK than in the US. Thus inequality measured by taking into account non-earned income and transfers and adjusted for family size was larger in the US than the inequality of wages of male heads of families. Also, the rise in post-transfer inequality of income in France was less than 1/3 of the rise in pre-transfer inequality between 1979 and 1984. The similar ratios for the UK and the US were 7/10 and 94/100 (between 1979 and 1986).

A third study by Gregg and Machin [12] reveals similar trends. Again inequality of earnings rose in the US in both the 1970s and the 1980s, in the UK between 1979 and 1989 and in France only slightly between 1979 and 1989.

Finally, this evolution is reflected in the Gini coefficient, shown in Table *A*4, which are taken from Atkinson, 1993.

TABLE *A*1

PROPORTION OF WORKERS RECEIVING THE MINIMUM WAGE

Year	Males	Females	Total
1972	1.8	4.6	2.7
1976	3.6	8.4	5.1
1979	3.0	6.2	4.0
1981	5.1	13.9	8.0
1983*	4.6	10.4	6.6
1985	6.2	16.2	9.7
1987	5.1	12.6	7.8
1989	5.2	13.9	8.2
1990	5.2	14.3	8.4
1991	3.6	10.3	6.1

* New series from 1983.

Source: BAZEN S. - MARTIN J.P. [1], SERVICE DES ETUDES ET DE LA STATISTIQUE, MINISTÈRE DU TRAVAIL, DE L'EMPLOI ET DE LA FORMATION PROFESSIONNELLE: *Premières Informations.*

---

[33] The greater rise in inequality in France may be attributable to the inclusion of part-time workers in his sample.

TABLE *A2*

CORRELATION BETWEEN CHANGES IN THE REAL VALUE OF THE SMIC AND CHANGES IN REAL WAGES OF BLUE-COLLAR WORKERS OF DIFFERENT SKILL LEVELS IN 1971-1988

rwage 1	0.96	*rwage* 5	0.86
rwage 2	0.93	*rwage* 6	0.88
rwage 3	0.92	*rwage* 7	0.80
rwage 4	0.90		

Legend,
rwagex = hourly real wage of a worker in skill group *x*,
x = 1-7 where 1 denotes the lowest skill level.

Source, INSEE.

TABLE *A3*

LOG WAGE DIFFERENTIAL AMONG MEN

Study	years	France		UK		US	
		90-10	50-10	90-10	50-10	90-10	50-10
Davis [1]	71	1.19	0.48	0.89	0.41	1.53	0.93
	79	1.19	0.47	0.87	0.42	1.73	0.96
	87	1.22	0.46	1.05	0.50	1.94	1.11
Gottschalk [2]	79	1.12		0.93		1.35	
	86	1.24 (84)		1.10		1.52	
Gregg [3]	73	1.18		0.91		1.24	
	79	1.19		0.88		1.30	
	89	1.22 (87)		1.17		1.49	

[1] Data for France is taken from *Declaration Annuelles de Salaires*. The measure of earnings is gross annual earnings, adjusted for differences among persons in annual hours worked for full time, full-year workers in private and semi-public firms.

Data for the UK is taken from the *New Earnings Survey*. It measures gross weekly earnings of full time employees, 21-64 years old, whose pay was not affected by absence during the survey period.

Data for the US is taken from the *Annual Demographic Files, Current Population Survey* (March). It measures weekly wage in the year prior to the survey of wage and salary earners, 18-64 years old, working at least 40 weeks and earning more than one-half the minimum wage on a full-time basis.

[2] Data source is *Luxembourg Income Study*. The data measures real annual gross wages and salaries for male heads of families, ages 25-54, not self-employed, working full-time. Data for France includes part-time workers.

[3] Data for the UK is taken from *UK New Earnings Survey*, and for France and the US from KATZ - LOVEMAN - BLANCHFLOWER, 1992. Both show hourly earnings. Earnings for the UK and the US are post tax but pre tax for France.

TABLE *A4*

GINI - COEFFICIENTS

	France	UK	US
73	38 (75)	27 (77)	36
79	36	28 (81)	37
89	37 (84)	35 (88)	40

Source, ATKINSON, 1993.

GRAPH 1A

MONTHLY REAL WAGE OF WORKERS
BETWEEN 25 AND 49 YEARS OF AGE
(1985 prices)

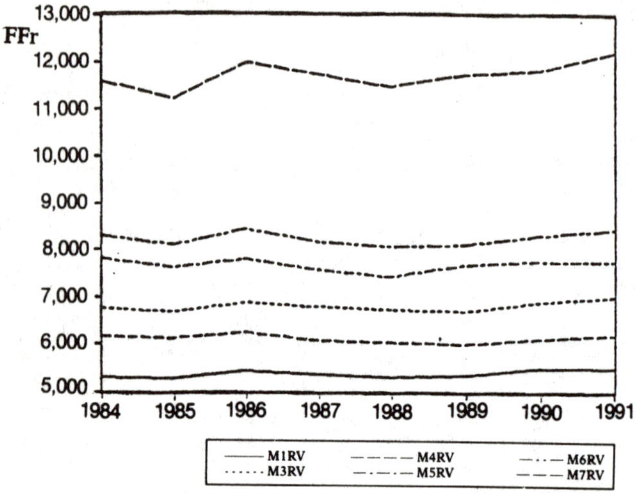

GRAPH 2A

MONTHLY REAL WAGE OF WORKERS
BETWEEN 15 AND 24 YEARS OF AGE
(1985 prices)

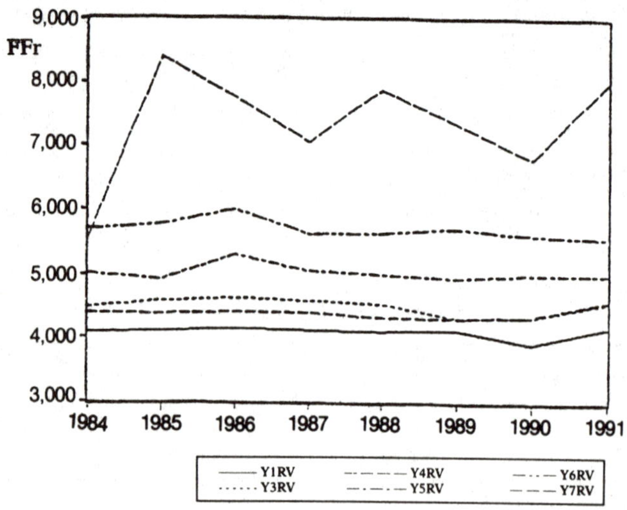

GRAPH 3*A*

MONTHLY REAL WAGE
OF WORKERS OVER 50
(1985 prices)

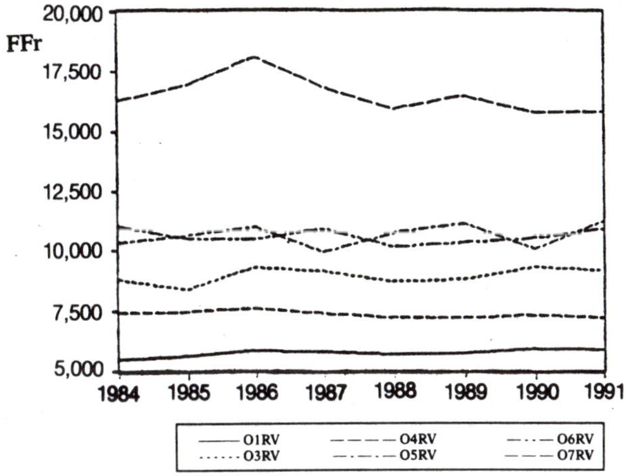

GRAPH 4*A*

THE RATE OF UNEMPLOYMENT
FOR WORKERS BETWEEN 25 AND 49 YEARS OF AGE

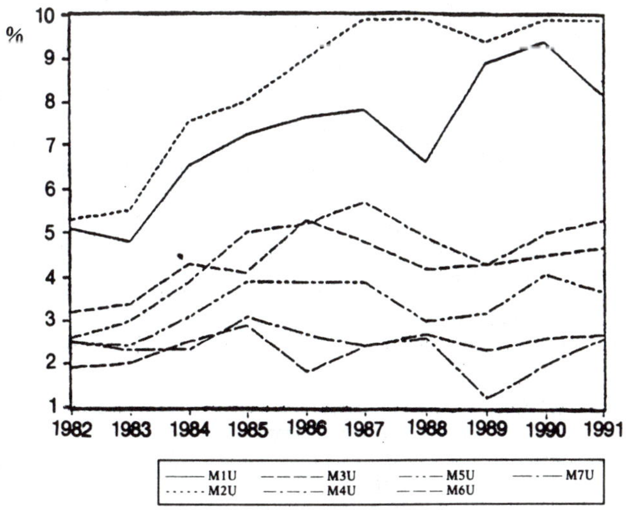

GRAPH 5A

THE RATE OF UNEMPLOYMENT
OF WORKERS BETWEEN 15 AND 24 YEARS OF AGE

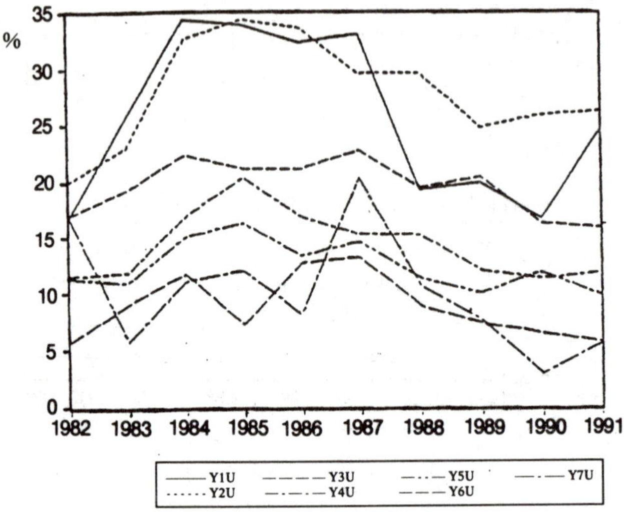

GRAPH 6A

THE RATE OF UNEMPLOYMENT
OF WORKERS OVER 50 YEARS OF AGE

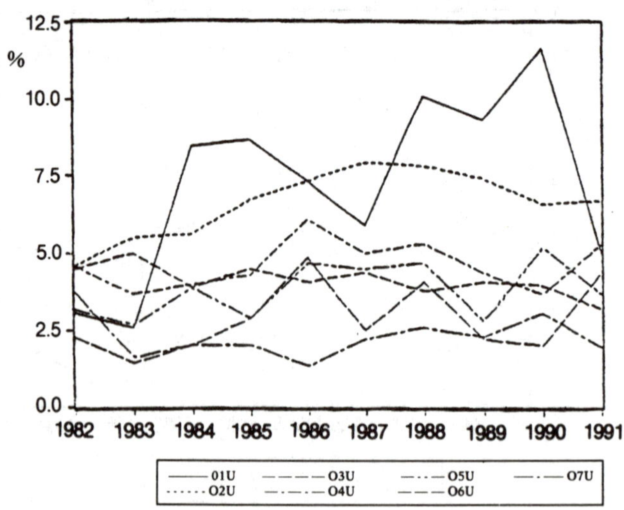

GRAPH 7*A*

RATE OF CHANGE OF REAL WAGES
OF TWO SKILL GROUPS OF MANUAL LABOR
AND THE REAL MINIMUM WAGE, 1974-1988

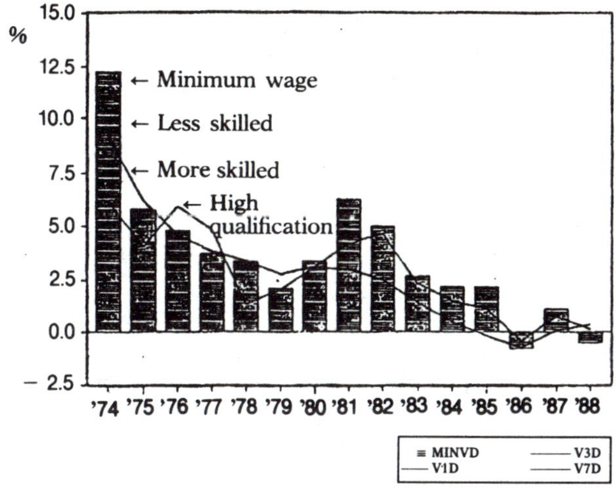

GRAPH 8*A*

LABOR FORCE PARTICIPATION OF WORKERS
BETWEEN 25 AND 49 YEARS OF AGE

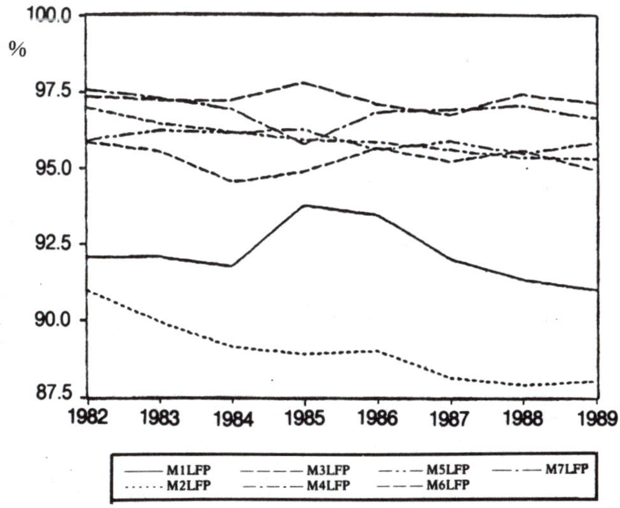

GRAPH 9*A*

LABOR FORCE PARTICIPATION OF WORKERS BETWEEN 15 AND 24 YEARS OF AGE

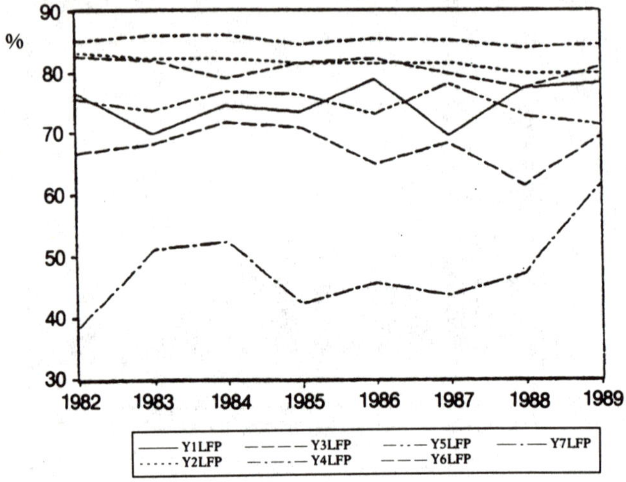

GRAPH 10*A*

LABOR FORCE PARTICIPATION OF WORKERS OVER 50

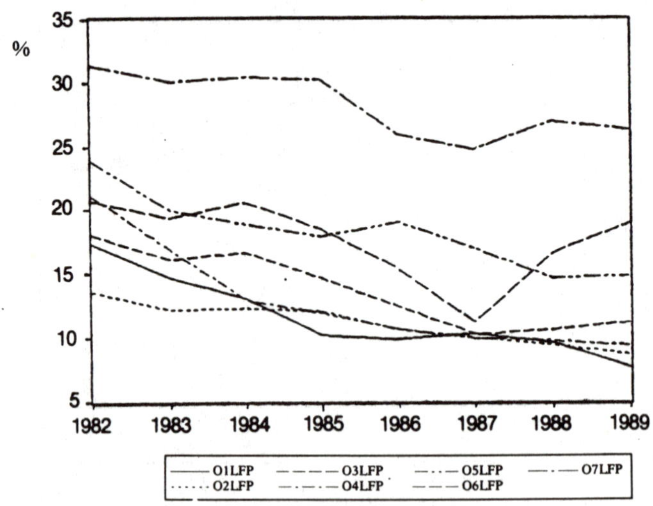

GRAPH 11*A*

MONTHLY REAL WAGE OF ALL WORKERS
(1985 prices)

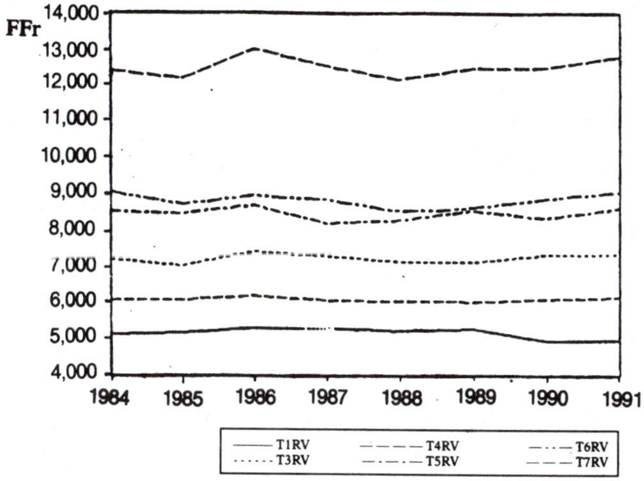

GRAPH 12*A*

THE RATE OF UNEMPLOYMENT FOR ALL WORKERS

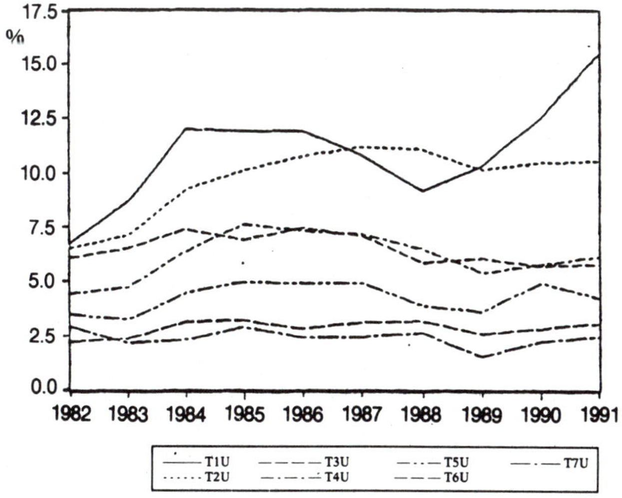

GRAPH 13A

LABOUR FORCE GROWTH IN FRANCE, UK, US
(from 1970 to 1990)

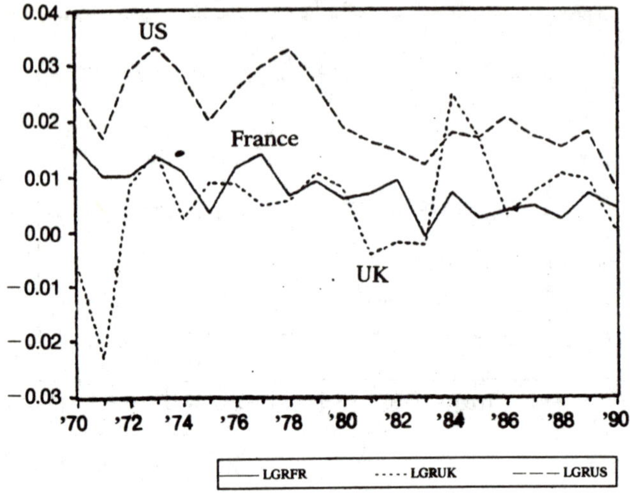

BIBLIOGRAPHY

[1] BAZEN S. - MARTIN J.P., «The Impact of the Minimum Wage on Earnings and Employment in France», OECD, *Economic Studies*, n. 16, Spring 1991.

[2] BERMAN E. - BOUND J., «Changes in the Demand for Skilled Labor within US Manufacturing Industries: Evidence from the Annual Survey of Manufacturing», NBER, *Working Paper*, n. 4255, 1993.

[3] BLACKBURN MCKINLEY L. - BLOOM D.E. - FREEMAN R.B., «The Declining Economic Position of less Skilled American Men» in BURTLESS (ed.), *A Future of Lousy Jobs?*, Washington (DC), Brookings Institution.

[4] BOUND J. - JOHNSON G., «Changes in the Structure of Wages during the 1980's: An Evaluation of Alternative Explanations», NBER, *Working Paper*, n. 2983, 1989.

[5] BURTLESS G., «The Contribution of Employment and Hours Changes to Family Income Inequality», *American Economic Review*, forthcoming 1993.

[6] COLES J.L. - HAMMOND P.J., «Walrasian Equilibrium without Survival: Existence, Efficiency and Remedial Policy», Firenze, Economic Department, European University Institute, *Discussion Paper*, n. 91/50, 1991.

[7] DAVIS S.J., «Cross-Country Patterns of Change in Relative Wages», NBER, *Working Paper*, n. 4085, June 1992.

[8] DEHEZ P. - FITOUSSI J.P., «Revenu Minimum, Allocations-Chômage et Subentions à l'Emploi: un Modèle Macroéconomique Simple», OFCE, *Document de Travail*, July 1992.

[9] FREEMAN R.B., «Evaluating the European View that the U.S. has no Unemployment Problem», NBER, *Working Paper*, n. 2562, 1988.

[10] GOTTSCHALK P., «Changes in Inequality of Family Income in Seven Industrialized Countries», *American Economic Review*, forthcoming 1993.

[11] GREGORY M., *Low Pay and Minimum Wage in Britain and the EC*, mimeo, Oxford, St. Hilda's College, 1993.

[12] GREGG P. - MACHIN S., *Is the UK Rise in Inequality Different?*, mimeo, London School of Economics, 1993.

[13] HIMANS S.H. - STAFFORD, F.P., *Divergence, Convergence, and the Gains from Trade*, mimeo, University of Michigan, 1993.

[14] JOHNSON G.E. - STAFFORD F.P., *Winners and Losers in the Globalized Economy*, mimeo, University of Michigan, 1993.

[15] —— - ——, *Models of Real Wages and International Competition*, mimeo, University of Michigan, 1992.

[16] JUHN C. - MURPHY K.M. - TOPEL R.H., «Why Has the Natural Rate of Unemployment Increased over Time?», *Brookings Papers on Economic Activity*, n. 2, 1991.

[17] KATZ L.F. - KRUEGER A.B., «The Effect of the New Minimum Wage Law in a Low-Wage Labor Market», NBER, *Working Paper*, n. 3655, 1991.

[18] KATZ L.F. - MURPHY K.M., «Changes in Relative Wages, 1963-1987: Supply and Demand Factors», *Quarterly Journal of Economics*, vol. CVII, February 1992.

[19] LAWRENCE R., «Sectoral shifts and the size of Middle Class», *Brookings Revue*, n. 3-11, 1984.

[20] LEVY F. - MURNANE R.J., «US Earnings Levels and Earnings Inequality: A Review of Recent Trends and Proposed Explanations», *Journal of Economic Literature*, vol. XXX, September 1992.

[21] MALINVAUD E., «The Segmented French Labor Market», NBER, *Conference on Unemployment and Wage Determination*, October 1991.

[22] MINCER J., *Schooling Experience and Earnings*, New York, Columbia University Press, 1974.

[23] ——, «Human Capital, Technology, and the Wage Structure; What do Time Series Show», NBER, *Working Paper*, n. 3581, 1991.

[24] MITCHEL D.J.B., «Shifting Norms in Wage Determination», *Brookings Papers on Economic Activity*, n. 2, 1985.

[25] MURPHY K.M., «Occupational Change and the Demand for Skil, 1940-1990», *American Economic Review*, forthcoming 1993.

[26] MURPHY K.M. - TOPEL R.H., «The Evolution of Unemployment in the United States: 1968-1985», *Brookings Papers on Economic Activity*, n. XX, 1987.

[27] MURPHY K.M. - WELCH F., «The Structure of Wages», *Quarterly Journal of Economics*, vol. CVII, February 1992.

[28] PHELPS E.S., *Economic Justice for the Working Poor through a Wage Subsidy*, Jerome Levy Institute, forthcoming 1993.

[29] ——, *Inflation Policy and Unemployment Theory*, New York, W.W. Norton, 1972.

[30] STAFFORD F.P., «International Competition and Real Wages», *American Economic Review*, forthcoming 1993.

German Reunification, Profit and Growth

Luigi Paganetto - Pasquale L. Scandizzo *
Università «Tor Vergata», Roma

1. - The Economic Cycle, Germany and the Role of Profits

The present international situation is characterized by a mild and long recession in a rather atypical economic cycle. After a long period of expansion, the duration of which has exceeded by about one year the corresponding period of the three preceeding cycles since 1970, first the UK and France, then the USA and gradually the other countries have entered the recessionary stage.

The first, main characteristic that makes the recessionary phase atypical, besides the fact that it follows a longer than usual expansion, is its asynchronic pattern and, as a consequence, its length. A full recessionary scenario for Germany and Japan, in particular, has materialized since the late winter of 1991. Moreover, while Japan seems to have recovered somethat since April 1993, the slump in Germany appears to be deepening.

The asynchronism among the world economies can be in part explained by the lack of a single source for a common contractionary shock. In particular, no supply shock has concerned oil or the other raw materials of which OECD countries are net importers. Prices of primary commodities, in fact, have displayed an overall downward trend, thus reducing, if anything, the intensity of the slump.

The asynchronism caused by the lack of symmetric shocks has been enlarged by some distinctively asymmetric shocks. On one hand,

---

N.B.: the numbers in square brackets refer to the Bibliography at the end of the paper.

German reunification has provided a localized, intense expansionary stimulus, which has been at the root of the late beginning of recession in Germany. On the other hand, the attempt of the USA to cure the domestic slump with an expansionary monetary policy has contrasted with the decoupling of monetary and fiscal policies attempted in the EMS under the German leadership.

In part as a consequence of these shocks, in part because of an underlying disequilibrium between demand and supply, the stylized facts between demand and supply, characterizing the present economic slump in the OECD countries, are rather atypical. In addition to the prolonged terminal phase, the present recession is in fact characterized by high unemployment and widespread deficit-financing. At the same time, however, long term interest rates are still high in Europe, where investment is also declining, while productivity appears to be rising in Europe and Japan. Inflation, which has been unusually moderate throughout the cycle, is mildly on the rise in Germany, but stationary in the other countries.

At the root of these seemingly contradictory features, we conjecture that the asymmetry of the factors affecting Germany plays a significant and perhaps determining role. German reunification, in fact, has made it possible to prolong the expansionary phase of the cycle, but this has occurred through a rather unusual mechanism: the rise of profit expectations via an induced imbalance between investment and savings.

The idea that enhanced profit prospects may significantly affect the business cycle was elaborated by Keynes ([12], Chapter 7) who, recalling an earlier discussion in his *Treatise on Money*, argued that a rise of expected profit, in excess of a "normal" income for the entrepreneur, was essentially the result and the root of a disequilibrium: «... As I now think, the volume of employment (and consequently of output and real income) is fixed by the entrepreneur under the motive of seeking to maximize his present and prospective profits (the allowance for user cost being determined by his view as to the use of equipment which will maximize his return from it over its whole life); whilst the volume of employment which will maximize his profit depends on the aggregate demand function given by his expectations of the sum of the proceeds resulting from consumption and investment respectively on various hypotheses... the expectation of an increased excess of Investment over Saving, given the former volume of employment and output, will induce entrepreneurs to increase the volume of employment and output».

In Keynes' discussion, the supply change (i.e. the entrepreneur's choice reguarding the rate of change of production and employment) depends on the expectation of profit over and above the «normal» level of income. But profit in turn depends on the excess of planned investment over planned savings. Expected excess demand, in other words, determines the change in supply that eventually drives the economy.

The demand-driven nature of the Keynesian cycle is of course well known, at least to the extent that it is predicated upon a (not necessarily absolute) failure of prices to adjust in response to a demand shift (see Romer [15] and Tobin [17] for a comprehensive discussion on this subject).

Less clear and much more detable appears however the link between demand and supply in a full Keynesian model, where the preference for liquidity and technology are explicitly considered. Earlier models of the accelerator by Kaldor [8], Goodwin [6], Ichimura [7] and others, take for granted that a supply increase will follow an anticipated excess of investment over savings, regardless of the effect of interest and profit rates on investment.

The more recent literature on this subject, however, is of a different opinion. As Stiglitz [16] persuasively argues, profits and firm equity levels, in addition to interest rates, are likely to be important determinants of investment behavior. Thus, earlier Keynesian models of growth and trade cycles (see, for example, Kaldor [9] and [10] and Kalecki [11]), once re-interpreted in the light of the more recent theoretical developments on the importance of the financial structure of the firm, can find firmer grounds for validation than in the past, when they were dismissed for «lack of microfoundations».

An interesting interpretation in this respect is provided by King [13], who discusses Gali's [5] results on the shocks accounting for fluctuations in gross national product at business cycle horizons. According to King, the *IS* shocks correspond to what Keynes would have seen as the outcome of "animal spirits" on investment demand.

While a positive *IS* shock has the effect of raising output and the nominal interest rate in the short run, however, its long run effects are reversed and more dramatic: a surge in the inflation rate, that rises permanently at all horizons, and a long term real interest rate *decline*.

Following the lead provided by the original Keynesian suggestions, we conjecture that a temporary increase in profit expectations may be at the root of the economic developments in Germany in the period after 1989. The main determinants of such a rise in profit expectations may be traced to three main causes. First, the general feeling of a reconstruction to be undertaken, similar in scope and size to the effort successfully performed after the Second World War, gave rise to a mobilization of entrepreneurship of unprecedented proportions. Second, the existence of many constraints to efficiency, which were the consequence of the socialist mode of organization, led to the belief that their removal could easily achieve dramatic profit increases.

For example, inefficient input procurement and inventory management had resulted in the past in widespread hoarding of both products and raw materials. The introduction of sound management practices and the sheer force of the market mechanism could reasonably be believed to produce large profits without much resource to new physical capital, by removing systemic bottlenecks and putting the ratio between current assets and production on a more rational basis (Various Authors [1], p. 6).

To these somewhat natural reasons for enhanced expectations, one must add the measures of financial support to the privatization program provided by the German government. Although these measures do not appear to correspond to a well coordinated and clear-cut concept of promotion (Bethkenhagen [2], p. 8), they certainly appear to favour expectations of large profits, specially for already successful entreprises. Moreover, the most important meassures of financial support favour immediate profit making by paying anticipated investment subsidies of up to 23% towards the construction of new plants, up to 20% towards investment in new plant capacity and up to 15% for rationalization investment.

Some data can give an idea of the size of private response that followed this combination of subjective and objective incentives.

Between January 1990 and March 1991, 331,000 new business were started in East Germany, while 34,000 businesses closed down (Various Authors [2], p. 4). In 1991, 6,000 out of 20,000 West German enterprises interviewed by the Chambers of Commerce declared that they had investment activities in East Germany. In March 1991 there were 117,000 private artisan firms contributing about 10% of the Eastern German GNP. At the same time, by the end of 1991, the large American companies had entered the arena, among them Ford, General Motors, Philip Morris, Reynolds, Coca Cola, Procter & Gamble and Otis Elevator.

Given this scenario, the rise in profit expectations provided a surge in private investment, which in the short run was concentrated on the removal of *X* inefficiencies and did not result, therefore, in large inflows of capital. The ensuing boom in economic activity that occurred both in West and East Germany while the other European countries were running into the recessionary phase of the cycle, caused the monetary authorities to react by keeping high interest rates, also as a consequence of a general pressure of the higher expected profits on the money market. Therefore, and this is our main contention, higher profits had the result of temporarily improving the economic situation in Germany at the expense of the other European countries. The overall effect of this process is however contractionary, as a longer and deeper recession resulted, even in Germany where the temporary shift of effective demand was paid with a rise of the rate of inflation over the long run.

2. - Profit Rate and Interest Rate: a Keynesian Model

Consider the hypothesis, originally advanced by Keynes, of profit emerging as a disequilibrium element in the investment-saving balance. Indicating with π the profit share, this hypothesis can be stated as follows:

$$\pi = \frac{I - S - F}{Y} \tag{1}$$

where: π = profit share
I = investment
S = domestic savings
F = balance of payment deficit (foreign savings)
Y = GNP

Totally differentiating both sides of *(1)* and solving for dY yields:

$$(2) \qquad dY = \frac{1}{(\pi + s)}(dI - dF - Yd\pi)$$

where s denotes the marginal propensity to save. From *(2)* it follows that the profit share has a negative effect on the multiplier both in terms of level (a higher share profit implies a lower multiplier) and in terms of change (an increase in π causes a *coeteris paribus* fall in GNP). The reason this occurs is that the disequilibrium specification in [1] causes an additional leakage to the multiplication process generated by consumption. The disequilibrium arising from an excess of investment over savings, in fact, implies that domestic absorption is limited to total expenditure net of total (domestic and foreign) savings and profits.

To complete the model, however, we have to consider first the nexus between expenditure and money, as in the *IS-LM* framework, and then the conditions for increase in production capacity and growth. An obvious and reasonable hypothesis to construct the first nexus is that investment is a positive function of the profit share[1] and a negative function of the interest rate:

$$(3) \qquad I = I(i_0, \pi, r)$$

$$\partial I / \partial i_0 > 0$$

$$\partial I / \partial \pi > 0$$

$$\partial I / \partial r < 0$$

[1] Assuming, as we do in the following, that the capital output ratio is constant, ensures that profit as a ratio to total output (i.e. the profit *share*) is proportional to profit divided by capital (i.e. the profit *rate*).

where I is investment, i_0 is an autonomous expense (e.g. public investment), and r the interest rate. Differentiating and substituting into *(2)* yields:

$$(4) \qquad dY = \frac{1}{\pi + s}(\alpha\, d\, i_0 + \beta\, d\, r + (h - Y)\, d\, \pi - d\, F)$$

where:

$$\alpha = \partial I / \partial\, i_0$$

$$\beta = |\partial I / \partial\, r|$$

$$h = \partial I / \partial\, \pi\,.$$

A higher expected profit share is also likely to be associated with a larger flow of foreign savings, while a higher interest rate will cause, through a revaluation of the currency, an increase in the balance of payment deficit. Thus:

$$(5) \qquad F = F(w, \pi, r)$$

$$\partial F / \partial\, w > \, < 0$$

$$\partial\, F / \partial\, \pi > 0$$

$$\partial F / \partial\, r > 0$$

where w is an exogenous shifter depending on world trade and other components of the "external" environment.

Differentiating *(5)* totally and substituting into *(4)* yields the final form of the *IS* function in disequilibrium:

$$(6) \qquad dY = \frac{1}{\pi + s}[\alpha\, d\, i_0 - \theta\, d\, w_0 + (h - \varphi - Y)\, d\, \pi - (\beta + \lambda)\, dr]$$

where:

$$\theta = \partial F / \partial\, w$$

$$\varphi = \partial F / \partial\, \pi$$

$$\lambda = \partial F / \partial\, r$$

The *IS* function is thus negative in φ, but can be either positive or negative in $d\pi$.

On the money side, assume that the money demand equation has the form:

$$M = M(PY, \pi, r) \tag{7}$$

where M denotes money and P the price level.

Expression *(7)* yields, by total differentiation:

$$dY = \frac{1}{mP} dM - Y\frac{dP}{P} + \frac{l}{mP} dr - b\,d\pi \tag{8}$$

where:
$$m = \frac{\partial M}{\partial (PY)}$$

$$l = \left|\frac{\partial M}{\partial r}\right|$$

$$b = \frac{\partial M}{\partial \pi}, \text{ are all } > 0$$

Demand for money, in particular, will be a positive function of the expected profit share, since a higher profit will make real business more attractive than financial activities.

By eliminating dY between *(6)* and *(8)*, and solving for dr:

$$dr = \frac{mp}{l(\pi+s)+(\beta+\lambda)\,mp} \cdot \tag{9}$$

$$\cdot \left[\alpha\, di_0 - \theta\, dw_0 + (h - \varphi - b - Y)\, d\pi \; + \right.$$

$$\left. - \frac{(\pi+s)}{mp} dM - \frac{(\pi+s)}{m} Y dP \right]$$

The derivative of the interest rate with respect to the profit share is:

(10) $$\frac{dr}{d\pi} = \frac{mp(h-\varphi-b-Y)}{l(\pi+s)+(\beta+\lambda)\,mp}$$

In order to interpret expression *(10)*, consider its version in terms of elasticities:

$$\rho_\pi = \frac{dr}{d\pi}\frac{\pi}{r} = \frac{\mu_y(j\,\eta_\pi - f\,\varepsilon_\pi - \eta\,\mu_\pi - \pi)}{|\eta_r|\,(\pi+s)+(j\,|\eta_r| + f\,\varepsilon_r)\,\mu_y}$$

where:

(11) $$\mu_y = \partial \log M / \partial \log (PY)$$

$$\mu_r = \partial \log M / \partial \log r$$

$$\eta_\pi = \partial \log I / \partial \log \pi$$

$$\eta_r = \partial \log I / \partial \log r$$

$$\mu_\pi = \partial \log M / \partial \log \pi$$

$$\varepsilon_\pi = \partial \log F / \partial \log \pi$$

$$\varepsilon_r = \partial \log F / \partial \log r$$

$$j = I / Y$$

$$f = F / Y$$

$$n = M / Y$$

Expression *(11)* states that the sign of the relationship between the profit share and the interest rate will be positive or negative depending on whether:

(12) $$j\,\eta_\pi + \eta\,\mu_\pi >< \pi + f\,\varepsilon_\pi$$

In other to explain this result more fully, consider again the form of the *IS* function obtained in equation *(6)*. An exogenous shift of the profit rate has two opposite effects on this function in the *Y, r* space (Graph 1). On the one hand, because of the positive link between expected profits and investment, a greater profit will tend to shift the function to the right. On the other hand, this expansive trend will be countered by two negative effects: *(i)* the reduction of the multiplier due to the fact that increased profit expectations increase the disequilibrium conditions of the economy and, *(ii)* the larger inflow of capital from abroad, with the ensuing deficit in the current account balance.

Because the *LM* curve shifts unequivocally to the left in response to a profit increase as money balances respond to business opportunities, the final effect on the interest rate is still undetermined.

If the initial situation is one of a current account surplus, expression *(12)* is more likely to be positive, however, since in this case the condition required is more easily respected, because of the negativity of f. Thus, even though the net effect remains undetermined, a country with a current account surplus (like Germany) is more likely to experience an increase in the interest rate that can be combined with a contractionary effect on income.

In Graph 1, if the initial equilibrium *A* is perturbed by an exogenous increase in profit expectations, the net effect of the ensuing shifts of the (disequilibrium) *IS* and *LM* curves may well be deflationary as a more than proportional increase in the interest rate is followed by a decline in output. The final point *D* corresponds to a higher interest rate and a lower income level.

From *(6)* and *(8)*, assuming that the production function is of the constant capital-output ratio variety and imposing the condition that demand be equal to supply, we obtain the expression for the steady state rate of warranted growth:

$$(13) \qquad g = \sigma \left[(s+\pi) - \frac{\mu_y}{|\mu_r|} (j\,\eta_r + f\,\varepsilon_r) \right]$$

where σ is the reciprocal of the capital output ratio.

GRAPH 1

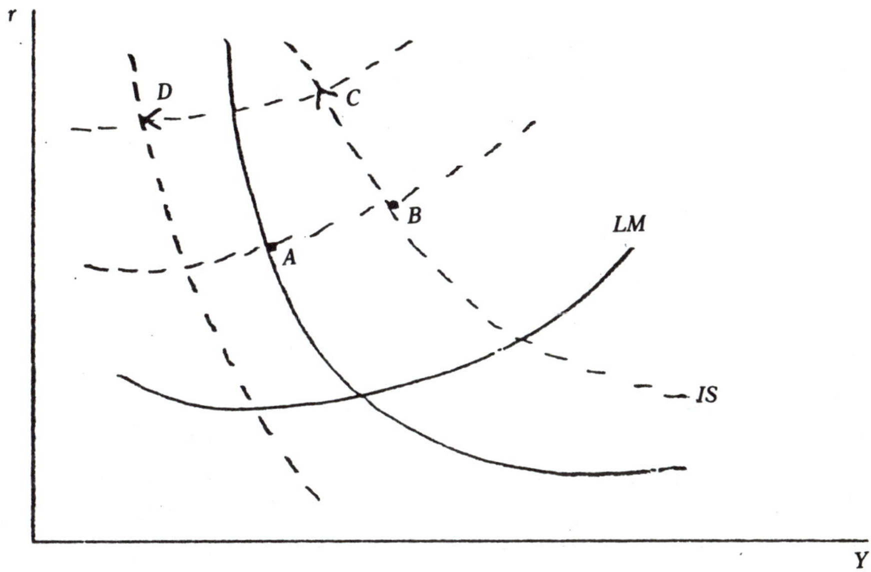

Expression *(13)* can be written, using *(12)*, as follows:

$$g = \sigma \frac{\mu_Y}{|\mu_r|} \frac{(j\,\eta_\pi + m\,|\mu_\pi| - f\,\varepsilon_\pi - \pi)}{\rho_\pi} \qquad (14)$$

Thus, the higher the elasticity of the interest rate with respect to profit, the lower the warranted rate of growth. On the other hand, expression *(13)* shows that such a rate will be higher than the "equilibrium" rate σs, since both profit and the sensitivity of the *IS* and *LM* schedules contribute to reduce the multiplier.

Indicating with $n+q$ the sum of the growth rate respectively of the labour force and of its productivity and equating it with the warranted rate in *(14)*, the steady state level of the current account deficit is found to be:

$$f = \frac{1}{\varepsilon_r}\left\{\left[\frac{n+q}{\sigma} - (\pi + s)\frac{|\mu_r|}{\mu_y}\right] - j\,\eta_r\right\} \qquad (15)$$

Using stars to denote the same quantities for the rest of the world, expression *(15)* implies:

$$j = \frac{1}{\eta_r}\left\{\left[\frac{n+q}{\sigma} - (\pi + s)\frac{|\mu_r|}{\mu_y}\right] + \right.$$
$$+ \frac{\varepsilon_r}{\varepsilon_r^*}$$
$$\left. + \left[\frac{n^* + q^*}{\sigma^*} - (\pi^* + s^*)\frac{|\mu_r^*|}{\mu_y^*}\right]\right\} - \left(\frac{\eta_r^*}{\varepsilon_r^*}\,\frac{\varepsilon_r}{\eta_r}\right) j^* \tag{16}$$

Expression *(16)* states that the steady state investment share in the home country is a negative function of the steady state share in the foreign country. It is noteworthy that an increase in productivity or a decrease in the profit share has the effect of increasing the investment share in the home country, regardless of whether it occurs at home or abroad. Viceversa, an increase in the profit share at home, even though it may have a transitory positive effect on investment, is bound to yield a lower level of investment and growth in the long run.

3. - Profit, Exports and Growth

Further insight on the possible impact of disequilibrium profit can be gained by analyzing its effect on a model where endogenous growth is caused by human capital accumulation via international trade (Paganetto and Scandizzo [14]).

Consider a country whose i-th firm is characterized by a linear homogeneous production function:

$$Q_i(t) = F_i(K_i(t), L_i(t)) \tag{17}$$

$$i = 1, 2, \ldots, N$$

where K_i denotes capital and L_i labour.

The economy is characterized by an aggregate function, affected by an externality:

$$Q(t) = A(t) \sum_{i=1}^{N} F_i(K_i(t), L_i(t)) \tag{18}$$

where $A(t)$ is a technical progress parameter whose growth depends on the level of export:

$$\dot{A}(t) = h(x(t)) \tag{19}$$

$$\partial h / \partial x > 0$$

where $\dot{A}$ denotes the time derivative and $x(t)$ is per capita net export, which is constrained by the equation:

$$x(t) = \dot{z}(t) - (r - n) z(t) \tag{20}$$

In *(20)*, $z(t)$ denotes credits with the rest of the world, r is the international rate of interest and n the growth of the labour force L.

Given the terminal condition:

$$\lim_{t \to \infty} e^{-rt} g(t) = 0 \tag{21}$$

we consider the optimization problem:

$$\max U_0 = \int_0^{\infty} e^{-rt} U(c(t))\, dt \tag{22}$$

where $U(c(t))$ is a well behaved social welfare function, subject to *(19)*, *(20)*, *(21)* and:

$$A(t) f(k(t)) (1 + \pi) = c(t) + \dot{k}(t) + nk(t) + x(t) \tag{23}$$

where the disequilibrium equation in *(1)* is expressed, taking into account *(18)* and *(19)* in terms of variables measured in per capita levels (lower case letters).

Forming the Hamiltonian, we find:

$$H(t) = e^{-rt}[U(c) + p((1+\pi) A f(k) - c - nk - x) + \qquad (24)$$
$$+ \lambda((r-n) z + x) + \mu h(x)]$$

where p, λ and μ are the appropriate multipliers.

From *(24)*, deriving the necessary conditions for a maximum, it can be shown (Paganetto - Scandizzo [14]) that the optimal growth rates, respectively of consumption and exports, are:

$$\frac{\dot{c}}{c} = \frac{1}{\eta}(A f_k + \rho - r - n) \qquad (25)$$

and:

$$\frac{\dot{x}}{x} = \frac{1}{\theta(U_c - \lambda)}[U_c(A f_k + \rho - f(k) h_x) - \lambda r] \qquad (26)$$

where:

$$U_c = \frac{\partial U}{\partial c}$$

$$\eta = -\frac{\partial^2 U / \partial c^2}{\partial U / \partial c} c$$

$$h_x = \frac{\partial h}{\partial x}$$

$$\theta = -\frac{\partial^2 h / \partial x^2}{\partial h / \partial x} x$$

where n is assumed zero for simplicity and ρ is the rate of return to capital resulting from the disequilibrium rate of profit:

$$\frac{\partial \pi}{\partial k} = \frac{1}{A f(k)}(\rho - \pi A f_k) \qquad (27)$$

With respect to the solution found in our earlier paper, equations *(25)* and *(26)* describe a higher growth path since expected profit has the effect of augmenting the rate of return to capital.

From *(26)*, hypothesizing that the same equation holds for the rest of the world, we can derive the level of the interest rate r that equates the growth rate respectively of the trade surplus $\dot{x}/x$ and of the rest of the world trade deficit $^{-}\dot{x}^*/x^*$:

$$\hat{r} = w \left[\frac{U_c}{\lambda} (A f_k + \rho - n - f(k)\, h_x \right] + \tag{28}$$

$$+ (1 - w) \cdot$$

$$\cdot \left[\frac{U_c^*}{\lambda^*} (A f_k^* + \rho^* - n^* - f^*(k)\, h_x^* \right]$$

where w is a weight defined as follows:

$$w = \frac{\frac{\lambda}{U_c} \theta (U_c^* - \lambda^*)}{\frac{\lambda^*}{U_c^*} \theta^* (U_c - \lambda) + \frac{\lambda}{U_c} \theta (U_c^* - \lambda^*)} \tag{29}$$

If $\rho \geq 0$ and $\rho^* \geq 0$, the world interest rate that ensures equilibrium in the export-import market will be higher than in the case with no extra-profits. In particular, if $\rho > 0$, and $\rho^* = 0$, the home country will experience two different effects on its rates of growth: one positive, due to ρ, and one negative, due to a higher r. The rest of the world, on the contrary, will only see the world interest rate increase and its growth rate contract as a consequence.

4. - Empirical Testing [2]

The analysis presented bears one major falsifiable implication: not only profits and interest rates in Germany should be positively

---

[2] The econometric work for this section was efficiently performed by Vincenzo Atella and Paola Manzini.

correlated over the period after the reunification, but also both the sign and the causality direction between the two variables should have changed in the same period from any preceeding time interval. In other words, if our hypothesis is right we should observe a major structural break in the sign of the relationship and in the direction of causality in Germany in the period 1989-1992, while no break should be observed in the other European countries.

In order to test this hypothesis we run a test of Granger causality between quarterly indices of stock prices and official discount rates for Germany, Italy and France over the period 1963.1 to 1992.4. The test was performed over two subsamples selected according to the date of German reunification (1989.4). The data has been transformed in logarithmic form and then filtered with the Hodrey and Prescott methodology, to isolate the cyclical component.

As shown in Table 1, the correlation between the share price index (a proxy for expected profit) and the interest rate (both the long term government rate and the official discount rate) in Germany is negative for the period 1963-1990 and positive for the period 1900-1993. Furthermore, as shown in Table 2, for the period 1963-1990 the test results lead to not reject the hypothesis that the share price was not deermined by the interest rate and to reject the hypothesis that the interest rate was not determined by the share price. Thus the data suggests a causal link running from the interest to profits. Viceversa, as conjectured, after the reunification, the test results suggest that reverse causality between share prices and the discount rate prevailed.

TABLE 1

GERMANY: CORRELATION COEFFICIENTS:
LOGARITHMS OF QUARTERLY DATA
TREATED WITH THE HODREY AND PRESCOTT FILTER

Variables	1963-1990	1990-1993
Share index-Official discount rate	−0.254	0.864
Share index-Long term gov. bond	−0.443	0.750
Share index-3 month int. rate	−0.268	0.802

TABLE 2

CASUALITY TEST

GERMANY

Null hypothesis:	F-statistic	Probability
SMPL: 1963.4 1989.4		
CLPSHARS is not Granger caused by *CLTUSS* ..	5.135994	0.0011
CLTUSS is not Granger caused by *CLPSHARS* ..	0.812623	0.5216
SMPL: 1989.4 1992.4		
CLPSHARS is not Granger caused by *CLTUSS* ..	1.586973	0.3327
CLTUSS is not Granger caused by *CLPSHARS* ..	12.21148	0.0163

ITALY

Null hypothesis:	F-statistic	Probability
SMPL: 1963.4 1989.4		
CLITPSHS is not Granger caused by *LITTUSS* ..	0.680816	0.6069
LITTUSS is not Granger caused by *CLITPSHS* ..	1.466376	0.2185
SMPL: 1989.4 1992.4		
CLPSHARS is not Granger caused by *CLTUSS* ..	0.324312	0.5840
CLTUSS is not Granger caused by *CLPSHARS* ..	0.182415	0.9312

FRANCE

Null hypothesis	F-statistic	Probability
SMPL: 1963.4 1989.4		
CLFRPSHS is not Granger caused by *LFRTUSS* ..	0.193236	0.9414
LFRTUSS is not Granger caused by *CLFRPSHS* ..	1.410664	0.2364
SMPL: 1989.4 1992.4		
Near singular matrix		

In the case of Italy we found no apparent structural break, nor did we in the case of France, for which it was not possible to test causality over the second period due to the constancy of the interest rate.

BIBLIOGRAPHY

[1] VARIOUS AUTHORS, «Altschudden Ost - Eine Schwere Last», *Informations Dienst des Instituts der Deutschen Wirtschaft*, vol. 17, n. 39, 1991, pp. 6-7.

[2] ——, «Die Kleinen Kommen», *Informations Dienst des Instituts der Deutschen Wirtschaft*, vol. 17, n. 19, 1991, pp. 4-5.

[3] BETHKENHAGEN J., «The Privatization and Structural Change in the Economic Transformation of Eastern Germany», paper presented at the 8th German-Korean Conference on *Consequences of German Unification and its Implications for a Divided Korea*, Seoul, 1991.

[4] FITOUSSI J.P. - PHELPS E.S., *The Slump in Europe*, Oxford, Blackwell, 1988.

[5] GALI J., «How Well Does the *IS-LM* Model Fit the Post-War U.S. Data?», *Quarterly Journal of Economics*, vol. 107, n. 2, May 1992, pp. 709-38.

[6] GOODWIN R., «Innovations and Irregularity of Economic Cycles», *Review of Economics and Statistics*, May 1946.

[7] ICHIMURA S., «Towards a General Macrodinamic non Linear Theory of Economic Fluctuations», in KURIHARA, K.K. (ed.), *Post Keynesian Economics*, New Brunowich (NJ), Rutgers University Press, 1954.

[8] KALDOR N., «A Model of the Trade Cycle», *Economic Journal*, March 1940.

[9] ——, «A Model of Economic Growth», *Economic Journal*, n. 68, December 1957, pp. 591-624.

[10] ——,«Capital Accumulation and Economic Growth» in LUTZ F.A. - HAGUE D.C. (eds.) *The Theory of Capital*, International Economic Association Conference, London, MacMillan, New York, St. Martin's, 1961.

[11] KALECKI M. *Essays in the Theory of Economic Fluctuations*, New York, Russel and Russel, 1939.

[12] KEYNES J.M., *The General Theory of Employment, Interest and Money*, London, MacMillan.

[13] KING R.G., «Will the New Keynesian Macroeconomics Resurrect the *IS-LM* Model?», *The Journal of Economic Perspectives*, n. 1, Winter 1993, pp. 67-82.

[14] PAGANETTO L. - SCANDIZZO P.L., «Quality, International Trade and Endogenous Growth», *Rivista di Politica Economica*, n. 11, November 1992, pp. 155-76.

[15] ROMER D., «The New Keynesian Synthesis», *Journal of Economic Perspectives*, vol. 7, n. 1, Winter 1993, pp. 5-22.

[16] STIGLITZ J.E., «Comments: Some Retrospective Views on Growth Theory», in DIAMOND P. (ed.), *Growth, Productivity Unemployment*, Cambridge (Mass), London, MIT Press, 1990.

[17] TOBIN J., «Price Flexibility and Output Stability: An Old Keynesian View», *The Journal of Economic Perspectives*, vol. 7, n. 1, Winter 1933, pp. 45-67.

The Italian Crisis of the 1990s: European Convergence and Structural Adjustment

Renato Brunetta - **Leonello Tronti***
Università «Tor Vergata», Roma Fondazione G. Brodolini, Roma

1. - The Specificity of the Italian Crisis

As the new decade began, the Italian economy found itself at a comparative disadvantage. Unlike those of other European countries, notably France. Italy's political and economic system had utterly failed to take advantage of the favorable conditions of the worldwide economic expansion of the 1980s to carry through the needed process of adjustment and correction of the disequilibria inherited from the turbulent 1970s.

In France the program of structural and financial rehabilitation got under way in 1983, when a hasty devaluation of the franc and extraordinary measures of public finance were required to curb the public sector borrowing requirement (Onofri - Tomasini [19]; Pennisi [20]). In Italy, by contrast, it was after 1985 that the pronounced degeneration of the public finances occurred, and with it the explosive growth of the public debt far beyond the level permitted in competitor economies. The latter part of the decade also witnessed a decline in Italy's international competitiveness, which ultimately entailed recession for Italian industry, beginning in the second half of 1989. Given this context of «bad policy», Italian deindustrialization has proven

---

Being the result of a completely agreed analysis, sections 1-3 were materially written by Leonello Tronti, sections 4 and 5 by Renato Brunetta.

* *N.B.:* the numbers in square brackets refer to the Bibliography at the end of the paper.

more severe: in fact, despite the protracted global economic expansion, since 1977 industrial value added has declined inexorably in relation to nominal GDP.

A further imbalance within the Italian economic structure stems from the differing sectoral price effects produced by variable degrees of exposure to international competition. Recent work (Milana - Scandizzo [18]; Barca - Visco [4]) has shown that since Italy's entry into the European Monetary System the constraint of fixed exchange rates vis-à-vis the currencies of Italy's European trading partners has enabled the sheltered sector to attain much greater income gains than the economy-wide average. That sector's relative prices have thus risen increasingly sharply, generating inflationary shocks on the rest of the economy and the country's export competitiveness.

Another recent study (Savona [23]) estimates price and productivity trends in the exposed sectors as distinct from those sheltered from international competition or assisted by public funds. In the course of the 1980s productivity in the former increased, on average, six times as fast as in the latter, and the entire inflation differential between Italy and its trading partners, which ultimately drove the lira out of the EMS, is accounted for by the sheltered sectors (Table 1)[1].

The fact is that the exposed sectors (manufacturing, food and food processing, parts of the financial and energy industries, tourism) are subject to a kind of implicit incomes policy dictated by the terms of competition, whose effect is the containment if not the reduction of prices[2]. By contrast, the sheltered sectors (government and public services, construction, and virtually all private services) are free of this pressure, and given the relative lack of competitiveness of domestic markets they enjoy a very considerable ability to maneuver relative prices. This independence enables them to widen profit margins when labour cost trends would prohibit it, and thus fuels inflation (Tronti [28]; Cucchiarelli - Tronti [12]).

---

[1] As the exposed sector accounts for less than 30% of Italian GDP and is reducing employment, while the protected sectors have long been creating jobs, the former has little political clout. The difficulty of righting the public finances is rooted in the predominant incidence of government-protected and government-assisted sectors.

[2] For the concept of implicit incomes policy, under the broader idea of the coordination of wage trends, see SOSKICE D. [25].

TABLE 1

OUTPUT AND EMPLOYMENT GROWTH RATES
IN THE EXPOSED AND SHELTERED SECTORS
OF THE ITALIAN ECONOMY

	1982	1986	1989	1990	1982-1986	1982-1990
PRE	− 3.5	−6.9	7.0	0.3	− 4.5	15.0
PRN	2.0	2.3	3.3	2.7	11.7	22.8
OCE	− 3.6	−0.6	−1.2	−0.4	−11.5	− 14.7
OCN	3.2	1.5	0.9	1.6	12.8	19.1
DPE	0.2	−6.4	8.3	0.7	8.0	34.8
DPN	− 1.2	0.8	2.4	1.1	− 0.9	5.7
ISE	15.2	5.6	5.2	2.7	55.3	79.1
ISN	17.6	9.1	6.0	8.9	84.1	139.1

Legend:
PRE = output of exposed sector
PRN = output of sheltered sector
OCE = employment in exposed sector
OCN = employment in sheltered sector
DPE = productivity in exposed sector
DPN = productivity in sheltered sector
ISE = inflation in exposed sector
ISN = inflation in sheltered sector

Source, SAVONA P. [24].

The end result of these conflicting patterns is the transfer of a part of the productivity gains achieved by the exposed sector to the sheltered sector. This process, which can be defined in Baumolian terms as a flow from the fast-productivity to the slow-productivity activities (Baumol [5]), diminishes the resources at the disposal of the exposed sector to the benefit of the sheltered, inflationary part of the economy. If the process is held within very definite limits, we have a usual Baumolian paradigm, generating unbalanced growth through the interplay between sectors of rapid and slow productivity growth, but nevertheless achieving dynamic equilibrium.

If, however, the slow-productivity sectors absorb the productivity gains of the rest of the economy even before they have been generated, or so substantially as to perceptibly curb wages, profits, and investment and raise the costs of the dynamic sectors by inflating the relative prices of their inputs, then we have a *perverse* Baumolian paradigm (for a formalized treatment of this approach, aimed at analyzing the Italian case, see Cucchiarelli - Tronti [13]). This pattern endangers the economy's very capacity for growth, and in any case distorts it structurally by fueling the unwarranted (and ultimately unsustainable) expansion of the sheltered sector.

In the case of the Italian economy, between 1980 and 1991 the prices of the sheltered sector rose 46.8% relative to those of the exposed sector, while the latter's share of GDP fell from 34 to 26.8% (Graph 1).

However, the operation of the perverse Baumolian paradigm, while it does characterize the prevalent form of market within the Italian economy, is not the only standpoint from which to view these deleterious developments. Quite a substantial body of work offers a different but complementary perspective, namely the comparative backwardness and underdevelopment of the "information economy"

GRAPH 1

EXPOSED SECTOR OUTPUT
AS PERCENTAGE OF GDP

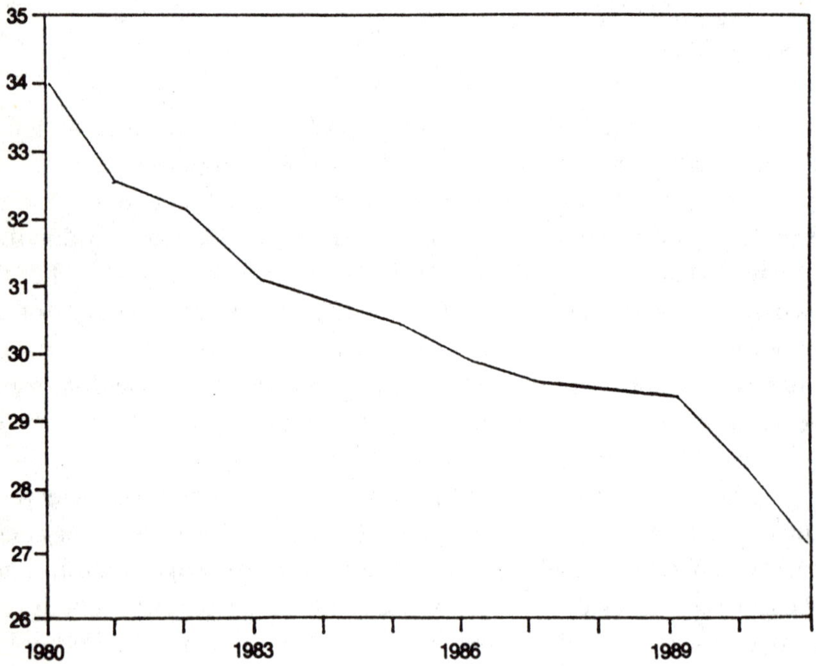

Source, based on ISTAT data.

in Italy[3]. The unsatisfactory working of the markets itself can be blamed in part on economic agents' lack of information, on informational asymmetries and the poor quality of the information available. From this point of view, the far-reaching tertiarization of the economy in the course of the last decade may not have been the product of the emergence of a virtuous information economy model (Tronti [29]).

The Italian economy's chances of resuming vigorous growth thus depend in part on its capacity to generate an adequate supply of high-quality information, with low entropy and high productive content. Only if the economic system succeeds in creating new "environmental conditions" (the relationship between the sheltered and exposed sectors, reliable, timely and valuable information, improved public finances, social productivity) to turn the perverse Baumolian paradigm around, to halt and reverse the process of deindustrialization (Faustini - Tronti [14]), will it be possible to achieve the essential goals of recouping competitiveness and reorienting the growth model to the development of foreign demand.

Accordingly, this transformation will entail more than just the restructuring of the exposed sector (which is already under way, again, on a large scale); it absolutely requires the profound restructuring of the sheltered sector as well, hence of the pubblic and private services, whose poor quality and inefficiency now represent one of the most severe impediments to the resumption of industrial growth. Today, in fact, the cost of the inputs produced by the sheltered sector (information, money, and more generally government and taxes) is at least as significant a handicap for the international competitiveness of Italian industry as the cost of labour.

2. - The Economic Policy Measures of the Amato Government

Consistent with Italy's undertaking with the European Community, in the summer of 1992 the Italian government enacted the

[3] For a general discussion, see among others PORAT M. [21]; TARANTELLI E. [26]; BAILY M.N. - GORDON R.J. [2]; RULLANI [23]; for an analysis with reference to the Italian economy, see also ANTONELLI C. [1]; BAUSSOLA M. [6]; MALERBA G. [17]; TRONTI L. - CUCCHIARELLI A. [30]; CAMPIGLIO L. [10].

first measures in an intensive program of structural and financial adjustment that, owing to the severity of the imbalances, will necessarily last for the rest of this decade.

The first action was Decree law 333 of 11 July, a supplementary budget package mandating 30 trillion lire in additional revenues and spending cuts in the second half of 1992. This was followed by the tripartite wage agreement of 31 July, confirming the abolition of the *scala mobile* (the Italian wage indexation system), freezing salaries and wage bargaining in the public sector and suspending company-level bargaining in the private sector. Next came Decree law 384 of 19 September, approved on the heels of the foreign exchange tempest that led to the devaluation of the lira on 13 September and the decision for free floating (16 September) with the suspension of Italian participation in the EMS (Exchange rate mechanism). This was followed by the enabling act for reform of social security, health care, public employment and local finances (Law 421 of 23 October), passed after a parliamentary vote of confidence, and the draft finance bill for 1993[4].

Italy thus initiated its strategic adjustment plan a decade behind France, and in greatly deteriorated international economic conditions to boot. These circumstances might well have counselled a decided emphasis on economic growth, but this is not the orientation that has emerged so far.

Essentially, the measures enacted are of four kinds (Pennisi [20], among others).

a) wage curbs: the renunciation of automatic, universal inflation adjustment, the suspension of company-level wage bargaining in the private sector, the freeze on bargaining and the imposition of a salary cap (in line with the "programmed" inflation rate) in the public sector. These measures are designed to eradicate the inflationary impulses engendered by wage bargaining (already significantly attenuated in the last few years, in any event), to slow the rise in labour costs and thus enhance export competitiveness, and to usher in a French-style

[4] The essential strategy behind the structural adjustment program is perhaps more readily perceptible in the government's *Economic and Financial Planning Document for 1993-1995*, approved on 31 July 1992, and the *Forecasting and Planning Report for 1993*, issued on 30 September 1992.

"implicit incomes policy", regulating the Baumolian paradigm by means of strict control of public salaries. This set of actions implies a return to the model of export-led growth, in which external demand can be profitably substituted for a portion of domestic demand. The measures were accompanied by the creation of a task force within the Office of the Prime Minister for action to sustain employment and protect occupational skills in the districts worst affected by the crisis, with a mandate to coordinate and deploy the resources and agencies assigned to job creation;

b) revenue increases: a series of measures posing no serious problems of effective collection, such as the capital tax on house ownership and on bank deposits, the minimum tax on the self-employed, new levies for municipal services, and increases in stamp taxes, excise duties and social contributions. In the medium term these measures will fit into the program for the reform of local finances, the improvement of the real estate market, and more efficient tax administration;

c) spending cuts, to be achieved in three ways: 1) following the French example, by curbing appropriations for public staff costs (slowdown in wage increases, new, private-law contractual instruments for public employees, the redefinition of the independent powers and responsibilities of public managers); 2) by reducing public investment, especially that of local authorities, and transfers to firms; 3) privatizations, and the disposal of public assets. In the medium term the trend and quality of public expenditure should be modified by the far-reaching reform of public employment, social security, health care and local finances that is set forth in the *Enabling Act,* whose implementing legislative decrees were passed promptly, in late 1992 and early 1993;

d) removal of constraints on competition: denationalizations and the disposal of public assets, deregulation, liberalization of monitored prices, public prices and charges, and protected markets (such as residential construction and distribution, especially the retail trade).

However, neither wage curbs nor the combination of budgetary measures, nor the program of privatizations, disposals and deregulation are sufficient to sustain the fourth and most fundamental cornerstone of the adjustment strategy, namely the defence of exchange rate stability, which is the prime condition of European convergence.

With the devaluation of 13 September the government acknowledged, in a traumatic fashion, the indefensibility of the previous exchange rate mechanism; in the twelve months ending 31 August 1992, the Bank of Italy expended more than half the country's foreign exchange reserves. Nevertheless, the devaluation, the present float and a future exchange rate mechanism consistent with the "law of purchasing power parity" are of great economic importance and an unquestionably legitimate component of the strategy for adjustment; this approach, though it many not be perceived at the moment of devaluation, facilitates the righting of external accounts and the resumption of export growth.

In brief, the supplementary budget deficit reduction package worth 30 trillion lire of July 1992 has been accompanied by salary measures with a disinflationary potential of 2 percentage points, a substantial devaluation (more than 15%), and further deficit reduction of nearly 93 trillion lire for fiscal year 1993. Revenue increases and spending cuts of comparable size will have to be enacted for 1994 and 1995 as well. The therapy is rigid, because the years wasted in the propitious circumstances of the 1980s now have to be recouped[5].

Apart form the magnitude of the fiscal packages and the effective improvement in the public finances that may be achieved, which depends on economic developments, the standard by which the corrective action should be assessed is the quality of the measures taken and the effectiveness of the instruments deployed. These are the key to the restoration of confidence, the reversal of pessimistic expectations, the return to normal conditions in the financial markets. The yardstick of success will be the reduction of the interest rates

[5] The preliminary budget out-turn for 1992 put the borrowing requirement net of settlements of past debts at 163 trillion lire, 8 trillion above the target set in the *Forecasting and Planning Report* in September. The overshoot was due mainly to the failure of the expected revenues from the disposal of public property (7 trillion lire) to materialize. The ratio of the deficit to GDP remained roughly the same as in 1990 and 1991, at 10.7%. Thus no significant progress was made towards rehabilitating the public finances, even though as Isco [16], observed, in view of the difficulties that emerged during the year, simply maintaining the ratio unchanged is quite an accomplishment.

demanded by subscribers of Italian government paper towards those prevailing in the rest of the Community (Banca d'Italia [3]).

The restoration of normal expectations, such as to hold the risk of inflation and of financial instability within narrow limits, will not only lower interest rates but also help to fix the value of the lira at more reasonable levels, pending reentry into the exchange rate mechanism. Regardless of cyclical difficulties, monetary stability, orderly public finances, the moderation of domestic production costs, gains in competitiveness and the high private sector propensity to save are the factors that can restore the confidence of households and firms and return the economy to sustained expansion of output and a lasting recovery in employment.

3. - The Employment Crisis

If the path of European convergence and the disarray of the public finances set severe constraints on the Government's ability to make effective use of exchange rate policy, budgetary and fiscal policy, and even industrial policy to adjust the terms of convergence, then the labour market becomes the chief, if not the sole variable subject to maneuver in the entire rehabilitation process. The consequences, for both "prices" and "volumes" in this market, are serious indeed.

The labour market figures for 1992 and 1993 signal the aggravation of the problems that emerged in 1991[6].

The *General Report* on the state of the economy *(Relazione generale sulla situazione economica del paese)* estimates a drop in total employment of about 0.9% in 1992, measured in standard labour units (i.e. about 200,000 full-time equivalent workers). The overall change resulted from the failure of the market services to compensate entirely for the employment decline in agriculture (−4.2%) and industry (−2.4%). The decline in industry, in turn reflected a sharp

[6] Eurostat's definitional standards were first applied in Italy in the October 1992 Labour Force survey; the effect was to modify the dimensions of employment and reduce unemployment (CNEL [11]).

contraction of 3.4% in manufacturing (including fuel and power products), which was not offset by a further gain in construction employment (+0.9%)[7]. The estimates for 1993 are even worse, so that about 410,000 jobs will have been last since 1991 (130,000 in 1992 and 280,000 in 1993).

The Office of the Prime Minister issued a *Note of Employment* in November 1992 which uses different definitions and indicators to spotlight the principal areas (both sectoral and geographical) of labour market crisis, identifying the zones of relative sag in the productive fabric.

Sectorally, as gauged by the number of hours of short-time compensation paid, the industries in greatest difficulty are engineering, basic metals, chemicals, construction, textiles, and clothing. Using the yardstick of early retirement, however, the weakness extends throughout manufacturing as a whole. Finally, considering "jobs at risk", the most exposed sectors are engineering, chemicals, basic metals, textiles, clothing, and construction.

Geographically, the indicators used result in sharply differing rankings. A broad index of "employment distress", combining seven separate indicators[8], finds the employment situation most difficult in the regions of Liguria, Valle d'Aosta, Basilicata, Campania, and Lombardy (in that order); those in the best relative conditions were Trentino Alto Adige, Lazio, Marche, Emilia Romagna, and Umbria. The regions with the least employment risk thus appear to be characterized by a productive fabric dominated by small and medium-sized businesses, which only confirms the fact that despite the prob-

[7] The drop in industrial employment is all the more worrying for several reasons. First, while jobs are being lost principally in larger corporations, which can more easily engage in restructuring, there are signs of weakness among small firms and "network systems" as well. Second, Mediobanca reports heavy indebtedness, especially among the large firms. And third, industrial employment is declining in the Centre and North while rising (albeit marginally) in the South, where the industrial fabric is least robust, which can only inspire skepticism as to the quality of the jobs being created. Combined with — and reflecting — the steady loss of competitiveness in years past, all these factors certainly bode no good for future employment.

[8] The "employment distress" index is a weighted average of the following indicators: unemployment rate: growth index (source: CONFINDUSTRIA); percentage decline in number of persons employed; percentage increase in number of unemployed; percentage increase in short-time earnings compensation; ratio of early retirements to employment: ratio of "jobs at risk" to employment.

lems cited, this segment remains the most vital component of Italian industry.

Table 2 reports long-term trends in a number of income maintenance programs, or social "shock absorbers". Judging by the number of jobs lost (workers laid off or definitively dismissed), the present crisis apperars less dramatic than that of the early 1980s,

TABLE 2

THE SOCIAL SHOCK ABSORBERS
(ITALIAN INCOME MAINTENANCE PROGRAMS, 1974-1993)*

	Programs used	No. workers losing jobs (temporally or definitively)	Expenditure (liras)
1st oil shock (1974-1976)	CIG, unemployment benefits	450,000/year (1.4 million total)	2.07 trillion/year (6.2 trillion total)
2nd oil shock Deverticalization & decentralization of firms (1981-1985)	CIG, unemployment benefits, early retirements	750,000/year (3.7 million total)	8.2 trillion/year (41 trillion total)
Economic expansion (1986-1990)	CIG, unemployment benefits, early retirements	400,000/year (2.1 million total)	5.7 trillion/year (28.5 trillion total)
1991	CIG, mobility allowance, unemployment benefits, etc.	510,000	7.5 trillion
1992	CIG, mobility allowance, unemployment benefits, etc.	560,000	8.8 trillion
1993 (optimistic scenario)	CIG, mobility allowance, unemployment benefits, etc.	650,000	9.6 trillion
1993 (pessimistic scenario)	CIG, mobility allowance, unemployment benefits, etc.	850,000	12 trillion

* CIG = Short-Time Earnings Compensation Fund.
Source, based on INPS data.

though this observation must be tempered by two considerations: first, that the features of the two crises are radically different, so the question cannot be restricted to the number of workers temporarily or permanently ejected from the productive system; and second, that the present crisis has yet to run its course, with no unequivocal sign so far of an upturn.

Even in years of buoyancy in the labour market (when total employment expands, perhaps even substantially), a significant number of workers are temporarily or permanently ejected (some 400,0000 a year from 1986 to 1990). This counsels great caution in using the number of workers (or jobs) "at risk" to infer the good or poor state of the labour market. But it also means that even in years of good labour market performance, government makes massive outlays on "shock absorption", as it becomes steadily clearer that the economy has moved into a new phase of continuous restructuring.

Trends in income mainenance expenditure are correlated positively and in synchrony with economic downturns and the inability of the system to create jobs. Trends in unemployment, however, follow cyclical downturns with a lag, precisely because of the operation of the social absorbers.

4. - The Amato Government's Labour Policies: Innovation or Continuity?

An initial, and clearly summary, response to the questions implicit in the foregoing analysis comes from the labour policy measures adopted in 1992 and 1993 under the premiership of Giuliano Amato.

Foreshadowing developments that would increase in amplitude in the course of the year, the beginning of 1992 was marked by increased resort to the traditional shock absorbers, notably short-time compensation and early retirement.

The prime economic policy objective of the Amato Government was the immediate curbing of inflationary pressures and a significant reduction of the budget deficit, to be achieved by a reform of the expenditure mechanisms and consistent use of the fiscal lever. A series of measures were announced: a supplementary budget package to reduce the 1992 deficit substantially; a draft enabling act for the reform of social security, health care, local finances, and public employment; and incisive action to control the rise in all nominal incomes, prices and public charges. The planning guidelines identified the conditions for broadening the employment base, namely economic expansion and removal of the rigidity and segmentation of the labour market.

Agreement was reached on a *Protocol on Incomes Policy, the Fight Against Inflation, and the Cost of Labour,* signed by government, unions, and employers on 31 July. The pact set forth incomes policy guidelines to curb inflation, recoup productivity and competitiveness, and relaunch employment, but without reducing the purchasing power of wages[9].

The *Protocol* is radically innovative and in the end will almost certainly modify the entire dynamics of collective bargaining and labour relations in Italy, as well as the very nature of the economic and political tradeoff that underlies the new round of incomes policy action[10].

This time, in fact, the recognition by unions and employers of the objective value of drastic disinflation is not simply a tradeoff for wage moderation, as in the classic tripartite accords of the 1980s, but is now flanked by a second, equally important objective: maintenance of the real value of salaries and pensions.

Price stability and the protection of the purchasing power of wages and pensions are thus considered public goods to be defended, especially with respect to those who enjoy them without helping to pay the costs. This is the case of the many public and private, individual and collective free riders who have profited over the years from unearned positions of strength. This ratifies the fundamental insight of Ezio Tarantelli, who was the first to treat price stability as a

---

[9] It can be noted at this point that this last objective was not attained: nominal wages rose 5.1% in 1992, while consumer prices rose 5.4%, and the gap appears to be widening further in 1993.

[10] For a more detailed analysis of the 31 July *Protocol* and the entire package of reforms adopted by the Government up to 18 April 1993, see BRUNETTA R. - TRONTI L. - CUCCHIARELLI A. [9]. For a thorough economic analysis of incomes and labour policies in Italy up to December 1993, see BRUNETTA R. - CUCCHIARELLI A. - NADDEO P. - TRONTI L. [8].

public good and to describe the wage inflation engaged in by the sheltered sector as free riding on that public good (Tarantelli [27]).

Implicit in the philosophy behind the new anti-inflation pact, accordingly, is the transition from conflictual to cooperative distribution of income, with the elimination of all automatic mechanisms and the attribution of the highest value to contract bargaining as the essential forum not only for the maintenance of purchasing power but also for the equitable distribution of productivity gains. This feature of the 1992 agreement has been wholly reconfirmed by the subsequent 1993 agreement (23 July), reforming the wage setting system.

The change is not a marginal one, in that it radically modifies the traditional causal sequence in the income distribution process. In the Keynesian model, firms set prices using the mark-up method and by independent investment decisions ultimately determine the shares going to wages and profits. Workers are left with nothing but the ability to bargain over money wages, and always subject to the threat of unemployment.

With the new model, given the constraints and objectives of European Union convergence, price stability (or in our case, disinflation) becomes a target variable to be pursued jointly by government, employers, and workers through coherent behaviour in terms of prices and public service charges, collective bargaining accords, and taxation. The second objective that the government undertook to pursue, i.e. the defence of real wages, represents the true, and in a sense historic, innovation implicit in the pact. This is no longer a generic *desideratum* to be verified after the fact but a serious commitment, treated (as we have noted) as a public good.

For the same volume of employment, then, the causal chain of income distribution is altered. Firms still set prices (in line with competitive conditions), but bargaining no longer concerns money wages, as in the past, with the safeguard of some indexation machinery such as the *scala mobile*; from now on, contract bargaining will focus directly on real wage trends (consistent with disinflation), under government guarantees effected through the tax system.

If incomes policy, in this way, is transformed into a long-run cooperative game (Brunetta - Carraro [7]), indexation systems no longer serve any purpose. However, long-run cooperative games must be credible and verifiable. And that is the reason why the following 1993 agreeent sets a two-step lateral concertation procedure aimed at checking and orienting macroeconomic behaviours.

Between September 1992 and 18 April 1993 the Amato government enacted a series of labour market measures, partly corresponding to the utterly traditional labour policy approach and partly conforming to the new line of action opened by the 31 July accord. This sharp internal contrast in philosophy also corresponds to the practical state of the labour market. With the second quarterly labour force survey, alarm over the incipient employment emergency began to spread, with the consequent need for urgent, short-term measures. On the other hand, spurred by the international recession and the European convergence obligations entered into at Maastricht, the government undertook a program of structural adjustment with far-reaching repercussions on the labour market.

Emergency employment action included Decree law 393, in late September, enacting *Urgent Measures Concerning Employment;* Decree law 398, in October, with its *Urgent Intervention to Safeguard Employment Levels* (presented anew in December as Decree law 478); the conference between central and regional governments, in early February, whose agenda consisted in the discussion of plans drafted by technical working groups setting out, region by region, all public works projects that could be started up promptly. The action of the task forse called for in the *July Protocol,* which began work on 23 October, also responded to the "employment emergency"[11].

First and foremost among the structural adjustment measures was Law 421 of 23 October, the enabling act whereby Parliament authorized the government to draft reforms of the National Health

---

[11] The *Task Force* surveyed the employment situation in December. Registrants with the state employment service numbered 2.6 million, 60% of them in the South. Unemployed workers (i.e. those having lost jobs) numbered 460,000, of whom 198,000 were in manufacturing; 62,000 workers had been placed on the mobility rolls, no fever than 36,000 of these having formerly been on special unemployment benefits; there were 146,000 newly unemployed workers in industry, almost all of them in the North. The gravity of the employment situation was apparently exacerbated by the declining job-creation capacity of the services sector, as it too is confronted with the necessity to improve efficiency and productivity, presumably through significant redundancies.

Service, public employment, social security, and local finances. The draft legislative decrees in implementation of the enabling act were presented to Parliament at the end of the year and all approved early in 1993.

Decree law 96 of 26 March 1993 terminated special development assistance for the south of Italy. As of 15 April, the Southern Italy Development Program no longer exists. Now, after decades of "extraordinary" assistance, the fate of the south is back in the hands of ordinary administration through the ministries for industry, public works, and budget.

A hybrid measure, halfway between the old and the new, between cyclical and structural action, between the short and the long term, was Decree law 1, presented by the government on 5 January 1993 but not subsequently ratified by Parliament. This provision, which would have created a *Fund to Increase and Sustain Employment*, later approved within Law 236/1993, was greeted by contrasting responses from the main union confederations[12].

From the standpoint of the change in approach to labour policy, one weakness of the proposal was the failure to distinguish clearly between "classical" unemployment (i.e., due to high labour costs) and "Keynesian" unemployment (due to insufficient demand). Whereas the first part of the decree (special appropriations, reindustrialization programs, the State Industrial Management and Holding Company, etc.) clearly focused on cyclical, Keynesian unemployment and accordingly proposed appropriate support for aggregate demand, the innovative portion of the proposed legislation tended to make structural changes suitable to the normal workings of the labour market (flexibility measures to eliminate that part of joblessness that can be attributed to excessive institutional rigidity). In short, the decree risked overlaying extraordinary (hence urgent) measures with structural actions that might have benefited from lengthier consideration.

---

[12] The CISL was open minded about the measures taken (in particular, it praised the government's acceptance of solidarity contracts), but the UIL was critical and the CGIL decidedly opposed, asking that the provisions on the entry wage, special first-job contracts, temporary employment, and individual hiring in agriculture be struck and resubmitted as separate legislation. Confindustria expressed a generally favorable opinion, with some reservations.

For that matter, the need for action to promote further flexibility in the Italian labour market has traditionally been controversial, as is confirmed by the continuing heated debate over the introduction of temporary employment agencies, approved in principle by the 23 July 1993 agreement but still lacking a regulation for actual implementation. One side of the industrial relations system views this innovation favorably, although international experience reveals that the employment potential of such institutions is quite modest, certainly inadequate to deal with Keynesian unemployment and capable at best of plugging a few gaps in the matching of labour demand and supply. The other side criticizes it as a dangerous step towards precarious employment relations, even though the first government plan — admittedly an imperfect draft, whose presentation as an (urgent) decree law was certainly questionable — moved in anything but that direction and in fact was so concerned with guaranteeing workers' rights as to appear utterly unworkable in practice, for simple pecuniary considerations.

5. - The Turning Point: the Role of Incomes Policy

In conclusion, it would be misleading to neglect the signs of change perceptible within the Italian economy. The signals are contradictory, in that indications of recovery are coupled with continuing difficulties, the momentum effect of the factors of hysteresis within the economy. What emerges clearly, though, is that Italy has been presented with a major opportunity, which if properly exploited has the potential to put the economy back on the path of sustained growth.

The turning point, whose nature is becoming ever clearer as the months pass, can be located in the foreign exchange crisis of September 1992. Much more than a simple, even sharp, devaluation, this episode took on the character of a new policy, imposed by the market in place of that pursued previously by the government.

The policy of the government up until the devaluation can be described in summary form as the effort to achieve balance-of-payments equilibrium through net capital inflows large enough to offset the outflow in the form of investment income on Italy's foreign debt. This required high interest rates and a reasonable amount of credibility, of confidence in the future of the economy and the political stability of the country.

When, in the wake of a political and institutional (and judicial) crisis, confidence in the Italian economy evaporated, the foreign exchange markets forced a devaluation of the lira (which in the meantime had withdrawn from the ERM) much steeper than that decided in September. The reason behind the present (under)valuation of the lira is the need for an exchange rate that can bring about a trade surplus large enough to offset the outflow of investment income. Otherwise, interest rates would have to be held for a considerable time at levels so high as to throttle the economy.

The devaluation resulted in a sudden, substantial gain in competitiveness for Italian firms doing international business. By itself, however, devaluation would not have accomplished much without a series of major complementary changes: the government averted bankruptcy and financial crisis, with courageous action for the structural rehabilitation of the public finances: the abolition of the *scala mobile* and the narrower scope for passing increases on to prices prevented inflation from following on the heels of devaluation, putting an end to the perverse mechanism that has dogged Italy's economic history, namely the spiral of devaluation, wage inflation, and price inflation.

For the achievements made possible by devaluation to become permanent, however, the objective of income stability must be pursued. For income from labour, this is possible thanks to the abolition of wage indexation: for income from capital, thanks to the lowering of interest rates that is taking place (in Italy and abroad); for profits, owing to the need to not lose recently regained competitiveness; for the services sector, owing to the narrower scope for earning, given the contraction of domestic demand.

Today, this would appear to be the main role for incomes policy, whose procedures and instruments were laid down by the tripartite agreement of 23 July 1993. Such an incomes policy could lay a solid foundation for the resumption of growth, which is a prerequisite to renewed expansion of employment.

The signs of recovery are unmistakably multiplying. Companies that are doing well — or at least starting to do well again — are appearing in scattered order, a bit like a leopardskin. Nevertheless, the pins in the map of Italy that stand for success are most heavily concentrated in a fairly well-defined area, ranging from Veneto through the Lombard hinterland to Emilia Romagna, with some outposts in the Marche region. It may be coincidence, perhaps, but one can hardly help noticing that these are all areas in which industry is not dominated by large firms.

As yet, the recovery is still selective. To a large extent the firms that have taken advantage of the scope for exports suddenly opened up in previously impenetrable markets have been medium-sized groups that have invested and made considerable progress in restructuring (Fazzolari [15]). Size counts, not only in output capacity but also in the ability to establish a market presence, because a company that is too small is unlikely to have an organizational structure enabling it to market its wares around the globe. The middle-sized firms, however, are flexible enough to shift promptly in response to demand.

Italy's crisis was first and foremost a crisis of political and financial credibility, while the real economy and the labour market in particular continued to perform reasonably well, despite the downturn into recession.

The improvement in the balance of trade and, hopefully, increased confidence in the Italian political and institutional system will result in an appreciation of the lira in the not-too-distant future, undercutting the recent gains in competitiveness. Predictably, then, there will be a seesawing advance (or, perhaps, a "cobweb" movement) towards the new equilibrium rate for the lira. If the development-oriented incomes policy described here is pursued during the course of these oscillations, Italy will come to the new equilibrium with an expanded productive base and increased employment. If not, today's opportunities will translate into the further financialization and deindustrialization of the economy. We shall have lost another chance offered to us by history.

BIBLIOGRAPHY

[1] ANTONELLI C., *New Information Technology and Industrial Change: the Italian Case*, London, Kluwer Academy Publishers, 1988.

[2] BAILY M.N. - GORDON R.J., «The Productivity Slowdown. Measurement Issues and the Explosion of Computer Power», *Brookings Papers on Economic Activity*, n. 2, 1988.

[3] BANCA D'ITALIA, *Bollettino economico*, n. 20, February 1993.

[4] BARCA F. - VISCO I., «L'economia italiana nella prospettiva europea: terziario protetto e dinamica dei redditi nominali», Roma, Banca d'Italia, *Temi di discussione*, n. 175, July 1992.

[5] BAUMOL W., «Macroeconomics of Unbalanced Growth», *American Economic Review*, n. 57, 1967.

[6] BAUSSOLA M., «Il settore dell'informazione in Italia: un'analisi macroeconomica», *Rivista Internazionale di Scienze sociali*, n. 2, 1990.

[7] BRUNETTA R. - CARRARO C., «Incomes Policies as Co-operative Strategies: Lessons from the Italian Experience of the 1980s», in BRUNETTA R. - DELL'ARINGA C. (eds.), *Labour Relations and Economic Performance*, Macmillan, London, 1990.

[8] BRUNETTA R. - CUCCHIARELLI A. - NADDEO P. - TRONTI L., *Politica dei redditi e struttura della contrattazione*, Roma, Ediesse - Edizioni Lavoro, forthcoming 1994.

[9] BRUNETTA R. - TRONTI L. - CUCCHIARELLI A., «Il mercato del lavoro italiano tra convergenza europea e aggiustamento strutturale», in MINISTERO DEL LAVORO, *Rapporto '91-'92. Lavoro e politiche della occupazione in Italia*, Poligrafico dello Stato, Roma, 1993.

[10] CAMPIGLIO L., «Informazione e attività economica in Italia: un nuovo indicatore coincidente», *L'industria*, n. 1, 1992.

[11] CNEL, *La situazione occupazionale in Italia*, Roma, 24 February 1993.

[12] CUCCHIARELLI A. - TRONTI L., «Inflazione, conflitto, concorrenza. La distribuzione dei guadagni di produttività in Italia dal 1970 al 1991», *Economia e Lavoro*, n. 4, 1992.

[13] ——— ——: *Produttività e distribuzione del reddito: equità ed efficenza in un modello a due settori*, AIEL 8th National conference, forthcoming, 1993.

[14] FAUSTINI G. - TRONTI L., «Ristrutturazioni e politiche del lavoro negli anni '90. Tendenze, strategie, strumenti», in FREY L. (ed.), *Politiche del lavoro*, Milano, F. Angeli, 1993.

[15] FAZZOLARI T., «Toh, rispunta il genio italico», *L'Espresso*, 18 April 1993.

[16] ISCO (ISTITUTO NAZIONALE PER LO STUDIO DELLA CONGIUNTURA), «*Rapporto semestrale. L'evoluzione congiunturale dell'economia italiana*», Rapporto 59, February, 1993.

[17] MALERBA G., «Tecnologia dell'informazione, strumenti informatici ed evoluzione della struttura professionale: una valutazione per l'economia italiana», *Rivista Internazionale di Scienze Sociali*, n. 2, 1990.

[18] MILANA C. - SCANDIZZO P.L., «Settori "esposti" e "non esposti" e politica dei redditi in Italia», in SCANDIZZO P.L. (ed.), *La politica dei redditi in Italia*, Roma, ISPE, 1992.

[19] ONOFRI P. - TOMASINI S., «France and Italy: a Tale of Two Adjustments», *Prometeia. Nota di Lavoro*, n. 9201, 1992.

[20] PENNISI, G., *Satrapi, mandarini e senza lavoro. Intervento nel Mezzogiorno e disoccupazione giovanile,* Roma, Ediesse, 1993.

[21] PORAT M., *The Information Economy,* Washington (DC), Dept. of Commerce. Office and Telecommunications, 1976.

[22] PRESIDENZA DEL CONSIGLIO DEI MINISTRI, *Nota sull'occupazione,* Roma, 20 November, 1992.

[23] RULLANI E., «Sopravviverà il capitalismo all'uso della scienza come forza produttiva?», *Economia e Politica Industriale,* n. 71, 1991.

[24] SAVONA P., «Sviluppo profitti e finanza in Italia», *Sviluppo economico,* n. 1, 1993.

[25] SOSKICE D., «Wage Determination: The Changing Role of Institution in Advanced Industrialized Countries», *Oxford Review of Economic Policy,* n. 4, 1990.

[26] TARANTELLI E., *Economia politica del lavoro,* Torino, UTET, 1986.

[27] ——, *L'utopia dei deboli è la paura dei forti,* Milano, F. Angeli, 1988.

[28] TRONTI L., «Distribuzione dei guadagni di produttività e livelli della contrattazione. Una proposta», *Economia e Lavoro,* n. 1, 1992.

[29] ——, «Il mercato del lavoro» in AUTORI VARI, *Gli studi di relazioni industriali in Italia negli anni '80,* Aisrt. Milano, F. Angeli, 1993.

[30] TRONTI L. - CUCCHIARELLI A., «Formazione e sviluppo economico», *Spazio Impresa,* n. 18, 1991.

III - THE POLITICAL ECONOMY OF THE 1990s SLUMP

Some Reflections on the Political Economy of Unemployment *

Alberto Alesina - **Gerald D. Cohen**
Harvard University, CEPR and NBER
Harvard University, Cambridge (Mass.)

1. - Introduction

Unemployment is both a cyclical and structural phenomenon. On the one hand, the level of unemployment fluctuates with the business cycle; on the other hand, several countries (in Europe in particular) have, in the last twenty years, experienced long periods of unemployment in excess of what is commonly thought of the natural level of unemployment[1]. Graph 1 displays the rate of unemployment for the last 20 years in several European countries[2].

The purpose of this paper is to establish and present ideas about what we do and do not know about the political economy of unemployment, namely how political and institutional factors influence the level of unemployment.

The paper addresses both cyclical and structural issues. We begin by considering the effects of the political cycle, by asking two questions. First, is there any evidence of an "opportunistic cycle" (Nordhaus [43], Lindbeck [42]) in which unemployment is reduced immediately before an election? Second, do different parties follow different policies when in office, generating a "partisan cycle" on

---

* We thank Ignazio Visco for useful comments to our previous version of the article.

N.B.: the numbers in square brackets refer to the Bibliography at the end of the paper.

[1] On unemployment persistence see Blanchard O.J. - Summers L.H. [23] and the references cited therein.

[2] This figure is taken from St. Paul G. [52].

unemployment (Hibbs [37], Alesina [1], [2]). More specifically, is unemployment higher when the left is in office than when the right is in office? A related question is how do the voters respond to these cycles, namely what is the effect of unemployment on voting behavior.

The next set of questions involve more structural considerations. We investigate how various institutional factors may influence the unemployment rate. For instance, several authors (Alesina [3], Alesina and Summers [8], Grilli, Masciandaro and Tabellini [35]) have argued that inflation is lower in countries with independent central banks. Alesina and Summers [8] have also noted that independent central banks have not paid for their success on the inflation front with higher unemployment rates; in this paper we investigate this issue further.

The second structural factor addressed is the effect of the European Monetary System (EMS). Is the EMS responsible, at least in part, for the recently experienced high levels of unemployment in Europe? This is, of course, a very difficult question to answer because it involves a comparison of the experience of EMS countries to what would have happened in these countries had they not joined the EMS. Since it is rather arbitrary to imagine "what would have happened" we follow the strategy of contrasting EMS countries (before and after they joined), with non-EMS, OECD countries (before and after the EMS was established). Utilizing this strategy, which in our view is the most straightforward, one can only gather suggestive, but possibly intriguing insights.

The type of electoral system with the associated party structure may also influence macroeconomic policy choices (Roubini and Sachs [51], Grilli, Masciandaro and Tabellini [35], Spolaore [53]). Large coalition governments have been slower in responding to the macroeconomic shocks of the early seventies, and have exhibited larger budget deficits. Can we detect a similar inefficiency in addressing the problem of unemployment? On the other hand, large coalition governments may insure moderation in policy formation, i.e. they reduce the magnitude of partisan swings. On the unemployment front, have coalition governments insured moderation or caused policy inaction, or have they made no difference?

Finally, a large body of literature (for example Bruno and Sachs [24] and Calmfors and Driffill [25]) has discussed the role of union organization in determining the level of unemployment. For instance, corporatist countries appear to have been associated with superior macroeconomic outcomes (Bruno and Sachs [24]). We briefly look at this effect by focusing on the index of corporatism proposed by Bruno and Sachs [24].

One advantage of considering all these different political and institutional determinants of unemployment at the same time is that we can also take into account the interaction between several of the factors. In addition, our large sample of countries allows analyses of these factors across countries as well as time. Our sample covers the quarterly unemployment rate from 1960 through 1987 for 17 OECD countries[3].

The conclusions of this paper can be summarized as follows. First we confirm and reinforce earlier results by Alesina and Roubini [6] on political cycles. We find no indication of opportunistic cycles, instead, we find robust evidence of short-term partisan cycles. Left wing governments pursue unemployment reducing policies which are successful only in the short-run (one or two years) after they come into office. After this early success, left wing governments are typically trapped in a high inflation equilibrium with no benefits in terms of unemployment. Conversely, unemployment is increased by right wing governments who fight inflation at the beginning of their terms of office. After inflation is reduced, unemployment tends to return to its natural level, while inflation remains low. It is important to note that unemployment is very persistent (Blanchard and Summers [23]). Thus, the recession which is needed to reduce inflation, may have a relatively "persistent" impact on unemployment.

Analyses of the effect of different institutions on the unemployment rate refer almost exclusively to cross-country comparisons. With the exception of the EMS, the institutions which we consider are "stable" within each country. That is, in our sample period we hold individual countries' institutional characteristics constant over time, without we believe, much distortion of reality.

---

[3] The specific country-by-country samples are listed in Appendix *A*1.

Our investigation confirms Alesina and Summers' [8] finding that independent central banks have not been associated with higher unemployment, despite their excellent record at fighting inflation. On the other hand, our results suggest that the countries which have joined the EMS do not show a superior record in terms of inflation reduction than countries which have not joined. Furthermore, unemployment rates seem to be higher in EMS countries that in non-EMS countries. Our results on the consequences of coalition governments and corporatism on unemployment are mixed. However, they generally point in the expected direction, that fragmented governments experience higher unemployment, and corporatism contributes to reduce unemployment.

This paper is organized as follows. Section 2 discusses the evidence on political business cycles; section 3 focuses on voting behavior; section 4 addresses several possible institutional determinants of unemployment; and the last section concludes. A description of the data and of data sources is in appendix.

2. - Political Business Cycles [4]

Nordhaus [43] and Lindbeck [42] have suggested an opportunistic cycle in which unemployment should fall before each election and increase immediately after, because of the opportunistic policies of politicians interested in being reelected. This model is based on three crucial assumptions:

1) the politicians can take advantage of an exploitable Phillips curve and can choose the desired level of unemployment at each point in time;

2) the voters are gullible; they do not understand, nor learn from past observations, that the good pre-electoral outcome will have to be paid with a post electoral recession;

3) the politicians care only about winning elections; there are no ideological differences between parties at least in economic policy.

---

[4] The results of this section are largely based on ALESINA A. - ROUBINI N. [6]. The reader is referred to that paper for more details on data, derivations and technical issues.

The empirical evidence is not very favorable to this model, which has been rejected on United States data by several authors (see Alesina and Roubini [6] and the references cited therein). Table 1 presents several tests of the opportunistic cycle which confirm these negative results for this model.

This table includes several panel regressions on the quarterly rate of unemployment for 17 countries for the sample 1960-1987. The countries included are: Australia, Austria, Belgium, Canada, Denmark, Finland, France, Germany, Ireland, Italy, Japan, the Netherlands, Norway, Sweden, Switzerland, the United Kingdom, and the United States.

TABLE 1

TEST OF OPPORTUNISTIC CYCLE ON UNEMPLOYMENT
dependent variable: U^{DIF}

Sample *	1960-1987 17-country	1960-1987 7-bipartisan	1960-1987 17-country	1960-1987 17-country
Variable	(1) coefficient (*t*-statistic)	(2) coefficient (*t*-statistic)	(3) coefficient (*t*-statistic)	(4) coefficient (*t*-statistic)
Constant........	0.169 (3.61)	0.015 (0.41)	0.163 (3.47)	0.174 (3.68)
$U^{DIF}(-1)$	1.317 (50.65)	1.405 (38.58)	1.319 (50.88)	1.317 (50.70)
$U^{DIF}(-2)$	−0.332 (−12.63)	−0.430 (−11.54)	−0.334 (−12.76)	−0.332 (−12.63)
NRD 6..........	−0.018 (−0.92)	−0.017 (−0.70)	—	—
NRD 4..........	—	—	0.007 (0.32)	—
NRD 8..........	—	—	—	−0.025 (−1.27)
R^2	0.99	0.98	0.99	0.99
Number of observations ..	1,341	634	1,341	1,341

* The estimated regressions include country fixed effects which are not reported in the table.

The dependent variable (U^{DIF}) is the difference between the unemployment rate in each country in each quarter and a proxy for a "world" average unemployment rate in the corresponding quarter. The world average unemployment rate is obtained as the average unemployment in the seven largest economies in our sample, weighted by each country's share of GNP over the total. The reason we want to consider the deviation from this world average variable is twofold. First, the politician's goal on domestic unemployment might be defined in relation with the rest of the world: a relatively high unemployment rate may be considered politically palatable in the middle of a major world recession, while the same rate of domestic unemployment is a political liability in the middle of a world expansion. That is, the crucial political variable is how the country is doing *relative* to the rest of the world. Second, regardless of the government goals, international trade and financial linkages make OECD economies highly interconnected[5].

We control for autocorrelation by including two lags of the dependent variable; this autoregressive specification is chosen as the "best" using standard techniques[6]. We also included fixed effects in the regression, namely we allowed for a different constant in each country; these country dummies are not explicity reported in Table 1 for space considerations.

The crucial variables which test the theory are the dummies *NRD*4, *NRD*6 and *NRD*8. They are defined as follows; the variables assume the value of 1 respectively in the 3, 5, and 7 quarters before an election and during the election quarter, and zero otherwise. Therefore a negative sign on the coefficient of these variables indicates that unemployment is lower in the year or two preceding an election. The dates of each election in each country are reported in appendix *A*2.

Column 1 of Table 1 shows that the coefficient on the *NRD*6 dummy is not statistically different from zero. As expected and

---

[5] An alternative way to correct for international effects would be to introduce the world variable as a regressor. None of the results of this paper would change qualitatively if we follow this alternative procedure. We choose to use the difference because of the high level of persistence shown by unemployment. The variable in differences is slightly less persistent than the variable levels.

[6] See ALESINA A. - ROUBINI N. [6] for further details.

indicated by the values of the coefficients on the lagged dependent variable, unemployment is extremely persistent[7]. The second column presents the same regression for a sub-sample of seven "bipartisan" countries with either a pure two-party system or a two-block system. These countries are: Australia, Canada, France, Germany, Sweden, the UK and the US. Once again the coefficient on *NRD*6 is insignificant. These results are similar to those reported by Alesina and Roubini [6].

The results presented in columns 3 and 4 reinforce those in columns 1 and 2. For the entire sample of countries, the coefficients on *NRD*4 and *NRD*8 are insignificant, although the latter coefficient has the expected sign and a t-static of almost -1.30. Thus, there is virtually no evidence of a fall in unemployment before elections.

In summary, one can find no systematic evidence of opportunistic cycles of the Nordhaus type. Unemployment does not appear to be particularly low during the pre-electoral period.

A contrasting view of political parties' behavior suggests that different parties follow diverse policies when in office. The left is relatively more averse to unemployment than the right; that is the left is more willing to risk inflation in order to fight unemployment than the right. The origin of these partisan preferences is in the distributional consequences of different combinations of inflation and unemployment. The lower middle-class suffers relatively more than the upper middle-class during recessions[8]. Hibbs [37], [38] argues that because of these distributional effects of unemployment, one should expect to see partisan cycles with permanently lower levels of unemployment when the left is in office as compared to right-wing administrations. Like Nordhaus' model, Hibbs' model relies on an exploitable Phillips curve with static or adaptive expectations.

Table 2 reports some tests of Hibbs' partisan cycle model. The

---

[7] The high level of persistence which is captured by the presence of lagged dependent variables in the regressions cause the R^2 in all these estimations to be remarkably high. This result is a common feature of quarterly macroeconomic time series.

[8] See Hibbs D.A. [38] for an extensive discusison of this point with specific reference on the United States and Alesina A. [3] for some observations on the same point for other countries.

TABLE 2

TEST OF PARTISAN CYCLE ON UNEMPLOYMENT
dependent variable: U^{DIF}

Sample *	1960-1987 15-country	1960-1987 7-bipartisan	1972-1987 15-country	1972-1987 7-country
Variable	(1) coefficient (*t*-statistic)	(2) coefficient (*t*-statistic)	(3) coefficient (*t*-statistic)	(4) coefficient (*t*-statistic)
Constant........	0.149 (3.27)	0.010 (0.31)	0.154 (3.17)	0.031 (0.88)
$U^{DIF}(-1)$	1.294 (48.87)	1.407 (39.97)	1.288 (40.62)	1.484 (35.04)
$U^{DIF}(-2)$	−0.308 (−11.55)	−0.430 (−12.02)	−0.306 (−9.63)	−0.511 (−11.96)
RADM (−1)	0.009 (0.87)	0.008 (0.63)	0.008 (0.53)	0.010 (0.67)
R^2	0.99	0.98	0.99	0.99
Number of observations ..	1,312	676	926	432

* The estimated regressions include country fixed effects which are not reported in the table.

dependent variable and the specification of the unemployment regression is the same as in Table 1. As in Table 1 we have included fixed effects in the regression but we have not explicity reported them in the table. The only difference is in the specification of the political dummy. The variable *RADM* assumes the value of 1 for periods with right-wing governments and −1 for periods with left-wing regimes in office. Thus, according to Hibbs' model the coefficient on the *RADM* variable should be positive. In addition, the *RADM* variable is lagged one quarter in order to incorporate delays in policy implementation[9]. The classification of right- and left-wing governments and the timing

[9] Different lags of the *RADM* variable were implemented, and the one-quarter lag was found to be the most generous to the theory. Estimations with larger lags are available upon request.

of changes of governments is described in Appendix *A*2 and follows Alesina and Roubini [6][10].

Column 1 reports results for the entire sample of 15 countries for the full sample period (1960-1987)[11]. The coefficient has the expected sign but is insignificant. Column 2 reports the results for the sub-sample of the seven "bipartisan" countries; one would expect to observe partisan difference in macroeconomic policies more markedly in these countries relative to other countries with coalition governments. The coefficient on *RADM* remains statistically zero[12]. In columns 3 and 4 we repeat the same regressions for the post-1971 sample (1972-1987). The motivation for these tests is that during the Bretton-Woods period, macroeconomic policies of economies linked by fixed exchange rates were less independent than in the post-Bretton-Woods period. Thus partisan differences in macroeconomic policies may appear more clearly after 1971. However, we again do not find any evidence of a partisan cycle as modelled by Hibbs. The coefficients on the *RADM* variables are insignificant.

In summary, one cannot find any evidence of a permanent partisan effect on unemployment[13].

Alesina [1], [2] has proposed a different partisan model which has been labeled the "rational partisan theory". As in Hibbs' model, the left is more unemployment averse than the right. However, contrary to Hibbs' model, the rational partisan theory is based on a

[10] The definition of what is left and what is right is generally straightforward; socialist and social democratic parties are considered left, conservative and Christian Democratic parties are considered right. In some cases of coalition governments one has to make some judgement calls. ALESINA A. - ROUBINI N. [6] describe this classification in more detail and argue that the general results on partisan cycles are not dependent on these few judgement calls.

[11] Japan and Switzerland are excluded from theses estimations because they do not experience changes of the party in power over the sample period.

[12] Similar results were reported by ALESINA A. - ROUBINI N. [6].

[13] In the last decade or more, a sequence of left leaning governments has experienced high levels of unemployment (Graph 1). If Spain were included in the sample for Table 2 the results would look even worse for Hibbs' model. There are two reasons why Spain is not part of our sample. First the data set for this paper is the same one as ALESINA A. - ROUBINI N. [6]. That paper did not include OECD countries which had not been democracies for the entire sample period 1960-1987. This choice was justfied by the consideration that transitions from dictatorships to democracies may represent exceptional periods which should not be considered together with normal government changes. Second, data availability for Spain is problematic.

neo-Keynesian specification of the Phillips curve based upon a sticky wage model with rational expectations[14]. Wage setters know the difference in the macroeconomic policies of the various political parties and have rational expectations. However, due to the electoral uncertainty, post-electoral policies cannot be predicted perfectly because, ex ante, nobody knows which party is going to win the election. Therefore, elections are associated with policy shocks. If the left wins, a positive aggregate demand shock materializes. This expansionary policy is partly unanticipated since the public had accounted for the possibility of a right-wing electoral victory. As a result, unemployment falls in the short-run. However, as soon as all the contracts can be adjusted to incorportate the new inflationary expectations, unemployment returns to its "natural" rate. In contrast, inflation remains high. In fact, since the left has an anti-unemployment bias, it suffers from an inflation bias, as in Barro and Gordon [19], [20]. Thus, a left-wing government should experience a short-run fall in unemployment at the beginning of its term of office and a build up of inflation which lasts throughout its term. A right-wing government experiences the opposite outcome.

When a new right-wing government takes power it fights inflation. This causes a recession and an increase in unemployment, because of the high inflation expectations built into the labor contracts. In fact, prior to the election, wage setters account for the possibility of a left-wing victory and incorporate this expectation into their wage demands. After the wages adjust to the new low inflation policy, unemployment returns to its natural rate. Inflation remains low because the right, being more inflation averse then the left, has less of a credibility problem on the inflation front. Therefore, this model predicts that partisan effects on unemployment should be observable only in the short-run, for no more than two years after a change of government[15]. Note however, that since unemployment is very persistent the consequences of the recession may be felt for a relatively long time. The recessionary "shock" after a right-wing

---

[14] The wage contract model by ALESINA A. [1] is a version of FISHER S. [33].

[15] A short-run effect of about two years is roughly consistent with a structure of overlapping wage contracts of an average duration of three years.

victory may fade away in a few quarters, but it may take several years before unemployment completes its adjustment process.

Table 3 tests the predictions of this model. Using the same estimation procedure as above we introduce a dummy variable *DRPT*6 which takes the values of 1 in the six quarters starting with a government change toward the right; −1 in the six quarters starting with a government change toward the left; and zero otherwise. The theory predicts a positive sign for this coefficient. The *DRPT*6 variable is lagged two quarters to incorporate well known delays in policy implementation, and in the effects of new policies on the economy. The first column of Table 3 includes all countries which have experienced changes in the party in power (thus Japan and Switzerland are

TABLE 3

TEST OF RATIONAL PARTISAN THEORY ON UNEMPLOYMENT
dependent variable: U^{DIF}

Sample *	1960-1987 15-country	1960-1987 7-bipartisan	1972-1987 15-country	1972-1987 7-bipartisan	1960-1987 17-country
Variable	(1) coefficient (*t*-statistic)	(2) coefficient (*t*-statistic)	(3) coefficient (*t*-statistic)	(4) coefficient (*t*-statistic)	(5) coefficient (*t*-statistic)
Constant	0.154 (3.39)	0.018 (0.56)	0.156 (3.23)	0.041 (1.15)	0.171 (3.66)
$U^{DIF}(-1)$	1.287 (48.43)	1.383 (38.83)	1.282 (40.40)	1.463 (34.26)	1.308 (50.15)
$U^{DIF}(-2)$	−0.301 (−11.25)	−0.410 (−11.40)	−0.300 (−9.43)	−0.493 (−11.51)	−0.324 (−12.29)
*DRPT*6 (−2)	0.057 (2.85)	0.087 (3.30)	0.058 (2.44)	0.083 (2.77)	0.062 (3.03)
*NRD*6	—	—	—	—	−0.019 (−0.98)
R^2	0.99	0.99	0.99	0.99	0.99
Number of observations ..	1,312	676	926	432	1,341

* The estimated regressions include country fixed effects which are not reported in the table.

excluded), for the entire sample period. The coefficient is positive and significant at extremely high levels of confidence. The second column includes only the seven bipartisan countries listed above. The coefficient is slightly larger and even more significant[16]. Columns 3 and 4 repeat the same regression for the post-1971 period, for the two samples of countries. The results suggest that there is no difference in partisan manipulations in the pre- and post-Bretton-Woods periods.

As a joint test of both Alesina's and Nordhaus' models, in column 5 we introduce both the *DRPT*6 and the *NRD*6 dummies. For the full sample period of all 17 countries, the *DRPT*6 variable remains significant, while the *NRD*6 is not statistically significant. This further confirms the results in Tables 1 and 3, which support the rational partisan theory. Finally, we have experimented with other specifications of the *DRPT* dummy, such as 4, 8 and 10 quarters of post-electoral influence. The results are robust: partisan difference are clearly strong for about 6 to 8 quarters after a change of government, they then fade away.

The size of the partisan differences implied by the coefficients of Table 3 are also substantial. For instance, the coefficients of the estimation in column 2, for the seven bipartisan countries suggest that seven quarters after a change in regime to the left unemployment is 1.5 percentage points lower than it would be after a change to the right.[17].

In Table 4 we test the second prediction of the model, namely that even though the unemployment effects are transitory, the impact on inflation is permanent. The specification of the inflation regression is analogous to those presented above with a longer lag structure for the inflation estimations than for unemployment. Also, rather than taking differences from domestic inflation from world inflation, we include a proxy for the average OECD inflation as a regressor[18]. The political dummy used is *RADM* which, as with the tests of Hibbs'

---

[16] These results are analogous to those presented in ALESINA A. - ROUBINI N. [6].

[17] ALESINA A. - ROUBINI N. [6] show that these favorable results for the rational partisan theory are replicated on GNP growth. Growth is higher than average at the beginning of the term of office of a left-wing government and lower than average at the beginning of the term of office of a right-wing government.

[18] The average is obtained as described above for unemployment.

TABLE 4

TEST OF RATIONAL PARTISAN THEORY ON INFLATION
dependent variable: π

Sample *	1960-1987 16-country	1960-1987 8-bipartisan	1972-1987 16-country	1972-1987 8-bipartisan
Variable	(1) coefficient (*t*-statistic)	(2) coefficient (*t*-statistic)	(3) coefficient (*t*-statistic)	(4) coefficient (*t*-statistic)
Constant........	−0.082 (−0.70)	0.590 (4.80)	−0.164 (−0.98)	1.417 (5.99)
$\pi(-1)$	1.085 (45.55)	1.211 (35.42)	1.112 (34.95)	1.198 (26.23)
$\pi(-2)$	−0.137 (−3.92)	−0.273 (−5.18)	−0.172 (−3.63)	−0.284 (−4.07)
$\pi(-3)$	−0.098 (−4.35)	−0.075 (−2.32)	−0.122 (−4.05)	−0.100 (−2.32)
πW............	0.146 (13.21)	0.128 (9.43)	0.152 (11.36)	0.134 (7.62)
RADM (−1)	−0.047 (−1.55)	−0.083 (−2.15)	−0.063 (−1.56)	−0.138 (−2.44)
R^2	0.94	0.95	0.94	0.94
Number of observations ..	1,792	896	1,024	512

* The estimated regressions include country fixed effects which are not reported in the table.

model, takes the value of 1 when right-wing governments are in office and −1 during left-wing administrations. Therefore, the rational partisan theory indicates that the coefficient on the *RADM* variable should be negative. Column 1 includes all 16 countries with changes in the party in power (including New Zealand, which has inflation data available) for the entire time period (1960-1987). The coefficient on the *RADM* variable has the expected negative sign, but is only borderline significant. Column 2 restricts the sample to the eight bipartisan countries (the seven listed above plus New Zealand). The coefficient on *RADM* is now larger in magnitude and significant at standard levels of confidence. Columns 3 and 4 repeat the same regressions for the post-1971 sample (1972-1987). The larger magnitudes of the *RADM* coefficients in columns 3 and 4 suggest that partisan inflationary differences are larger for the post-Bretton-Woods period. This results concurs with theories of larger inflationary pressures to which governments must react in the post-Bretton-Woods period. However, as Cohen [27] indicates, even during the 1960s, the US public perceived Republicans as much stauncher inflation fighters than Democrats.

In summary, the results of this section, which has reviewed and extended previous results by Alesina and Roubini [6] on political busines cycles on unemployment, can be summarized by three points:

1) there is virtually no evidence of an opportunistic cycle in which the party in office manages to reduce unemployment right before an election;

2) partisan effects are widespread but are temporary in nature. Unemployment rates exhibit rational partisan cycles;

3) partisan cycles are most evident in two-party or two-bloc systems. They are less detectable in countries with large coalition governments, which are countries with proportional electoral systems.

3. - Do the Voters Care?

One of the results of the previous section is that politicians are not successful in reducing unemployment immediately before an election. The next question is why this is the case. One possibility is that the voters do not particularly care about unemployment, therefore it is not worth it for the politicians to even try to do much about unemployment before an election.

Economists and political scientists have studied the effects of economic conditions on voting behavior; the literature is particularly rich for the Unites States[19]. Several researchers agree that in the

[19] The path-breaking contribution on this point is KRAMER G. [40]; see also FAIR R.C. [30], [31]; FIORINA M.P. [32] and ALESINA A. - ROSENTHAL H. [9].

United States the state of the economy in the election year is a very important determinant of presidential election results. The economic variable which is most successful in explaining voter behavior is the rate of income or GNP growth in the election year, but unemployment it also important.

Research on other OECD countries has also concluded that economic conditions are an important determinant of voting decisions (Lewis-Beck [41]). In conducting this research one must take into consideration several issues which are specific to various countries with different institutions, party structures and electoral laws and history. However, it can be safely concluded that in Europe as well as the United States, the economy matters when electorates make their decisions.

To be sure, St. Paul [52] notes that, generally, European electorates have been more tolerant of unemployment than the American one. European governments are routinely reappointed even with rates of unemployment which are well above levels which would be considered a political catastrophe for an American administration. One can think of several explanations for this differences. First, social welfare programs and social insurance schemes are generally more widespread in Europe than in the US. Without these social programs, unemployment has more visible social costs. To be unemployed in the US is more damaging than to be unemployed in Europe, where the costs of unemployment are spread out to the taxpayers who pay, in more or less visible ways, for social insurance schemes. Second, electorates in Europe may have become accustomed to high levels of unemployment and view them, correctly or erroneously, as a result of structural phenomena such as labor market rigidities (St. Paul [52]), which have little to do with macroeconomic policies. Therefore, the voters do not perceive the governments as responsible for high unemployment. Third, the European electorate may be more ideological than the American one and more strictly follow party line voting. Fourth, the electorate may not know how to place the blame in countries run by large coalition governments.

In any case, despite all these caveats, even the European electorate respond to unemployment. St. Paul [52] argues that it is not so much the level of unemployment that matters but changes in this level. Lewis-Beck [41], on the other hand, reviews a vast literature and concludes that not only the change but also the level of unemployment affects voting decisions in several European countries.

In summary we are left with a bit of a puzzle. The level of unemployment, or its rate of change, has an influence on the electoral fortunes of incumbent governments, but incumbent governments do not seem to be able to take advantage of this opportunity. In fact, as we have discussed in section 2, the unemployment rate is not particularly low in election years. Alesina and Rosenthal [9] provide an argument which may help to explain these apparently contradictory observations. The idea is that different governments may have different levels of competence in handling macroeconomic problems, such as unemployment[20]. More competent governments manage to reduce unemployment without increasing inflation; less competent ones do not succeed in doing so. In other words, competent governments manage to lower unemployment without trying to exploit a Phillips curve which may be vertical or extremely steep. The electorate cannot perfectly distinguish the effects of government competence from those of random shocks which hit the economy. If the electorate observes high unemployment, it assigns some probability to the fact that the government is not good at fighting unemployment and some probability to the possibility that the economy is suffering from an adverse shock. If the public performs such an analysis, then the level (or rate of change) of unemployment will affect electoral results, even though the government may not be able to systematically influence the rate of unemployment, because it faces a vertical Phillips curve. Thus, the voters evaluate the competence of the government by observing the state of the economy, but the government cannot systematically alter the average level of unemployment in election years[21].

---

[20] The original proponents of "competence" models are ROGOFF K. - SIBERT A. [50]; see also ROGOFF K. [49]; PERSSON T. - TABELLINI G. [48]. The model by ALESINA A. - ROSENTHAL H. [9] described in the text builds upon and then departs from this earlier literature.

[21] In a related model by PERSSON T. - TABELLINI G. [48] the government can take advantage of asymmetric information on its own competence and generate Nordhaus' type political business cycles. However, the assumption of asymmetric information needed to generate these rational opportunistic cycles is rather artificial. For instance,

This argument raises an interesting question: are voters rational in attributing blame and praise to governments? More precisely, do voters use all available information in their attempt to disentangle the effects of government competence and random shocks? Or, conversely, do they simply vote against the government when the economy is doing poorly so that good governments are punished for bad luck and vice versa?

It is not easy to answer these question. Tests of rationality are always complex and imperfect. In order to test rational behavior, one has to make stringent assumptions about what the agents know and do not know. In addition, every test is «model dependent», since one crucial assumption of these tests is that rational agents should know the model and act accordingly.

Alesina and Rosenthal [9] provide the first formal test of rationality in voting behavior in US elections. They conclude that the American electorate pays too much attention to the short-run state of the economy to be consistent with rationality and all the other auxiliary assumptions necessary for these tests. The American voter does not seem to make much effort at disentangling the effects of random shocks from government competence in handling the economy.

Similar tests of European elections are not available. This is in fact an excellent topic for future research: are incumbent governments in OECD democracies systematically punished for bad luck as well as for incompetence? The answer to this question has potentially important consequences for policy. For instance, if the voters do not distinguish between bad luck and injurious policies, governments have an incentive to avoid poor outcomes at all costs even when the best policy is to do nothing. Or, it may be difficult to implement hard stabilization policies if the voters have a tendency to not "see through" the necessity of the bad tasting medicine.

In summary, the voters do care about unemployment, or its rate of change. In fact, evidence from the US suggests that the voters may care even too much about the short-run state of the economy. Thus,

---

the voters are supposed to observe unemployment first and then with a substantial lag, the rate of inflation. Not only do these assumptions appear unnatural, but no evidence of opportunistic cycles is found in the data.

why don't politicians take advantage of this fact by reducing unemployment in election years?[22]

The answer has to be that they cannot. Aggregate demand policies, which are the traditional tool for achieving quick movements in unemployment, may be too imperfect and unreliable for politicians to achieve their goals. This does not of course imply that aggregate demand policies are not useful, it just stresses that it is difficult for the incumbent to systematically alter the state of the economy in election years.

4. - Institutions and Unemployment

4.1 *Central Bank Independence*

Independent central banks in OECD economies have been associated with low and stable inflation rates[23]. The argument is that independent central banks are more insulated from political pressures to ease monetary policy, and can more effectively commit to a low inflation policy[24].

Alesina and Summers [8] suggest that this success on the inflation front has not been paid with higher unemployment. They find no correlation between average levels of unemployment and a measure of central bank independence. In this section we attempt to advance their simple observation, by adding their measure of central bank independence to our panel regressions. Appendix *A*3 reports this index.

Alesina and Summers [8] obtained their measure of central bank independence by combining two previously used indices of indepen-

---

[22] The fact that they try to be opportunistic is demonstrated by ALESINA A. - COHEN G.D. - ROUBINI N. [10] and [12]. They find that monetary and fiscal policies tend to be loose in election years; budget deficits tend to increase, and monetary growth tends to be high. These results suggest that politicians have a tendency to be opportunistic, but they cannot affect unemployment.

[23] See BADE R. - PARKIN M. [15], ALESINA A. [3], ALESINA A. - SUMMERS L. [8], GRILLI V. - MASCIANDARO D. - TABELLINI G. [35], CUKIERMAN A. - WEBB S. - NEYAPTI B. [28].

[24] See ROGOFF K. [49] on this point and ALESINA A. - GRILLI V. [5] for more discussion in the context of the EMS.

dence. The first index was originally proposed by Bade and Parkin [15] and was later updated, and extended by Alesina [3]. This is an index of political autonomy which ranks independence as a function of the type of relationship between the governing body of the central bank and the executive and the legislature of the country. The second, more sophisticated measure, was proposed by Grilli, Masciandaro and Tabellini [35]. This index has two components: a political element, similar in spirit to the Bade and Parkin [15] index; and a component of economic independence. The latter is basically defined as a function of whether or not and how much the central bank is compelled to monetize budget deficits[25].

The Alesina and Summers' index *CBIND*, assumes values from 1, the least independent to 4, the most independent. Therefore, the theory indicates that the coefficient on the *CBIND* variable should be negative, indicating lower inflation for countries with a more independent central bank. Table 5 includes the *CBIND* index panel estimations on inflation. The table presents results for the full (1960-1987) sample for the 13 countries for which a measure of central bank independence is available (hence Finland, Austria and Ireland are excluded). These estimations do not include fixed effects because the central bank independence index (*CBIND*) variable is constant throughout time for each country and thus acts as a substitute for the fixed effects[26].

The table demonstrates that, concurring with the theory, the coefficient on the *CBIND* variable is negative and strongly significant. The implication of this estimation is that differences in the rates of inflation across countries may be explained by differences in the independence of each country's central bank. These results are further confirmed by the coefficients on the fixed effects of Table 4. That is, the coefficients on the fixed effects are positive and significant for countries like Italy and New Zealand in which the *CBIND* variable takes on a low value, and negative in Germany and the United States

---

[25] For more details about the construction of these indexes see ALESINA A. - SUMMERS L. [8].

[26] That is, the *CBIND* variable can be separated into a linear combination of the country fixed effects. Therefore, if both the *CBIND* variable and the fixed effects were included in a regression they would be perfectly collinear.

TABLE 5

EFFECT OF CENTRAL BANK INDEPENDENCE ON INFLATION
dependent variable: π

Sample	1960-1987 13-country	1960-1987 13-country
Variable	(1) coefficient (*t*-statistic)	(2) coefficient (*t*-statistic)
Constant	0.730 (6.17)	0.768 (6.44)
$\pi(-1)$	1.152 (43.56)	1.149 (43.42)
$\pi(-2)$	−0.191 (−4.81)	−0.191 (−4.80)
$\pi(-3)$	−0.086 (−3.44)	−0.086 (−3.43)
πW	0.122 (10.83)	0.122 (10.82)
CBIND	−0.255 (−5.96)	−0.262 (−5.13)
RADM(-1)	—	−0.070 (−2.39)
R^2	0.94	0.94
Number of observations	1,456	1,456

with independent central banks[27]. Lastly, column 2 includes the *RADM* variable and indicates that, for the entire sample of countries, controlling for differences in central bank independence, one finds larger and statistically significant partisan differences in inflation.

In Table 6 the same central bank independence index is incorporated into our unemployment estimations. Theories produce mixed

[27] These estimations do not include Switzerland which has an independent central bank and low inflation. If Switzerland were added to the data set, the central bank independence results illustrated in Table 5 would be even stronger.

TABLE 6

EFFECT OF CENTRAL BANK INDEPENDENCE ON UNEMPLOYMENT
dependent variable: U^{DIF}

Sample	1960-1987 12-country	1960-1987 12-country
Variable	(1) coefficient (*t*-statistic)	(2) coefficient (*t*-statistic)
Constant	0.053 (1.29)	0.060 (1.48)
$U^{DIF}(-1)$	1.282 (43.83)	1.270 (43.21)
$U^{DIF}(-2)$	−0.287 (−9.71)	−0.275 (−9.27)
CBIND	−0.008 (−0.51)	−0.011 (−0.68)
DRPT(−6)	—	0.075 (3.25)
R^2	0.99	0.99
Number of observations	1,081	1,081

implications concerning the impact of independent central banks on unemployment. On the one hand, independent central banks, by keeping inflation low, may stabilize expectations, reduce uncertainty, and stimulate growth. Therefore, independent central banks might be associated with low unemployment. Thus, the coefficient on *CBIND* should be negative. On the other hand, arguments based on the Phillips curve theory suggest that low inflation can only be achieved at the expense of higher unemployment. Thus, according to this view, the coefficient on *CBIND* should be positive. Column 1 of Table 6 attempts to control for differences in country unemployment by replacing the fixed effects with the *CBIND* variable. Column 2 then includes the *DRPT6* variable as a further test of the rational partisan theory. In both cases the coefficient on *CBIND* has a negative sign, but it is insignificant. The sign on the *CBIND* variable indicates that as central bank independence increases, unemployment decreases. However this variable is not significantly different from zero, thus indicating that central bank independence has no effect on unemployment.

In summary, these results reinforce previous research by Alesina and Summers [8] independent central banks have contributed to reduce inflation without increasing unemployment. In other words, independent central banks don't pay for their lower average inflation with higher average unemployment.

4.2 *Unemployment and the EMS*

Several commentators have argued that the EMS has contributed to a reduction in the inflation rates of the member countries because it has introduced a deflationary bias in the monetary policies of all countries which have linked themselves to the Bundesbank[28]. Table 7 presents a simple test of this hypothesis on inflation. These estimations recreate those conducted in Tables 4 and 5 by including a dummy variable labelled *EMS* to our standard inflation panel. The *EMS* variable takes on a value of 1 during the time period when a country is a member of the *EMS*, and zero otherwise. Thus the *EMS* variable takes on a value of 1 from 1979 through 1987 (the end of the sample) in Belgium, Denmark, France, Germany, Ireland, Italy, and the Netherlands.

The theory described above implies that the coefficient on the *EMS* variable should be negative. The results of the estimations indicate that only in column 3 is the coefficient on the *EMS* variable the expected negative sign. However, in no case is the coefficient on the *EMS* variable statistically different from zero. This outcome is robust to different specifications of the model, such as the inclusion of

---

[28] See Begg D. - Wyplost C. [21] for a history of the EMS, as well as, an excellent and balanced survey of various arguments in favor and against this institution.

Table 7

EFFECT OF EMS ON INFLATION
dependent variable: π

Sample *	1960-1987 16-country		1960-1987 13-country
Variable	(1) coefficient (*t*-statistic)	(2) coefficient (*t*-statistic)	(3) coefficient (*t*-statistic)
Constant	−0.124 (−1.05)	−0.087 (−0.71)	0.767 (6.43)
$\pi(-1)$	1.087 (45.60)	1.085 (45.54)	1.148 (43.40)
$\pi(-2)$	−0.137 (−3.92)	−0.137 (−3.92)	−0.191 (−4.80)
$\pi(-3)$	−0.098 (−4.36)	−0.098 (−4.35)	−0.085 (−3.40)
πW	0.148 (13.41)	0.146 (13.20)	0.122 (10.82)
SME	0.021 (0.24)	0.014 (0.16)	−0.026 (0.33)
RADM (−1)	—	−0.047 (−1.54)	−0.070 (−2.39)
CBIND	—	—	−0.261 (−6.05)
R^2	0.94	0.94	0.94
Number of observations	1,792	1,792	1,456

* Estimations (1) and (2) include country fixed effects which are not reported in the table.

fixed effects in columns 1 and 2, and the *DRPT6* and *CBIND* variables in columns 2 and 3.

These results indicate that EMS member countries do not exhibit lower inflation (that is, a faster disinflation in the eighties) than non-EMS countries. One explanation for this finding is the EMS has not particularly helped in fighting inflation. The alternative explanation is that if the EMS did not exist, EMS countries would have had much higher rates of inflation. In other words, several countries which joined the EMS did so precisely because they knew that they would not have managed to reduce inflation without the help of an external monetary anchor. In this respect, the EMS provided a way for "weak currency" countries to commit to low inflation (Giavazzi and Giovannini [36]).

As a further test of the possible impact of the EMS, Table 8 assesses the impact of the EMS on unemployment. The specification

Table 8

EFFECT OF EMS ON UNEMPLOYMENT
dependent variable: *UE*

Sample *	1960-1987 15-country	1960-1987 15-country	1960-1987 12-country
Variable	(1) coefficient (*t*-statistic)	(2) coefficient (*t*-statistic)	(3) coefficient (*t*-statistic)
Constant	0.015 (0.28)	0.021 (0.40)	−0.005 (−0.10)
UE (−1)	1.320 (50.51)	1.317 (50.35)	1.346 (47.06)
UE (−2)	−0.357 (−13.98)	−0.355 (−13.86)	−0.363 (−12.78)
UEW	0.058 (6.79)	0.057 (6.69)	0.028 (3.46)
SME	0.152 (4.22)	0.151 (4.19)	0.087 (2.72)
*DRPT*6 (−2)	—	0.032 (1.74)	0.058 (2.74)
CBIND	—	—	−0.009 (−0.61)
R^2	0.99	0.99	0.99
Number of observations	1,312	1,312	1,081

* Estimations (1) and (2) include country fixed effects which are not reported in the table.

of these estimations are slightly different from the unemployment regressions presented earlier. Rather than using the difference between the country's unemployment rate and the world average (U^{DIF}) as our measure of unemployment, we use the level of unemployment (*UE*) itself. This specification was chosen because close to half of our defined "world" is made up of countries in the EMS. Thus, use of the difference variable (U^{DIF}) may bias the results. Therefore, the specification of the regression has the level of unemployment (*UE*) as the dependent variable, and includes the world unemployment rate (*UEW*) as one of the regressors.

The results of the estimations outlined above are quite surprising. In all the specifications displayed in Table 8 the *EMS* variable has a very significant positive coefficient, indicating an adverse effect of EMS membership on unemployment. This result is statistically robust and does not disappear in every other specification which we tried, including using the U^{DIF} specification estimated in the earlier tables[29]. The value of the coefficient on *EMS* is also quite large. For example, the value of this coefficient in column 1 indicates that in the steady state, it costs on average four percentage points of unemployment to be a member of the EMS[30].

As was the case for the impact of the EMS on inflation, one can view the results for unemployment in two different ways. One is to argue that the EMS did indeed introduce a recessionary bias in member countries' economies. Blanchard, for instance, emphasized the role of high real interest rates as an important explanatory factor for European unemployment. EMS countries might have experienced high interest rates in linking themselves to German policies. In contrast to the above view, what may appear to be a consequence of the EMS, may instead be the effect of higher persistence in European unemployment relative to non-European countries. That is, the oil shock of 1979-1980 and the recession of the early eighties might have had more persistent effects in Europe than in other parts of the world. Our *EMS* variable may be capturing this persistence which might be

[29] All of these results are available upon request.

[30] The reader should also note that Spain is not included in our sample. Spain joined the EMS in 1986, and has continued to have very high unemployment during the that time (see Graph 1).

explained, for instance, by characteristics of European labor markets which have nothing to do with the EMS. It should be noted however, that EMS countries have had high unemployment even relative to other non-EMS European countries.

Finally, it is interesting to note that the *DRPT6* variable remains significant and the central bank independence variable remains insignificant, when they are included in a regression with the EMS dummy. In summary, our results are not very encouraging for enthusiastic views of the EMS. Many reasons, discussed above, may fairly easily "rescue" the EMS. However, it is a fact that the macroeconomic benefits of the EMS do not immediately "catch" the eyes of the observer.

4.3 *Coalition Governments and Unemployment*

Coalition governments are often held responsible for costly delays in policy responses to crises, particularly with reference to budget deficits. For example, Alesina and Drazen, 1991, and Spolaore [53] discuss theories of delays in implementation of fiscal stabilization in coalition governments. Roubini and Sachs [51] and Grilli, Masciandaro and Tabellini [35] present evidence on the effect of coalition governments on the accumulation of debt. On the other hand, our results in section 2 concerning the larger partisan impact in the sub-sample of bipartisan countries, suggest that coalition governments may reduce the extent of partisan cycles in macroeconomic policies in general, and unemployment cycles in particular. (For more evidence on this point see Alesina and Roubini [10]). An interesting question is whether or not this lower partisan variance has been "paid for" with higher average unemployment. In other words, we investigate whether unemployment is higher in coalition governments, possibly as a result of the lack of decisive actions on the unemployment front.

In order to assess the impact of fragmented governments on unemployment, we have added a dummy variable *COAL*, which is the same one used in Roubini and Sachs [51] in their work on budget deficits, to our standard unemployment regression (with U^{DIF} as the dependent variable). The *COAL* variable takes the following values: 0

in a one-party majority parliamentary government, or a presidential government, with the same party in the majority in the executive and legislative branches; 1 in a coalition parliamentary government with two coalition partners, or in a presidential government with different parties in control of the executive and legislative branches; 2 in a coalition parliamentary government with three or more coalition partners; and 3 in a minority parliamentary government[31]. The above theory suggests that the coefficient on the *COAL* variable should be positive, indicating that the more coalition partnes, the more unstable the government, the higher the average unemployment.

The results of estimations which include fixed effects and the *COAL* variable are depicted in Table 9 for the full sample (1960-1987) for the 13 countries with *COAL* data (Roubini and Sachs did not collect data for Australia and Canada). The table indicates that the coefficient on *COAL* has the expected positive sign but is not statistically significant at standard levels. In addition, inclusion of the *DRPT6* and *EMS* yield results which concur with the rational partisan theory and the adverse impact of the EMS discussed above. However, the magnitude and significance of the *COAL* variable decreases. These results suggest that, even controlling for the moderating effects of coalition governments does not abrogate the existence of post-electoral partisan swings. Consequently, in general there is some indication that government instability yields higher unemployment, but these results are dependent upon the specification of the model.

4.4 *Unions, Corporatism and Unemployment*

A large literature (see Bruno and Sachs [24] and the references cited therein) has emphasized the role of labor market organizations as an explanatory variable for macroeconomic outcomes. In particular, corporatist systems are generally thought of as more likely to experience superior macroeconomic outcomes. Corporatism can be defined as "a mode of social organization in which functional groups

---

[31] Details on the construction of the index for each particular country can be found in Roubini N. - Sachs I. [51].

TABLE 9

EFFECT OF COALITION GOVERNMENTS ON UNEMPLOYMENT
dependent variable: U^{DIF}

Sample *	1960-1987 13-country	1960-1987 13-country	1960-1987 13-country
Variable	(1) coefficient (*t*-statistic)	(2) coefficient (*t*-statistic)	(3) coefficient (*t*-statistic)
Constant..................	0.101 (1.57)	0.112 (1.74)	0.082 (1.26)
$U^{DIF}(-1)$	1.306 (43.44)	1.287 (43.03)	1.293 (42.97)
$U^{DIF}(-2)$	−0.319 (−10.47)	−0.311 (−10.18)	−0.317 (−10.36)
COAL	0.030 (1.48)	0.025 (1.24)	0.022 (1.10)
*DRPT*6 (−2).............	—	0.062 (2.62)	0.058 (2.44)
EMS	—	—	0.105 (2.55)
R^2	0.99	0.99	0.99
Number of observations....	1,017	1,017	1,017

* The estimated regressions include country fixed effects which are not reported in the table.

rather than discrete individuals wield power and transact affairs" (Bruno and Sachs [24], p. 222). In the sphere of labor market institution, a corporatist system is one in which bargaining on wage and work conditions are carried out by encompassing organizations rather than at the individual or firm level. Often, in a corporatist system, representatives of the government are also present at the labor negotiating table along with union and employer representatives. The idea is that large encompassing organizations have a better chance of taking into account the aggregate interests of the country, rather than specific interests of a particular firm or sector. Cooperative income policies are more likely to be implementable in highly corporatist systems. Therefore the presumption is that corporatist economies should do better than non-corporatist ones.

Aggregate indexes of corporatism are hard to come by. Here we use the index proposed by Bruno and Sachs [24] in Table 11.3 p. 226. For more details on the construction of this index the reader is referred to that source.

In Table 10 we add Bruno and Sachs' [24] measure of corporatism *(CORP)* to our unemployment estimations. The index is defined so that the expected sign of the coefficient is negative. That is, the more corporatist is the government, the greater the index number, the less unemployment should be expected. In addition, as with the

TABLE 10

EFFECT OF CORPORATISM ON UNEMPLOYMENT
dependent variable: U^{DIF}

Sample	1960-1987 14-country	1960-1987 14-country	1960-1987 14-country	1960-1987 7-bipartisan
Variable	(1) coefficient (*t*-statistic)	(2) coefficient (*t*-statistic)	(3) coefficient (*t*-statistic)	(4) coefficient (*t*-statistic)
Constant........	0.031 (2.16)	0.033 (2.28)	0.029 (2.03)	0.025 (1.76)
$U^{DIF}(-1)$	1.300 (48.32)	1.289 (47.66)	1.281 (47.41)	1.380 (38.90)
$U^{DIF}(-2)$	−0.305 (−11.21)	−0.295 (−10.77)	−0.297 (−10.90)	−0.406 (−11.45)
CORP	−0.003 (−0.47)	−0.004 (−0.59)	−0.015 (−2.08)	−0.025 (−2.83)
*DRPT*6 (−2)....	—	0.064 (3.05)	0.058 (2.75)	0.082 (3.12)
EMS	—	—	0.123 (3.59)	0.094 (2.41)
R^2	0.99	0.99	0.99	0.98
Number of observations ..	1,263	1,263	1,263	676

CBIND variable, the *CORP* variable is constant throughout time for each and thus acts as a substitute for the fixed effects[32]. The results depicted in columns 1 through 3 of Table 10 indicate that for the full sample of 14 countries (Bruno and Sachs [24] do not measure corporatism in Ireland), the coefficient on *CORP* has the expected negative sign, but only when both the *DRPT* and the *EMS* variable are included does the coefficient on *CORP* become statistically significant at conventional levels. Finally, column 4 of the table presents a test of the impact of corporatism by including the *CORP* variable in a sub-sample of countries such as the seven bipartisan countries. This estimation yields a larger and significant impact of the *CORP* variable. In addition, for both the 14-country and 7-bipartisan estimations the coefficients on the *DRPT6* and *EMS* variables concur with results presented earlier.

In summary, there is some indication of a significant negative impact of a corporatist system on the rate of unemployment. That is corporatist economies tend to have lower unemployment. However, the statistical significance of the coefficient on the *CORP* variable is dependent upon the specification of the model[33].

5. - Conclusions and Discussions

The purpose of this paper is to present models and test for evidence of how political and institutional factors influence unemployment. In doing so we deal with both cyclical and structural factors.

The first task of this paper was to test for the existence of economic cycles which are dependent upon elections and/or electoral change. We further confirmed the existence of partisan cycles of

---

[32] As discussed in note 26, if both the *CORP* variable and the fixed effets are included in the estimations, they would be perfectly collinear.

[33] CALMFORS L. - DRIFFIL [25] argue that the effect of corporatism on unemployment and other macroeconomic variables is *U* shaped, rather than linear. That is, the most successful countries are those at the very high and very low ends of this scale. In addition, they propose a classification of countries which is slightly different than BRUNO M. - SACHS L. [24] measure. We leave to future research a more detailed discussione of the impact of corporatism on unemployment.

short-lived, post-electoral fluctuations in unemployment which occur after changes in government.

The results of these estimations suggest some very interesting implications concerning voter behavior. Tests of retrospective voting indicate that the electorate responds to pre-electoral economic outcomes. However, tests for opportunistic cycles indicate that governments cannot manipulate pre-electoral outcomes. Thus, incumbent governments are faced with an uncomfortable predicament. They are judged on the basis of a pre-electoral economy which they are unable to manipulate to their advantage.

The second goal of this study is to analyze how various institutional factors such as central bank independence, the EMS, coalition governments, and corporatist economic systems, impact unemployment. Estimations of these structural factors on unemployment yield suggestive results. As expected independent central banks reduce inflation, however, they do not "pay" for it with higher unemployment. Second, based upon our results it is hard to pinpoint the benefit of joining the EMS in terms of inflation and unemployment.

Third, our estimations weakly suggest that coalition governments might have reduced the variability of partisan cycles, but at the expense of somewhat higher unemployment. However, these results are not strong, and are subject to the specification of the model. Therefore, further research in this area would be beneficial.

Finally, this paper explores the impact of corporatist economic systems on macroeconomic outcomes by constructing models which attempt to factor out a country's institutional characteristics. Our results suggest that other institutional characteristics are controlled for, a variable which measures corporatism, perhaps imperfectly, appeared to have an impact on unemployment.

In conclusion, this paper has found that political and structural factors have both short- and long-run implications for an economy. Further research on these issues, with an emphasis on the long-term impact of political-economic institutions, may be very beneficial because it will deepen our understanding of the economic implications of future institutional reforms.

APPENDIX

TABLE *A*1

DESCRIPTION OF DATA

Inflation: inflation is obtained as: $\pi_t = [(P_t - P_{t-4}) / P_{t-4}] \times 100$, where P_t is the consumer price index in quarter t. For all countries the sample is 1960.1-1987.4, and CPI is taken from line 64 of IMS-IFS.

Output and unemployment: country-by-country sample and sources *.

Australia	GDP - real quarterly GDP from OECDMEI (1960.1-1987.4). Unemployment - unemployment rate - adjusted - OECDMEI (1965.1-1987.4).
Austria	GDP - real quarterly GDP from IMF-IFS (1960.1-1987.4). Unemployment - unemployment rate - total - adjusted - OECDMEI (1969.1-1987.4).
Belgium	GDP - quarterly industrial production from OECDMEI (1960.1-1987.4). Unemployment - unemployment rate - total insured - adjusted - OECDMEI (1960.1-1987.4).
Canada	GDP - real quarterly GDP from IMS-IFS (1960.1-1987.4). Unemployment - unemployment rate - total - adjusted - OECDMEI (1960.1-1987.4).
Denmark	GDP - real annual GDP from IMF-IFS (1960.1-1987.4), (converted into quarterly data by assuming that quarter-to-quarter annual change corresponds to year-to-year change). Unemployment - unemployment rate - registered - unemployment - adjusted - OECDMEI (1970.1-1987.4).
Finland	GDP - real quarterly GDP from IMF-IFS (1970.1-1987.4). Unemployment - unemployment rate - total - adjusted - OECDMEI (1960.1-1987.4).
France	GDP - real quarterly GDP from IMF-IFS (1965.1-1987.4). Unemployment - unemployment rate - total - adjusted - OECDMEI (1967.1-1987.4).

* Countries which use other measures of GDP do so because real quarterly GDP is not available.

Germany	GDP - real quarterly GDP from IMF-IFS (1960.1-1987.4). Unemployment - unemployment rate - adjusted - OECDMEI (1965.1-1987.4).
Ireland	GDP - quarterly industrial production from OECDMEI (1975.1-1986.4). Unemployment - unemployment rate - adjusted - OECDMEI (1967.1-1987.4).
Italy	GDP - real quarterly GDP from IMF-IFS (1960.1-1987.4). Unemployment - unemployment rate - adjusted - OECDMEI (1960.1-1987.4).
Japan	GDP - real quarterly GDP from IMF-IFS (1960.1-1987.4). Unemployment - unemployment rate - adjusted - OECDMEI (1965.1-1987.4).
Netherlands	GDP - quarterly industrial production from OECDMEI (1960.1-1987.4). Unemployment - unemployment rate - registered unemployed - OECDMEI (1971.1-1987.4), no adjusted available.
New Zealand	GDP - real annual GDP from IMF-IFS (1960.1-1987.4), (converted into quarterly data by assuming that quarter-to-quarter annual change corresponds to year-to-year change). Unemployment - not available.
Norway	GDP - real annual GDP from PNL IMF-IFS (1960.1-1987.4), (converted into quarterly data by assuming that quarter-to-quarter annual change corresponds to year-to-year change). Unemployment - unemployment rate - adjusted - OECDMEI (1972.1-1987.4).
Sweden	GDP - real quarterly GDP from IMF-IFS (1969.1-1986.4); Unemployment - unemployment rate - total insured - adjusted - OECDMEI (1969.1-1983.4).
Switzerland	GDP - real quarterly GDP from IMF-IFS (1967.1-1986.4); Unemployment - ratio of total unemployed to labor force - adjusted - OECDMEI (1974.4-1987.3).
UK	GDP - real quarterly GDP from IMF-IFS (1960.1-1987.4); Unemployment - unemployment rate - registered - civilian - adjusted - OECDMEI (1960.1-1987.4).
USA	GDP - real quarterly GDP from IMF-IFS (1960.1-1987.4); Unemployment - unemployment rate - total - adjusted - OECDMEI (1960.1-1987.4).

TAV. *A2*

ELECTION AND REGIME CHANGE

E = election; *CH L* change left; *CH R* change right

Australia: endogenous timing, 3 yrs

1961.4	*E*	*RIGHT*	*a*
1963.4	*E*		
1966.4	*E*		
1969.4	*E*		
1972.4	*E*	*CH L*	
1974.2	*E*		(*) *b*
1975.4	*E*	*CH R*	
1977.4	*E*		
1980.4	*E*		
1983.1	*E*	*CH L*	
1984.4	*E*		(*)
1987.3	*E*		

Austria: endogenous timing, 4 yrs

1959.2	*E*	*RIGHT*	*c*
1962.4	*E*		
1966.1	*E*	*CH R*	
1970.1	*E*	*CH L*	
1971.4	*E*		(*)
1975.4	*E*		
1979.2	*E*		
1983.2	*E*	*CH R*	*c*
1986.4	*E*	*CH R*	

Belgium: endogenous timing, 4 yrs

1961.1	*E*	*RIGHT*	
1965.2	*E*		
1968.1	*E*	*CH L*	
1971.4	*E*		
1973.1		*CH R*	
1974.1	*E*		
1977.2	*E*	*CH L*	
1978.4	*E*		(*)
1981.4	*E*	*CH R*	
1985.4	*E*	*CH L*	
1987.4	*E*		

Canada: endogenous timing, 5 yrs

1962.2	*E*	*RIGHT*	
1963.2	*E*	*CH L*	(*)
1965.4	*E*		
1968.2	*E*		
1972.4	*E*		
1974.3	*E*		(*)
1979.2	*E*	*CH R*	
1980.1	*E*	*CH L*	(*)
1984.3	*E*	*CH R*	

Denmark: endogenous timing, 4 yrs

1960.4	*E*	*LEFT*	
1964.3	*E*		
1966.4	*E*		
1968.1	*E*	*CH R*	(*)
1971.3	*E*	*CH L*	
1973.4	*E*	*CH R*	
1975.1	*E*	*CH L*	(*)
1977.1	*E*		
1979.4	*E*		
1981.4	*E*		
1982.3		*CH R*	
1984.1	*E*		
1987.3	*E*		

Finland: endogenous timing, 3 yrs

1962.1	*E*	*LEFT*	
1963.4		*CH R*	
1966.1	*E*	*CH L*	
1970.1	*E*		
1972.1	*E*		
1975.3	*E*	*CH R*	
1977.2		*CH L*	
1979.1	*E*		
1983.1	*E*	*CH R*	
1987.1	*E*	*CH R*	

a RIGHT or *LEFT* indicates the type of government in power at the beginning of the sample which is 1959.1. We also indicate for each country whether election dates are endogenous or exogenous and the official number of years between two elections.

b Elections denoted with an asterisk (*) are not included in tests of the political business cycle theory because they are too close (less than two years) to previous elections. They are however included in tests of the opportunistic endogenous election model.

c Both Germany and Austria had grand coalitions of left and right parties. Thus, a finer administration variable was used in the *RPT* inflation and partisan (Hibbs) regressions. This also explains the occurrence of a rightward shift from an already central right leaning party.

Source, election dates are obtained from BANKS A. [16]; dates of changes of government and their classification of "right" and "left" are obtained from ALT J. [13] and BANKS A. [16].

TABLE *A2 continued*

France: endogenous timing, 5 yrs

1962.4	*E*	*RIGHT*	
1967.1	*E*		
1968.2	*E*		(*)
1973.1	*E*		
1978.1	*E*		
1981.2	*E*	*CH L*	
1984.3		*CH R*	
1986.1	*E*	*CH R*	

Germany: endogenous timing, 4 yrs

1961.3	*E*	*RIGHT*	
1965.3	*E*		
1966.4		*CH R*	*c*
1969.3	*E*	*CH L*	
1972.4	*E*	*CH R*	
1976.4	*E*		
1980.4	*E*		
1982.4			
1983.1	*E*	*CH R*	
1987.1	*E*		

Ireland: endogenous timing, 5 yrs

1961.4	*E*	*RIGHT*	
1965.2	*E*		
1969.2	*E*		
1973.1	*E*	*CH L*	
1977.2	*E*	*CH R*	
1981.2	*E*	*CH L*	
1982.1	*E*	*CH R*	(*)
1982.4	*E*	*CH L*	(*)
1987.1	*E*		

Italy: endogenous timing, 4 yrs

		RIGHT	
1962.4		*CH L*	
1963.2	*E*		
1968.2	*E*		
1972.2	*E*		
1974.4		*CH R*	
1976.2	*E*	*CH L*	
1979.2	*E*		
1983.2	*E*		
1987.2	*E*		

Japan: endogenous timing, 4 yrs

1960.4	*E*	*RIGHT*	
1963.4	*E*		
1967.1	*E*		
1969.4	*E*		
1972.4	*E*		
1976.4	*E*		
1979.4	*E*		
1980.2	*E*		(*)
1983.4	*E*		
1986.3	*E*		

Netherlands: endogenous timing, 4 yrs

1959.1	*E*	*RIGHT*	
1963.2	*E*		
1965.2		*CH L*	
1967.1	*E*	*CH R*	
1971.1	*E*		
1972.4	*E*		(*)
1973.2		CH L	
1977.2	*E*		
1977.4		*CH R*	
1981.2	*E*	*CH L*	
1982.3	*E*	*CH R*	(*)
1986.2	*E*		

New Zealand: endogenous timing, 3 yrs

1960.4	*E*	*RIGHT*	
1963.4	*E*		
1966.4	*E*		
1969.4	*E*		
1972.4	*E*	*CH L*	
1975.4	*E*	*CH R*	
1978.4	*E*		
1981.4	*E*		
1984.3	*E*	*CH L*	
1987.3	*E*		

Norway: exogenous timing, 4 yrs

1961.3	*E*	*LEFT*	
1965.3	*E*	*CH R*	
1969.3	*E*		
1971.4		*CH L*	
1972.4		*CH R*	
1973.3	*E*	*CH L*	
1977.3	*E*		
1981.3	*E*	*CH R*	
1985.3	*E*		
1986.2		*CH L*	

a,b,c, see previous notes.

TABLE *A2 continued*

Sweden: exogenous timing, 3 yrs since late 60s constitutional reform				Switzerland: exogenous timing, 4 yrs		
1960.3	*E*	*LEFT*		1959.4	*E*	*RIGHT*
1964.3	*E*			1963.4	*E*	
1968.3	*E*			1967.4	*E*	
1970.3	*E*			1971.4	*E*	
1973.3	*E*			1975.4	*E*	
1976.3	*E*	*CH R*		1979.4	*E*	
1979.3	*E*			1983.4	*E*	
1982.3	*E*	*CH L*		1987.4	*E*	
1985.3	*E*					

UK: endogenous timing, 5 yrs				USA: exogenous timing, 4 yrs		
1959.4	*E*	*RIGHT*				*RIGHT*
1964.4	*E*	*CH L*		1960.4	*E*	*CH L*
1966.1	*E*		(*)	1964.4	*E*	
1970.2	*E*	*CH R*		1968.4	*E*	*CH R*
1974.1	*E*			1972.4	*E*	
1974.3	*E*	*CH L*	(*)	1976.4	*E*	*CH L*
1979.2	*E*	*CH R*		1980.4	*E*	*CH R*
1983.2	*E*			1984.4	*E*	
1987.2	*E*					

a,b,c, see previous notes.

TABLE *A3*

CENTRAL BANK INDEPENDENCE

Country	Average index of central bank independence
Australia	2.0
Belgium	2.0
Canada	2.5
Denmark	2.5
France	2.0
Germany	4.0
Italy	1.75
Netherlands	2.5
New Zealand	1.0
Norway	2.0
Sweden	2.0
United Kingdom	2.0
United States	3.5

Source, ALESINA A. - SUMMERS L. [8].

BIBLIOGRAPHY

[1] ALESINA A., «Macroeconomic Policy in a Two-Party System as a Repeated Game», *Quarterly Journal of Economics*, n. 102, 1987, pp. 651-78.

[2] ——, «Macroeconomics and Politics» in FISHER S. - BLANCHARD O. (eds.), *NBER Macroeconomic Annual 1988*, Cambridge (MA), MIT Press, 1988, pp. 13-61.

[3] ——, «Politics and Business Cycles in Industrial Democracies», *Economic Policy*, n. 8, 1989, pp. 58-98.

[4] ALESINA A. - SACHS J., «Political Parties and the Business Cycle in the United States, 1948-1984», *Journal of Money, Credit and Banking*, n. 20, 1988, pp. 63-82.

[5] ALESINA A. - GRILLI V., «The European Central Bank: Reshaping Monetary Policy in Europe», in CANZONERI M. - GRILLI V. - MASSON P. (eds.), *Establishing a Central Bank: Issues in Europe and Lessons from the United States*, Cambridge, Cambridge University Press, 1992, pp. 49-77.

[6] ALESINA A. - ROUBINI N., «Political Business Cycles in OECD Economies», *Review of Economic Studies*, n. 59, 1992, pp. 663-88.

[7] ALESINA A. - TABELLINI G., «A Political Theory of Fiscal Deficits and Government Debt in a Democracy», *The Review of Economic Studies*, n. 57, 1990, pp. 403-14.

[8] ALESINA A. - SUMMERS L., «Central Bank Independence and Macroeconomic Performance: Some Comparative Evidence», *Journal of Money, Credit and Banking*, n. 25, 1993, pp. 151-62.

[9] ALESINA A. - ROSENTHAL H., *Partisan Politics, Divided Government, and the Economy*, New York (NY), Cambridge University Press, 1993.

[10] ALESINA A. - COHEN G.D. - ROUBINI N., «Macroeconomic Policy and Elections in OECD Democracies», *Economics and Politics*, n. 4, 1992, pp. 1-31.

[11] ALESINA A. - LONDREGAN J. - ROSENTHAL H., «A Model of the Political Economy of the United States», *American Political Science Review*, n. 87, 1993, pp. 12-33.

[12] ALESINA A. - COHEN G.D. - ROUBINI N., «Electoral Cycles in Industrial Democracies», *European Journal of Political Economy*, n. 9, 1993, pp. 1-23.

[13] ALT J., «Political Parties, World Demand, and Unemployment: Domestic and International Sources of Economic Activity», *American Political Science Review*, n. 79, 1985, pp. 1016-40.

[14] ANDERSON T.W. - HSAIO C., «Formulation and Estimation of Dynamic Models Using Panel Data», *Journal of Econometrics*, n. 18, 1982, pp. 47-82.

[15] BADE R. - PARKIN M., *Central Bank Laws and Monetary Policy*, Unpublished 1982.

[16] BANKS A., *Political Handbook of the World*, State University of New York at Binghamton, CSA Publications, 1987, 1989.

[17] BARRO R., «US Deficits Since World War I.», *Scandinavian Journal of Economics*, n. 88, 1986, pp. 195-222.

[18] ——, «On the Determination of the Public Debt», *Journal of Political Economy*, n. 87, 1979, pp. 940-71.

[19] BARRO R. - GORDON D., «Rules, Discretion, and Reputation in a Model of Monetary Policy», *Journal of Monetary Economics*, n. 12, 1983, pp. 101-22.

[20] ————, «A Positive Theory of Monetary Policy in a Natural Rate Model», *Journal of Political Economy*, n. 31, 1983, pp. 589-610.

[21] BEGG D. - WYPLOST C., *The European Monetary System: Recent Intellectual History*, Unpublished 1993.

[22] BHARGAVA A. - SARGAN J.D., «Estimating Dynamic Random Effects Models from Panel Data Covering Short Time Periods», *Econometrica*, n. 51, 1983, pp. 1653-9.

[23] BLANCHARD O.J. - SUMMERS L.H., «Hysteresis and the European Unemployment Problem.» in FISHER S. (eds.), *NBER Macroeconomic Annual 1986*, Cambridge (MA), MIT Press, 1988, pp. 15-78.

[24] BRUNO M. - SACHS L., *Economics of World Stagflation*, Cambridge (MA), Harvard University Press, 1985.

[25] CALMFORS L. - DRIFFILL, «Bargaining Structure, Corporatism and Macroeconomic Performance», *Economic Policy*, n. 6, 1988, pp. 13-61.

[26] CHAPPEL H.W. Jr. - KEECH W.R., «The Unemployment Consequences of Partisan Monetary Policies», *Southern Economic Journal*, n. 55, 1988, pp. 107-16.

[27] COHEN G.D., *Polls, Partisan Politics and Financial Markets: Evidence from US Elections*, Harvard University, mimeo, 1993.

[28] CUKIERMAN A. - WEBB S. - NEYAPTI B., «The Measurement of Central Bank Independence and its Effect on Policy Outcomes», *The World Bank Economic Review*, n. 6, 1992, pp. 353-98.

[29] DOWNS A., *An Economic Theory of Democracy*, New York, Harper and Row, 1957.

[30] FAIR R.C., «The Effects of Economic Events on Votes for President», *Review of Economics and Statistics*, n. 64, 1978, pp. 159-72.

[31] ——, «The Effect of Economic Events on Votes for President: 1984 Update», *Political Behavior*, n. 10, 1988, pp. 168-79.

[32] FIORINA M.P., *Retrospective Voting in American National Elections*, New Haven (CT), Yale University Press, 1981.

[33] FISCHER S., «Long Term Contracts, Rational Expectations and the Optimal Money Supply Rule», *Journal of Political Economy*, n. 85, 1977, pp. 191-206.

[34] FREY B. - SCHNEIDER F., «An Empirical Study of Politico-Economic Interaction in the United States», *The Review of Economics and Statistics*, n. 60, 1978, pp. 174-83.

[35] GRILLI V. - MASCIANDARO D. - TABELLINI G., «Political and Monetary Institutions and Public Finance Policies in the Industrial Democracies», *Economic Policy*, n. 13, 1991, pp. 341-92.

[36] GIAVAZZI F. - GIOVANNINI A., *Limiting Exchange Rate Flexibility: The European Monetary System*, Cambridge (MA), MIT Press, 1989.

[37] HIBBS D.A., «Political Parties and Macroeconomic Policy», *The American Political Science Review*, n. 7, 1977, pp. 1467-87.

[38] ——, *The American Political Economy: Macroeconomics and Electoral Politics*, Cambridge (MA), Harvard University Press, 1987.

[39] HSIAO C., *Analysis of Panel Data*, New York (NY), Cambridge University Press, 1986.

[40] KRAMER G., «Short-Term Fluctuations in US Voting Behavior, 1986-1964», *American Political Science Review*, n. 65, 1971, pp. 131-43.

[41] LEWIS-BECK M.S., *Economics and Elections: The Major Western Democracies*, Ann Arbor (MI), University of Michigan Press, 1988.

[42] LINDBECK A., «Stabilization Policies in Open Economies with Endogenous Politicians», *American Economic Review*, Papers and Proceedings, pp. 1-19.

[43] NORDHAUS W., «The Political Business Cycle», *Review of Economic Studies*, n. 42, 1975, pp. 169-90.

[44] ——, «Alternative Models to Political Business Cycles», *Brookings Papers on Economic Activity*, n. 2, 1989, pp. 1-68.

[45] PALDAM M., «Politics Matter After All: Testing Alesina's Theory of RE Partisan Cycles», Aarhus University, *Working Paper*, 1989.

[46] ——, «Politics Matter After All: Testing Hibbs' Theory of Partisan Cycles», Aarhus University, *Working Paper*, 1989.

[47] ——, «Is There An Electoral Cycle?», *Scandinavian Journal of Economics*, n. 81, 1979, pp. 323-42.

[48] PERSSON T. - TABELLINI G., *Macroeconomic Policy, Credibility and Politics*, New York (NY), Harwood Academic Publishers, 1990.

[49] ROGOFF K., «Equilibrium Political Budget Cycles», *American Economic Review*, n. 80, 1990, pp. 21-36.

[50] ROGOFF K. - SIBERT A., «Equilibrium Political Business Cycles», *Review of Economic Studies*, n. 55, 1988, pp. 1-16.

[51] ROUBINI N. - SACHS I., «Political and Economic Determinants of Budget Deficits in the Industrial Economies», *European Economic Review*, n. 33, 1989, pp. 903-33.

[52] ST. PAUL G., «On the Political Economy of Labor Market Flexibility», *NBER Macroeconomics Annual 1993*, forthcoming 1993.

[53] SPOLAORE E., *Policy-Making Systems and Economic Efficiency: Coalition Governments versus Majority Governments*, Harvard University, mimeo, 1993.

[54] TABELLINI G. - ALESINA A., «Voting on the Budget Deficit», *American Economic Review*, n. 80, 1990, pp. 37-52.

[55] TAYLOR J., «Aggregate Dynamics and Staggered Contracts», *Journal of Political Economy*, n. 88, 1980, pp. 1-23.

[56] TUFTE E., *Political Control of the Economy*, Princeton (NJ), Princeton University Press, 1978.

Coordination and Independence in Monetary and Fiscal Policies[1]

William D. Nordhaus
Yale University, New Haven (CT)

As of summer 1993, few countries are satisfied with their macroeconomic policies. Virtually all countries complain that their fiscal-monetary mix is skewed in an undesirable direction. Countries find their fiscal deficits reduce national saving while interest rates are also too high to sustain recovery. Moreover, this monetary-fiscal syndrome has been a feature of the macroeconomic landscape for more than a decade. How can we explain that countries persist in following policies that they believe undesirable?

One answer might be that policy makers do not know what they are doing. This seems unlikely. While there are disagreements about many economic issues, most schools of macroeconomic thinking hold that monetary and fiscal policies do affect the economy. In the modern mainstream neo-Keynesian view, monetary and fiscal policy have a first-order impact upon output, unemployment, and inflation through their impact upon aggregate demand. But by the «common-funnel theorem», in the short run monetary and fiscal policies affect unemployment and inflation primarily by affecting aggregate demand — in effect, going through the common funnel of aggregate demand. There are second-order impacts, however, because monetary policies affect interest rates, exchange rates, and some prices directly, while tax policies can affect prices directly. In addition, there are important

1 The author is grateful for comments by Robert Mundell and James Tobin.
N.B.: the numbers in square brackets refer to the Bibliography at the end of the paper.

differential impacts upon the composition of output, such as that tight money will lead to a squeeze on tradeable-goods sector and investment while tight fiscal policy will squeeze government purchases or consumption, and policies have quite different impacts on the growth of potential output. It is possible that the current fiscal-monetary mix is in fact desired by many governments, but this view would require a cynical view of politics that holds that government policies have no connection to their goals or pubblic pronouncements.

An alternative possibility is that decision makers are caught in an interaction that locks them into high deficits and tight money. The economic analysis of monetary and fiscal policies often overlooks the fact that monetary and fiscal policies have different degrees of coordination or independence in different countries. Macroeconomists in an earlier era worried about the lack of coordination of policies, fearing that monetary policy might be pulling in one direction while fiscal policy was pulling in another. In the early 1980s, the fiscal deficits of the Reagan administration were pulling the economy toward a high-consumption strategy, while the tight, anti-inflationary monetary policies of the Volcker Federal Reserve were pulling the economy toward a low-investment strategy. The effect was a sharp decline in US national saving along with the highest real interest rates in decades.

More recently, Russia has witnessed a sharp divergence between the austere policies of the Gaidar government in early 1992 and a Russian central bank that seemed to find no loan or credit unworthy of an advance. The result was an accelerating inflation fueled by monetary expansion even as fiscal policy was tightened.

Most recently, the Clinton administration has proposed a bold deficit reduction package that proposed reducing the US structural budget deficit by almost $200 billion over five years. The paradox is that we find a left-of-center government, one which ran on a promise of job creation, proposing fiscal austerity as the centerpiece of its economic program. The fiscal package is a gamble that monetary policy will offset the fiscal contraction through an anticipatory monetary expansion. It should be clear that this policy is indeed a gamble, for conventional macroeconomic models would predict that, without a monetary offset to the Clinton fiscal contraction, the 1996 Clinton reelection campaign will be disadvantaged by the Clinton economic package.

This essay attempts to pursue the issue of coordination of policy in greater depth in two dimensions. In the first section, I propose a game-theoretic approach to fiscal and monetary coordination. This approach provides an enormously rich set of possible outcomes depending upon the degree of coordination or independence, on the objectives of the two institutions, and on the dynamics. Then in the second section, I apply this approach to the Clinton package by examining the likely time path of the major economic variables with a business-as-usual monetary reaction.

1. - An Analytical Approach to Monetary and Fiscal Coordination

1.1 *Background*

The textbook treatment of macroeconomic policy takes monetary and fiscal policy as exogenous to the economic system. Policies are taken with certain macroeconomic objectives in mind, and we then trace out the implications of those policies for output, employment, and inflation. One school of thought has endogenized policy in the analysis of the «political business cycle», an approach which attempts to examine the impact of electoral forces on the setting of macroeconomic policy. In this essay, I examine the impact of the separation of powers among macroeconomic policy makers.

There is a vast literature on the making of monetary and fiscal policy, but relatively little addresses the implications of independence or dependence in the making of policy. The theory of policy as developed by Tinbergen visualizes a unitary policymaker optimizing policy in the face of economic constraints and uncertainties. The possibility of conflicts amongst policy makers was formally analysed in an early study by Pindyck [11], which examines the general problem of conflicting objectives among policy makers. The most thorough dissertation is that of Ribe [12], which deals with the impact of coordination or lack of coordination on the efficiency of macroeconomic policy. Ribe analyzed the impact of differences in both preferences and in the structure of the economy and concluded that there is a significant potential for inefficiency if monetary and fiscal policy are not coordinated. Blinder [1] analyzed issues of coordination in the case where policy makers have two or three discrete options and suggested that the game takes the form of a prisoners' dilemma (also see Dixit and Nalebuff [4]).

This study is confined to the case of the implications of independence of the central bank along with differences in objectives among the monetary and fiscal authority upon the conduct and outcome of macroeconomic policy. It is customary in a modern economy to separate monetary and fiscal functions. The degree of separation differs from country to country, with the Bundesbank retaining a fierce independence of both branches, the US Federal Reserve maintaining considerable but less fierce independence accompanied by a ritual obeisance to the legislative branch, the Japanese central bank being accountable to the Ministry of Finance, and the Russian central bank after 1991 being a toady to the Parliament and the military-industrial complex. Fiscal institutions also differ greatly across countries, but in almost all democracies, fiscal authority is in the hands of the legislature, and, where the executive is separate from the legislature (as in the United States), there may be some divisions in the conduct of fiscal policy.

In most countries, the central bank takes a stance that emphasizes austerity and low inflation. This central banker's credo was expressed by Arthur Burns shortly after he retired as Chairman of the Federal Reserve in the following words: «By training, if not also by temperament, [central bankers] are inclined to lay great stress on price stability, and their abhorrence of inflation is continually reinforced by contacts with one another and with likeminded members of the private financial community»[2]. He contrasts the central bankers' perspective with that of the government: «In fact, much of the expanding range of government spending was prompted by the commitment to full employment... "Maximum" or "full" employment, after all, had become the nation's major economic goal — not stability of the price level»[3].

---

[2] See BURNS A.F. [3], p. 4.
[3] See BURNS A.F. [3], p. 16.

1.2 *The Model*

Although the analysis can apply to a wide variety of situations, it is most applicable to a closed economy, to a large open economy with a relatively small foreign-trade sector, or to a country with fixed exchange rates and relatively closed financial markets. For purposes of this essay, I will consider an economy in which the monetary authority is responsible for monetary policy as represented by the real interest rate, r; while the fiscal authority is responsible for the structural fiscal surplus ratio, or the government surplus at high employment divided by potential GNP, S. For purposes of this section, I will consider a single-period model (which might be thought of as either the year or the electoral period). In addition, I assume that the two policy authorities have preferences over the macroeconomic outcomes, inflation *(p)* and unemployment *(u)*, and in addition they may have views on the monetary and fiscal variables (r and S). We can write the preferences of the authorities as:

$$U^F = V^F(u, p, r, S) \quad (1.1)$$

$$U^M = V^M(u, p, r, S) \quad (1.2)$$

where U^k is the preference or utility level of policy authority k ($k = F$, M) and V^k is the preference function. In the analysis that follows, we assume that both authorities desire levels of unemployment and inflation that are lower than is feasible. In addition, the fiscal authority prefers higher deficits, *ceteris paribus*, because that allows greater spending or lower taxes, while the monetary authority prefers a higher surplus because that will increase national saving and investment and take pressure off financial markets. Neither has any intrinsic interest in interest rates.

A major issue for policy is the existence of a tradeoff between inflation and unemployment in the short run. For purposes of this study, we assume that the decision of both fiscal and monetary agencies can affect these variables (thus rejecting the new classical view in which unemployment cannot be affected by predictable or predicted policies). Most empirical macroeconomic models determine that fiscal and monetary policies have enduring impacts for at least four years, and this period is sufficiently long to raise concerns among political actors whose electoral accountability is not much longer than that span. We also hold to the common-funnel theory by which both output, unemployment, and prices are functions of the combined impact of fiscal and monetary policies (along, of course, with other non-policy variables) on aggregate demand. These assumptions yield the following equation:

$$p = p(u; p^e) \tag{1.3}$$

Equation *(1.3)* is the medium-run Phillips curve, where p^e is the (exogenous) expected rate of inflation. The Appendix shows that the exogenous expected rate of inflation can be suppressed without affecting the analysis.

Unemployment is a function of the two policies (along with other exogenous variables):

$$u = u(r, S) \tag{1.4}$$

Combining *(1.3)* and *(1.4)* with *(1.1)* and *(1.2)* yields the preference of each agencies with respect to the policy variables:

$$U^F = V^F[u(r, S), p\{u(r, S)\}, r, S] = U^F(r, S) \tag{1.5}$$

$$U^M = V^M[u(r, S), p\{u(r, S)\}, r, S] = U^M(r, S) \tag{1.6}$$

where U^M and U^F are the implicit preferences as a function of the policy variables.

1.3 *Aggregate Demand Curves and Bliss Points*

We can picture the preferences of the different agencies in Graph 1. The monetary agency aims for a combination of policies that leads to its «aggregate-demand curve» given by the line *M*. The monetary authorities have a more restrictive target than the fiscal

GRAPH 1

BASIC STRUCTURE *

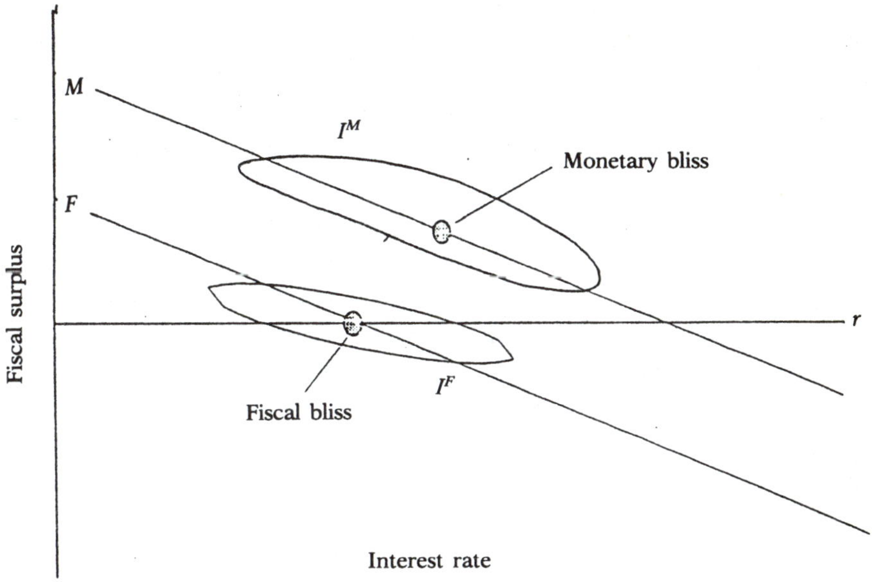

* Indifference contours of monetary authority (I^M) and fiscal authority (I^F), with bliss point of most preferred outcomes. *M* line and *F* line show the combinations of monetary and fiscal policies that give the target aggregate demand for monetary and fiscal authorities.

authorities, whose target aggregate demand is given by the line *F*. The fiscal and monetary authorities' bliss points lie at the intersection of their aggregate demand lines and their desired level of fiscal surplus. In Graph 1, the monetary authority has a slightly more contractionary target for aggregate demand (reflecting its mission to contain inflation) along with a higher targeted government surplus (reflecting its desire to increase private investment). The fiscal authority has a relatively expansionary attitude toward aggregate demand (reflecting the distaste commonly expressed by voters toward high unemployment and the lag of inflation behind low unemployment) and an inclination to run fiscal deficits (to finance everything from supply-side tax cuts to health care and infrastructure). In this essay, we will concentrate on the pattern of preferences that is shown in Graph 1, although from time to time (as in Russia) we find preference reversals and anomalies.

1.4 *Cooperative Equilibrium*

Given the preferences of the two authorities, the macroeconomic outcome will be determined by the extent of cooperation or independence. The first and presumably happiest case would be that of cooperation, shown in Graph 2. The heavy contract curve shows the locus of interest rates and fiscal stances that will result from agreeing jointly on policies and pursuing them cooperatively. Not surprisingly, the cooperative policies will be a compromise of the views of the two parties. One might suspect, however, that in fact the government, which is the fiscal authority, would be the heavyweight in the discussions and that the monetary authority would pretty much follow the lead of the government. In this case, the outcome would be close to the fiscal bliss point, with relatively high inflation and deficits in the long run and a tendency to counter recessions aggressively in the short run.

GRAPH 2

COOPERATIVE EQUILIBRIUM*

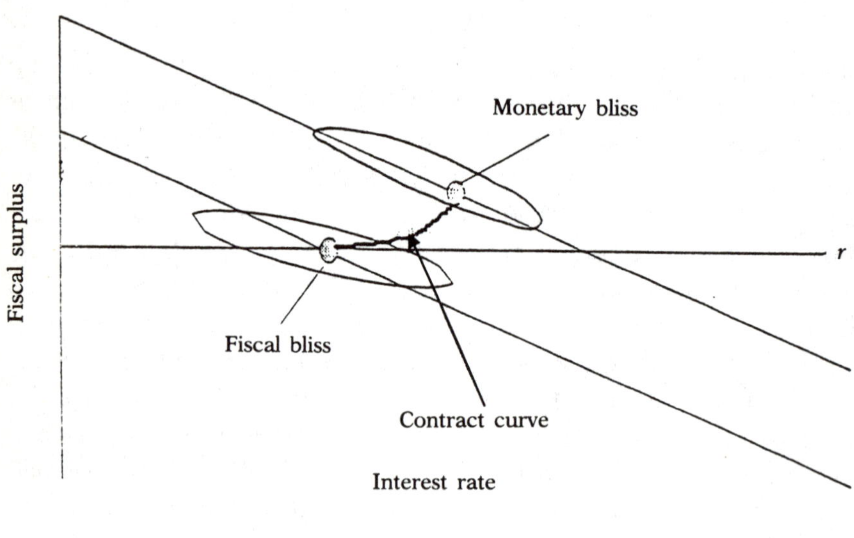

* Heavy line shows the cooperative equilibrium or contract curve of policies.

1.5 *Non-Cooperative Equilibrium*

In many countries, monetary and fiscal policy are separated, and the monetary authority is directed to meet specific objectives, such as ensuring price stability. In such a situation, central banks will have their own governing bodies and will make decisions in part independently of the fiscal authorities. It is useful to analyze this process as a two-person, non-zero-sum game. There are two players, *M* and *F*, and each decides on its policies taking into account the policies of the other. For the most part, I will analyze the situation as a one-shot rather than repeated game, although some pseudo-dynamics will be introduced.

The Appendix derives the major propositions for the reactions functions for the case of quadratic utility functions in which the real interest rate does not enter directly into the utility of either party. Among the results are the following: the reaction functions have a negative slope; the slope of the monetary reaction function is (in absolute value) steeper than that of the fiscal reaction function; and the optimal combination of policies for the two authorities (their «bliss points») are such that that of the monetary authority will have a higher optimal level of surplus (but not necessarily a higher level of real interest rates) than the fiscal authority.

We begin by assuming that each authority behaves in a non-cooperative manner by setting its policies assuming that the other's policies will not change, leading to the Nash equilibrium solution. Graph 3 shows the reaction functions of the two players. The monetary reaction function coincides with the aggregate-demand line of the monetary authority, shown as *M* in Graph 3. For the assumed tastes, the fiscal reaction function is less steep than the fiscal aggregate demand target line *(F)*, and the reaction function passes through the fiscal bliss point.

One important result that emerges from this analysis is that the monetary reaction function is independent of the central bank's preferences about fiscal policy if the central bank follows a Nash policy. This has important implications for an evaluation of the central bank's reaction to deficit-reduction packages which will be explored later.

GRAPH 3

REACTION FUNCTIONS AND NON-COOPERATIVE EQUILIBRIUM

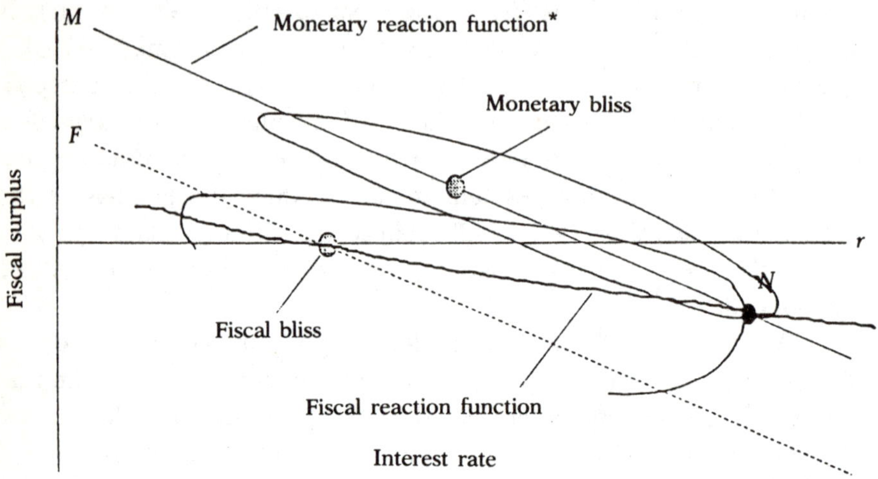

* Monetary reaction function coincides with monetary aggregate demand line. Fiscal reaction function is flatter. *N* shows the Nash or non-cooperative equilibrium.

Graph 3 also shows the Nash equilibrium for our monetary-fiscal game at point *N* along with the players' indifference curves that generate the Nash equilibrium[4]. This graph shows the central result of this paper. The characteristics of the non-cooperative outcome are distinctly familiar and unhappy:

1) the equilibrium is one in which the deficit is higher than the desired deficits of either party. This results from a conflict between the different objectives. The fiscal authority attempts to lower unemployment by raising the deficit; this is countered by the monetary authority raising interest rates to fight inflation; and so forth. At the end of this struggle, because the two parties pursue their different objectives, the deficit is the big loser;

[4] It can also be seen that the monetary-fiscal game is not prisoners' dilemma because the players do not have dominant strategies. Rather, the Nash equilibrium is not Pareto efficient.

2) in the non-cooperative equilibrium, the interest rate is also higher than either party would wish and for analogous reasons[5];

3) the level of inflation and unemployment is a compromise between the fiscal and monetary authorities; the extent to which the outcome is closer to fiscal or monetary preferences depending upon the two reaction functions.

This syndrome is familiar to students of recent economic history. In the United States in the last three decades, a combination of policies from political business cycles to supply-side tax cuts to fiscal gridlock has led to a upward trend in the structural fiscal deficit. The result has been an increase in the real interest rates and a decline in national savings. A more recent episode is found in Germany where, after German unification, the fiscal authorities did not take steps to offset the large demand stimulus. The result was soaring interest rates, with a contractionary impact spilling over to the rest of Europe.

1.6 *A Monetary Rule*

In a repeated game like that concerning the fiscal-monetary mix, the participants will surely recognize that the other has an approach, perhaps even a strategy, toward economic management. Of the two, monetary policy makers have developed a more coherent approach, while fiscal policy tends to be dictated by elections, personalities, the power of opposing or blocking coalitions, and by changing fads in economic theory.

To recognize the likelihood that the parties will recognize the repeated nature of the game, we assume that the monetary authority has selected a clear and publicly stated approach. It might be one in which interest rates are pegged, as was the case for monetary policies from World War II until the accord of 1951. Alternatives would be a fixed-*M* rule, targeting nominal GNP, targeting the price level, pegging

[5] Points *i* and *ii* were results in Ribe F.C. [12], who found that preference disagreements tended to push each player's policy in the direction that would emphasize that player's relative emphasis; i.e a player who wanted relatively more stimulus would push its instrument far in the stimulative direction relative to the cooperative equilibrium.

Graph 4

MONETARY RULE*

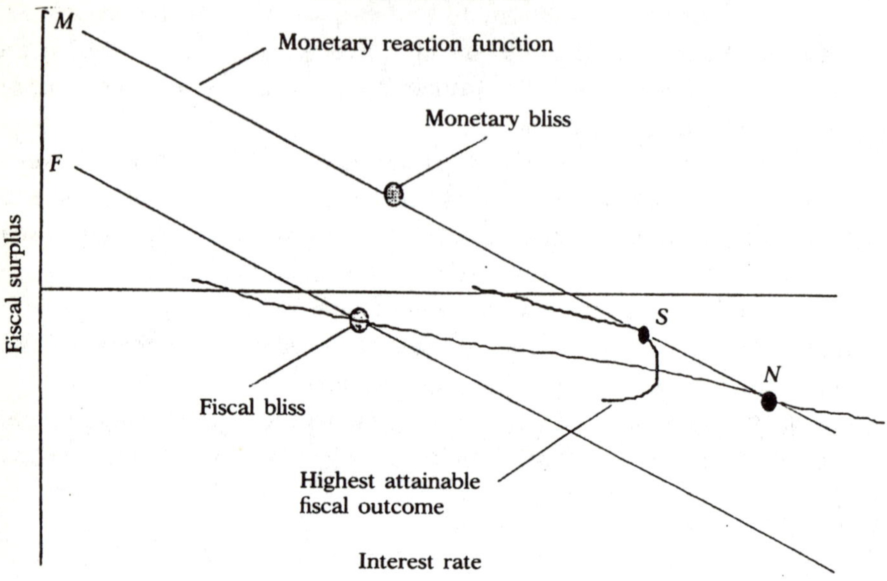

* If monetary authority announces a credible rule and fiscal authority maximizes subject to the rule, equilibrium is at S. There is no effect on inflation or unemployment, but outcome shows improved monetary-fiscal mix for both players.

the exchange rate, or enforcing a sliding peg. We assume that the rule is articulated by the central bank, understood by the fiscal authority, and credible in terms of durability.

Graph 4 shows the case of a monetary rule that is reflected in the monetary reaction function. We assume that the fiscal authority then optimizes with respect to the monetary rule, choosing the level of the fiscal surplus that leads to the highest attainable level of utility for the fiscal authority. This leads to an equilibrium at point *S*, which compares with the Nash equilibrium at point *N*. Note that the monetary-rule approach leads to the following:

a) the outcome is an improvement for *both* fiscal and monetary participants in that the outcome improves the utility level of both;

b) the outcome has a lower government deficit and a lower level of interest rates, and therefore higher investment, than the Nash solution;

c) a major surprise is that use of a monetary rule improves utility but has no effect upon inflation or unemployment because the monetary authority's reaction function corresponds to its aggregate-demand curve.

One of the most popular themes in analyzing monetary policy concerns whether the monetary authority should take a tough, anti-inflation stand rather than try to accomodate political forces. In the framework of a non-cooperative game between the monetary and fiscal authority, surprisingly, the effect of the central bank taking the lead is not to affect the inflation or unemployment rates, which are determined by the monetary authority in any case. Rather, by taking the leadership in the game, the central bank improves the fiscal-monetary mix.

1.7 *Effects of Deficit-Reduction Strategies*

In the next section I examinc thc implications of a shift in the preference function of the fiscal authority using the example of the Clinton deficit-reduction package. Graph 5 shows the results schematically. The lower fiscal line shows the Reagan-Bush policy. Assume that a new government comes into power and decides to "get tough with the deficit". The preference of the new government has a bliss point shown as the black circle on the "Clinton" line; the reaction function is given by the heavy "Clinton" line. There are a number of different strategies that the new administration might follow. A myopic policy would follow a tatonnement from the old Reagan-Bush Nash equilibrium at *N-RB* to the new Clinton Nash equilibrium at *N-C*, and the arrows show how such a dynamic might occur. The economy would cycle toward the new equilibrium, but there would be an initial period in which unemployment would be raised to induce the monetary authority to lower interest rates. Under a far-sighted policy, the government might move immediately to the new equilibrium at *N-C*, which would lower the deficit more quickly but produce even higher near-term unemployment than the myopic policy. Or the government might optimize as shown in Graph 4, picking a fiscal stance that optimizes the government's utility subject to the central,

GRAPH 5

IMPACT OF DEFICIT-REDUCTION PLAN*

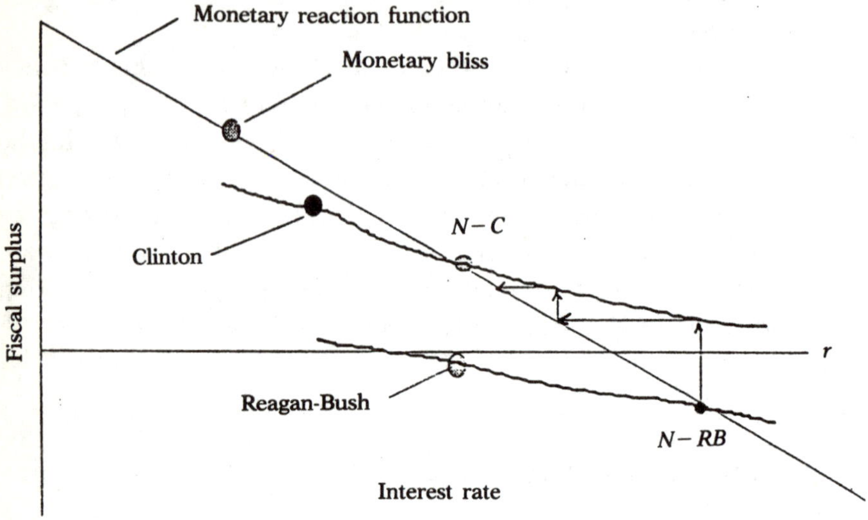

* If preferences of fiscal authority shift toward lower targeted deficit, then equilibrium shifts from *N−RB* to *N−C*. In the tatonnement along the way, there is likely to be a transition period of high unemployment.

bank's reaction function; this would lead to an even larger deficit-reduction policy and to even higher unemployment than the Nash equilibrium shown in Graph 5. The major conclusion here is that any non-cooperative deficit-reduction strategy would tend to raise unemployment in the short run as a way of inducing the central bank to lower interest rates.

1.8 *Is the Independence Game Worth the Candle?*

It is common currency in economics to extol the independence of the central bank. The analysis used here allows us to examine that presumption in a game-theoretic context. We showed earlier that there may be large losses from non-cooperative policies. Graph 6 shows a case where monetary capitulation is superior to indepen-

Graph 6

IS MONETARY INDEPENDENCE WORTH THE COST*

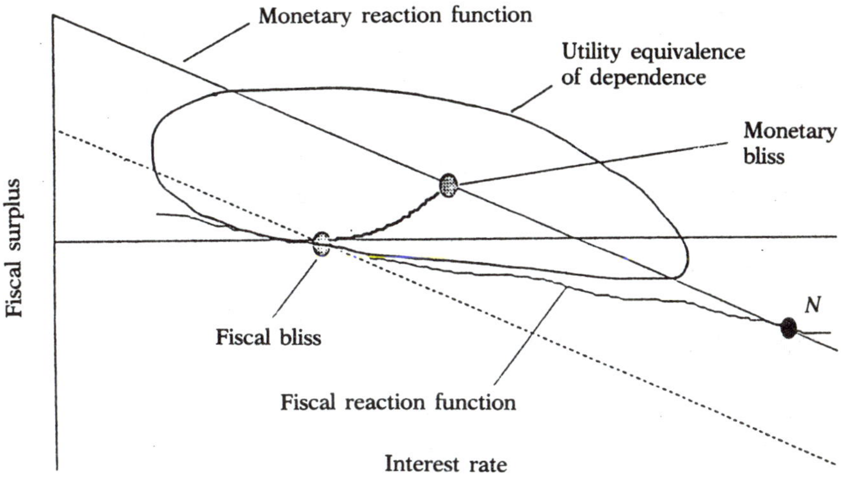

* Non-cooperative equilibrium with monetary independence puts equilibrium at *N*, while dependence puts economy on the contract curve. Indifference oval labelled "utility equivalence of dependence" shows the combination of policies that is equally preferred by monetary authority to complete subjugation to fiscal authority. Any equilibrium outside the indifference oval is worse for both players than dependence.

dence *for both parties*. When the fiscal-monetary game turns into fiscal-monetary wars, the outcome may diverge sharply from either parties' preferred solution, as does the Nash equilibrium *N* from the contract curve. In addition, we have drawn the indifference contour for the monetary authority that goes through the fiscal bliss point. If capitulation occurs, we would expect that the monetary authority will give in to the fiscal authorities in the government; the reverse is hardly likely. Graph 6 shows a case where capitulation is superior to the non-cooperative equilibrium from the point of view of the central bank. Of course, in this case, inflation will be higher than with an independent central bank; but the gains in other objectives will outweigh the losses from higher inflation from the point of view of both policy making bodies.

2. - The Clinton Economic Plan as an Example of the Monetary-Fiscal Game

2.1 *Outline of the Approach*

The last section showed how different preferences and strategies could lead to a wide variety of outcomes — some desirable, others quite perverse. In this section, we go beyond theory to provide a concrete example by examining the dynamics of policy and response that might arise to the original Clinton economic package (we examine the original package because it comes closer to a coherent fiscal package than what eventually emerged). The Clinton administration proposed taking stern deficit-reduction steps over the next five years. We use a simple model of the economic and of the monetary reaction to estimate the impact of the *Clinton Plan* — and its chance of success — on the macroeconomic outcomes of output and unemployment.

The basic structure will follow the outlines of the model laid out in section 1. We first outline the structure of the economy and then consider the behavior of the fiscal and monetary authorities. Potential, $Q(t)$, is determined by exogenous labor force, $L(t)$, exogenous technology, $A(t)$, and endogenous capital, $K(t)$:

$$Q(t) = A(t)\, K(t)^{\alpha}\, L(t)^{1-\alpha} \tag{2.1}$$

In what follows, all lower case Greek letters are parameters. Actual output, $X(t)$, is determined by exogenous forces $[\beta_0(t)]$, fiscal policy measured by the ratio of the high-employment surplus to potential GNP, $S(t)$, and by endogenous monetary policy represented by the short-run real interest rate, $r(t)$:

$$\log[X(t)] = \beta_0(t) + \Sigma\, \beta_{1j}\, S(t-j) + \Sigma\, \beta_{2j}\, r(t-j) \tag{2.2}$$

The unemployment rate, $u(t)$, is determined by Okun's law:

$$u(t) = u^n(t) - \Sigma\, \gamma_{1j}\,[x(t-j)/Q^{(t-j)} - 1] \tag{2.3}$$

where $u^n(t)$ is the exogenous natural rate of unemployment.

The inflation rate follows the natural rate hypothesis:

$$p(t) = \Sigma\, \theta_{1j}\, p(t-1-j) + \Sigma\, \theta_{2j}\, u(t-j) \qquad (2.4)$$

$$\Sigma\, \theta_{1j} = 1$$

where $p(t)$ is the inflation rate.

The equations for investment and capital assume that increases in the government deficit "crowd out" investment. For purposes of the simulation, we take Modigliani's stock version of the crowding-out hypothesis, which holds that government debt displaces private capital in the nation's portfolio. More precisely, we assume that an increase in the net outstanding debt of $D(t)$ leads to a decrease in the net private wealth that is a fraction, λ, of the change in net debt. This leads to the following equation for the capital stock:

$$K(t) = K^*(t) - \lambda\, D(t) \qquad (2.5)$$

where $K^*(t)$ is the capital stock that would obtain without the deficit-reduction program, λ is the crowding-out or capital-displacement fraction, and $D(t)$ is the change in the net government debt from the Clinton policy [6].

The final issue concerns the strategic assumptions about fiscal and monetary policy. For this experiment, we assume that fiscal policy is determined by the complicated and unpredictable interaction of the executive and legislative branches. The important assumption is that fiscal policy is *exogenous* in that it is independent of the state of the economy and of the strategy of the monetary authority. Hence, the deficit reduction in the Clinton package is assumed to be 100% effective and not to substitute for future deficit reduction.

Monetary policy is, however, taken to be endogenous. We assu-

---

[6] This formulation simplifies by assuming that the deficit-reduction package has no effect on investment other than through the impact on the government debt. It may therefore overstate the amount of capital if the deficit reduction reduces output and lowers investment through the accelerator mechanism. By omitting the cyclical impact of the package on investment, we can avoid the necessity of including an investment equation in our simulation. The effect of this and the assumption concerning crowding out will probably be to overstate the amount of additional investment that will be generated by the Clinton package.

me that the central bank has a preference function, $V^M(u, p, r, S)$. The central bank then determines real interest rates by maximizing this preference function, which leads to a reaction function of the following generic form:

$$V^M r(u, p, r, S) = 0 \tag{2.6}$$

Again, note that this reaction function is reactive and non-cooperative, responding to the actual and past state of the economy and not to the actions of the fiscal authority. The most important assumption is that monetary policy is determined by *outcomes*, rather than forecasts, fiscal policies, monetary variables, or exchange rates. In this respect, it falls short of the optimizing central bank, which would use forecasts or conjectural variations on both exogenous and fiscal actions in determining monetary policy. On the other hand, it is tuned to the state of the economy rather than some arbitrary intermediate objective, such as reserves, debt, the money supply, or some monetarist operating rule.

A full discussion of the nature of the monetary reaction function will not be given here (again, see particularly McNees [8]). Monetary policy in the United States has responded to varying influences, election returns, fads, ideologies, and economic theories over the twentieth century, and the coefficients of the reaction function have varied with these influences, but the significance of inflation and unemployment (or output) comes through loud and clear in past empirical studies [7].

2.2 *Empirical Implementation*

Rather than constructing an elaborate econometric model, we have relied upon a combination of calibration and estimation of the simplified model. The equations have been fitted where that is sensible

---

[7] There is a vast literature on the actual and optimal behavior of the monetary authorities. It is quite rare that empirical macroeconomic models assume an endogenous central bank. For examples in macroeconomic models, see FAIR R.C. [5]. For empirical studies of the Federal Reserve behavior, see KETTL D. [7], GOLDFELD S. [6], MCNESS S.K. [8] and PERRY G. - SCHULTZE C.L. [10].

and calibrated to existing models and findings where that seems more appropriate. The estimation period is 1954.Q1 to 1992.Q4 unless otherwise noted.

The specific equations are derived as follows: in equation *(2.1)*, we have estimated potential output using the Okun's Law relationship in equation *(2.3)* assuming that the capital elasticity is $\alpha = 0.25$. Future potential output growth is taken from CBO projections. The parameters of equation *(2.2)* are derived from macroeconomic modeling exercises, particularly the estimates of the impact of monetary and fiscal policy from Bryant *et* Al. [2]. It is assumed that the semi-logarithmic multiplier of fiscal policy on GDP is -2.0 (that is, a one percentage point increase in the ratio of the high-employment surplus to output lowers output by 2%). The semi-logarithmic multiplier of the real short-term interest rate on GDP is -1.0. Both policies are assumed to have a geometrical declining impact with an average lag of 5 quarters. Th Okun's law coefficient in equation *(2.3)* is estimated to be 2.1. The inflation equation is fitted to quarterly data with a single lag. The crowding-out coefficient is assumed to be $\lambda = 1$ in light of experience in the 1980s, while the depreciation rate of the capital stock is taken to be 10% per annum at a declining balance rate.

For the crucial monetary policy equation we have taken a number of different approaches. The major difference of this model from other studies is that we are modeling the *real interest rate*, while most other studies have examined the reaction function of the nominal interest rate. We focus on the real interest rate to simplify the analysis and to guarantee that the model will be dynamically stable (recall that output is a function of the real interest rate).

In the purely historical estimate, I assume that monetary policy adjusts real interest rates in an adaptive manner, reacting to the unemployment rate and the (quarterly) inflation rate, all variables measured in natural numbers. The equation is then fitted to observations over the period in which monetary policy has been relatively activist, 1975.Q1 to 1992.Q4, which yields:

$$(2.6a)\; r(t) = 0.00398 + \underset{(0.048)}{0.917}\; r(t-1) - \underset{(0.09)}{0.0345}\; u(t) + \underset{(0.19)}{0.0495}\; p(t)$$

$$R^2 = 0.866, \quad SEE = 0.0098$$

A second approach assumes that the Federal Reserve has a utility function of the form $U^M = V^M (u, p^2, \Theta = w_0 + w_1 u + w_2 p^2 + \Theta$, where Θ are adjustment terms. Assuming that all shocks were from other equations, we can estimate the parameters of this utility function from the observed relationship of u and p^2. From these, we derive an alternative reaction function:

$$(2.6b)\quad r(t) = 0.00204 + \underset{(0.0438)}{0.916}\, r(t-1) - 0.1\, [u(t) - 16.8\, p(t)^2]$$

$$R^2 = 0.866 \quad SEE = 0.0097$$

A third approach is one that is forward-looking and bases current monetary policy on forecasted future unemployment and inflation. This structure assumes that monetary policy moves in anticipation of future economic conditions. For this reaction function, we take a reaction function that is approximately ten times as reactive to inflation and unemployment as has been the case historically. This is designed to determine how a more responsive Federal Reserve might offset the projected contractionary impact of the deficit-reduction program:

$$(2.6c)\qquad r(t) = 0.5\, r(t-1) + 0.5\, [2\, p(t) - 5\, u(t+2)]$$

Note that this equation fits the data very poorly because it is so reactive. The best equation with such a rapid reaction has a standard error of estimate at least 50% higher than equations *(2.6a)* and *(2.6b)*.

Finally, it might be asked whether there is evidence that the Federal Reserve tends to move in a cooperative way in response to fiscal actions. We have estimated the coefficient of the fiscal surplus in equations *(2.6a)* and *(2.6b)*. According to the underlying econometric model, to offset fiscal policy would require a negative coefficient of around 2 (i.e. 200 basis points lowering of short term interest rates simultaneous with every 1 percentage point increase in the ratio of the fiscal surplus to potential GNP). Estimated coefficients for various periods have the wrong sign; for the period 1975.Q1 to 1992.Q4, the coefficient is 0.18 with a standard error of 0.16, which pretty definitely rules out that monetary policy responds appropriately to fiscal policy rather than the state of the economy.

The "baseline" fiscal forecast was taken from the *CBO*'s baseline projection. The alternative "Clinton" forecast was taken by assuming that the deficit reduction package was enacted as proposed. The Clinton package was, in brief, a small expansion package (which was scrapped by the Congress), followed by a deficit-reduction program which would reduce the high-employment deficit by slightly under 2% of GNP over a 5-year period, that is to 1998. For the two projections, we then held the 1998 estimate of the surplus ratio, *S* (1998) constant for the rest of the projection period [8].

An alternative approach to estimating the macroeconomic impact of the Clinton deficit-reduction package is to use an existing macroeconomic model. The only model that is suitable for this purpose [9] is that of Fair, which has an endogenous monetary policy (see Fair [5] for the latest results). Professor Fair graciously made a version of his model available for these simulations. To estimate the impact, I simply entered the baseline and Clinton fiscal proposals into the Fair model with endogenous monetary policy and calculated the impact upon the economy [10]. This simulation can then be compared with estimates for

---

[8] In all simulations, we assume that the change in government programs takes the form of reductions in government spending on current goods and services with no changes in tax or transfer programs and that Barro's Ricardian hypothesis does not hold. This assumption is likely to overstate the impact upon aggregate demand. If half the programs is tax and transfer programs with a marginal propensity to spend of 0.80, and there is no correction for the Ricardian hypothesis, then the impact upon actual output would be approximately 90% of the estimates shown below with no change for the impact upon potential output. If the strict Ricardian hypothesis holds, then the impact upon aggregate demand would be maintained as long as deficit reduction took the form of expenditure cuts but would be completely erased if the deficit reductions were tax cuts; however, there would be no increase in investment or capital in the Ricardian case, so there would consequently be no increase in potential output.

[9] The standard approach to estimating the short-run impact of fiscal policies assumes that the money supply is fixed. This approach implicity assumes much too rapid a reaction of interest rates to output or monetary shocks to be consistent with past Fed behavior.

[10] The monetary reaction function in the Fair model is a more elaborate version of the one developed in equation *(2.6a)*. It uses the nominal 3-month treasury bill rate, and the lag is virtually identical to that used here. The reaction is a function of the rate of inflation and the ratio of actual to potential output with very similar coefficients to those determined in equation *(2.6a)*. In addition, Fair's model includes variables on the growth rate of GDP, a money-supply variable, a dummy variable, and rates of change of interest rates. For the sample period, the standard error of the equation is about 60% of that for equation *(2.6a)*.

the minimodel developed in this section. The Fair model holds potential output exogenous, however, so the impact could only be measured on actual output, and we must use the model in this section for the impact upon potential output.

2.3 *Results of Simulation*

The results of the experiments can be broken into two parts — the impact upon actual output and that on the growth of potential output. For the first, we have performed simulations of the impact upon unemployment assuming no increase in potential output. Graph 7 shows the impact for the three different reaction functions in

GRAPH 7

ALTERNATIVE ESTIMATES
OF IMPACT OF CLINTON PROGRAM
ON UNEMPLOYMENT RATE

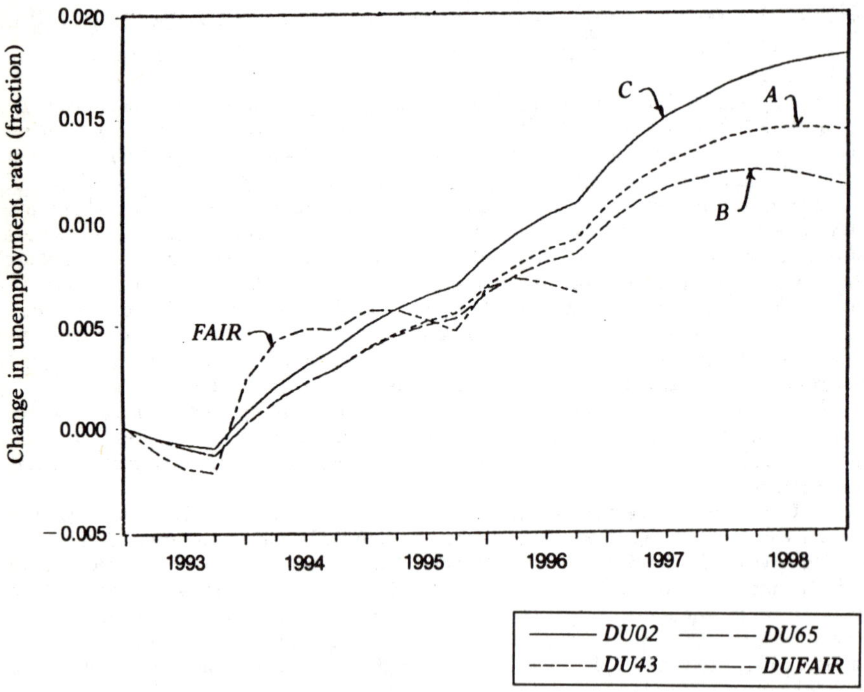

equations *(2.6a)* through *(2.6c)* for the period 1993.1 through 1999.4, as well as the simulation for the Fair model for the period 1993.1 through 1996.4. The major result of the simulation is that, even with endogenous and responsive monetary policy, the Clinton deficit-reduction package will produce a significant increase in unemployment over the next few years.

Surprisingly, there is relatively little disagreement among either the three reaction functions or between the model presented here and the Fair model. For example, at the end of 1996, the range of estimates is for the unemployment rate under the Clinton program to be from 0.6 to 1.1 percentage points higher than the baseline. The difference between the estimated response under the Fair model and that of the model used here arises largely because of the difference in the non-monetary sector rather than in the response of monetary policy to the state of the economy.

Why is there such a large effect of a fiscal deficit on the economy after four years even with a reactive monetary policy? The reasons are two. The first and obvious condition is that fiscal policy matters; if fiscal policy has no impact on aggregate demand, then there will be no impact on unemployment in the short or the long run. The second and less obvious condition is that there are lags of policies which imply that a monetary policy based on performance rather than fiscal policies will act too late, and to this is added the tendency of the Fed to act too little. A simple example will show why the contractionary impact of deficit reduction will not be dampened much by monetary policies. Assume that fiscal policy has a one year lag; that monetary policy reacts instantaneously in response to output changes and has a one year lag in its impact upon the economy; and that interest rates adjust halfway toward that level that would remove the gap in a year. With this set of assumptions, monetary policy would not begin to offset the contractionary impulse for two years and would offset only one-half of the contraction after three years.

The purpose of the Clinton deficit-reduction package is obviously not to increase unemployment but rather aspires to raise long-term economic growth by increasing investment. The next step is to estimate the increase in potential output that arises from the change in the monetary-fiscal mix. To estimate this impact, we take the estimated ratio of capital to potential output at the end of 1992 and assume this ratio is constant in the base case. We then take the estimated cumulative surplus from the Clinton package, multiply this by the crowding-out ratio which is assumed to be unity ($\lambda = 1$), and thereby obtain the increase in the capital stock from the lower government debt. Applying the elasticity of output with respect to capital of 0.25, we can estimate the difference between potential output with and without the Clinton program.

The results of this estimate is shown as the "potential" line in Graph 8. According to this estimate, the increase in potential output is around 1.5% by the turn of the century and about 4% by 2010. This estimate is probably on the high side because it assumes the crowding-out ratio is 100%, because it ignores the depressing effect of lower output on investment, and because it assumes that net foreign investment has a rate of return equal to that of domestic capital.

A potential offset to this overestimate would arise if there are externalities of investment, particularly investment in equipment. If the estimated social return from conventional production functions underestimates the social return, the impact on potential output would be higher than otherwise calculated. This second approach is unlikely to add up to much, however if, as most models suggest, only a small fraction of the lower deficit turns up in higher investment spending [11].

The actual effect shown is also shown in Graph 8. This graph takes the unemployment rate estimate from Graph 7 and converts it to an output deviation using Okun's law. This estimate suggests that the contractionary impact of the deficit-reduction program peaks at slightly under 3% of output in 1998, and then gradually diminishes.

The total effect takes the sum of the effects on actual and potential output and is shown by the curve marked "total" in Graph 8. This calculation indicates that the contractionary impact on actual

---

[11] For example, an estimate of the impact of the change in the monetary-fiscal mix using the *DRI* macroeconomic model suggests that a $ 50 billion reduction in the federal deficit accompanied by a monetary stimulus to keep the unemployment rate constant would increase investment spending by $ 66 billion of which only $ 15 billion would take the form of business fixed investment and under $ 10 billion would be higher investment in equipment (see NORDHAUS W.D. [6]).

GRAPH 8

TOTAL IMPACT OF CLINTON PACKAGE
ON POTENTIAL AND ACTUAL
OUTPUT WITH MONETARY REACTION

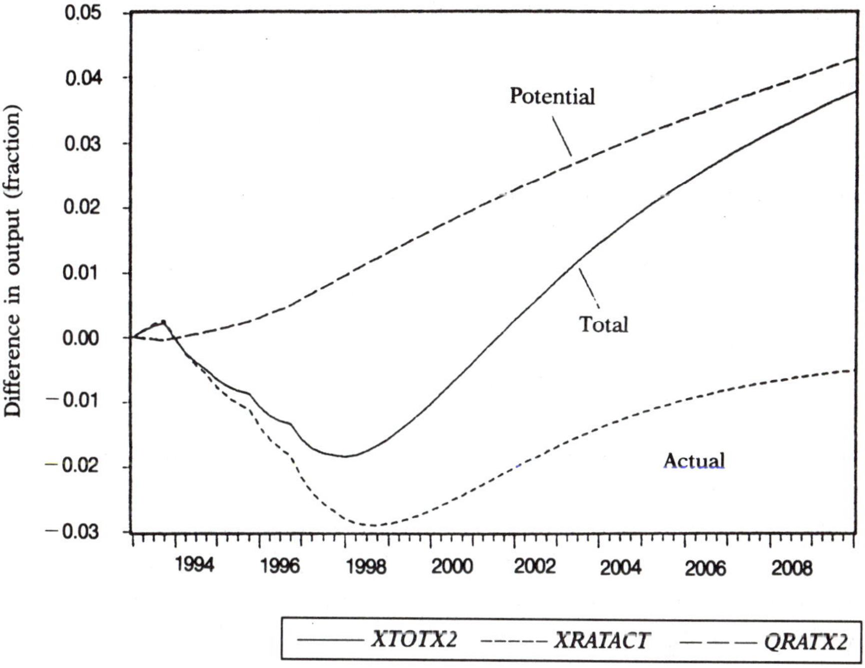

output dominates in the near term; that the growth-enhancing impact catches up with the contractionary impact around the year 2001; and that after 2001, output is actually higher. By the end of the period, output is almost 4% higher than it would be without the deficit-reduction (and investment-enhancing) fiscal program.

These calculations are subjected to all the reservations that have been noted above and should be viewed as having large potential error due to problems of misspecification, uncertainties about the appropriate construction of the Federal Reserve reaction function, uncertainties such as those surrounding the Ricardian hypothesis or the extent of externalities in equipment investment.

Subject to these reservations, two striking conclusions emerge from these results. The first is that it would require a brave political leader to undertake a massive deficit-reduction program in the face of a stagnant economy. The increase in unemployment and the decline in aggregate demand are unlikely to be offset by any increase in productivity or real wages within an electoral cycle of most industrial democracies. Given the timidity of many policy makers, there can be little surprise that elected officials hesitate to undertake massive deficit-reduction policies. The consequence is just the monetary-fiscal equilibrium that has been established in most democracies.

The second point is that the losses from lack of coordination, and the potential gains from coordination, are extremely high. A coordinated macroeconomic policy would be one in which the interest rate reaction came simultaneously with, and in sufficient strength to offset the contractionary impact of, the fiscal contraction. A coordinated policy would avoid the need for the contractions and internal inconsistencies of the Clinton package, which imbeds a stimulus and deficit-increasing package within a contractionary and deficit-reducing policy. More important, a well-coordinated monetary policy could avoid the unpleasant side-effect of contraction. For comparative purposes, we can inquire into the gains from coordination in the scenario shown in Graph 8. A coordinated monetary-fiscal package could erase the contraction, so that the actual line would coincide with the potential line in Graph 8. The total gain in output from coordination over the period would be one quarter of a year's GNP, or $ 1.75 trillion undiscounted in 1993 prices.

Are fiscal and monetary policy out of step? Apparently, they are, and the cost to society is more than bad timing or discordant policies. It is likely to be an outcome in which economies settle into a high-deficit, low-investment equilibrium out of which no politician dares break for fear of the twin evils of political economy-economic recession and electoral defeat.

APPENDIX

Derivation of Reaction Functions

The purpose of this appendix is to derive the reaction functions for the case of quadratic preferences. The preference functions of the policy makers are given by:

(A1) $$U^F = V^F(u, p, r, S)$$

(A2) $$U^M = V^M(u, p, r, S)$$

which will be taken to be quadratic and separable and can be written as:

(A3) $$U^F = -(u-u^*)^2 - \beta^*(p-p^*)^2 - \gamma^*(S-S^*)^2$$

(A4) $$U^M = -(u-u^{**})^2 - \beta^{**}(p-p^{**})^2 - \gamma^{**}(S-S^{**})^2$$

The variables with *'s refer to the most desired outcomes for the fiscal authority and those with **'s refer to the bliss points of monetary authority. The economy can be written succinctly as:

(A5) $$u = \mu_S S + \mu_r r$$

(A6) $$p = -\alpha u + p^e = -\alpha \mu_S S - \alpha \mu_r r + p^e$$

Maximizing the preference leads to the following first-order conditions:

(A7) $$\partial U^F/\partial S = -2(u-u^*)\mu_S + 2\beta^*(p-p^*)(\alpha\mu_S) - 2\gamma^*(S-S^*) = 0$$

(A8) $$\partial U^M/\partial r = -2(u-u^{**})\mu_r + 2\beta^{**}(p-p^{**})\alpha\mu_r = 0$$

Substituting *(A5)* and *(A6)* and reducing yields:

(A9) $$(u-u^*)+\beta^*(u-u^+)\alpha^2+\gamma^*(S-S^*)/\mu_S=0$$

(A10) $$(u-u^{**})+\beta^{**}(u-u^{++})\alpha^2=0$$

to u^+ and u^{++} are the unemployment rates that correspond to the desired inflationary rates, p^* and p^{**}, respectively:

Solving for the optimal policies for each policy maker, we obtain:

(A11) $$\mu_S S+\mu_r r=[u^*+\beta^*\alpha^2 u^+-\gamma^*(S-S^*)/\mu_S]/[1+\beta^*\alpha^2]$$

(A12) $$\mu_S S+\mu_r r=[u^{**}+\beta^{**}\alpha^2 u^{++}]/[1+\beta^{**}\alpha^2]$$

To simplify, we can without loss of generality change units of S so that $\mu_S=1$; further define

$$\phi^*=1/[1+\beta^*\alpha^2] \text{ and } \phi^{**}=1/[1+\beta^{**}\alpha^2]$$

This yields

(A13) $$S=-\mu_r r+\phi^*[u^*+\beta^*\alpha^2 u^+-\gamma^*(S-S^*)]$$

(A14) $$S=-\mu_r r+\phi^{**}[u^{**}+\beta^{**}\alpha^2 u^{++}]$$

which gives us the reaction functions of the fiscal authority:

(A15) $$S^F(r)=-[\mu_r/(1+\phi^*\gamma^*)]r+$$
$$+\phi^*[u^*+\beta^*\alpha^2 u^+ +\gamma^* S^*]/[1+\phi^*\gamma^*]$$

We write the reaction function of the monetary authority as an implicit function for transparency:

(A16) $$S=-\mu_r r^M(S)+\phi^{**}[u^{**}+\beta^{**}\alpha^2 u^{++}]$$

Equation *(A15)* is the reaction function of the fiscal authority, while equation *(A16)* is the reaction function of the monetary authority. The interpretation is that $S^F(r)$ is the surplus set by the fiscal authority as a function of the monetary policy and other variables, while $r^M(S)$ is the interest rate set by the monetary authority as a function of fiscal policy and other variables. We can determine the slope (in terms of the change in S per unit change in r) of the reaction functions as follows:

$$\partial S^F/\partial r = -\mu_r/[1+\gamma^* \phi^*] \tag{A17}$$

and:

$$\partial S/\partial r^M = -\mu_r \tag{A18}$$

Because γ^* and ϕ^* are both positive constants, the slope of the fiscal reaction function in *(A17)* is less in absolute value than that of the monetary authority in *(A18)*. This is the relationship shown in Graphs 1 through 6.

The location of the reaction functions will depend upon all the parameters. We can locate the bliss points for each policy maker by finding the intersection of the optimal aggregate demand line with the optimal fiscal position. For example, for the fiscal authority, the maximum of *(A3)* with respect to both r and S will yield the optimal level of aggregate demand and the optimal fiscal posture. By the common-funnel theorem, there are only two independent targets (aggregate demand and the fiscal surplus), so these can be perfectly reached by the combination of r and S. It is obvious that if the monetary authority has a lower target for aggregate demand (say because it has a higher target for unemployment and a lower target for inflation) along with a higher target for the fiscal surplus, then its bliss point lies above (although not necessarily to the left) of the bliss point of the fiscal authority. Since each policy maker's reaction function goes through its bliss point, this shows that the shape of the reaction function will be as shown in Graphs 1 through 6.

For completeness, we will show this proposition for the simplest case in which we assume that all parameters of the preference functions are the same except that the target unemployment rate of the authority is higher than that of the fiscal authority, so that

$u^{**} > u^*$. Evaluating the reaction functions in *(A13)* and *(A14)* at $S = S^*$, and equating all parameters other than u^* and u^{**} to the fiscal parameters, we have:

(A19) $$S^F = -\mu_r r + \phi^* [u^* + \beta^* \alpha^2 u^+]$$

(A20) $$S = -\mu_r r^M + \phi^* [u^{**} + \beta^* \alpha^2 u^+]$$

Because ϕ^* is a positive constant, the level of the surplus along the monetary reaction function in *(A20)* evaluated at the same level of r will be higher by the amount $\phi^* [u^{**} - u^*]$. This implies that the monetary bliss point will be above that of the fiscal bliss point as long as the optimal fiscal surplus desired by the monetary authority is higher than the optimal fiscal surplus desired by the fiscal authority. It is conceivable that, if the central bank's most preferred fiscal surplus is extremely high, the monetary bliss point will be above and to the left of the fiscal bliss point. This would indicate that the monetary authority has a lower desired real interest rate than did the fiscal authority. Showing the position of the reaction function for other parameter values will be omitted.

Finally, note that as long as the monetary authority follows a Nash strategy, the monetary reaction function coincides with its aggregate demand line — i.e., with that combination of interest rates and fiscal surpluses that would optimize aggregate demand. Put differently, there is no impact of the central bank's fiscal preferences on the central bank's reaction function. This is easily seen in the monetary reaction function, which contains no parameters that reflect the central bank's preference concerning the fiscal surplus.

BIBLIOGRAPHY

[1] BLINDER A.S., «Issues in the Coordination of Monetary Policy», in FEDERAL RESERVE BANK OF KANSAS CITY, *Monetary Policy Issues in the 1980s*, Federal Reserve Bank of Kansas City, proceedings of a conference of August 1982, pp. 3-34.

[2] BRYANT R.C. - HOLTHAM G. - HOOPER, P., *Empirical Macroeconomics for Interdependent Economies*, Washington (DC), Brookings, 1988.

[3] BURNS A.F., *The Anguish of Central Banking*, Jacobbsen Lecture delivered to the IMF-World Bank Annual Meeting, Belgrade, September 1979.

[4] DIXIT A.K. - NALEBUFF B.J., *Thinking Strategically*, New York, Norton, 1991.

[5] FAIR R.C., *Testing Macroeconomic Models*, New Haven, Cowles Foundation, 1993.

[6] GOLDFELD S., «The Demand for Money Revisited», *Brookings Papers on Economic Activity*, n. 3, 1973.

[7] KETTL D., *Leadership at the Fed*, New Haven, Yale University Press, 1986.

[8] MCNESS S.K., «Modeling the Fed: a Forward-Looking Monetary Policy Reaction Function, *New England Economic Review*, November-December 1986, pp. 3-8.

[9] NORDHAUS W.D., «The United States», in LLEWELLYN J. (ed.), *Policies for the 1990s*, Oxford, Basil-Blackwell, 1991.

[10] PERRY G. - SCHULTZE C.L., «Is this Recession Different? Are All Recessions Different?», paper presented at the *Brookings Papers on Economic Activity*, April 1993.

[11] PINDYCK R.S., «The Cost of Conflicting Objectives in Policy Formulation», *Annals of Economic and Social Measurement*, vol. 5, n. 2, 1976.

[12] RIBE F.C., *Effects of Decentralization on the Efficiency of Stabilization Policy*, Ph. D. Dissertation, London, Yale University, 1980.

Rejection of the *Common Funnel Theorem* *

Robert A. Mundell
Columbia University, New York

Upon reading this interesting paper I gained the impression that I could agree with Professor Nordhaus on most of the details if only we agreed on the fundamentals.

Our disagreement on the fundamentals lies over the *Common Funnel Theorem.* According to this Yale-intensive proposition, monetary and fiscal policies have equivalent first-order effects on aggregate demand. As far as first-order effects are concerned, policies affecting inflation and unemployment are funneled through their impact on aggregate demand. A fiscal policy that delivers one billion dollars of additional aggregate demand could be offset exactly by a monetary policy that delivers one billion dollars of redution in aggregate demand. Graph 1 depicts the sense of the theorem, in which monetary *m* and fiscal *f* effects are fed into the funnel of aggregate demand and these effects are then combined to produce an impact on unemployment *u* and the rate of inflation *p*.

The *Common Funnel Theorem (CFT)* was contested by supply-side macroeconomics. You will not therefore be surprised by my opposition to it! Undoubtedly the most controversial feature of supply-side economics was its proposition that it was possible to reduce unemployment and inflation at the same time. Monetarists and Keynesians had both rejected this proposition, the former on the grounds that there is a "natural" rate of unemployment that cannot be

* Comment on *Coordination and Independence in Monetary and Fiscal Policies* by William D. Nordhaus.

altered, the latter on the grounds that the Phillips curve is stable and cannot be shifted by economic policy. Nordhaus' opposition to this idea is based on the idea of a fixed Phillips curve embodied in his appendix equation *A*5, which is $p = -au$. The supply-side policy mix of tight money and tax cuts demonstrated that the Phillips curve could be shifted, with unemployment and inflation falling at the same time, as they did during the great expansion of 1983-1989.

The key difference between supply-side economics and the other schools was the *Supply-Side Theorem:* that monetary and fiscal policies are independent instruments that can be used to achieve employment-growth and inflation-depreciation targets simultaneously. Specifically, fiscal policy has a comparative advantage with respect to employment-growth objectives and monetary policy has a comparative advantage with respect to inflation-depreciation objective. Tax reduction can promote expansion at the same time that monetary restraint is reducing inflation. The sense of the *Supply-Side Theorem* is provided by the vertical line inserted inside the funnel within Graph 1.

Because the difference between Nordhaus and myself stands or

GRAPH 1

THE COMMON FUNNEL THEOREM

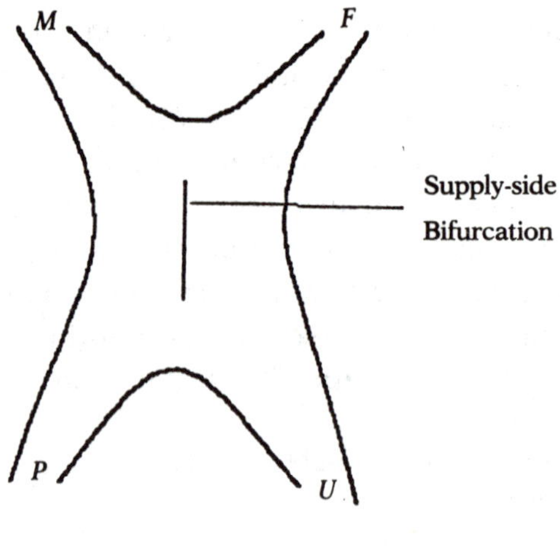

falls on the validity of this theorem — and at the same time by a rejection of the *CFT* — I will devote the first part of my remarks to the case for the supply-side proposition and the case against the funnel theorem.

1. - The *Supply-Side Theorem*

A theorem is only as good as the model from which it is derived. I argue that the assumptions on which the *CFT* is based are not relevant to the cyclical problems most countries face in the real world.

On January 8, 1981, the «*Wall Street Journal*» published an article, titled *Once More, With Feeling*, elaborating the theory of the supply-side policy mix, arguing that monetary policy should focus on controlling inflation, while employment and growth are accelerated by a tax cut. This brought a retort from Nordhaus' colleague at Yale, Professor James Tobin who, in a letter to the *Journal* on January 20, 1981 — the day President Reagan was inaugurated — challenged the *Theorem* as follows: «If a west-bound locomotive is harnessed to one end of an Amtrak train in New Haven and an east-bound engine to the other end, will the train go simultaneously to New York and Boston? If a Volcker monetary locomotive pulls the economy one way while a Kemp-Stockman fiscal engine pulls it the other, will the train reach both destinations, disinflation and expansion?

«Your editorial attributes to Bob Mundell the old dictum that you need as many policy levers as goals but omits the crucial qualifications he knows, the words 'at least'. When the levers are connected to the goals by identical mechanisms, it does no good to have as many levers as goals, or even more. The dominant mechanisms relating fiscal and monetary levers to price and output goals are the same; both policies work via the pressure of demand on productive resources. The policy mix does matter, to be sure, for other objectives, e.g., the dollar exchange rate, capital formation.

«It's best to be realistic about stagflation. It can't be solved by assigning disinflation to the Fed while tax cuts and defense spending 'get the economy moving again'. The train may creep in one direction or the other, but the main result will be high interest rates, nominal and real».

Let me make a comment first on subsequent history. It is true that, because the Volcker monetary lever was pulled more than a year before the tax cut lever came into place, the economy went into sharp recession with rising unemployment[1]. But after the tax cuts had been implemented, by 1983, the economy moved into one of its two greatest expansions ever. Graph 2 depicts inflation-unemployment space and the positions at Reagan's inauguration, the pit of the recession in November 1982 and the successful reduction in both unemployment and inflation by the fall of 1984. Low unemployment and inflation would persist until the recession that began in June 1990.

GRAPH 2

REAGANOMICS

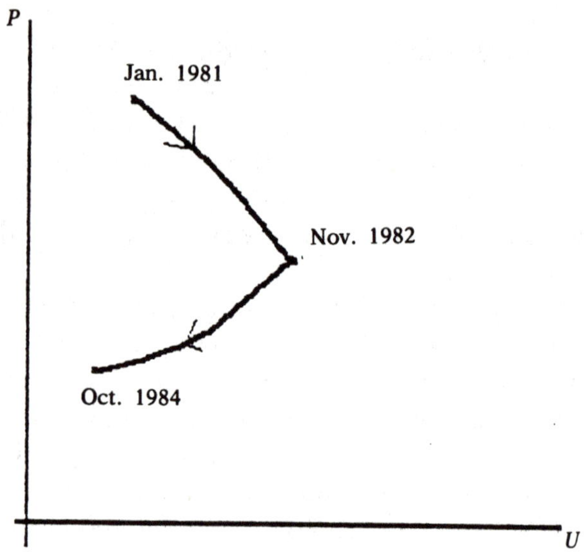

[1] The plan lowering tax rates in three stages in the *Economic Recovery Act* of 1961 (as in the original Kemp-Roth bill) may have been a political necessity but it was, from an economic standpoint, a mistake insofar as it created incentives to shift production and taxable income from 1981 and 1982 to 1983 in order to take advantage of lower future taxes; this income-shifting bears part of the blame for the recession of 1981-1982.

The Reagan expansion was comparable to that which followed the Kennedy-Johnson tax cuts of 1964; the stock market rose four-fold from July 1982 to the end of Reagan's term in office. The *Supply-Side Theorem* worked in the 1960s under a Democratic President, why did Professor Tobin think it would not work in the 1980s under a Republican president?

One difference between the two periods is that the exchange rate was fixed in the former, and was flexible in the latter. In the 1960s, the tax cut was needed to spur economic growth while monetary policy was required to maintain equilibrium in the balance of payments. In the 1980s, the tax cut was again needed to spur economic growth while monetary policy was required to bring about disinflation. In theory, the policy mix should not be changed because of the shift from fixed to flexible exchange rates.

Consider first the case of fiscal policy with unchanged monetary policy under a situation where the exchange rate is flexible. In the supply-side analysis, a cut in marginal tax rates increases both demand and supply, generating an investment boom, an expansion of output and employment, increased supply of new securities and an increased demand for money. With the money supply under restraint, interest rates rise, giving rise to a capital inflow which results in an appreciation of the currency with disinflationary effects as the current account of the balance of payments goes into deficit. The tax cut stimulates output and employment and at the same time brings about disinflation shifting the Phillips curve (if it exists) downward. The shift from fixed to flexible exchange rates therefore does not vitiate the policy mix. On the contrary, the appreciation of the currency associated with the policy aids and abets the disinflationary process. This was indeed the sequel that followed the Reagan tax cuts after 1982.

We have just considered the case of fiscal expansion with monetary restraint and shown that, if timed correctly, it increases output and reduces inflation. Now consider the opposite policy mix of monetary expansion combined with fiscal contraction. In the very short run, we could assume, as in Keynesian theory, that expectations are not yet reformulated to take account of inflation. In this case the increase in the rate of monetary expansion would lead to a fall in the rate of interest, an outflow of capital, a depreciation of the currency, an improvement in the trade balance and a more rapid increase in the price level. Concurrently, if money wages stay constant, the decline in real wages increases profits which leads to a boom in the stock market, and the expansion of output and employment[2]. In this short-run analysis of the effects of monetary expansion, output may increase, as in the case of the tax cut, but the rate of inflation increases.

It is necessary also to take into account fiscal effects. Suppose that tax brackets are not indexed for inflation so that monetary acceleration that brings on an increase in the price level in the context of a progressive tax system shifts individuals and corporations into higher tax brackets, reducing real disposable wages and after-tax real profits, and lowering the marginal efficiency of capital and the stock market. Fiscal constraint will cancel out all or part of the formerly favorable effects of monetary expansion on output. Monetary acceleration combined with fiscal constraint may therefore offset one another with respect to the rise in output, but the net effect will nevertheless be a rise in the price level. This price level effect will be accentuated as higher tax rates lead to higher wage demands as workers and their unions seek to maintain disposable income. Even in this very short-run analysis, therefore, monetary acceleration has a comparative advantage in affecting the rate of inflation.

But the very short-run is not an adequate time framework for analyzing macroeconomic policy over the business cycle. It is unrealistic to assume that expectations about the effects of policy will not influence decisions. Monetary acceleration will almost certainly change expectations of inflation. This will have consequences for both interest rates and wage rates. In the financial markets in the very short run, unexpected monetary acceleration might lower short-term interest rates for a few days; but once the monetary acceleration becomes apparent, the bond market will crack and then both long-term and (later) short-term interest rates will rise. In the labor market

---

[2] The higher profits may also attract equity capital from abroad, an effect which would tend to worsen the current account. The net effect on the exchange rate and the current account would depend on whether the outflow of portfolio capital induced by the fall in interest rates exceeds or falls short of the inflow of direct investment induced by the increase in profits.

GRAPH 3

THE SUPPLY-SIDE POLICY MIX

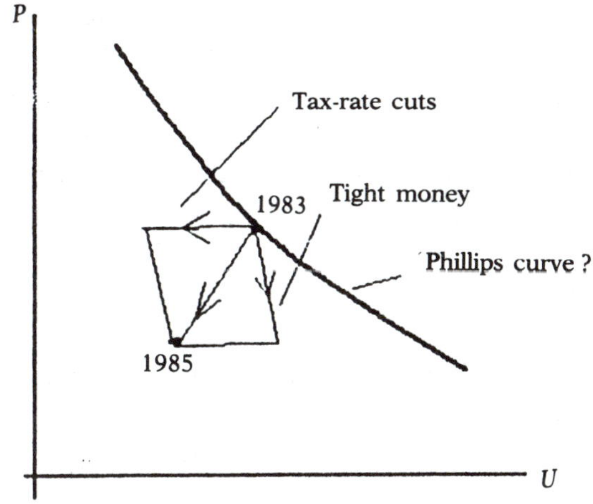

expectations of higher inflation will result in higher wage demands as old contracts expire, raising marginal costs of production and lowering profits and the marginal efficiency of capital. When expectations effects are taken into account, the policy mix of monetary acceleration and fiscal tightness leads to higher inflation, currency depreciation, stagnation[3] and falling real stock prices. These were indeed stylized facts of the US economy in the late 1970s when monetary acceleration was combined with automatic fiscal tightness.

It is clear from this analysis that monetary policy has a comparative advantage with respect to control of inflation and the exchange rate, whereas tax reduction has a comparative advantage in affecting employment and growth. Thus Graph 3 plots the "fixed" Phillips curve from which, according to the *CFT*, the economy cannot escape by any combination of monetary and fiscal policy. On the contrary, the *Supply-Side Theorem* asserts that tight money and tax cuts do not cancel each other out, but move the $u-p$ situation along the vectors

[3] The effect of monetary acceleration and fiscal tightness on output and employment obviously depends on how strongly each policy is pursued. In the 1970s the tightness of the fiscal policy was automatically determined by the rate at which tax brackets were shifted.

indicated, moving to the more favorable position actually achieved in the fall of 1984.

It may even be the case that fiscal tightness, in the form of tax increases, far from being deflationary, is actually inflationary. Suppose the government raises marginal tax rates to over 90% (as they were in the United States during World War II). This would cause such a collapse of production that, with a given stock of money, the price level would increase! Once supply-side incentive effects are taken into account, the Keynesian assumption that tax increases will not raise prices is incorrect.

The proposition that monetary and fiscal policies have different effects on output and the price level is not restricted to large economies like that of the United States; it applies equally, if not more so, in other countries. There is no tax policy unaccompanied by monetary expansion that can lead to hyperinflations of the kind experienced by several countries after World Wars I and II. No fiscal policy can lead to hyperinflation unless it is accompanied by rapid monetary expansion[4].

In many countries, of course, fiscal and monetary policies are closely connected. Rapid inflations are usually caused by monetary expansion but rapid monetary expansions in the modern world are nearly always caused by budget deficits financed by the central bank; the budget deficit determines the rate of monetary expansion. Even in this case, however, the *Supply-Side Theorem* remains true in the sense that monetary acceleration has a comparative advantage in, and is the *sine qua non* of, stopping inflation, whereas fiscal policies have real effects. the *Supply-Side Theorem* is part of a more general principle that when money illusion is absent, nominal instruments of policy should be assigned to nominal targets, real instruments to real targets. The money supply is a nominal instrument that should be assigned to nominal variables such as the price level and the nominal

[4] There is one exception where fiscal policy without monetary expansion can lead to hyperinflation; and that is where marginal tax rates are increased to such an extent that they shut down production almost entirely; the reader will note that in this case, contrary to the Keynesian argument, fiscal tightness leads to a higher price level. While this case is an extreme one, these supply-side effects exert an inflationary influence at all tax rates.

exchange rate; fiscal policy is a real variable that can be assigned to real variables such as the balance of trade, the level of employment or the rate of growth.

2. - Criticism of the Model

It will be clear from the above that I am not an enthusiast of the kind of model used by Nordhaus. His equation *(1.3)* relates the inflation rate to the level of unemployment, with the expected rate of inflation treated as an exogenous variable, and in fact held constant. In the policy equations $u = u\ (m,\ f)$ and $p = p\ (m,\ f)$ the *CFT* (and Nordhaus' equation) implies that the Jacobian of u and p with respect to m and f vanishes.

It is totally unrealistic, however, to assume that the expected inflation rate is independent of the actual inflation rate or the variables that determine it. Suppose, for example, that the *Clinton Plan* fails to achieve the growth desired and that the government is forced to pressure the Federal Reserve into more expansionary monetary policy. This will affect the expected inflation rate: 1) directly through its announcement effect; 2) indirectly through its impact on actual inflation; and 3) indirectly again through its impact on the exchange rate. When more expansionary monetary policies are expected to increase the inflation rate they will also increase wage demands and so on. The assumption of constant inflationary expectations when changes in monetary and fiscal policy are being undertaken is too unrealistic to serve as a reliable guide to economic policy.

Nor am I in sympathy with Nordhaus's equation *(1.4)*, which makes unemployment a function of the real interest rate r and the fiscal variable, S, intended to designate a surplus. My complaint is not that unemployment is unaffected by these variables — everything affects everything else in a general equilibrium system. It is rather that r and S are not policy variables in the strict sense of the word. How in heaven's name does the Federal Reserve or any other central bank change the real rate of interest as a policy variable?

The real interest rate is governed by a complex of forces in the economy, most importantly by the rate of return to capital. The Fed's policy variable is an open market operation. Whether it can affect the real rate of interest or not is a moot question in economics the answer to which depends, *inter alia*, on how expectations are affected.

When taxes are under consideration, it is necessary to make a distinction between the after-tax and the before-tax real interest rate. A change in tax rates will alter the wedge between the two interest rates. It will also tend to change the general level of real interest rates. The fiscal policy of the government may have more influence on real interest rates than the monetary policy of the central bank.

Another objection I have to the Nordhaus model is the failure to discriminate between alternative mechanisms of fiscal policy. Changes in tax rates have a profoundly different impact on the economy than changes in government spending. I think the best comparison is between the tax reductions in US economic policy in 1981-1988, and the increases in government spending to finance unification in Germany in 1990-1993. Sensible government spending can also have supply-side effects, but not so strong or growth-promoting as tax reductions.

It is necessary to disaggregate the fiscal policy variables to take into account changes in individual tax rates and changes in specific types of government expenditure. It makes a difference whether government expenditures are productivity-enhancing or mere consumption; and whether corporate taxes, income taxes, capital gains taxes or other taxes are taken into consideration. Some tax increases will lower rather than increase government revenues along the lines of Laffer-curve analysis.

As far as budgetary policy is concerned, it would be a mistake to ignore the relevance of the double-valued relation between tax rates and tax revenues that became known as the Laffer curve, but which could equally have been called after Ibn Khaldun, Jonathan Swift, David Hume, Adam Smith, Alexander Hamilton or even John Maynard Keynes[5]. This schedule reflects the impact of diminishing returns

[5] Why, it may be asked, did the introduction of the Laffer curve into economics have to wait for the 1970s? At first this seems to be a puzzle, because the idea that revenues from increasing tax rates first rise and then fall was not exactly new. It must have been known to revenue-hungry finance ministers fixing tax rates in the ancient world. The Muslim philosopher and historian, Ibn Khaldun, in the 14th century, wrote:

applied to increasing tax rates. From a tax rate of zero, an increase in the tax rate will initially raise some revenue but soon increasing tax rates yield smaller increments to revenue until a point is reached at which revenue ceases to increase as tax rates are raised. Increases in tax rates beyond this maximum revenue position will yield less, not more, revenue.

The Laffer curve phenomenon arises because rising tax rates create two effects working in the opposite direction. A rise in tax rates would, on the hand, raise revenues for a given tax base, but, on the other hand, it would reduce the tax base. Maximum tax revenue is

---

«At the beginning of the dynasty, taxation yields a large revenue from small assessments. At the end of the dynasty, taxation yields a small revenue from large assessments».

Jonathan Swift, writing in 1728, wrote: «I will tell you a Secret, which I learned many years ago from the commissioners of the customs in London: they said, when any commodity appeared to be taxed above a moderate rate, the consequence was to lessen that branch of the revenue by one half; and one of those gentlemen pleasantly told me, that the mistake of parliaments, on such occasions, was owing to an error of computing two and two to make four; whereas in the business of laying heavy impositions, two and two never made more than one; which happens by lessening the import, and the strong temptation of running such goods as paid high duties». A few pages later, he wrote: «High taxes, sometimes by diminishing the consumption of the taxed commodities, and sometimes by encouraging smuggling, frequently afford a smaller revenue to government than what might be drawn from more moderate taxes».

Swift's catchy phrases were picked up by other economists, like Hume: «We ought, however, always to remember the maxim of Dr. Swift, that in the arithmetic of the customs, two and two make not four, but often make only one. It can scarcely be doubted, but if the duties on wine were lowered to a third, they would yield much more to the government than at present».

Referring to indirect taxation, Hume wrote that: «a duty upon commodities checks itself; and a prince will soon find, that an encrease of the impost is no encrease of his revenue».

Adam Smith wrote: «High taxes, sometimes by diminishing the consumption of the taxed commodities, and sometimes by encouraging smuggling, frequently afford a smaller revenue to government than what might be drawn from more moderate taxes».

Alexander Hamilton wrote: «It is a signal advantage of taxes on articles of consumption that they contain in their own nature a security against excess. They prescribe their own limit, which cannot be exceeded without defeating the end proposed that is, an extension of the revenue... If duties are too high, they lessen the consumption; the collection is eluded; and the product to the Treasury is not so great as when they are confined withinm proper and moderate bounds».

These examples illustrate that the Laffer curve concept was by no means a new idea. What was new, however, was the application of the Laffer curve idea to macroeconomic stabilization policy. Read any textbook on macroeconomics written between 1935 and 1975 and try to find an explicit recognition that a tax reduction must increase tax revenues when tax rates are above the maximum tax rate. If any economists were aware of it, they kept it a secret.

achieved when the positive effects on revenue of increasing the rate exactly equals the negative effects on revenue of reducing the base. If tax rates are lower than the maximum revenue tax, an increase in taxes will raise revenues; but if tax rates are above the maximum revenue tax, a reduction in tax rates will augment tax revenues.

Nordhaus' paper implies that US tax rates are well below the maximum revenue position. This may be true for some taxes but not for others. From the stand point of both economic theory and policy, it is necessary to distinguish between different types of Laffer curves.

Consider, for example, a reduction in the tax rate on corporate profits[6]. Out of a given GNP this would raise or lower corporate tax revenues depending on whether the initial tax rate was above or below the maximum revenue peak of the Laffer Curve; in Graph 4, lower taxes would raise or lower corporate-tax revenues depending on whether the actual tax rate was at a position like *C* or a position like *A*, on the Laffer curve for corporate profits, *OABC*.

The curve *OABC*, however, does not determine the effect of a change in corporate tax rates on the government budget. Because, a reduction in the corporate tax rate would increase investment[7], it would raise GNP and its rate of growth, and thus increase the revenues from other taxes, including income and excise taxes. The *relevant* Laffer curve for (say) corporation profits taxes has to take into account not only the change in taxes paid by corporations, but also the changes in revenues from all other taxes. It must also take into account the increase in revenues from state and local taxes. The general equilibrium Laffer curve, *OA'B'C'* lies entirely to the right of the partial equilibrium curve *OABC*.

---

[6] The corporate tax rate is objectionable on many grounds: it discourages the formation of corporations in favor of less efficient entities; because it is progressive it encourages the proliferation of small corporations for tax rather than economic reasons; it discourages equity finance in lieu of bond finance (because interest is deductible from pre-tax profits); it is asymmetrical, with inadequate allowance for carrying forward past losses; it drives a wedge between the marginal efficiency of capital and the rate of interest, distorting the choice between present and future consumption; it creates double taxation on equity capital income (because capital income is also taxed at the personal income tax rate).

[7] A fall in the tax rate on corporate profits raises the capitalized value of future profits and therefore the price of capital goods, which induces a shift of resources into the capital goods industry, increasing investment; it therefore raises the marginal efficiency of capital.

GRAPH 4

GENERAL AND PARTIAL EQUILIBRIUM LAFFER CURVES

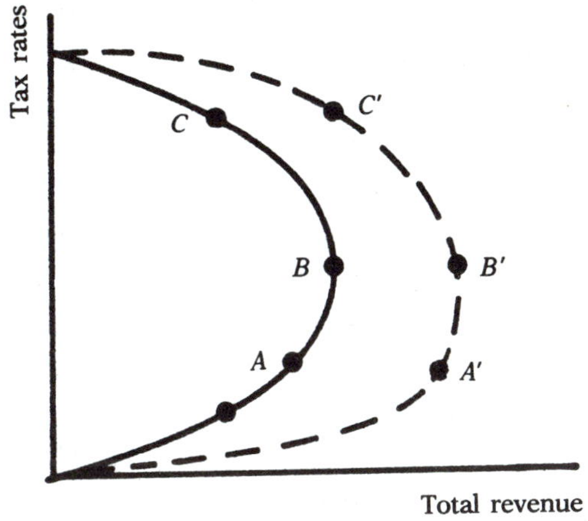

Because of the interdependence among tax rates — each tax affects the revenue from both its own and other taxes — there is a general equilibrium problem associated with finding the maximum revenue position. Tax revenues in general would be maximized only by adjusting each tax rate until, at the maximum point, small changes in either direction would not change total revenue[8].

---

[8] The importance of the relationship between tax rates and tax revenues looms larger when it is generalized to allow for possible changes in output and employment. Just as there is a separate Laffer curve for each tax, so there is a distinct curve for each level of employment. A tax cut can help to reduce a budget deficit even in the context of a Keynesian model. In conventional Keynesian theory, a tax cut results in a multiplied increase in income and therefore in a smaller reduction in tax revenue than if income had stayed constant. If, however, the tax reduction stimulates investment, a budget deficit may actually be reduced, or a budget surplus be increased, by a tax cut.

The application of Laffer curve analysis is not confined to the conventional tax system. It applies also to the revenue obtainable from the inflationary "tax". Real government proceeds from printing money are maximized at that rate of inflation at which the elasticity of real balances with respect to the rate of monetary expansion is unity, a proposition which, in slightly different form, was first demonstrated by Martin J. Bailey in his 1956 paper, «The Welfare Effects of Inflationary Finance», *Journal of Political Economy*, 64.

The same logic applies to bond finance: at sufficiently high levels of the public debt and of the budget deficit, additional debt finance will sink bond prices; revenue from bond finance is maximized at the point where the falling value of bonds sold by the government is just equal to the reduction in bonds sold. This point provides an extreme upper limit on the feasible budget deficit.

Of course it is not government's business to maximize revenue! The legitimate function of government is to maximize social welfare. This requires a comparison of the marginal social utility of government expenditure with its marginal private utility. There is a strong presumption that the tax rate that maximizes social welfare is lower than that which maximizes government revenue[9].

The significance of these relationships has I believe been lost on economic policy makers, particular in the Bush and Clinton administrations, and on many economists. The best policy to balance the budget is to achieve a higher rate of economic growth.

3. - Conclusions

Nordhaus completes his tour of the policy domain with "two striking conlusions". I disagree with both of them. His first conclusion is that "it would require a political leader who is either brave, foolish or ignorant to undertake a massive deficit reduction program in the face of a stagnant economy". On the contrary, I believe that a stagnant economy presents an opportunity for deficit reduction by closing the gap between potential and actual output. The mechanism for closing the gap is to increase investment by increasing its after-tax profitability. How can this be achieved?

The answer lies in a completely different strategy from that adopted by the Clinton administration in 1993. The Clinton strategy is to raise taxes now and hope that Alan Greenspan, the Chairman of the Board of Governors of the Federal Reserve System, will bail the economy out by an expansionary monetary policy. I doubt that Greenspan will be so foolish, but even if he were, the strategy would not work. Whenever this policy mix has been tried — the first two years of the Kennedy administration and all four years of the Carter administration are the best examples — it has failed.

The correct strategy is to give primary emphasis to increasing

[9] The equation of marginal cost with marginal revenue necessary to achieve the maximum revenue tax violates the condition of a welfare optimum, so that if government has maximized revenue from a particular tax it has raised the tax rate above its optimal rate.

economic growth and achieving full employment. There are four steps I would recommend to further these ends, in decreasing order of urgency: 1) reduce the capital gains tax to 15%; 2) reduce the corporation income tax to 25%; 3) ease depreciation allowances; 4) reinstate the investment tax credit.

These changes would have an electric effect on the stock market and the cost of capital. They would promote reinvestment of corporate profits and increase investment, employment, output and growth. It would render unnecessary a shift to an inflationary monetary policy and enable an expansion of employment without reigniting inflation. In short, it would shift whatever the Phillips curve is meant to be downward and to the left.

I have different reasons for disagreeing with Nordhaus' second conclusion, that "the losses from lack of coordination, and the potential gains from coordination, are extremely high". In theory, with perfect knowledge, perfect coordination should be better than imperfect coordination. An all-knowing commissar in a socialist economy would opt for perfect coordination. But such a world does not exist and I for one hope it never does exist. I think it is better for the monetary authorities to be assigned primary responsibility for either fixing the exchange rate (as in the exchange rate mechanism of the EMS) or stabilizing the inflation rate at the targeted level. I prefer the German system with a quasi-independent Bundesbank (the Minister of Finance still has official control over the exchange rate), which is assigned the responsibility for inflation, or the quasi-independence of the Federal Reserve Board, responsible to Congress.

Here again, my views are conditioned by my concept of relationships in the economy. If I believed in Nordhaus' fixed Phillips curve model, I would probably share his views. But I believe his model has validity over a period that is too short to be useful for macroeconomic policy, and that it gives seriously misleading conclusions capable of great damage in the long run.

Finally, Nordhaus' pessimistic conclusion, that we are probably doomed to a "high-deficit, low-investment equilibrium out of which no politician dares break for fear of the twin evils of political economy-economic recession and electoral defeat" may be close to the mark if the Clinton administration continues on its current path.

However, I am more optimistic. I believe here that the political cycle which Nordhaus analyzes could in fact come to our rescue. I would therefore like to make a prediction. It is that the history of the Kennedy-Johnson administration will repeat itself in the Clinton administration. If you remember, Kennedy had campaigned on a promise to get the country moving again. But for two agonizing years, following the so-called neo-classical synthesis policy mix of easy money and tight budget, the economic situation worsened. At the end of two years, Kennedy dramatically announced the reversal of the policy mix to tight money to protect the balance of payments and a tax cut to spur economic growth. The result was a politician's dream, matched two decades later (but under flexible exchange rates) by the Reagan repeat performance.

I believe history will repeat itself here. By the end of 1994, facing either continued stagnation or the prospect of a new recession, Clinton will see that his re-election chances in 1996 depend upon a thriving economy. This highly-intelligent, gifted president has shown himself to be adaptable and is unlikely to remain for long wedded to a failing policy. By the end of 1994, therefore, I predict that he will tell his economic advisers to take another look at the policies that proved to be successful for the Kennedy-Johnson administrations and for the Reagan administrations and prepare a plan to put his with these successful administrations. Tax cuts on business, the motor of the economy, combined with stabilizing monetary policy, are the twin pillars on which Clinton's economic success will have to rest.

The Role of Legislation and Labour Policies in Explaining Structural Unemployment

Carlo Dell'Aringa
Università Cattolica «Sacro Cuore», Milano

Introduction

The purpose of the present paper is to review some of the recent literature regarding unemployment and the functioning of the labour market. The perspective adopted in the paper assigns to the labour market and to its functioning the role of reabsorbing excess unemployment. The main arguments are essentially based on a comparative analysis of the phenomenon in question; in particular, we compare the aspects which characterise European unemployment with those that characterise unemployment in the other major areas of the industrialised world.

The paper is divided into three sections, as follows: the first describes the growth of unemployment and summarises the main explanations for the phenomenon. The second deals with those problems concerned with the institutional setting which introduce frictions in the functioning of the market mechanism. The third section reviews other political-institutional factors which, unlike those mentioned above, can facilitate and accelerate the adjustment process towards lower unemployment rates.

1. - The Nature of Unemployment

Conceptually, unemployment can be split into a cyclical and a trend component. The cyclical component is generally considered as falling within the field of action of aggregate demand policies, while the trend component generally concerns structural measures. There exist different criteria for splitting the two components. Namely, one can use the Beveridge curve approach (where data exists), or else the relation between unemployment and production capacity utilisation, or finally the (short-term) relation between unemployment and the acceleration of inflation. What one currently observes for a series of countries, (OECD [8])*, is that the unemployment rate associated respectively to a given job-vacancy rate level, or to a given production capacity utilisation rate, or alternatively to a stable (short-term) inflation, has increased significantly in the last 10-15 years. This series of countries includes almost all European countries. On the contrary, in Japan and in the US, the growth of the trend component of the unemployment rate has been considerably lower, if not almost absent. Univariate analyses of historical series of unemployment provide similar results: in European countries unemployment displays only a slight tendency to return, after a shock, to its initial level. The trend in unemployment is usually interpreted as an effect of structural factors which are present in the economic system. If this is true — as it appears to be — we need to understand the role and nature of structural factors.

One, useful, conceptual framework for classifying the role and nature of these factors draws on the concept of equilibrium unemployment defined as that rate of unemployment which persists in the equilibrium of the macroeconomic system and, in particular, under conditions of stable inflation (in the long term). When adopting such a framework, it is important to ask (and attempt to reply) whether the increase in the trend of unemployment in European countries is a state of equilibrium or simply represents a slow adjustment process towards equilibrium conditions.

---

* *N.B*: the numbers in square brackets refer to the Bibliography at the end of the paper.

It should be clarified at this point that no clear and definite response has yet been provided to this question.

Neither can this paper offer such a response. We would simply point out that the empirical evidence produced by much of the literature on the issue would appear to exclude that the increasing trend in European unemployment produces an increase in the equilibrium level of unemployment. We shall refer on the one hand to those studies that attempt to measure the evolution of structural unemployment over time (due to mismatch) and on the other hand to those works that attempt to identify the role played by unemployment in the wage determination process. With regard to the former, the increase in mismatch would not appear to account for the strong increase in unemployment and able to explain above all the difference in the increase in unemployment experienced by various European countries (Padoa Schioppa [9]). With respect to the latter, it should be borne in mind that in estimated wage equations for OECD countries (using either the standard Phillips curve specification or the real wage specification) the actual level of unemployment almost always shows an important statistically significant role. For many countries, the change in unemployment is also significant, however it is the level of unemployment that is often the dominant variable and this empirical result, together with that quoted above (concerning "mismatch") would appear to indicate that the growth in equilibrium unemployment (granting that such phenomenon exists) is not the most important factor in explaining the increase in actual unemployment. The level of the latter, though high, continues to play an important role as a "discipline device" for the dynamics of nominal and, above all, real wages.

Is it therefore possible that the situation we are observing is essentially a disequilibrium state and that we are merely experiencing a slow and difficult process of adjustment of European labour markets? I would stress that it is not certain that this is the case, even though there are solid grounds for believing so. If it is the case, we should understand where and when this process ran into difficulties. There are two possibilities that should be taken into consideration.

The first is that the process ran into difficulties during the wage moderation phase — i.e., when wages were reacting to unemployment. The second is that the process jammed in the phase following wage moderation — i.e., when unemployment was recovering, that is to say when labour demand was reacting to improved supply conditions (represented by lower labour costs).

2. - Factors Slowing Down the Adjustment Process

Until a few years ago, most of the existing literature on these issues concentrated its attention on the stickiness of nominal and real wages (Dell'Aringa [5]). It was shown that, in general, the persistence of unemployment was negatively correlated across-countries with the coefficient (elasticity) of wage dynamics *vis-à-vis* unemployment. The latter was largely the result of the oil shocks and in this respect European economies had shown their feeble capacity to adjust quickly. The empirical evidence was supported by an important explanation of this phenomenon which argued that the degree of centralisation in the wage bargaining process regulated the degree of flexibility of nominal and (above all) real wages *vis-à-vis* unemployment (Tarantelli [10]).

This explanation may still be considered valid, but I do not believe that it can provide a comprehensive explanation in view of the high and growing unemployment rates of recent years. We should first bear in mind that wage moderation is a reality (dating back many years) for a number of countries (above all European countries). If we take for example the labour share of income on value-added, we can see that this share significantly decreased during the 1980s, in particular: in France, Germany, Denmark, Ireland, the Netherlands and Spain. These countries experienced, in the same period, a strong increase in unemployment. We should therefore conclude that the high and growing unemployment produced the expected result, namely strong wage moderation. The argument is not conclusive. There are undoubtely many reasons which can explain why the functional distribution of income is subject to changes and it is not certain that a fall in the labour share can be attributed to wage moderation alone. Other factors (related to tecnology and the market structure) can help to explain the phenomenon observed. It is however a stylised fact that almost all and *only* European countries experienced this phenomenon. If we were to apply the concept of "real wage gap" adopted until recently in some of the most influential studies on these issues (Bruno-Sachs [2]) we would come to the conclusion that in most of the Eureopean countries the situation was completely reversed during the 1980s with respect to the previous decade when they were ranked in the first places with respect to the "positive real gap".

We would add a further consideration concerning the degree of centralisation in the wage bargaining as an explanation of unemployment. We would point out that Scandinavian countries (led by Sweden) are quickly losing places in the list of virtuous countries. In Sweden, for example, unemployment has more than doubled with respect to the level prevalent until few years ago. The explanation of the low Swedish unemployment rate, which was based in large part on the "corporatist" industrial relations model of the Nordic countries, should now be at least carefully reconsidered (Calmfors [4]).

Without denying that wage stickiness may still play an important role in explaining the low speed of the adjustement process, it is obvious that more attention should be paid to the factors and reasons that can explain the inertia of labour demand when faced with changed and more favourable conditions of labour costs. All countries have experienced turbulence of one kind or another following the oil shocks; examples of such turbulence which has affected the labour market include the consequences of increased international competition, the effects of technical progress (both factors have influenced the structure of labour demand). All countries have experienced "turbulence" of this nature. Yet, while some countries have managed to react creating millions of replacement and additional jobs (i.e., the USA and Japan), European countries show a different performance, they have created few replacement jobs and despite the lower demographic pressure on the labour market, unemployment has been increasing disproportionately. It should be said that there are also social and institutional aspects, related to the characteristics of social legislation and active labour policy, which can diminuish the level, of flexibility of employment and the capacity of labour demand to react quickly to the improved conditions in terms of lower wages. It is not the scope of the present paper to summarise the extensive literature that exists on this subject. We shall however indicate which structural factors may have played an important role. We shall attempt to provide a list of them (albeit not in order of importance).

First and foremost there are those factors that influence labour supply and the job-search activities. Unemployment benefit is one of these factors. The generosity and duration of these benefits prolong the time spent searching for a job. Among empirical studies, those showing greater effects are "cross-country" studies. It is clear why this is so: these studies capture not only the effects on individual behaviour, but also the macroeconomic effects which go through the wage determination process. Income support for the unemployed reduces the advantage for workers and unions of accepting a wage moderation policy. A similar effect is produced by measures intended at reducing the labour supply: early-retirement and reductions in working hours are the most common examples. The freezing of labour supply slows down the adjustment process. It only affects the symptoms of the illness and not its roots. This problem is particularly serious in Belgium and the Netherlands.

There are also institutional factors (perhaps more important given the present situation) which influence the behaviour of firms. Among these we can list those related to legislation and union behaviour which tend to protect existing jobs. These factors are generally referred to as hiring and firing costs.

It can be stressed that protecting unemployment, or better, ensuring stable employment, entails important externalities. It is also an opportunity that workers and firms often exploit to the best. This is the case in several countries, and Japan is one of them. However, it is equally true that in many countries, above all European countries (and particularly in Italy) this type of protection is viewed by companies as a constraint. It is an obstacle that is circumvented whenever possible and, when not possible, represents a source of increased costs. In particular, it makes firms more careful and selective when hiring new workers. This behaviour (which is typical of big and medium-sized companies rather than small companies) determines a lower adjustment process for employment levels (Bentolilla-Bertola [1]), and hence can explain, to a certain extent, the persistence of unemployment.

There are also factors of an institutional nature which, while not directly affecting the behaviour of workers and firms, do affect the functioning of the labour market. We would mention in particular: labour legislation and collective bargaining which tend to reduce wage differentials. These measures take different forms and range from minimum wages (as in France) to collective bargaining (as in Germany and Italy) which tend to reduce wage differentials. Obviously the rigidity of wage structures reduces factors mobility and slows down the adjustment process. This is likely to be more relevant the larger are the disparities between the unemployment levels of the different categories of workers.

Finally, we would mention the possibility that the factors indicated above interact negatively with each other, aggravating their effects in the labour market. As an example, we would cite the manner in which the effects of minimum wages and job protection legislation combine with each other. Less skilled workers are the most affected: they are excluded from work experience, they become long-term unemployed and at the same time firms become more selective and adopt discriminatory practices towards them. This is the segment of the labour market for which European countries have created the least jobs and it is also the segment in which unemployment has increased the most. To conclude, we would point out that Germany, France, the United Kingdom and Italy are among those countries which experienced a more-than-proportionate increase in long-term unemployment. Italy currently has the dubious honour of having the highest percentage of long-term unemployed.

3. - Active Labour Policies

The labour legislation and policies mentioned above are directed at ensuring equity, but in doing so undermine the system's level of efficiency. In other words (and more precisely), policies for protecting and ensuring minimum standards are directed first and foremost at short-term rather than long-term objectives. One example will suffice: measures to limit dismissals may guarantee relief in the short term but may be harmful in the long term. One cannot reduce the stock of unemployment by limiting the inflow into this stock! Between the two variables (volume of the inflow and stock) does not exist, at least theoretically, a direct functional relation. Rather, across countries, if it does exist, there is a negative empirical relation.

What is to be done? Can labour policy and welfare legislation be transformed so as to eliminate those elements which make the process of unemployment adjustment hazardous? In addition, is it possible to transform them not into an obstacle but rather into a positive factor which will endow the labour market with greater flexibility?

These questions are generally answered by saying that labour policy should not be "passive" but rather "active". How is this to be realised? Below, we summarise the main results of the empirical literature on this matter. Here again, our review is not complete, as it is limited to those contributions which are considered the most important.

As regards the limits of the effects of "passive" measures, it is held that those measures which tend to reduce potential labour supply should be reduced to the minimum, secondly, the system of income supplementation benefits paid to the unemployed and to those worker with jobs at risk should be revised. To this end, it is necessary to reduce the "waste" effect associated to these measures (which prolong the time to find a new job without providing any benefit as regards the quality of the worker-firm match) and fight the frequent abuse of such systems. Combining control with the assistance for workers in their search activity would appear to provide better results (Meyer [6]). An alternative way of reducing moral hazard effects is to internalise the social costs of unemployment (whether total or partial). There are various ways: one is to make workers' representatives and firms responsible for managing available resources. Another way is to adjust workers' contributions to the funds to their actual use of the fund (experience rating).

As regards job protection legislation, it should be relaxed in those countries where it is stronger (Italy, France, Belgium, and to a certain extent Spain). Otherwise firms could be allowed to legally by-pass this obstacle by stipulating short-term job contracts (fixed-time contact, temporary work contract). Where this possibility has been granted (France and Spain), the response on the firm's side has been very positive as regards the creation of additional jobs and in terms of labour demand reacting to the business cycle.

As regards the so-called "active" labour policies, there is a literature (albeit still small) on the assessment of existing shemes, this literature helps identify those measures which may give a useful result (OECD [7]). Active labour policies include measures such as assisting workers to find jobs and firms to find workers. Information collection and diffusion, advice and guidance techniques have improved greatly during recent decades. Additionally there are measures designed to facilitate mobility, training and retraining, youth programmes to facilitate the transition from school to work, employment subsidies, job-creation schemes. In general active labour policies can improve the functioning of the market by making the labour supply more mobile and active, facilitating the process of demand-supply matching and limiting to the maximum long-term unemployment.

A few general conclusions can be drawn from these assessment studies. The most promising measures from the point of view of results (and also as regards costs) are those in the fields of: 1) job search assistance; 2) the transition from school to work; 3) the retraining of employed workers, above all of those workers who are at risk of losing their jobs.

Employment subsidies and direct job creation would appear to have produced much results which are less significant if not discouraging in some cases.

It should not be forgotten that the so-called active labour policies also have some problems. It is often said, for example, that they can result in deadweight costs (as they are inefficient) or substitution and/or displacement effects (as they favour some workers while damaging others). It should also be borne in mind that active policies can have the same negative effect on the wage determination process wich is usually attributed to "passive" policies, i.e., they can strengthen the power of insiders during the bargaining process and simultaneously reduce the "competition" effect of outsiders. In fact, we cannot exclude that active policies amy also, in one way or another, "freeze" the labour supply which will in turn slow down the adjustment process. Research on this phenomenon started with the case of Sweden and north European countries (which were the reference model for active policies) (Calmfors [4]) and is of considerable interest as far as the possible developments it opens for both research and reflection on this issue. If the results of these early studies are confirmed for these and other countries, we would have to conclude that the role of the so-called active policies should be thoroughly re-evaluated.

Conclusions

The purpose of the present paper is not to present strong statistical evidence in favour of one particular aspect of unemployment, but rather to survey and summarise the results of a rich, though not conclusive, empirical literature on the possible nature of unemployment in Europe. The conclusions are therefore based on a series of assumptions supported by the existing empirical evidence and by preliminary interpretation of that evidence.

The high level of unemployment in Europe would appear to be the result of a slow process of adjustment rather than the physicological and structural growth of its permanent component. The adjustment process pertains not so much and solely to the realisation of wage moderation which, in some countries in particular, would appear to have been operating some time now (in Italy, more recently), but rather to the lack of growth in labour demand *vis-à-vis* the reduction in the level of labour costs. The reduced employment flexibility-elasticity may derive, to a large extent, from institutional factors (labour legislation, labour policies) which on the one hand make firms careful and selective in their hiring practices and, on the other, isolate the workers from the market, reducing their labour supply and their job-searching activities.

We have to find a way of moderating these factors without excessively abandoning the objectives of equity for which the aforementioned measures appear to be pursued. In any case, the trade-off between equity and efficiency (to the extent that it exists) can be improved, transforming labour policy measures from passive into active.

Finally, the institutional set-up which regulates wage determination does not appear as important as in the past in promoting wage moderation. It may be important for guaranteeing the necessary flexibility of wage differentials. This flexibility has, to date, been little exploited in Europe to readjust the imbalances (of various nature) of the labour market. This may be one of the main factors which explain the difference between the performance, in terms of job creation, of the USA and that of the European countries.

BIBLIOGRAPHY

[1] BENTOLILLA S. - BERTOLA G., «Firing Costs and Labour Demand: How Bad is Eurosclerosis?», *Review of Economic Studies*, n. 57, 1990.

[2] BRUNO M. - SACHS L., *The Economics of Worldwide Stagflation*, Oxford, Basil Blackwell, 1985.

[3] CALMFORS L. - NYMOEN R., «Real Wage Adjustment and Employment Policies in the Nordic Countries», *Economic Policy*, n. 11, 1990.

[4] CALMFORS L., *Centralization of Wage Bargaining and Macroeconomic Performance: a Survey*, mimeo, Paris, OECD, 1993.

[5] DELL'ARINGA C., «Il mercato del lavoro italiano nel contesto internazionale», in MICOSSI S. - VISCO I. (eds.), *Inflazione, concorrenza e sviluppo*, Bologna, il Mulino, 1993.

[6] MEYER B.D., «Policy Lessons from the US Unemployment Insurance Experiments», NBER, *Working Paper* n. 4197, 1992.

[7] OECD, *Evaluating Labour Market and Social Programmes*, Paris, 1991.

[8] ——, *High and Persistent Unemployment: Assessment of the Problem and Its Causes*, mimeo, Paris, 1993.

[9] PADOA SCHIOPPA F., *Mismatch and Labour Mobility*, Cambridge, Cambridge University Press, 1991.

[10] TARANTELLI E., *Economia politica del lavoro*, Torino, UTET, 1986.

IV - ECONOMETRIC MODELS

How to Decrease Unemployment

Olivier J. Blanchard
MIT, Cambridge (Mass.) and NBER

I do not share the view which has dominated in this volume, that nothing short of a dramatic and painful overhaul of the supply side of our economies will reduce unemployment. I believe unemployment in Western Europe can be reduced, can be reduced to low levels, and that this need not involve much pain.

Let me present my argument in four steps. The first one goes back in time, to the origins of the increase in unemployment in the late 1970s and early 1980s. It is very important to go back, because doing so disqualifies a number of currently fashionable explanations, or at least makes them much harder to defend. The second turns to the question of why unemployment has persisted at such a high level for so long, now for more than a decade. The third asks, in the light of my diagnosis for both the increase and the persistence, whether there is room for a decrease in unemployment. The fourth articulates the specific measures which should be taken now, as well as the measures which might be taken but which, to my mind, are not of the essence in decreasing unemployment in the short and medium run.

1. - The Origins of the Increase in Unemployment

Let me turn to the origins of the increase in unemployment. As you all know, unemployment crept up in the 1970s, from the first oil shock on. But the major increase in unemployment was actually quite dramatic and quite concentrated in time. It usually took place for each country within two to four years, and for the group of countries that comprises the EC, between 1978 and 1983. That's an important point. The way unemployment became high is not that it crept upwards from 2% to 10% at the rate of 0,5% per year, but that is basically doubled in the span of a over few years to reach roughly the level that we see today.

What is at the origin of this very sharp increase in unemployment? I think the answer is uncontroversial: there was a change in regime in the early eighties. There was a change in the way that governments perceived their role in the economy. Most governments became convinced, and rightly so, that less government intervention would be a good thing. This was half of it. The other half was their perception that one of the preconditions to allow market forces to work well, and for price signals not to be contaminated by distortions and noise, was to reduce inflation. Measures were taken to reduce the role of the State, to improve the functioning of many markets, to reduce various types of barriers; on the macro front, there was an all-out attack on inflation. This was done in the conventional way, namely, by a sharp increase in nominal rates, and an even sharper rise in real rates as inflation was going down. This part of the overall story is the easy part to tell.

2. - The Persistence of High Unemployment

Let me turn to the second step, the persistence of high unemployment. The widely held expectation was that, once inflation was rooted out of the system — something which was mostly accomplished, depending on the country, between 1983 and 1985 — we would see a gradual process along which the unemployment rate would decrease to something like the pre-monetary contraction unemployment rate, 4 or 5% at most. We did not see that. The question is why.

While this is admittedly post facto, I think that there is now little doubt as to what happened. Actual unemployment became, over time, "structural". There is a strong interaction between actual unemployment and structural unemployment: through a variety of mechanisms, high actual unemployment steadily turns into structural unemployment; put another way, the pressure of high unemployment on inflation steadily decreases with time. Before I turn to what these mechanisms are and how they work, let me register my profound dislike for the word "structural" here. Once current unemployment has been defined as "structural", there is only a short step to the conclusion that demand policies cannot be used. As I shall argue later, I do not believe that. Therefore, I very strongly resist the term. I shall use instead "equilibrium unemployment" which is not great, but is a less loaded word.

What are the channels through which high actual unemployment becomes equilibrium unemployment? Many of us have worked on this question in the last decade. Snower and Karanassou presented some of the answers from their work with Assar Lindbeck. I am not sure that we have all the answers, but I think we have many of them.

High unemployment leads to a change in the distribution of unemployment durations across workers. When unemployment is low, average duration is low; when unemployment is high, average duration typically increases, and the proportion of the long-term unemployed increases. This is very much a mechanical effect of the level of unemployment on the distribution of durations. One of the very interesting facts given Llewellyn in his paper is that, at this point in Europe, more than half of the unemployed have been unemployed for more than a year, a number which is orders of magnitude higher than the corresponding number in the United States. So, high unemployment leads to a higher proportion of long-term unemployed.

This in turn affects labor supply. The long-term unemployed adapt to unemployment. They give up looking for work, because they basically find the probability of getting work too small to justify intensive search. They find ways of surviving, very often by relying on the other earners in the family. They return home. The 1980s have been characterized by an increase in the proportion of teenagers and young workers living at home; I suspect this comes not from an improvement in family relations, but rather by the need to actually get free rent. In short, people adjust — not happily, but they adjust — to unemployment. And, although they might be formally looking for work, and therefore be classified as unemployed, many no longer effectively are, and, therefore, they put very little pressure on wages.

On the labor demand side, firms look at the long-term unemployed as less employable than the short-term unemployed. From the point of view of firms, this may not be a major decision. The evidence is that, when firms have no choice and just have long-term unemployed coming to fill a vacancy, they will hire the long-term unemployed. But when, in a depressed labor market, vacancies generate a very large number of applications, firms need simple ways of ranking people. One simple way, once you have accounted for the objective characteristics of workers, is to rank according to the length of time for which people have been out of work. Other things equal, someone who has been out of work for a longer time is likely to be slightly less employable than somebody who has not, either because of intrinsic charcteristics that the market has recognized, or just because work habits have deteriorated and this person might be slightly harder to train. As a result, firms rend to hire the short-term unemployed first and the long-term unemployed next — unless governments have explicit programs for the hiring of the long-term unemployed, which exist in a number of countries.

This clearly is tough on the long term unemployed; but why is this relevant to the macro question of unemployment persistence? Because it implies that if you are still employed, you are much less scared about your own labor market prospects than the aggregate unemployment number would suggest: you know that, if you were to lose your job, you would actually be ahead of a number of a people in the labor market, namely, all the long-term unemployed. To the extent that firms have a policy of hiring first people who have been out of work for a short time, your prospects as an employed worker are actually much better than the prospects of the typical unemployed worker, who has been unemployed for a longer period of time. Indeed, one fascinating number we unearthed with Summers a few years back was from a poll of English workers, in which they were asked what they thought their probability of finding a job would be, were they to be laid off. The question was asked twice. It was asked in the 1970s, when the labor market was relatively tight and the probability of finding a job was relatively high. It was asked in 1985, at a time when things were terrible in England and when the average exit rate from unemployment was extremely low. The probability of finding a job easily, as perceived by employed workers, was no lower in 1985 than in 1978... Part of it was probably just an inability to fully understand the facts of life. But some of it was probably due to the fact that they thought of the long-term unemployed as no competition and, therefore, did not care much about the high aggregate rate. As a result, the pressure of unemployment in wages, the willingness to accept wage concessions, was relatively small.

These factors point a more general and more diffuse effect at work here, namely that society, in its many dimensions, also adapts to high persistent unemployment. When unemployment and the proportion of long-term unemployed becomes high, society is compelled, mostly through the political process, to actually make life bearable for those who are long-term unemployed. Through unemployment benefits, safety nets, real or pseudo- training programs, governments basically make sure that people do not starve. This is obviously the humane thing to do. It is the normal response both from a normative and a positive point of view to high unemployment. Nevertheless, it has very much the same effect as the factors I talked about earlier, namely that, by making unemployment bearable, it decreases the pressure on wages. This is not to say it should not be done, just to explain why the effects of high unemployment on wages decrease with time. Summers and I have explored a twist on this argument, which we think is empirically important, and that we have called fiscal increasing returns. As unemployment increases, the tax base shrinks. This forces governments to increase taxes on the remaining employed workers, which goes very much in the same direction of decreasing labor demand.

All these factors lead to the conclusion that equilibrium unemployment, rather than being constant, tends to adjust over time in the direction of actual unemployment. And while the amplitude of the movement in equilibrium unemployment is unprecedented — at least during the post-war period —, it is not a new phenomenon, and maybe we should have been less surprised to see it at work in Europe in the 1980s than we were. It has been a running joke in the United States, long before there was a slump in Europe, that the equilibrium, or the so-called natural rate of unemployment was the average of the last three years' actual rate. That remark was first made, I believe, by

Solow in the 1960s and has proven fairly reliable as an econometric finding since.

My conclusions, so far, are thus that the initial shock was mostly due to demand, and the fact that unemployment has remained so high is due to the dynamics of labor markets themselves. We may want to call these factors which cause persistence "supply factors", as long as we understand what they are and are not.

3. - Factors Behind the Scene

I now come to the third point, which is: if what was initially a demand contraction has indeed transformed into an increase in equilibrium unemployment, what can we do about unemployment today?

The first question to tackle is the following. Suppose that my diagnosis is indeed right, that, at the margin, unemployment increased initially because of lower demand and has remained high because of the persistence mechanisms I have just discussed. This does not exclude that other factors have come into play, behind the scene, and that as a result, Europe cannot decrease its unemployment rate below some high level. Here there is a long list of candidates, many of which have been discussed in this volume. Let me take a few.

There has clearly been, in Europe and elsewhere, a steady shift in labor demand away from unskilled workers towards skilled workers. It has been documented at length in all countries, and was summarized very ably by Fitoussi-Zoega in their paper for this volume. This could imply that, because of minimum wage legislations, or other social or institutional restrictions on the spread of the wage distribution, the unemployment rate of unskilled workers cannot be lowered very much. I see the Fitoussi-Zoega paper as looking at that question. I read it as saying that, somewhat surpisingly, there is very little relation between the minimum wage in relation to the average wage, and the level of unemployment across countries. Even more surprisingly, there does not seem to be much relation between the minimum wage and the unemployment rate of young, unskilled workers. I find this result very striking, given my strong belief that the minimum wage, which might be justified on other grounds, is probably a bad thing for the employment of young and unskilled workers.

It is true that high unemployment in Europe is associated with very high unemployment of unskilled workers; it is often associated with high unemployment of young people as well, with exceptions which come from the specific market institutions of the country. Should we conclude from the high unemployment rate of unskilled workers that they are indeed unemployable? Surely not. The way labor markets work is basically through up- and down-grading. When unemployment is high, firms, instead of hiring somebody with a high school degree, hire somebody with a college degree, because they are available. This goes all the way down the education and skill ladder. The people who end up suffering the most from unemployment are the unskilled. It does not say anything per se about their employability.

In short, it would be a serious mistake to conclude from the high rate of unemployment among unskilled workers that there is a deep structural problem here. There is surely a long run problem. The shift in relative demand requires either a shift in relative wages and an increase in income inequality, which may be socially hard to accept in Western Europe, or the training of unskilled workers, something which is not easy to achieve. This problem is of the essence for the next ten to twenty years. But it is not the source of unemployment today, nor are training and education policies the way to solve the unemployment problem in the short and the medium run.

Another set of factors which has been discussed at length, at this conference and elsewhere, comes under the heading "labor market rigidities". It holds that Europe has deep labor market rigidities and, that therefore, it is inconceivable to decrease the unemployment rate unless and until those are fully removed. I strongly disagree.

I think we have to be very careful here. The labor market is not a market for potatoes. Workers value their wage, but they also value the security of their job. A well functioning labor market is a market which finds the right balance between protection of workers and efficiency, not a market which removes all protection. What is now fashionable to call "rigidities" is a remarkable set of institutions which emerged after the war in Europe in order to protect workers.

Designed in a period of strong growth, it was quite viable then. Now growth has decreased. Foreign competition is higher. Uncertainty facing firms is higher. And it is clear that the package of insurance and job protection which can be offered by firms has to change. It is clear that firms cannot promise life-time employment. It is clear that firms have to have the ability to fire workers if demand conditions warrant it.

At the same time, it is utterly crazy to think that less protection is always better. Europe has to find the right mix for the new environment. Tremendous movement was made in the right direction in the 1980s. There are many more flexible contracts, part-time contracts, fixed term contracts. I am not convinced that more needs to be done. I think the burden of the proof is on those who believe that protection is still excessive. So far, I have heard slogans, but no evidence. We should never be slaves to intellectual fashions, and this one strikes me as one of the most dangerous to come along in a long time: it is socially divisive, painful on those who suffer from reduced protection. We had better make sure that such remedies are needed before we use them.

In short, I see no solid argument for the notion that, short of drastic supply measures, unemployment must remain very high. I am quite sure Europe cannot return to the 2 or 3% rates of the 1960s. There have been too many changes in the labor market. The amount of reallocation of labor requires a higher rate of unemployment than in those years. But to put numbers on things, 6% strikes me as a perfectly reasonable goal.

4. - The Measures to Be Taken

How do we get there? Even if my diagnosis is right that high equilibrium unemployment comes from an initial demand shock and labor market dynamics rather than ridigities and such, can the process work in reverse?

One can think of good arguments for why it may not. Think, for example, of a story — which I do not believe but which is logically consistent — in which high unemployment leads long-term unemployed to permanently lose their skills or work ethic. Think of the analogy to drinking. People may not be predisposed to take to drinking. But, if by accident, they do and get addicted, it is hard to get them to stop. In that case, the fact that it is the history of actual unemployment that led to high equilibrium unemployment is no great blessing. Nothing short of the unemployment equivalent of a massive "Alcoholics Anonymous" program is needed to get out of high unemployment. And, like "Alcoholics Anonymous", these programs do not always work.

Thus, what matters here is the exact nature of the mechanism which led to high equilibrium unemployment. Is it the case that the people who got discouraged can turn around and become active again when the labor market turns around? This is a difficult question. Once again, we cannot pretend to know the answer for sure. But we have bits and pieces to go on.

We have bits and pieces about the behavior and the productivity of long-term unemployed workers once they are hired by firms. The evidence there is is that, after a while, they perform well. The loss of skills or work ethic does not appear irreversible. This should not be terribly surprising, as we are talking mostly about workers who are unskilled. What they need to learn or re-learn, can often be learned in a week, or a month at most.

The other piece of evidence is more macro-economic in nature, and comes from the rapid output expansion in the UK in the late 1980s. The point is not to advocate that other countries follow the UK lead. It is clear — and was actually clear at the time — that the expansion was too rapid; the result was not catastrophic, but was higher inflation, and one more episode of UK stop and go policies. The point is that we can learn from what happened in the labor market during that expansion. Is it for example the case that the short-term unemployed got the new jobs, and that the long-term unemployed remained unemployed? No. Somewhat to my surprise, I found, when looking at the data, that, as activity picked up, the exit rates from unemployment did not depend very much on unemployment duration. In the expansion, the long-term unemployed actually got jobs at nearly the same rate as those who had been unemployed for less time.

This suggests that the problem is that there are not enough jobs, not that the unemployed are unable to fill them.

Thus, my assessment of that part of the evidence is that, although long-term unemployment surely will leave some permanent scars, much of the damage is reversible, and relatively quickly. An increase in the demand for labor can decrease actual and equilibrium unemployment, although one cannot promise that this will happen without transitory wage pressure, and some transitory increase in inflation.

This takes us to the last question. What actual measures should be taken to increase the demand for labor? And here, in contrast to Llewellyn, I believe that there is a magic bullet: aggregate demand. The problem is that the magic bullet is awfully hard to fire. The government has instruments which affect aggregate demand, more or less reliably; but these instruments have to serve other functions as well, and aggregate demand moves a whole lot apart from government interventions. Indeed, most of the movements in aggregate demand have nothing to do with policy. Policy is, at best, able to add here or subtract there.

What can and should governments do? Governments have three main macrotools, fiscal policy, monetary policy, and words. Let's look at them in turn.

I think that, for the time being, we have reached the limits of fiscal policy. I fully agree with the proposition that current deficits are primarily the result of high unemployment. They are induced rather than the result of reckless policies. In fact, most of the recent movement has been in the direction of fiscal consolidation, at a given level of activity. But, with current activity being so weak, the deficits are very large. Does this imply that fiscal deficits can be increased? No. What determines the accumulation of debt and the potential medium run perverse effects of fiscal policy is the accumulation of debt, no matter why, induced by activity or not. At this stage I think that the room for fiscal play is very limited. Given current levels of debt, starting levels of deficits, and current real interest rates, the reaction of financial markets to large increases in fiscal deficits, even through tax cuts, is likely to be extremely negative. And we have learned that expectational effects in financial markets can more than offset the direct expansionary effects of fiscal policy.

The second tool, interest rates, should definitely be used. Here the terms of the debate are well understood. I shall not repeat them. At this stage, I believe short real interest rates should be equal to zero, or even negative. Not doing so is wrong. I see no reason, if this is part of a coherent package, for long real rates not to follow suit. Low interest rates are exactly what Europe needs, both for aggregate demand today, and for capital accumulation later. This being said, I do not expect the effects of lower interest rates per se on aggregate demand to be either large, quick, or magic. We have learned that these effects are diffuse and slow. And this takes me to the third tool that governments have, words.

What is of the essence today is to change expectations, to eliminate the gloom. The reason for the current recession, in most countries, is that consumers have become extremely pessimistic; and as long as their expectations, as well as those of firms, remain pessimistic, demand will not pick up very much. The job of governments is to change their own discourse, and to explain and repeat that Europe is fundamentally sound, that fundamentals are favorable, and that the only problem is, basically, *that spending is not there.* After ten years of another discourse, this is a difficult task. I think however that it can be achieved. I believe that, if demand comes, Europe can have sustained growth and low inflation, and much lower unemployment.

This will make it easier to implement the other measures needed to sustain growth. I have indicated my reservations about labor market rigidities and what this may include, but it is clear that improved training and education programs are of fundamental importance for the medium and long run. They may hold the key to eventually getting unemployment down to, say 4%. As such programs are hard to design, we have to work on them now. The important thing is to realize that they have little to do with why unemployment is high today.

The Role of Transfers and Monetary Reform in the Current Economic Slowdown

Bruce C. Greenwald
Columbia University, New York

1. - Introduction

This paper represents an attempt to translate recent developments in macroeconomic theory which are rooted in the microeconomics of imperfect information into current economic diagnoses and policy prescriptions. The theoretical models in question fall under the heading of what Phelps [1] has described as structuralist models in the sense that business cycle phenomena are ascribed fundamentally to real market imperfections, although monetary disturbances may alleviate or exacerbate the macroeconomic impact of these imperfections. Within the broad framework of structuralist explanations, the developments on which we will focus are primarily related to capital market imperfections (and to an extent the broader impact of government policy on the dynamics of firm investment). Finally, within the area of capital market imperfections, the paper will focus on the issue of wealth transfers rather than financial market efficiencies. The final distinction is the one which we wish to emphasize since it is probably the least well-developed aspect of the literature on information-related structural market imperfections.

---

[1] See PHELPS E.S. [10].

N.B.: the numbers in square brackets refer to the Bibliography at the end of the paper.

There is already a considerable body of work which attempts to apply contact based models of imperfect financial information to analyzing current macroeconomic conditions [2]. Applications of this approach typically proceed from the idea that financial institutions, especially banks, which have developed long-term relationship with borrowers and have special informational advantages with respect to those borrowers, may suffer from lack of funds as a result of banking panics, loan losses and/or contractionary monetary policies. As a result the borrower firms in these relationships must turn to other less well informed lenders and in doing so must pay generally higher rates of interest. Empirical attempts to identify the effects in question have focused on either fluctuations in bank credit, on the composition of business borrowing (as business are forced to rely on non-bank sources of financing) or the spreads between safe lending rates and market-based business borrowing rates (as outside investors demand greater returns to replace inside providers of funds) [3]. The difficulties with this approach are both theoretical and empirical. Empirically, the central problem is that these factors are very difficult to separate from traditional interest-rate-based approaches to macroeconomics. Bank credit typically varies in response to changes in the money supply (and hence in the traditional view with interest rates) and, yield spreads often vary directly with interest rates. Indeed, this credit related version of imperfect information macroeconomics is a tale dependent on variations in the cost of funds and, therefore, suffers from the same empirical difficulties as all interest-rate-based business cyclic models; namely that investment does not seem to respond sufficiently to interest rates to account for observed cyclical variations in investment levels. Moreover, in the latest recession in the United States, declines in bank credit do not seem to have played a significant role [4]. Theoretically, the difficulty is that all these models rule out external equity as a source of finance by assumption. In doing so, they introduce an implicit second source of cyclical variability that by itself accounts for many of the same basic phenomena, but whose conse-

---

[2] See most recently BERNANKE B. - LOWN C. [1].

[3] See GERTLER M. - GILCHRIST S. [2], and KASHYAP A. - STEIN J. - WILCOX D. [6].

[4] See BERNANKE B. - LOWN C. [1] and also evidence against this approach in MIRON, 1992.

quences and implications are both different and more far-reaching than those of the contract models themselves [5]. It is this latter family of financial imperfection models that we propose to examine.

Equity levels are critical to firm behavior quite apart from borrowing constraints for a number of reasons. Most importantly, if decision-makers are averse to risk, then equity serves the critical role of absorbing the risk of firm operations and spreading them among a broad base of investors. Assuming that firm-related risks increase with the scale of firm operations, then the alternative means of controlling risk is to adjust the firm's scale of operation by reducing investment, output and employment. Thus, if firms are unable for familiar "lemons" related reasons to issue new equity [6], the levels of internal equity determined by exogenous economic factors (taxes, monetary policy or demand disturbances) will determine the level of risk that firm decision-makers will be prepared to assume and, in turn, the scale of firm operations. An analogy can be drawn in this regard between fluctuations in net household wealth (i.e. household equity) and household purchasing behavior. The effect of equity-related capital market imperfections is to introduce wealth (equity) effects into the theory of firm behaviour in a way in which they have hitherto only been regarded as affecting households. Individual firm levels of activity are determined, not just by the usual marginal trade-offs that the firm faces - i.e., *substitution effects* - but also by changes in overall wealth (equity) - i.e., *income effects*. The importance of this distinction is that while substitution effects depend upon marginal conditions and hence marginal tax rates and the marginal effects of changes in prices, income effects depend upon average conditions and hence average tax rates. In looking for the causes of change in the scale of economic activity, we will focus on the average impacts of tax, regulatory and price changes and the associated transfers that lead to changes in firm equity levels [7].

---

[5] See Greenwald B. - Stiglitz J. - Weiss A. [3] and Stiglitz J. - Weiss A. [10].

[6] See Greenwald B. - Stiglitz J. - Weiss A. [3] or Myers S. - Majlux N. [7].

[7] There are other factors that become important in equity constrained firm models in addition to the wealth (equity) effects described. In particular, government policies that reduce the variability of the economic environment will allow a given equity base to support a greater level of firm activity. Also, the multiplier effects of reductions in firm equity should be kept in mind. As firms reduce activity in response to deteriorations in

In order to address these questions, this paper consists beyond this introduction of four parts. Section 2 describes briefly the family of imperfect information models which underlie the empirical analysis. Section 3 then describes expropriation model of the determination of firm investment and activity with very similar conclusion to those of the imperfect information models. This to done both to reinforce the usefulness of the basic framework for macroeconomic analysis and to avoid confusion between the two models. Section 4 then describes and tests the empirical conclusions of the models by looking at data for the United States. Finally, Section 5 describes their application to analyzing the current worldwide economic slowdown.

2. - Asymmetric Information and Macroeconomic Behavior

Models of imperfect information in financial markets have altered the traditional view of firm behaviour in two important ways. First, if information is asymmetrically distributed between the buyers and sellers of financial instruments, then certain financial markets, such as that for equities, may break down or be severely limited — a form of the lemons problems identified by Akerlof, 1970 — and accordingly the free access to all forms of financing envisaged by Modigliani-Miller many not exist. In loan markets, there may be credit rationing. In these cases financial structure and position matter and affect firm behavior. Second, if information is asymmetrically distributed between those who make decisions (agents) and the theoretical beneficiaries of those decisions (principals), then the reward functions which govern firm decision-making may not have the form of simple valuation maximization assumed in the neoclassical theory. Here we examine the consequences of both kinds of imperfections for the behavior of firms and for macroeconomics.

We will assume for expository purposes that at the beginning of each of T periods (indexed $t=1, \ldots, T$), firms decide on a single

their equity positions, they reduce demand, prices and the profits of other firms. The lower profits of other firms lead to deteriorations in their equity positions and further reductions in output.

variable, i_t, which represents the scale of the firm's activity which we will refer to as investment. For expositional simplicity we will assume that prior investments have fully depreciated so that i_t reppresents the firm's capital stock in period t[8]. The firm's profits during period t are a random function of this level of investment, where

$$\pi_t = \theta_t i_t \equiv \text{operating firm profits in period } t$$

and θ_t is a random return variable with mean $\bar{\theta}_t$. Also at the beginning of period t, the firms has an inherited equity stock a_t and the difference between a_t and the level of investment i_t must be borrowed at a rate of interest r_t. Finally, we assume that the firm is subject to a tax, m_t, which we will assume is independent of profitability, so that there is no confusion of the substitution and income effect of such a tax. The firm's period t profit is, therefore,

$$\theta_t i_t - (i_t - a_t) r_t - m_t$$

and its end-of-period equity position is:

$$a_{t+1} = \theta_t i_t - (i_t - a_t) r_t - m_t + a_t$$

or:

$$a_{t+1} = (\theta_t - r_t) i_t + ((1 + r_t) a_t - m_t) \tag{1}$$

The critical aspect of this equation *(1)* is that a_{t+1} cannot be changed by selling new equity.

We assume that the firm's decision-makers are risk averse and maximize a utility function of the firm's end-of-period equity value, which we will unite as

$$u \{b [(\theta_t - r_t) i_t + (1 + r_t) a_t - m_t] + w\} \tag{2}$$

---

[8] This assumption could be altered at the cost of some complexity but it would not affect the basic implications of the analysis.

where the constants b and w are inserted entirely for expositional convenience. The constraint on equity issue plus appropriate risk aversion will guarantee that an interior optimum level of investment exists.

An objective function similar to that of equation *(2)*, or at least with similar implications, emerges from a wide range of imperfect information models. For example, an entrepreneur with wealth, w, who owns a fraction of his firm b will maximize such a function. But the distinction between owner-managed and professionally managed firms is not especially significant here. When professional managers' actions are unobservable, in effect managers become part owners of their firms' equity capital. The managers' wealth then consists of their holdings, w, plus a fraction b of the terminal equity (profit) of the firm which they are able to appropriate to their own use. Since this latter part of their wealth is non-fungible and since the managers, like owners, should be deterred from issuing shares by informational considerations, managers will be maximizing a function similar to that of equation *(2)*. Alternatively, if agency arrangements are made with risk averse managers and these arrangements are limited for practical reasons to pay-offs which are linear in the profits of the firm, an objective function identical to that of equation *(2)* will emerge, with the variable, b, now representing the slope of the pay-off function and w now being the intercept of the pay-off function plus private wealth. If the firm faces a cost of bankruptcy, we have shown elsewhere that the behavior generated by maximizing expected profits minus an expected cost of bankruptcy (the cost of bankruptcy times the probability of bankruptcy) is similar to that generated by equation *(2)* under plausible restriction on the firm's cost and probability of bankruptcy. Thus, if professional managers are subject to an agency arrangement which either explicitly or informally rewards them with a share of profits, but imposes a large penalty in the event of bankruptcy (i.e., dismissal with a stigma which significantly impairs future earnings), then the resulting objective function produces behavior almost exactly identical with that of equation *(2)*[9], when (as

[9] See GREENWALD B. - STIGLITZ J. [5]. This requires that bankruptcy costs increase with the size of the firm (as they appear to do in practice).

we will assume here) the utility function is characterized by decreasing absolute risk aversion.

In order to see the effect on optimal investment of changes in average tax rates (m_t) or the firm's inherited equity, a_t, we will first consider the case of constant relative risk aversion. Then, the optimal solution to the firm's decision problem will be homogeneous of degree one in the initial wealth variable and can be written:

$$(3) \qquad i^*_t = k\,[(1 + r_t)\, a_t - m_t + w]$$

where k depends on r_t, $\bar{\theta}_t$, the variance of θ_t, and the degree of risk aversion implicit in the utility function (we have assumed without loss of generality that $b = 1$). More generally, if the utility function is characterized by declining absolute risk aversion, i^*_t will be increasing in the wealth term, $(1 + r_t)\, a_t - m_t + w$.

The macroeconomic implications of the microeconomic behavior described by equation *(3)* are straightforward. Aggregating across firms and equating the investment demand with a saving function yields an *IS* curve that shifts to the right as firm wealth, including presumably both equity and the private wealth of entrepreneurs and managers increases. These fluctuations in firm investment will thus translate directly into aggregate fluctuations in overall investment growth and economic activity [10]. The wealth effects involved are, it should be stressed, not overall wealth level for an economy as a whole but rather the wealth of firms and firm decision makers (e.g., manager,). Thus changes in m_t may reflect not only an increase in overall tax level (both present and anticipated future levels), but also shifts in the tax burden between firms and investors on the one hand and households on the other. Similarly changes in inherited equity may occur at the expense of households (given overall levels of output) as well as through overall economic growth. Debt deflation may for example, represent a loss in firm wealth through its impact on future economic activity, but the larger effect is likely to be the

---

[10] A full general equilibriun macroeconomic model of this sort is developed in GREENWALD B. - STIGLITZ J. [5].

associated redistribution of wealth between debtor firms and creditor households.

A further element in this situation is the banking systems. For the purpose of macroeconomic analysis banks may be regarded as maximizing an objective function like equation *(2)* with the i_t^* level of investment being loans to other firms. In this interpretation, the banking sector does not increase investment demand directly, but increases in loan supply generate demand for investment by borrower firms. Thus, if banks are aggregated together with other business firms in the *IS* sector (the *LM* curve would then stand for equilibrium in financial markets which determines a baseline rate of interest), an increase in bank equity would lead to a rightward shift of the *IS* curve in the same way as any other increase in business sector wealth [11]. Bank wealth for a period t is:

$$(r_t - d_t)\, D_t + (1 + r_t)\, a_t - m_t$$

where d_t is the effective rate banks must pay on demand deposit (including the effect of reserve requirements) and D_t is the level of deposits determined by the monetary authorities. In practice, historical restraints on bank competition (e.g. interest rate prohibitions of demand deposits in the United States from the depression through the late 1960s) usually meant that d_t was well below r_t so that expansionary monetary policy lead to significant increases in effective equity (as D_t rose). Elimination of restrictions on competition may, therefore, have greatly reduced the overall level of business sector (including bank) subsidies from households reducing both growth and the potential influence of monetary policy.

A final point is that government policies which reduce economic instability (e.g., particularly after World War II) have an expansionary impact on the level of investment by increasing k in equation *(3)*. The stimulative effect of such stabilizing policies (including those in agriculture) is the principal point which differentiates the imperfect information model of this section from the expropriation model of the next section.

---

[11] See GREENWALD B. - STIGLITZ J. [4].

3. - Dynamic Interactions and Fiscal Policy

An alternative specification which produces implications similar to those of the imperfect information model outlined above is a model of expropriation bargaining and it is worth describing briefly for two reasons. First, in attempting to identify both the underlying determinants of the current economic slowdown and possible remedies, there are a variety of forces at work and establishing the extent to which these forces have similar implications serves to clarify the remaining points at issue. In the case of the dynamics of expropriation, there is an established formal literature applying these models to problems of investment in developing economies [12] and in general theoretical contexts. There is an equally well established informal tradition in which issues of potential government expropriations of *ex post, quasi-rent* returns to fixed investment play an important part. Since the operational considerations involved — average tax rates and wealth transfers — are similar to those in the imperfect information models of the previous section of this paper — it is worth investigating the role that they play in an expropriation context. Second, since the basic factors at work are so similar, especially in contrast to the marginal concerns of more traditional models, there is a danger that the two models — expropriation and imperfect information — will be taken to be identical. They are not identical in their implications (we have already noted the stabilization effects which apply only to the imperfect information model) and it is worth examining the differences in some details to avoid confusion. The key to investment behavior in expropriation models is not the general risks associated with investment, but the fact that fixed investment once in place cannot usually be undone in response to subsequent negative tax and other developments.

Fixed capital once in place is subject to a variety of demands that may reduce the net return to the owners of that capital. Unionized workers may capture any post-investment embedded rents by wage (and employment) demands. Regulatory authorities may impose unanticipated demands for environmental controls, worker safety, train-

[12] See RODRIC D. [9].

ing, job security and/or worker benefits (e.g., day-care). Licensing fees, whether officially sanctioned or not, may be imposed. And a whole range of taxes — beyond merely corporate profit taxes — may be imposed after facilities are in place. These include sales taxes, export fees, value-added taxes, royalties, taxes on critical inputs, payroll taxes and property taxes and fees.

It might be possible to analyze separately the effect of each of these subtractions from the flow of profits that accrues to a particular investment. However, there are several factors that may vitiate the usefulness of any such analysis. First, there ought both in theory and practice to be interactions among the several powers that may lay claim to returns to capital once in place. Both the importance and the complexity of these interactions are likely to complicate any agent-by-agent approach beyond the realm of feasible models. Second, in many cases different instruments may interact in ways that actually simplify the analysis and it is important to take advantage of these simplications. For example, unions may control both wages and employment. In looking at wages alone, the union will be concerned with the employment response of a company and an analysis of employment responses to wage increases will be a necessary part of the overall model. But, if the union can also control employment, the firm's employment decision is irrelevant and the problem is merely one of how to extract as much overall surplus as possible. Third, and finally, the process of determining expropriations — whether by governments or others — is clearly a dynamic one. Firms will react to the potential for expropriation by reducing their exposure; both the level and form of their original investment and the level and form of employment. This possibility will, in turn, affect the behavior of expropriators. However, in trying to react expropriating authorities cannot usually commit themselves to perpetual policies. Unions are democracies (of sorts) and prior wage promises may not be binding on future leaderships. Similar conditions affect governments which cannot promise to fix either tax rates or regulatory impositions once and for all. Thus, time consistency is a critical problem in the overall situation and is difficult to analyze in a detailed partial equilibrium model. At the same time, by ruling out certain contracts, time consistency problems may actually simplify the analysis.

For all these reasons what follows below is a very simple model of the macroeconomic implications of the interaction between a firm and those with a potential claim on the profits of its investment. We will begin by asssuming that firms make investment decisions at the beginning of each of a number of discrete periods indexed $t = 1,2, \ldots$ In doing so they know the level of tax to which they will be subject during period t. At the end of period t, the firm has a residual capital stock, which depends on its investment decision in period t and the rate of capital depreciation, and an after-tax profit that it distributes (i.e., that is not subject to tax in any subsequent period). The tax (or expropriating) authority makes its period $t + 1$ decision knowing this capital stock.

In order to focus on issues of investment, we will assume that the firm's labor force is constant and that the firm's output per worker depends on capital-per-worker (i.e., the overall production function exhibits constant returns to scale). Thus, the following notation will be used.

i_t $\equiv$ investment per worker undertaken by the firm in period t,

k_t $\equiv$ the firm's capital per worker entering period t,

$f(k_t)$ $\equiv$ net return per worker (over the cost of variable inputs), where $f' > 0$, $f'' < 0$,

δ $\equiv$ rate of depreciation of capital so that:

k_t $\equiv (1 - \delta)\, k_{t-1} + i_t$,

w_t $\equiv$ tax per worker imposed on the firm and

π_t $\equiv$ firm's profit per worker $= f(k_t) - w_t$, which we will assume that the firm receives at the end of period.

The firm maximizes:

$$\sum_{t=1}^{\infty}\left(- i_t + \frac{f(k_t) - w_t}{(1 + r)}\right)\left(\frac{1}{1 + r}\right)^t$$

where r is the firm's cost of capital, assumed for simplicity to be exogeneously determined and constant. In solving its decision problem we assume that firm's managers act as a single player which can commit itself to a single intertemporal strategy [13].

---

[13] Later we will consider the case of many firms.

In contrast, government authorities cannot as a rule commit themselves beyond their current period of authority and we will, therefore, treat the authority in each period as a separate player. The strategy spaces of the government in each period consist of a level of w_t for each prior history of firm investments on entering the period. In practice, since governments make single period decisions they need only condition their tax strategies on the capital stock of the firm at the beginning of the period in which they set taxes. However, we will assume that the government in any period is concerned not with just current taxes, but more generally with the full net present value of taxes. The objective function of the government in period t is, therefore, to maximize:

$$\sum_{j=0}^{\infty} \frac{w_{t+j}}{(1+g)^j}$$

where g is the subjective discount rate of the governement. The government in each period chooses a strategy to maximize this function conditional on the strategies of the firm and governments in future and past periods. Thus, although each government controls only a single period's taxation its concerns are long-lived.

The strategy space of the firm in any period may be conditioned on the entire past history of taxes and investment. But, since each government regime is a single-period-lived entity, investment in any simple period need only be conditioned on the tax rate that will reign in that period and the firm's capital stock at the beginning of the period. Under these circumstances, Proposition 1 describes Nash equilibrium strategies for the governments in each period and the firm.

Proposition 1: for the model described above, Nash equilibrium strategies for the firm and taxing authorities are respectively:

$$(4) \qquad i_t = \begin{cases} k^* - k_{t-1}(1-\delta) & \text{if } \; w_t \leq w^*(k_{t-1}) \\ 0 \text{ otherwise} & \end{cases}$$

and:

$$w_t = \begin{cases} f(k_t(1-\delta)) & \text{if} \quad k_{t-1} > k^* \\ w^*(k_{t-1}) & \text{if} \quad k_{t-1} \leq k^* \end{cases} \tag{5}$$

where:

$$w^*(k_{t-1}) = f(k^*) - (1+r)\,[k^* - (1-\delta)\,k_{t-1}]$$

and k^* is determined by the equation:

$$\frac{f(k^*) - f(k^*(1-\delta))}{\delta k^*} = \frac{(1+r)}{(1+g)}\left(\frac{g+\delta}{r+\delta}\right)(r+\delta) \tag{6}$$

Proof: consider first the maximization problem of the firm given the strategies of the several taxing authorities. As long as $k_t \leq k^*$ in every period, the firm's maximand is:

$$\sum_{t=1}^{\infty}\left(-k_t + k_{t+1}(1-\delta) + \frac{f(k_t)}{(1+r)} - \frac{f(k^*)}{(1+r)} + [k^* - (1-\delta)k_{t-1}]\right) \tag{7}$$

$$= \sum_{t=1}^{\infty}\frac{f(k_t) - f(k^*)}{(1 \mid r)} + (k^* - k_t)$$

Therefore, the derivative of the firm's objective function with respect to k_t is:

$$\frac{f'(k_t)}{(1+r)} - 1 > 0 \text{ for } k_t \leq k^{**} \tag{8}$$

where k^{**} is defined by $f^1(k^{**}) = (1+r)$. Therefore, if $k^* < k^{**}$, the condition of equation *(8)* holds and among all $k_t \leq k^*$, $k_t = k^*$ maximizes the firm's objective function. In general k^* as defined by equation *(6)* will be less than k^{**}. Thus, among $k_t \leq k^*$, the optimal k_t is equal to k^*. But k_t can never exceed k^* since under those circumstances the next period's taxing authority confiscates all profit. Thus, k^* is the optimal period t capital stock and:

$$i_t^* = k^* - k_{t-1}(1 - \delta)$$

Moreover, it should be clear that for $w_t < w^*$, $k_t = k^*$ will continue to be the optimal level of investment. However, since at $k_t = k^*$, the value of the firm's objective function is zero, for any $w_t > w^*(k_{t+1})$, the firm's optimal policy is not to invest at all, which produces zero loss. Hence the optimal of the policy of the firm is defined by equation *(4)* for the firm.

Next consider the situation of one government given that other governments follow the policy of equation *(5)* and the firm follows the policy of equation *(4)*. If the government choses w_t to exceed w_t^*, then it might as well expropriate everything since $i_t = 0$ for any $w_t > w_t^*$. Furthermore it never pays the authority to set $w_t < w_t^*$ since this does not elicit any further investment. Thus, the choice of the taxing authority is between:

$$\text{(9)} \qquad w_t^e = f(k_{t-1}(1 - \delta)) - \text{expropriation}$$

and:

$$\text{(10)} \quad w_t^n = f(k^*) - (1 + r)[k^* - (1 - \delta)k_{t-1}] - \text{non-expropriation}$$

If prior and future governments follow the strategy of equation *(5)* and the firm follows the strategy of equation *(4)*, then the firm inherits a capital stock k^* from period $t - 1$. If the government in period t decides to expropriate, then the capital stock at the end of period t is $(1 - \delta)k^*$, since the firm does no investment. Also, the wage in period $t + 1$ is:

$$\text{(11)} \qquad w_{t+1} = f(k^*) - (1 + r)[k^* - (1 - \delta)^2 k^*]$$

since $k_{t+1} = (1 - \delta)k^* < k^*$ and the $t + 1$ government is assumed to follow the strategy of equation *(5)*. Beyond period $t + 1$ wages remain $w^*(k^*)$.

If the government in period t decides not to expropriate, then the capital stock at the end of period t is k^* and the wage in period $t+1$:

$$w_{t+1} = f(k^*) - (1 + r)\,[k^* - (1 - \delta)\,k^*] \tag{12}$$

with wages beyond period $t + 1$ again being w^* (k^*). Thus, the difference in the government's objective function consists solely of differences in period t and $t+1$ wages between the expropriation and non-expropriation choices. After some algebraic simplification, this difference is:

$$f(k^* - \delta k^*) - f(k^*) + (1 + r)\,\delta k^* \left(\frac{g + \delta}{1 + g}\right)$$

which is increasing in k^* if $g \geq r$ (and even if g is less than r under many circumstances). Thus, if $g \geq r$, there is a unique k^* such that the advantage of expropriation is zero. Above this level expropriation is better than non-expropriation. Below this level expropriation is inferior to non-expropriation. Thus, an equilibrium k^* occurs where:

$$f(k^*) - f(k^* - \delta k^*) = (1 + r)\,\delta k^* \left(\frac{g + \delta}{1 + g}\right)$$

or where:

$$\frac{f(k^*) - f(k^* - \delta k^*)}{\delta k^*} = \left(\frac{1 + r}{1 + g}\right)\left(\frac{g + \delta}{r + \delta}\right)(r + \delta) \tag{13}$$

as in equation *(6)* [Q.E.D.].

Several points follow from Proposition 1. First, the effect of potential expropriative taxes on the level of investment depends importantly on the factor:

$$M = \frac{(1 + r)}{(1 + g)}\left(\frac{g + \delta}{r + \delta}\right) \tag{14}$$

since the left-hand side of equation *(6)* is the average of the marginal product of capital between k^* and $k^* - \delta k^*$ and $r + \delta$ is what this would equal in a competitive market (i.e., the first best). If the government discount rate, which should never be less than the private discount rate, is equal to the private discount, (i.e., $r = g$), this expression is always equal to one and as a result the overall level of investment in a mean value sense is optimal. The heuristic reason for this is that the firm's strategy implicitly recognizes the potential for ex-post government expropriation and invests only if the tax rate allows for full recovery of the cost of investment (i.e. $(1 + r)\ i^*$) within the period. In a sense, therefore, the government is forced to act as a purchaser rather than a renter of capital (i.e., paying $(r + \delta)\ k^*$).

If the government is myopic, then (with $g > r$) M will be greater than one and investment will fall. Moreover, as short-term pressures on the government mount (e.g., health care expenses, needs for reunification, services to an aging population) or changes in the composition of the voter population to which the government responds (e.g., an older population) make it more short-sighted, the discount rate g will rise and equilibrium investment levels will fall. In the short run, of course, such pressure may appear as declining employment and output growth.

A second critical factor (given $g > r$) is the depreciation rate δ. The lower this rate of depreciation, the higher M will be and the lower will be the equilibrium level of investment and capital stock. But "depreciation" here can be interpreted in several ways. Since there is no explicit definition of period length in the model, this is an important determinant of the depreciation rate, δ. If the period during which a government agency is constrained to maintain tax rates is long, because for example institutional structures (e.g., democratic legislatures) effectively rule out rapid changes, then for any given technology the amount of depreciation during that period δ, will be correspondingly high. On the other hand, if policy may shift rapidly, then the "period" of the model will be short and the depreciation factor will be low. Since large depreciation leads to a lower marginal product of capital, institutional constraints will tend to raise the level of capital investment and reduce the impact of expropriate tax policy.

The intuition here is straightforward. The threat possessed by firms in response to government impositions is to stop investing. The harm that this does to the government in power depends on the size of the reduction in capital stock that such a non-investment position engenders. This, in turn, is positively related to the depreciation factor, δ. Higher levels of threat to government are then able to deter expropriation at existing levels of the capital stock and, hence, permit higher levels of capital and investment. In the long run, this is of course in the government's interest also so that, paradoxically, government vulnerability actually enhances government welfare.

Other possible sources of a high "depreciation" factor are government stability over long periods or government concern for investment levels beyond the immediate "period". Then the period over which a government can effectively and credibly commit itself to a set of tax rates, and hence the "period" of the model, is relatively long. In each of these cases, whether because of commitment or a long government time horizon, the effect is to increase investment and, in macroeconomic terms, employment and output.

In practice, higher future average taxes reduce returns to investment (to the extent they fall on firms) and, in the implicit bargaining process between firms and government, reduce future investment even in the absence of capital market imperfections. Thus, in a sense all the expropriation model provides is an explanation of the determinants of average tax rates and an alternative rationale for the impact of average tax rates (and hence transfers) on investment and economic activity [14].

A simple extension of the model does, however, suggest the importance of factors quite different from those of the imperfect information model. If we assume than there is more than one competing government expropriator (i.e., different independent levels or agencies of government or governments plus unions), then the level of investment in the expropriation model decreases rapidly. With n expropriating agencies equation *(6)* becomes:

$$\frac{f(K^*) - f(k^* - \delta k^*)}{\delta k^*} = n(r + \delta)M$$

[14] The process interpreted here as taking place between a government and a single firm applies equally well to expropriations between a government and multiple firms as long as the government is assumed to deal differentially with each different class of firms.

with a consequent rapid reduction in the level of the equilibrium capital stock. The reason for this dramatic increase in the effective marginal cost of capital is the fact that with many potential expropriators each one must worry about pre-empting the others. There are significant externalities when one agency restrains its tax (or wage) demands to encourage investment. The resultant induced investments benefits all expropriators (equally in a symmetrical model), so that each individual expropriator enjoys only $1/n$ part of the benefits of its own restraint. Thus, the deterrent consequences in terms of a lower capital stock must be n times as large to deter expropriation and the capital stock consequently lower (although equilibrium taxes will again be just sufficient to allow investment for a stable capital stock). For practical purposes, this suggests that increasing tax demands by multiple agencies (e.g., the European Community and national governments) may, if firms understand the potential for expropriation, deter investment, employment and economic activity well in advance of any measurable increase in taxes.

4. - Testing the Model

Broadly speaking the important exogenous factors that will drive investment and economic activity in the models of the kind described in the past two sections are those which affect present and future firm equity and, the mirror image of this, reduce external subtractions from firm profits and equity, where equity here should be broadly interpreted to include bank equity and the private wealth of enterpreneurs and professional managers. Other considerations are the number of independent agencies with potential power to expropriate firm profits and changes in economic structure (including those due to conscious government policies) that serve to attenuate market fluctuations. The problem in attempting to test the model explicitly is that there are a very large number of these factors which are in many cases difficult to quantify and many different kinds of investment (organizational, human capital and technological) which are often difficult to track. However, broad changes in government attitudes towards business should be correlated with many of these. If elections are exogenous events (as their timing is in the United States), then one possible test would be look at the consequences of political change for physical capital investment and ultimately productivity growth (as the consequence of both tangible and intangible investment).

The most dramatic recent period of such change in the United States was the shift from the Carter administration of the late 1970s to the Reagan administration in the 1980s.

Comparisons of investment experience across these years has the further advantage of posing a stark test of the models of this paper against traditional interest rate driven models of investment. The transition from Carter to Reagan at the end of 1980 coincides roughly with both a rapid increase in real interest rates and, perhaps not coincidentally, with an equally rapid rise in the real United States government deficit. In traditional terms, these factors should have led to a marked decline in capital investment during the 1980s. In contrast, the more favorable attitude of Reagan towards business in both tax and regulatory terms should have had the opposite effect.

In looking at changes in the capital stock data, we have actually chosen the periods 1947-1973, as a benchmark, 1973-1979 and 1979-1989. The choice of 1979 as the transition year was made to eliminate cyclical effects. In each case, we are using peak-to-peak business cycle periods. The choice of 1973 was made because it is the prior cyclical peak to 1979. Fortunately, the period of low real deficits and low real interest rates extends back to 1973 and the important change in the attitude of the Reagan administration was a break with the Ford and Nixon administration attitudes also (although not perhaps as dramatic as the break with the Carter administration).

The raw data on annual average changes in capital-labor ratios are given in column 1 of Table 1. These were then adjusted to reflect changes in the composition of economic activity between the periods using two-digit *SIC* industry classifications. The procedure for doing this is straight forward. The aggregate capital-labor ratio is:

$$k = \sum_i k_i L_i$$

where k_i is the capital-labor ratio in sector i and L_i is the fraction of the labor force in sector i. The change in the capital-labor ratio consists, therefore, of the sum of the effects of changes in the industry level capital-labor ratios, k_i, (with which we are concerned) and of changes in the composition of employment, L_i. Formally:

$$\frac{\Delta k}{k} = \sum \mu_i \frac{\Delta k_i}{k_i} + \sum \mu_i \frac{\Delta L_i}{L_i}$$

where μ_i is the fraction of the capital stock in industry. The second term in this expression is the change in the capital labor ratio due to changes in the composition of economic activity, which would occur even if there were no change at all in the industry level capital-labor ratios. It is precisely this effect which we would like to eliminate. Thus, we computed:

$$\left(\frac{\Delta k}{k}\right)_i \equiv \frac{\Delta k}{k} - \Sigma \mu i \frac{\Delta L_i}{K_i} \tag{15}$$

and these numbers appear in column 2 of Table 1. The pattern that they reveal of a sharp decline in the growth of capital labor ratios in the 1973-1979 period and a recovery in 1979-1989 tends to support the arguments of this paper [15].

TABLE 1

ANNUAL PERCENTAGE GROWTH RATES
IN AGGREGATE CAPITAL-LABOR RATIOS
IN US PRIVATE NON-FARM BUSINESS

	(1) actual	(2) adjusted
Equipment		
1947-1973	3.80	4.22
1973-1979	2.88	3.01
1979-1989	2.40	3.10
Structure		
1947-1973	1.57	2.11
1973-1979	0.49	−0.21
1979-1989	0.45	1.15

[15] The data are these from unpublished work by Steve Oliner of the Board of Governors of the Federal Reserve System.

A more general test would be to examine the impact of changing political regines on the level of productivity growth itself. This was done for the United States from 1948 through 1992. Annual percentage changes in non-farm business productivity were regressed on dummies for each presidency during that period and a business cycle variable (the constant term was arbitrarily set to 1.7% the average level of productivity growth over the period). In principle, productivity growth differences should not line up with changes in regime but rather with specific economic measures. And, given the widespread uncertainty concerning the determinants of productivity, it is not at all clear on what those changes should be.

It is somewhat surprising, therefore, and consistent again with the models of this paper, that there are significant differences in the productivity performances of different administrations.

The difference between the Reagan and Carter administrations, apparent in the investment data shows up strongly in the productivity data, as does the rise in business and upper income taxes and regulatory burdens in the Bush administration. The Eisenhower administration also shows up negatively, especially with respect to contemporaneous administrations, perhaps due to the fact that there were few tax changes and regulatory initiatives during the administra-

TABLE 2

DETERMINANTS OF US PRODUCTIVITY GROWTH 1940-1992

Variable	Coefficient	Standard error
Business cycle	(1.2)	0.45
Administrations		
Truman	1.9	0.63
Eisenhower	0.5	0.45
Kennedy	1.5	0.73
Johnson	1.1	0.57
Nixon	0	0.54
Ford	0.2	0.80
Carter	(1.5)	0.63
Reagan	(0.3)	0.45
Bush	(0.9)	0.63

tion and the administration's stabilization record appears to have been worse than both its predecessor and successor. There is also a pronounced negative trend in the data that corresponds to the widely observed phenomenon of declining productivity growth. It coincides with steady increases in government spending and regulatory burdens, although it is probably best not to make too much of this with the available data. Taken together with the investment data, the productivity growth figures for the United States at least suggest that considerations of overall business sector burdens, transfers from the business sector to households and potential changes in such burdens are an important component in aggregate economic performance.

5. - The Current Economic Slowdown

Application of the basic approach of this paper strongly suggests both a rationale for the current slowdown and a prognosis for the future. First, trends toward higher health care expenditures that affect the United States, Canada and Europe and which are increasingly funded by direct taxes upon business and business-related individuals are likely to represent present and future drains of equity accumulation that will inhibit growth and investment. Environmental improvements achieved through mandated business changes that represent in many cases lump sum impositions on existing plants may have exacerbated this situation and are likely to continue to do so. In Germany, the social expense of reunification has substantially increased government spending and promises to continue to do so (Table 3). To the extent that the incidence of the associated tax burden falls on the business sector, it will inhibit equity accumulation, investment and growth. At the same time many traditional business subsidies are being phased out in the pursuit of deregulation. In the United States, the most striking instance of this has been the effective abolition of zero interest rate ceilings on demand deposits. The result has been a gradual withdrawal of an important equity subsidy to the banking sector and, to the extent that the models of this paper apply, a reduction in the efficacy of monetary policy as it no longer controls the level of this subsidy. In Japan, these forces (which include

TABLE 3

LEVELS OF GERMAN GOVERNMENT
EXPENDITURE AS A FRACTION OF GNP

1975	31.1
1980	30.1
1985	30.7
1988	30.3
1989	29.2
1990	29.3
1991	32.5

inherited wage commitments to older workers) have been exacerbated by widespread declines in the values of corporate assets which have by themselves meant substantial reductions in firm equity. Finally in Europe, divided government authority between the European Community and national governments may mean increased pressures on business returns as these authorities compete to impose their separate social agendas. Taken together such forces seem likely to account for a substantial part of the slowdown in growth and appear unlikely to change any time soon.

BIBLIOGRAPHY

[1] BERNANKE B. - LOWN C., «The Credit Crunch», *Brookings Papers on Economic Activity*, vol. 2, 1992, pp. 205-39.

[2] GERTLER M. - GILCHRIST S., «The Role of Credit Market Imperfections in the Monetary Transmission Mechanism: Arguments and Evidence», *NYU Discussion Paper*, 1992.

[3] GREENWALD B. - STIGLITZ J. - WEISS A., «Informational Imperfections and Macroeconomic Fluctuations», *American Economic Review Paper and Proceedings*, vol. 74, 1984, pp. 194-9.

[4] GREENWALD B. - STIGLITZ J., «Macroeconomic Models with Equity and Credit Rationing» in HUBBARD G., (ed.), *Asymmetric Information, Corporate Finance and Investment*, NBER, University of Chigaco Press, 1990.

[5] ——-——, Financial Market Imperfections and Business Cycles», *Quarterly Journal of Economics*, forthcoming 1993.

[6] KASHYAP A. - STEIN J. - WILCOX D., «Monetary Policy and Credit Conditions: Evidence from the Composition of External Finance», *American Economic Review*, forthcoming 1993.

[7] MYERS S. - MAJLUF N., «Corporate Financing and Investment Decisions when Firms Have Information that Investors Do not Have», *Journal of Financial Economics*, vol. 2, 1984, pp. 187-221.

[8] PHELPS E.S., «Pro-Keynesian and Counter-Keynesian Implications of the "Structuralist" Theory of Unemployment and Interest Under the Classic Two-Sector View of Capital and Production», New York, Columbia University, *Discussion Paper*, n. 494, August 1990.

[9] RODRIC D., «Redistributive Taxation Without Excess Burden», *Economics and Politics*, vol. 5, n. 1, March 1993, pp. 53-60.

[10] STIGLITZ J. - WEISS A., «Credit Rationing in Markets with Imperfect Information», *American Economic Review*, vol. 71, 1981, pp. 393-410.

Do the Main Structural Forces of the 1970s and 1980s Account for the 1990s Slump As Well?

Edmund S. Phelps - **Gylfi Zoega**
Columbia University, New York and EBRD - University of London and OFCE

There is a movement in macroeconomics toward a new perspective on employment determination. The aim is to understand the long swings and secular shifts in the level of economic activity rather than the high-frequency fluctuations absorbing Keynesians and neoclassicals. The approach seeks non-monetary mechanisms by which non-monetary shocks — structural shifts and changes in real conditions — disturb the path of unemployment. What broad changes in the structure of demands and supplies have driven unemployment rates over the postwar era? What institutional provisions have moderated unemployment and what institutional developments have made it worse? This structuralist approach differs from the monetary and aggregative perspectives of the older schools of macroeconomic thought [1].

The theoretical task posed by this approach has been to develop supporting theoretical models that are neither monetary nor neoclassical - models based on the incentive problems and market imperfections without which there could be no widescale and persistent unemployment. The empirical task has been to compare the behavior of actual data with the behavior of the theoretical models. Phelps's forthcoming book presents some intertemporal and international

---

[1] A recent survey of the various extant approaches is PHELPS E.S. [7].

N.B.: the numbers in square brackets refer to the Bibliography at the end of the paper.

models of the necessary theoretical type, models that endogenize the path of the natural rate of unemployment [2]. In their open-economy versions these models suggest how economies participating in the global economy are connected by the world real interest rate set in the global capital market and by real exchange rates coming from the global tradeable goods markets. Further, both in this book and the latest report of the *OFCE International Panel,* we construct and estimate a reduced-form econometric model for the purpose of testing the main implications adduced from the theoretical models [3]. Remarkably, the causal variables in this cross-section time-series study of OECD unemployment rates were estimated to operate in directions consistent with the models and generally to a statistically significant degree.

In theoretical work, however, it is always necessary to choose the sorts of shocks to be modeled. The determinants — state variables and parameter shifts — of the equilibrium path of the unemployment rate (and the current value of the natural rate of unemployment, defined as the stationary rate) in the theoretical models of the open economy were the world (or rest-of-the world) interest rate and various supply and demand factors of traditional interest. These models were designed primarily in the hope that they would support certain intuitive contentions about demand and supply shocks (which, on the whole, they did):

— if a small open economy faces overseas demand or supply shocks driving up the rest-of-the-world real interest rate (say, increased overseas public debt or increased overseas public expenditure or a decreased overseas capital stock), the effects are a rise of domestic real interest rates and a real depreciation, and hence (on both counts) a drop of the demand wage and thus a contraction of employment;

— if a small open economy of the customer-market type experiences such shocks, pushing up domestic interest rates and causing a real appreciation, an expansion of employment is possible. (It occurs if the appreciation overcomes the higher interest rates);

---

[2] See Phelps E.S. [8].
[3] See Fitoussi J.P. *et* Al. [1].

— if such an economy experiences the same shocks on the same scale as occur overseas, and is representative in its structure of the world as a whole, there is no real appreciation, hence no expansion of labor demand on that account, and there is no depreciation either, hence no contraction of labor demand on that account. But the consequent upward push on real interest rates results in an unemployment contraction.

Some earlier models, inspired by the increases in unemployment in the 1970s and the 1980s, showed how a shift in the equilibrium unemployment path could be caused by an oil price shock and by the escalation of disincentives brought by the rise of the welfare state [4]. Our econometric equation for explaining the countries' natural unemployment rates contains these "old" factors alongside our own: the world real interest rate, the world real oil price, and, among the national variables, some familiar macroeconomic factors (public expenditures, the capital stock, certain tax rates, and so forth) and a set of national characteristics pertaining to institutions and social policy [5]. (In addition the first difference of the inflation rate was used to proxy for high-frequency effects of disturbances coming through monetary channels, which disturb unemployment away from its natural-rate path).

The question that now looms over our work is whether the events subsequent to the theorizing and the testing can be explained by the same factors operating in the same way. If each new slump requires a new structural explanation — first oil, then real interest rates, then something else — the value of the structuralist approach is put in doubt. If, on the contrary, our equations interpret the present slump as either a rise of the natural rate that is explained by our causal variables or a perturbation of essentially monetary origin around the

---

[4] Among the recent econometric studies one highlighting institutional factors in LAYARD R. - NICKELL S. - JACKMAN R. [2]. A study somewhat similar to ours as regards the rate of interest is MANNING D. [3]. See also MCKIBBIN W.J. - SACHS J.D. [4]. Among econometric forerunners one must mention, besides Sachs, the econometric work in NEWELL A. - SYMONS J. [5]. Other authors of recent econometric work on national unemployment rates include Bean C., Blanchard O., Oswald A., Taylor J. and in a paper for this volume Minford P. and Riley J.

[5] The global variables were in turn explained by the world levels of the latter national variables.

natural rate path, the null hypothesis that our equations remain satisfactory is not rejected.

The present semi-global slump, not unlike its recent predecessors, has indeed brought forth hypotheses of new causal forces of the structuralist type not previously operating, a veritable plethora of imaginative hypotheses. One of these is the hypothesis that a deterioration of balance sheets at banks or at enterprise or households (or some or all of the above) is the cause of the worsened business conditions. Yet, proponents of this view admitted a year ago that if balance sheets greatly improved while the economy did not they would have to downgrade the importance of this factor; in fact, in the United States and to a lesser extent the United Kingdom at least, balance sheets are much improved while the economy is much less improved. Another structural factor that is receiving increased attention is the rate of progress in total factor productivity, which can be shown in a number of models to be contractionary for employment: from China to Britain, new or restructured firms seem suddenly to have learned how to produce the same output with sharply less labor input. Yet it is not obvious that the World Bank's announcement of the world growth rate for the 1990s will exceed by much if at all the improved world growth rate reported for the 1980s. A third hypothesis, which is more in the Keynesian than the structuralist spirit but which can be accomodated with no problems, is that a crisis of confidence has discouraged households from making consumer durables commitments and firms from making new employment commitments. Yet in the United States high share prices are being paid in the stock market by the same households, and producers durables purchases have been holding up well in relation to national output; the loss of confidence seems to be curiously selective.

Quite another category of hypotheses, which is clearly outside the structuralist domain, are essentially monetary. From the viewpoint taken here, these alternative hypotheses assert a widening deviation of the unemployment rate above a more-or-less unchanged path of the natural rate rather than a bulge or elevation to a new plateau of the natural rate itself. According to one of these hypotheses, a wave of deregulation of banks spread over several countries in the late 1980s with the result that inflation rose unexpectedly, pulling unemployment down yet finally triggering a move toward tighter money that has pulled inflation back down but only at the cost of sending unemployment well above the natural rate, at least for a time. The other monetary hypothesis is that the German central bank was forced to raise interest rates to curb the increased inflation brought by German unification, and the resulting swing of the unemployment rate above the natural rate in Germany was at the same time shared by those other European countries that chose to keep their exchange rates at a fixed parity with the Deutschmark.

Application of the "traditional" structural approach as found in our study must instead look to increases in the world real interest, in the world price of oil and, among national factors, increases in tax rates, especially ones critical for unemployment decisions, in order to explain the 1990s slump. At once it may be objected by some readers that real interest rates have not been notably higher in the 1990s than in, say, the second half of the 1980s. However, as Graph 5 illustrates, a conventional estimate of the long-term world real interest rate indicates a movement from a level around 4% in the last two years of the 1980s to a plateau around 5% in the 1990s [6]. Furthermore, when observers point to the moderation of real rates in several of the countries that are in a slump, they are confusing a cyclical real rate with the structural real rate. If the dollar, the pound and the lira, for example, have experienced large real depreciations relative to most currencies in east Asia and Latin America and the unified Germany, the prospect of a partial (and *a fortiori* a full) return of the latter currencies to their previous levels implies lower real interest rates in terms of the former currencies on this account; once recovery of both economic activity and the real exchange rate take place, with no further exchange-rate recoveries in prospect, real rates will again be as high as in the rest of the world, where they seem to be undiminished.

It is of great interest, therefore, to see to what extent the increased unemployment rates of the 1990s, and the dip of these rates in the late 1980s, can be explained by our econometric equations

---

[6] There was a much more pronounced rise of the world short-term real interest rate.

either as a fall and subsequent rise in the natural rate of unemployment of the affected countries resulting from a fluctuation in world real interest rates, energy prices, tax rates and so forth, or as a perturbation of the unemployment rate around a little-changed natural rate path that is explained by a rise and subsequent drop of inflation. The finding of an important increase of the natural rate would suggest the necessity of new remedies — structuralist remedies! — while a finding that the dip and subsequent sharp rise of unemployment is primarily of monetary origin would indicate the use of traditional anticyclical therapies as the policies of choice. On the other hand, a finding that neither of these explanations works well in the 1990s would point the way toward renewed efforts to identify new or awakened structural forces now at work.

1. - The Econometric Study

The cross-section time-series study is an attempt within the limits of data availability to represent the structuralist theory embodied in the three kinds of theoretical models in Phelps (in press). Pooling the time series data of many countries greatly increases the degrees of freedom with which to estimate the effects of national and global variables. Such pooling need not exclude cross-country differences both in the constant term and in the "deflator" by which one country's coefficients may differ across the board from another's.

Although the theoretical models determine only the equilibrium unemployment path, the data on the actual unemployment path in any country unquestionably reflects both the influence of monetary shocks and the operation of non-monetary shocks through monetary mechanisms. In our study we seek to control for such disturbances around the equilibrium path by introducing as an added explanatory variable the change in the inflation rate, $d(inflw_t)$, where d is the first-difference operator. The hypothesis is that unemployment is below its equilibrium path (u^*) when inflation is increasing, above when decreasing; the boost to world consumption from an episode of below-equilibrium world unemployment may be guessed to reduce, transiently at any rate, the world real interest rate. To put this another way: the inflation change term proxies for the discrepancy between the actual unemployment rate and the equilibrium unemployment in the current period, and thus makes possible the use of the actual unemployment path for the purposes of the regression rather than the equilibrium unemployment path, which is unobservable.

The equilibrium unemployment path is driven by the set of exogenous variables contained in the structuralist models, with the exception that the domestic stock of (resident or overseas) customers is not an available series, and is hence a missing variable. These variables fall into three categories: global variables, domestic time-variant variables, and domestic time-invariant variables, or characteristics [7].

Among the domestic variables are those affecting the domestic real interest rate or exchange rates and hence domestic labor demand, given the world real interest rate: the shock of central-government public debt (B), the domestic capital stock (K), defense expenditure (Gd) and government non-defense expenditure (Gnd) [8]. The domestic variables also include those impacting on labor incentives and hence the wage locus: revenue collected through direct taxation as a proportion of total household income (t), the proportion of the labor force (called workers) between 20 and 24 years of age (*youth*), a rolling average of the rate of growth of the labor force (*lgrowth*) [9]. Finally we

---

[7] As the closed-economy models portray, the world real interest rate is in turn determined by the equality of world supply and dermand of the (tradeable) consumer goods. The exogenous variables driving this equilibrium are the world level of public debt, the world capital stock, world military spending, world government spending on non-military goods and the transitory component of oil prices. Government spending is divided into the two components based on the possibility that military expenditures fall to a greater extent on capital goods. In addition the world price of oil also affects labor demand and unemployment directly. This exercise will not be repeated in the present update of our econometric study.

[8] The preceding variables are written on a per augmented labor unit basis. The labor force measure used is a 5 year rolling average of the OECD annual labor force data. The rate of labor augmenting technical progress is determined such that the output-augmented labor unit ratio in the US have no trend - assuming that the US was close to steady state during the period. In calculating the growth rate, the sample was split in 1973. This gave a higher rate in the period 1955-1973 (1.82%) than in 1974-1989 (0.9%).

[9] The rolling average is used to prevent the 'discouraged worker effect' from creating a negative correlation between the rate of unemployment and this variabe.

have a vector, C_i, of country characteristics that are not time dependent. (This can be either because the object they measure does not change over time or because the measures of it exist for only one point in time). These are variables that can affect either labor demand or incentives. Some of them reflect labor market institutions, such as unions and legislation, while others reflect general government policy.

The global variables are the real price of oil (*rpoil**) [10] and the world real long-term rate of interest (*rlong**) [11].

As explained above, the inflation shock term provides for the possibility that unemployment is above its equilibrium level when inflation is decreasing and below when inflation is increasing. Hence the remaining right-hand side variables of the unemployment equation are the determinants of the equilibrium rate itself.

This gives rise to 17 augmented Phillips curves, one for each of 17 OECD countries [12], for the years beginning in 1957 to 1989. These are estimated together, subject to cross-country restrictions [13].

The coefficient restrictions imply that the ratio of any two coefficients is the same across countries. Thus the countries differ only in the degree of sensitivity of their labor markets, as reflected in the slope of the labor demand and the wage locus, and the intercept term, a_i. The coefficient c_i is a measure of this labor market sensitivity, or real wage flexibility.

Owing to adjustment costs, firms respond partly with a lag to changes in the right-hand side variables. It is assumed that a simple geometric lag representation is sufficient to capture this effect. This requires the estimation of only one additional coefficient, which is the parameter of the lag distribution.

---

[10] The oil price variable is equal to the ratio of US PPI for crude petroleum to overall US PPI.

[11] The interest rate variable is equal to a weighted average of the real rate of interest on 10 year government bonds in the G7 countries where inflation expectations are measured by the simple average of the current year's and next year's inflation. PPP-adjusted GDP is used for weights.

[12] The countries are: Australia, Austria, Belgium, Canada, Denmark, Finland, France, Germany, Ireland, Italy, Japan, the Netherlands, Norway, Spain, Sweden, the UK and US.

[13] This is a fixed effect model which controls for the possibility of unobservable country-specific effects which may be correlated with some of the included variables.

The equation to be estimated is:

$$u_{it} = k_i \cdot u_{it-1} + c_i \cdot [a_i + b \cdot (B_{it} + K_{it}) + \\ + c \cdot K_{it} + d \cdot Gd_{it} + f \cdot Gnd_{it} + g \cdot t_{it} + h \cdot youth_{it} + \\ + i \cdot lgrowth_{it} + j \cdot rlong^*_t + k \cdot rpoil^*_t + l \cdot d(infl_{it})]$$

$$i = 1,2,\ldots, 17; t = 1957, \ldots 1989.$$

Based on a prior estimation, the coefficient of lagged unemployment, k_i, was constrained to take the same value for countries belonging to the same group. One group is Canada and Europe, excluding Scandinavia and Finland, the other group includes Norway, Sweden and Finland. The US, Japan and Australia were treated separately.

The equations were estimated jointly using iterative, non linear, weighted least squares. This method corrects for cross-equation heteroskedasticity by weighing each equation by an estimate of the inverse of the standard error of the equation [14].

An iterative Cochrane-Orcutt procedure was used to correct for any possible autocorrelation of residuals over time. Due to the presence of the lagged dependent variable it would lead to inconsistent coefficient estimates [15] if not corrected for. The estimation results follow.

The equality of the coefficients of the two types of government expenditure was tested and could not be rejected at the 95% level. The restriction was then imposed in the final estimation. This suggests the absence of a serious endogeneity bias as far as public expenditures are concerned, assuming that defense expenditures do not respond much to changes in unemployment.

The coefficients have the expected sign. An increase in wealth tends to decrease unemployment and also increases government

---

[14] Since some unobserved shocks are likely to affect all countries simultaneously the equations were also estimated using Zellner's method (SURE) to take into account any cross-country correlation of residuals. The results turned out to be qualitatively the same as below.

[15] In order to prevent the Cochrane-Orcutt procedure from converging to a local minimum which is not a global minimum, a grid search was applied. Thus the procedure was started from values of the autocorrelation coefficient ranging between −1 and 1. All estimations gave the same coefficient estimates.

TABLE 1

DEPENDENT VARIABLE : u_{it}
(Estimation method: iterative, nonlinear weighted least squares
number of observations: 32 · 17 = 544)

Variable name	Coefficient estimate	Standard error
$B_{it} + K_{it}$	−0.0682	0.0341
K_{it}	0.1725	0.0711
$Gd_{it} + Gnd_{it}$	−0.5223	0.3015
t_{it}	8.8537	4.1611
$youth_{it}$	6.4796	6.6048
$lgrowth_{it}$	9.0954	7.6574
$d(infl_{it})$	−0.0342	0.0155
$rlong^*_t$	11.8937	4.5039
$rpoil^*_t$	1.5101	0.6235

expenditures. Direct taxes as a proportion of total household income, the proportion of recent entrants into the labor force, the rate of growth of the labor force and the capital stock [16] turn out to increase unemployment. This suggests that, of the direct taxes, taxes on wage income dominate taxes on non-earned income. Most importantly both the world real rate of interest [17] and the real price of oil have negative effects on unemployment. The coefficients of the variables denoting labor force growth (*lgrowth*) and the proportion of recent entrants in the labor force (*youth*) are least significant. The sign of these coefficients is though a robust feature of the data, not sensitive to the inclusion or exclusion of any variable [18].

[16] This indicates substitutability between labor and capital in production.

[17] The interest rate and oil price variables are of course endogenous for the world as a whole. The rationalization for their inclusion in the reduced form equation is that for each country the degree of endogeneity is smaller. However, to the extent that one country can affect the world real rate or oil prices this results in biased estimates.

[18] Indirect taxes, calculated as the ratio of tax-revenue and private consumption, were also included in the estimation. Their coefficient turned out to be insignificant and was omitted.

Data on payroll-taxes, calculated as a ratio of the sum of social security contributions and pension funds contributions and total private sector wage payments, was available for 15 of the 17 countries. This variable had a very significant, positive coefficient (t = 2.28) but was not included in the table above due to its limited coverage.

The size of the sensitivity coefficient (c_i) across countries conforms with our prior expectations. Thus the Scandinavian countries have low values — indicating real wage flexibility — while others, such as Spain, the United Kingdom and the Netherlands, have a high value of this coefficient [19]. The relatively high value for the United States was deceptive. The estimates of the coefficient of lagged unemployment is low (insignificantly different from zero), indicating that the effect of shocks is more immediate than elsewhere and persistence lower. Thus the total effect of shocks is smaller than for the high unemployment European and Asia countries. Japan, not surprisingly, has a low value of the sensitivity coefficient. However, the coefficient of lagged unemployment is high for that country. The fourth column shows the autocorrelation coefficients for the residuals.

The table also contains the unadjusted coefficient of determination of multiple regression and standard error for each of the countries.

TABLE 2

COUNTRY-SPECIFIC COEFFICIENTS

Country	c_i	a_i	k_i	$AR(1)$	R^2	s.e.
Australia	1.00	−4.24	0.57	0.10	0.91	0.94
Austria	0.52	−2.80	0.51	0.11	0.92	0.55
Belgium	1.28	3.57	0.72	0.27	0.98	0.67
Canada	1.02	−4.79	0.72	0.20	0.86	1.05
Denmark	0.81	−2.99	0.72	0.29	0.95	0.95
Finland	0.76	−3.85	0.51	0.66	0.84	0.88
France	0.71	−2.56	0.72	0.05	0.99	0.38
Germany	0.89	−4.59	0.72	0.14	0.95	0.71
Ireland	1.08	−2.80	0.72	0.38	0.97	0.95
Italy	0.52	−1.73	0.72	0.33	0.95	0.42
Japan	0.14	0.06	0.67	0.17	0.93	0.19
Netherlands	1.70	−4.88	0.72	0.40	0.98	0.70
Norway	0.33	−2.67	0.51	0.60	0.54	0.67
Spain	2.08	−2.79	0.72	0.36	1.00	0.60
Sweden	0.46	−2.88	0.51	0.49	0.69	0.35
UK	1.45	−2.80	0.72	0.22	0.96	0.82
US	1.67	−0.77	−0.06	0.61	0.71	1.55

[19] The sensitivity coefficient is positively correlated across countries with Tarantelli's index of corporatism. The greater the centralization of wage-bargaining, the lower is the sensitivity of unemployment to shocks, and presumably the greater is real wage flexibility. Also, a higher level of public labor market expenditures and a lower replacement ratio have the same effect.

2. - The Implied Natural (or Stationary) Rate Series in the 1990s

The estimated unemployment equations can now be used to calculate for each year the stationary, or steady-state, level of the unemployment rate for each of the 17 countries ($u_t = u_{t-1}$). The inflation shock term is excluded. Thus, this calculation can be looked upon as a proxy varible for the *natural* rate of unemployment, to which equilibrium paths tend under any reasonable assumption set. Following a monetary shock, the actual unemployment rate, since it will approach the equilibrium unemployment-rate path provided the inflation change variable is damped, will by the same token approach the path of the natural rate.

Graph 1 shows the weighted average of the 17 countries' steady-state rates alongside their actual unemployment rates for the period

GRAPH 1

WEIGHTED AVERAGE OF WORLD ACTUAL AND STEADY-STATE UNEMPLOYMENT

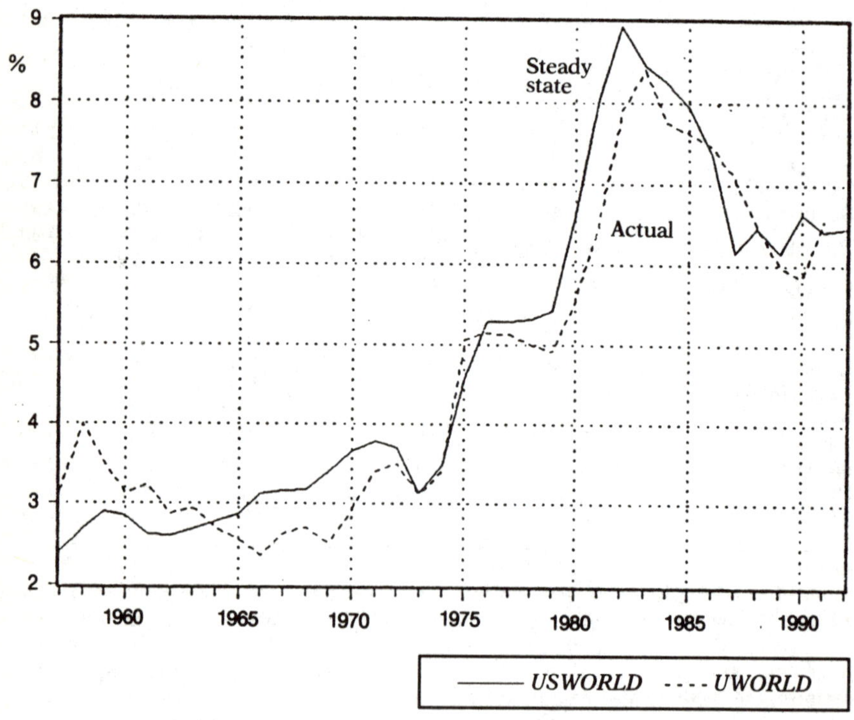

1957-1992. The labor force is used as weights. The years 1990-1992 are out of sample and therefore of more interest.

2.1 *Implications for the 1990s*

The natural rate appears to have increased in 1990 by about half a percentage point (or 50 basis points). The rise in the long-term world real interest rate in 1990, shown in Graph 5 to be about 50 basis points, can be seen to push up the OECD natural rate that year. The oil-price rise in late 1990 is another factor driving up the steady-state unemployment rate in that year. These two factors are largely responsible for the rise of the OECD natural rate in 1990, which returns it to the level it had in 1986 before some further progress in the remaining years of the decade [20]. (The movement of the actual unemployment rate can be described as a downward approach toward the path of the steady-state rate than as the upward movement in the steady-state rate).

Thereafter the calculated natural rate fluctuates slightly, falling back a little in 1991 along with the long-term real interest rate, then rising very slightly in 1992. There are, it may be remarked, some secular forces making the natural rate inch up a little each year in the absence of countervailing cyclical forces. However, the econometric system here cannot be said to imply that slowing defense expenditures has recently been pushing the natural rate up since, according to the underlying models and as confirmed by the coefficient estimates, the beneficial effect in moderating the world real interest rate is more than enough to offset the effect in each country of the slowdown in its own defense expenditures.

Graphs 2, 3 and 4 depict a similar but more pronounced picture for the US, UK and Italy. In addition to the steady-state unemploy-

[20] It is true that, according to the estimate here, a 100 basis point increase of the long-term real rate would have only a 12 basis point effect on the current-period equilibrium unemployment rate (taken as a decimal so as to be in the same units as the interest rate in the data processing). But the feedback through the lagged unemployment rate raises the effect on the steady-state, or natural, unemployment rate, to a coefficient on the order of some multiple of 12, depending on the country. In Italy and the other European countries, for example, the effect is about 50 basis points.

GRAPH 2

DECOMPOSITION OF THE RATE
OF STEADY-STATE UNEMPLOYMENT
AND THE RATE OF ACTUAL UNEMPLOYMENT

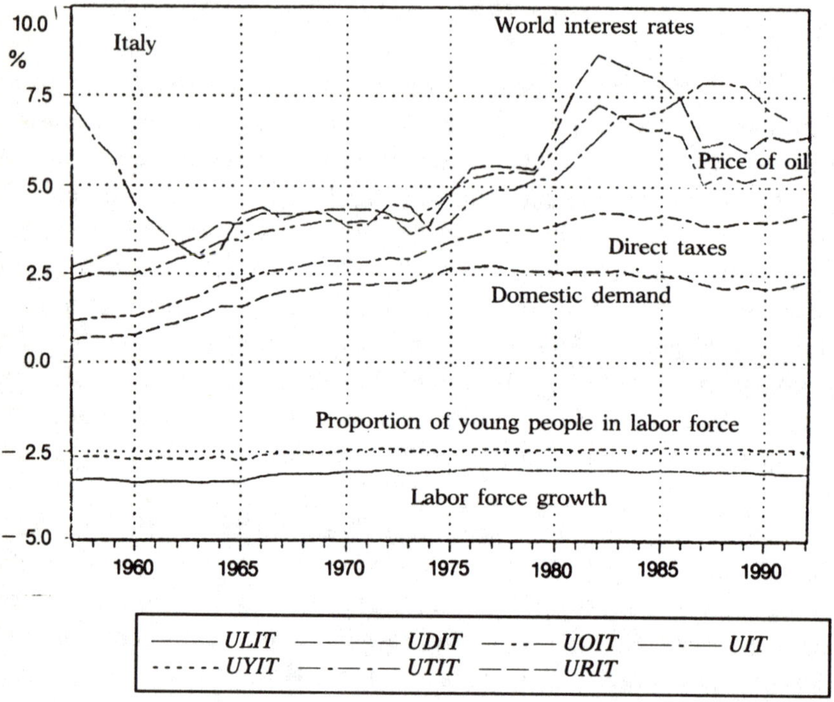

ment rate, these three charts show the cumulative influence of the explanatory variables. The top line, the excess of which over the next-highest line measures the contribution of the world real long-term interest rate, shows the impact of all explanatory variables other than the inflation shock term.

In Italy, the steady-state rate rises about a whole percentage point in 1990 because of the increases in the world oil price and in world interest rates. It then falls slightly in 1991 because of lower oil prices but only partially because interest rates persist at the higher level. In addition, there is a continuation of an upward trend in the rate of direct taxes, starting in the mid-1970s, until 1990. Actual unemployment starts rising in 1980 and reaches a peak in 1987-1988 and then

Graph 3

DECOMPOSITION OF THE RATE
OF STEADY-STATE UNEMPLOYMENT
AND THE RATE OF ACTUAL UNEMPLOYMENT

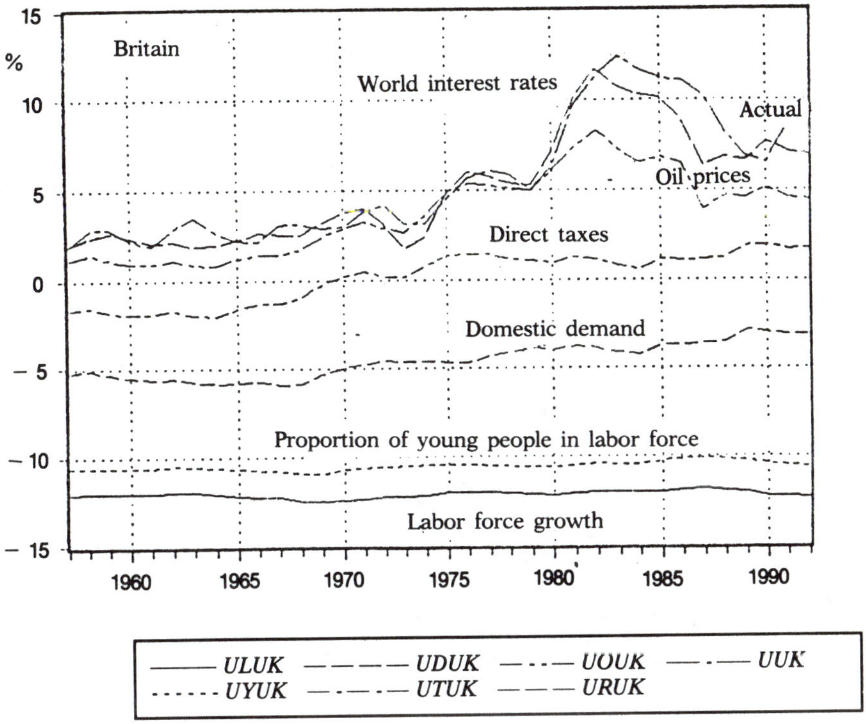

declines gradually in 1989-1991 towards the predicted steady-state level.

The UK has a higher sensitivity coefficient, c_i, and the steady state is thus more affected by the rise in the price of oil and world interest rates in 1990. Direct taxes declined in the 1980s, at least until 1989. The rise in observed unemployment in the past three years can be seen as an overshooting of the steady-state rate. It is reasonable to lay this wayward drift of the actual unemployment rate to the overvaluation of the pound and to the high real interest rates needed to achieve it during the period ending in October 1992 when the pound was finally cut loose from the EMS. It is interesting, however, that the

GRAPH 4

DECOMPOSITION OF THE RATE
OF STEADY-STATE UNEMPLOYMENT
AND THE RATE OF ACTUAL UNEMPLOYMENT

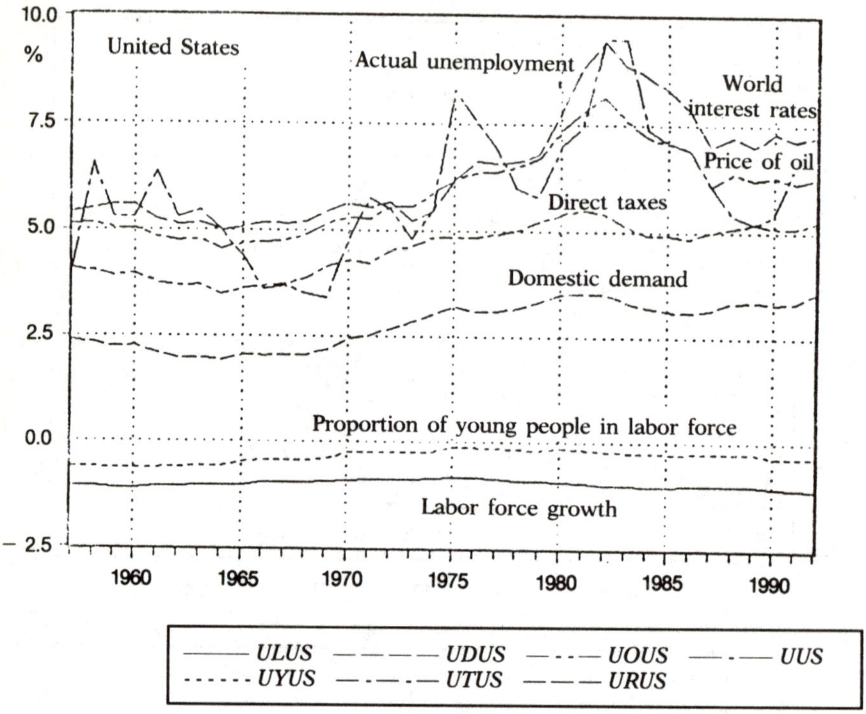

same upward drift relative to the natural rate does not seem to have occurred in Italy, which seemed to be suffering the same difficulties.

In the US the natural unemployment rate has been subject to wide swings in military expenditures. One can see the expansionary effect of the increased defense spending in the late 1960s and the first half of the 1980s on steady-state unemployment. In more recent history, the effect of the reduction in defense spending after 1985 is also apparent. The US is different from the two European countries in the sense that unemployment since 1983 has been much lower than the estimated steady-state level. The recent surge in unemployment is thus, according to the present equation, a return to the slightly rising steady-state rate. So far as we can tell, the US unemployment rate is

Graph 5

WORLD LONG-TERM REAL INTEREST RATES

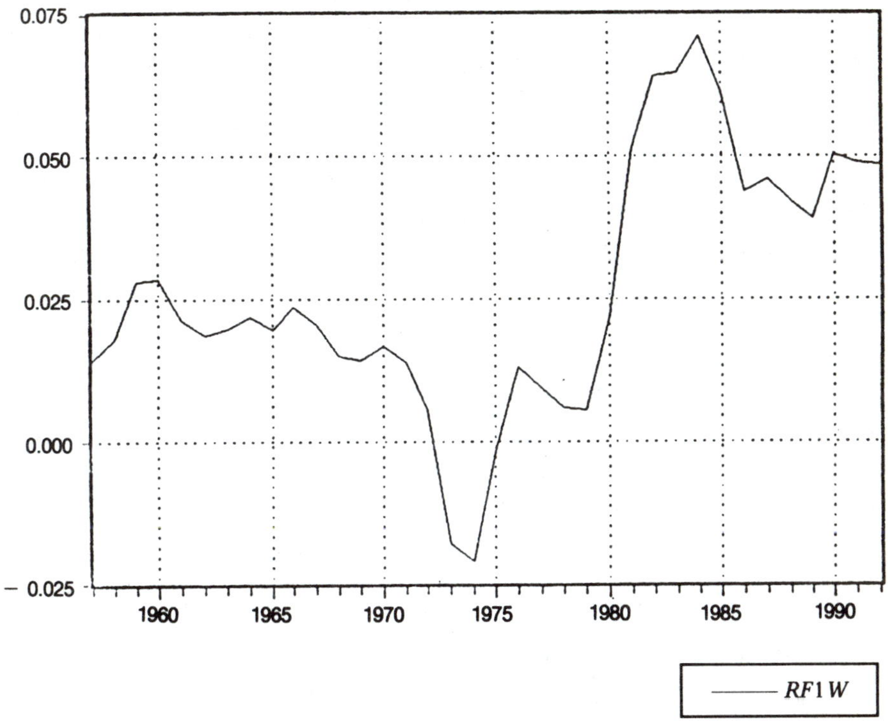

now in the neighborhood of the natural rate, though the latter may still be trending up slightly with the unwinding of previous decisions to cut or postpone military spending [21].

There is an interesting, and somewhat puzzling, contrast in these recent records. Both in the UK and the US there seems to have been a stimulus driving unemployment down relative to the path of the natural rate path over two or more years in the latter half of the 1980s. This episode was followed by a counterbalancing period in the early 1990s in which the unemployment rate rose in relation to the natural rate. These calculations lend support to the widespread feeling

---

[21] The slowdown in military spending would show no net effect on the natural rate in the United States if it were accompanied by equal developments in the rest of the world. But such has not so far been the case.

that a boom developed through monetary channels in the former years — a boom fed by financial regulation and countenanced by the central banks — and that the ensuing increases in the rate of inflation finally persuaded the central banks to tighten monetary policy in the latter years. If this hypothesis is broadly correct, the good news is that the natural rate, though a little worse than in the late 1980s, remains much better than in the several years before 1988.

Italy, on the other hand, seems to show the mirror-opposite pattern of deviations from the path of the natural rate. This country had its episode of tightness or the equivalent of tightness originating spontaneously in the private sector in the latter half of the 1980s, but it was to be followed by an episode of apparent expansiveness or toleration of exuberance in the private sector in the 1990s. However, in all three countries the rate of inflation and the expectations thereof are sufficiently low that unemployment in the neighborhood of the natural rate seems to be rather quickly attainable and, where already attained (as in the United States), sustainable over the future.

3. - Concluding Remarks

The main finding of the present paper can be put as follows. There is evidence that the world long-term real interest rate in the 1990s is on a plateau at the level to which it had returned in 1986, but which it slipped below as the decade wore on. On this account taken alone, the prediction of our econometric study is a return of the natural unemployment rate to the level of 1986, a level which the natural rate likewise slipped below in the latter half of the 1980s. In fact, conveniently enough, the other factors have not added much to the 1990s story.

How, then, can one explain why the actual OECD unemployment rate, which had been in the neighborhood of our estimate of the natural rate in 1991, departed for a higher level in 1992 and has at this writing (June 1993) penetrated into vastly higher territory? In the view taken by our study there are, as commented in the introduction, two kinds of eligible explanations: other structural factors have operated to raise the natural rate to a much higher level in the 1990s than is captured by our econometric study, *or* monetary factors and non-monetary factors operating through monetary channels have been forcing the actual unemployment rate to rise much more than the natural rate.

There may be a good deal of truth in both of these possibilities. The development of insufficient capital at banks in the latter half of the 1980s and the efforts of the banking system to restore their capital positions in the 1990s is a plausible factor that operates both ways — both to raise the natural rate and, at the same time, to induce a disinflationary shock tending to drive up the actual unemployment rate relative to the natural rate. Another plausible factor, also operating in this two-fold way, is the cumulative worsening of enterprise indebtedness over the 1980s. It must be noted, however, that the importance of these two factors has presumably noderated as banks have succeeded in raising increased amounts of capital and corporations have managed to retire some of their debt. The recent rise in unemployment in Europe comes at the very time when these factors are apparently diminishing.

A better-timed factor of the structural sort is the curious surge of restructuring going on at large numbers of companies in Europe and North America. The resulting productivity growth is not simply the usual phenomenon that occurs as firms coming out of recession find they can resume larger levels of output with less-than-proportional increases in labor, so much of their labor input being overhead labor, since output has hardly increased much at most European and North American firms [22]. Rather, there seems to have been a "productivity surprise" at a great many manufacturing operations. In general, a one-time shift (of Harrod-neutral type) in the level of productivity need not cause any shift of the natural rate path, only a proportional shift of the equilibrium real wage path (and of nonwage incomes). The peculiarity of this surprise is that its incidence seems to have fallen largely on unemployment and hardly at all on output. If so, that would suggest that something happened reducing demand for manufactures — possibly it was the increased competition from the emer-

---

[22] See PERRY G.L. - SCHULTZE C.L. [6].

ging economies of east Asia and other areas — while at the same time spurring manufacturers to shed labor or restrict hiring.

In a formulation in the spirit of the theory underlying the present econometric study, firms train newly hired workers as an investment for the future. If the profitability of any given stock of employees would grow as a result of a rising stock of customers were no new employees added, the rate of hiring (and thus the cumulative number of workers hired) will be a function of the expected real rate of interest *less* the expected growth rate of stock of customers. In this view, if these firms were forced to revise sharply downwards their estimate of the growth rate of their market, owing to the new competitors, the volume of hiring (and even the retention of employees) that would have made sense when a high growth rate in the stock of customers was expected would no longer be judged profitable. In a closed economy, very possibly, a reduction of the growth rate will generally be accompanied by a somewhat similar drop in the real interest rate, but that will not be the case in a small open economy or a group of large ones. The world real interest rate will not fall if the reduced growth rate of customers for some countries is mirrored in an enhanced growth rate of customers for some other countries.

The other kind of eligible explanation for the rise of unemployment well in excess of the rise of our estimate of the natural unemployment rate path are hypotheses of monetary disturbances. The outstanding example, of course, is the rise of real interest rates in Germany following unification in 1990, which implied a real appreciation matching the Deutschmark appreciation in those countries wishing to maintain the old exchange-rate parity in the European Monetary System and required of them a loosely matching increase of real interest rates in order to maintain the parity. It is now increasingly clear that the countries that held out longest before suspending their operation within the EMS or opting for a new parity have generally suffered the largest increases of the unemployment rate: France on the way to a larger increase in the unemployment rate than Britain (and perhaps Spain) experienced — the case of Italy being clouded by the gathering political crisis in 1993.

The hope in Europe must be that the natural rate has indeed risen about as little as has been estimated here, and that, as natural rate theory allows and suggests, the actual unemployment rate will soon subside in Europe back toward the little-changed natural rate path [23]. In this case, monetary policy can play the familiar role of speeding up that process of adjustment, though at the cost of circumventing the fall of the inflation rate over the subsequent future that would have been a side-benefit of continued tight money.

The worry is that the peculiar effects of the increased competition from overeseas, the impact of which falls more strongly on future prospects than on immediate revenues, have shifted up the natural rate path well above the increase estimated here — perhaps by a full percentage point or even two, in some countries at any rate, in the early years. In this case, many structural impediments to a high unemployment rate will be candidates for reconsideration, their costs compared with their welfare-state attractions: lengthy and generous unemployment compensation will have to be reevaluated. Such a reevaluation may fail to produce a persuasive case for such measures, however.

If the removal of impediments is judged infeasible or ineffective, or such an eventuality is judged likely, governments will be well advised to begin consideration of structural assistance in the form of subsidies to enterprises for their employment of labor, especially low-wage labor. These subsidies, which could be financed by higher value added taxes or else by taxes on the unemployment of high-wage labor, will serve to increase the demand for low-wage workers and thus, except insofar as an increase of their wage results (also a welcome effect), to raise their employment rates. Since there is already a strong case for such subsidies as a device to pull up the wage rates of the working poor, there is less than the usual reason to wait and see before preparing to act.

---

[23] We carn try to get a rough idea of how little the natural rate has risen and how much the rise of European unemployment is driven by German unification within the EMS by examining the magnitude of the unemployment increases in a number of nonEMS countries with significant manufacturing exports—Austria, Australia, Canada, and perhaps one or two more. The United States is probably not a very reliable guide since its manufacturing base has already shrunk considerably over recent decades. (It is true that much of American manufacturing will inevitably go on being "traded" within the national borders in view of the size of the country; but by the same token much of European manufacturing will go on being traded within Europe). This examination is not very encouraging, but at least these countries have not seen their unemployment rates in 1993 rise as fast as they have in France and the other countries still maintaining their parity with the Deutschmark.

BIBLIOGRAPHY

[1] FITOUSSI J.P. *et* AL., *Taux d'Intérêt et Chômage*, Second Annual Report of the International Panel on Macroeconomic Policy of the OFCE, Seuil, 1993, and *Real Interest and Unemployment*, Oxford, Oxford University Press, forthcoming.

[2] LAYARD R. - NICKELL S. - JACKMAN R., *Unemployment: Macroeconomic Performance and the Labor Market*, Oxford, Oxford University Press, 1991.

[3] MANNING D., «Productivity Growth, Wage Setting, and the Equilibrium Rate of Unemployment», Conference on *Unemployment and Wage Determination*, National Bureau of Economic Research, 17-18 October 1991.

[4] MCKIBBIN W.J. - SACHS J.D., *Global Linkages: Macroeconomic Interdependence and Cooperation in the World Economy*, Washington (DC), Brookings Institution, 1991.

[5] NEWELL A. - SYMONS J., «Wages and Employment between the Wars», London, University College, *Discussion Paper*, n. 8702, pp. 1-36, reprinted in *Recent Developments in Macroeconomics*, vol. III, Hants (GB), Edward Elgar, 1991, pp. 432-67.

[6] PERRY G.L. - SCHULTZE C.L., «Was this Recession Different? Are They All Different?», *Brookings Papers on Economic Activity*, Fall 1993.

[7] PHELPS E.S., *Seven Schools of Macroeconomic Throught*, Oxford, Oxford University Press, 1991.

[8] ——, *Structural Slumps: the Modern Equilibrium Theory of Employment, Interest and Assets*, Cambridge (Mass.), Harvard University Press, forthcoming.

V - STRUCTURAL VERSUS MONETARY FACTORS

The UK Labour Market: Micro Rigidities and Macro Obstructions *

Patrick Minford - **Jonathan Riley**
University of Liverpool
Business School, Cardiff and CEPR
Business School, Cardiff

Introduction

In recent months UK unemployment has again reached 3 million. A number of economists have suggested that it will not fall much below 3 million in the foreseeable future. The implication of such a view is that the UK "equilibrium" or natural rate is of this order. In this paper we set out an alternative view based on our work in Liverpool and embodied in the Liverpool model of the UK.

This model (a full account of it in its early annual form is Minford *et* Al. [6] and in its latest quarterly version in Minford *et* Al. [7]) is new classical in approach, though it includes a unionised sector which strikes collective wage bargains. These bargains generate a fairly slow rate of real wage adjustment, which underlies the model's slow rate of adjustment of real variables. By contrast there is little nominal rigidity in the model (notably in Minford *et* Al. [7]) so that inflation rapidly reaches its equilibrium (apart from some modest adjustment element contributed by real variables such as real balances). Nominal disturbances have their effect through interest rates and wealth effects. Real

---

* We are grateful for useful comments to Samuel Brittan, Andrew Britton, and others. This work has been partly supported by a grant from the Esmee Fairbairn Trust.

N.B.: the numbers in square brackets refer to the Bibliography at the end of the paper.

disturbances come from changes in "supply-side" variables such as tax rates, benefits and union power.

In what follows we discuss first the model estimate of the natural rate, U^*, and the contribution to it of different exogenous variables. Secondly we look at the deviation from U^* of the actual unemployment rate and the elements contributing to this. Finally we discuss the contrast between this set of findings and the more pessimistic claims referred to at the start.

1. - The Natural Rate

This is calculated in the model from the equilibrium version of four behavioural equations:

1) a wage equation, treated as the supply price of labour. Real wages are a function of unemployment, real benefits grossed up for direct taxes, the unionisation rate, and (with only a small impact) surprise movements in prices. Because there is assumed to be a non-negligible non-union sector this is not a "bargaining" equation as eg in Layard and Nickell [2] and their many followers. It is identified by the exclusion of current influences on labour demand, as noted by Manning [3]. The non-union wage depends on benefits and unemployment (the proxy for labour supply); but the average wage also includes the union wage whose mark-up depends on unionisation (and unspecified expected future developments) subject to lagged adjustment;

2) a price-cost relation (with a cyclical mark-up which drops out in equilibrium), derived from the implicit (constant returns) production function;

3) a wage-marginal product relation for (un)employment where marginal product is conditioned on expected output. This too comes from the implicit production function. (Given that prices are set mainly in relation to long run average costs, this set-up implies that output and labour demand respond in the short run to aggregate demand, with capacity utilisation variable in the production function);

4) the previous three equations give rise to an "open economy supply curve" of output, with the real exchange rate as its principal

argument (an increase, or decline in competitiveness, causes more supply because this lowers import prices enabling home suppliers to pay higher real consumer wages while still maintaining their producer price to cost margin). The fourth equation is for the current (external) balance, a function of home and foreign output, and the real exchange rate: the effect of net interest, profits and dividends related to accumulated net foreign assets is neglected as second order (inclusion of it would produce a small hysteretic influence on the equilibrium). We assume that in equilibrium stocks of net foreign assets cannot be changing: this is an approximation to the stock-flow equilibrium condition that all asset holdings be increasing at the steady state growth rate, effectively assuming net foreign assets to be close to zero. Also we should realise that for a fast-growing economy (eg an LDC) this condition is too stringent, as one would expect large capital inflows in this case for long periods. However this is not relevant for a mature economy with a moderate steady growth rate. On our assumption we can turn this equation into a long-run demand relation, where output is related to the real exchange rate (negatively) and to world output (or trade).

Of course in the long run capacity utilisation must be normal and so we can illustrate the system by a four-quadrant diagram adapted from Parkin and Bade [9] and for a detailed derivation see Minford [8], Chapter 8, Appendix. Notice that capital is completely endogenous in this solution: capital flows in from abroad or from domestic savings until normal profit is restored. It is the (world) cost of capital that is exogenous here.

Graph 2 shows the overall natural rate we obtain over the last two decades from the resulting long-run equations (in the Appendix we set out the equations used). It rose to a peak of 3 million in 1981-1983 and since then has fallen to below 1 million today.

We now proceed to decompose this rather striking pattern of change in the natural rate into its constituent determinants. Graphs 3-8 show the results.

Interestingly the flat profile of benefits during the 1970s rules them out as having contributed to U^* changes in that decade. However in the 1980s the sharp rises in council house rents, fully compensated in unemployment benefits, but only partially in in-work benefits, substantially raised the benefit package. Besides this contributory role, the key role of benefits is in giving the labour supply schedule a fairly high elasticity (a degree of real wage rigidity, due to the presence of a reservation wage).

The main elements producing change are unionisation, followed by taxes of various sorts. The former rises steadily to 1980 before steadily falling back. The tax rates move in largely offsetting ways until 1983 when their net effect is to lower unemployment, led by falling employer taxes on labour.

Besides these we can see that the trend elements (productivity and world trade trends) produce a tendency to improvement which is reversed by the serious world recession of the early 1980s. Thereafter the ground is gradually recaptured over the 1980s.

One way to summarise this story is to say that trends in productivity and world markets managed after the world recession of 1982 to dominate (just) the effect of rising benefits, while 1980s supply-side influences reducing union power and lowering taxes had further reduced equilibrium unemployment by 1991 to below the level of 1970, restoring it (at 0.6 million) well towards the natural rate of the 1950s (put by the annual model at about 0.3 million).

2. - $U-U^*$ - the Story of "Temporary" Unemployment

We put temporary in quotes because it can take a long time before unemployment reaches its natural rate. There are two sources of $U-U^*$, the "unemployment gap".

First as U^* changes it takes time — about three years — before U is fully affected. This lag can be thought of as the delay in investment taking advantage of new profit opportunities or being run down as losses are realised. It follows that changes in U^* affect the unemployment gap in a manner illustrated in Graph 9: falling U^* raises the gap while rising U^* lowers it. The net effect on $U-U^*$ of the estimated changes in U^* is shown in Graph 10. In the early 1970s this factor generated a fluctuating but on average small gap. But by the late 1970s and early 1980s, as U^* grew steadily, this had become substantially negative, peaking in 1981 at minus 0.7 milion. From 1981, as U^*

levelled off, the gap dropped to zero and then from 1983 as U^* has fallen the unemployment gap rose, to a peak of 0.7 million in 1984. It then fluctuates before falling away as U^* levels off in the late 1980s.

The second element is the effect of shocks to demand. We do not attempt to decompose this element here. In Matthews and Minford [5] we did attempt it (using the earlier annual Liverpool model) for a purely floating period from 1980-1986. On this occasion we are faced with a much longer period and a regime change — the shadow ERM 1987-1988 and the ERM proper 1990-1992 — which upset this floating transmission in a manner that is not easy to model. Instead of formal decomposition we make some informal comments about the demand pressures revealed by this second (residual) element.

Graph 11 shows this demand element. During most of the 1970s fluctuations in it were fairly modest. There was a peak of demand-induced unemployment of 0.3 milion in 1976, against a trough of −0.4 million in 1973, a not-implausibile net swing of 0.7 from the Barber boom to the recession after the first oil price rise. Thereafter the swings become larger. In the 1979 expansion it falls to −0.6 in 1979 before emerging into the trauma of the 1980s.

During the early 1980s demand-led unemployment fluctuates between 0.2 and −0.2 million before the lagged effects of persistent deflation (Matthews - Minford [5]) come through from 1984 onwards. The peak of demand-induced unemployment is 1.2 million in 1986 (much in line with Matthews - Minford [5]). From then the recovery begins to reduce the total, bringing it down to 0.7 million in 1990.

At this point we run into the phase of deflation associated with the aftermath of the 1988 boom and the entry into the ERM. According to these figures demand-led unemployment had reached no less than 2.3 million by the end of 1992. They clearly indicate that this deflation has been of an extraordinary magnitude.

Clearly these numbers must be treated with more than the usual caution. There are high standard errors around natural rate estimates. Nevertheless the direction and size of these movements in the natural rate and their broad decomposition into supply- and demand-driven components does in our view indicate four main things. First, that there was a large rise in the natural rate between the 1960s and the early 1980s. Second, that this rise was probably more than reversed by the somewhat draconian labour market reforms of the 1980s. Third that there have been two major deflationary episodes with sharp effects on unemployment in the 1980s. Fourth that of these the second, associated with ERM entry was the more deflationary and had the sharper unemployment effect, on a scale comparable with that of the 1930s.

3. - Interpretation and Contrast

The picture drawn in these pages could not be in greater contrast with the generality of comment one reads about the UK economy today. This is true of most forecasting houses as it is of economic commentators, business or academic. The general view seems to be that the UK has little excess capacity and that in the labour market wage pressures will restart at unemployment rates not much below 3 million, most of these unemployed being considered to exert little if any market pressure on wages because of the power of "insiders".

There is of course a natural human tendency to extrapolate current experience. This tendency is all the greater in a world of rapid change, today's par excellence; it is hard to rely on past regularities when these are being upset with equally alarming regularity.

But this tendency can be overdone. This chronic Lucas Critique condition does not imply that we should jettison all modelling relationships in favour of a know-nothing random walk model whose implication is that one should extrapolate the present endlessly into the future. We must try to separate out the shifting from the stable relations, adjust our models rather than throw them away. In this paper we have made some adjustments to our model, notably for the ERM and the productivity shifts induced by the major tax reforms of Nigel Lawson. But we can see no reason to chuck the whole thing away: indeed though we have not dwelt on this aspect here, what exercises we have done on the model's forecasting capacity have been reasonably encouraging (Matthews - Minford [5]; Matthews - Minford - Riley [4]; Andrews *et* Al., [1]).

What sort of evidence is adduced for the agnostic random walk position against our own? There are three main pieces of which we are aware:

First it is argued that wage behaviour became aggressive again as unemployment fell below 2.5 million in 1988. Wages grew by 10% by 1990, after averaging 8% through the mid-1980s;

Second, unemployment itself is argued to be on a rising ratchet-like trend. In the latest boom it fell only to 1.6 million (in mid-1990), against 1.3 million in the last cyclical upturn of 1979. In spite of the February unemployment fall it is commonly forecast that unemployment will reach 3.4 million or more in the current contraction against 3.3 million in 1986, the last peak;

Finally on capacity it is said that there is limited excess capacity because of accelerated write-offs of plant during this recession. As evidence we are pointed to the latest CBI survey's answer to the below-capacity question— Graph 12 (showing only 70% below capacity as against 83% in 1980) and to the high import penetration figures and balance of payments deficits in the midst of severe recesion, but starting from 1988.

This is a daunting charge sheet on the key trio of wages, unemployment and capacity; we may have left out some further charges but these are perhaps the major ones and certainly enough to be getting on with.

We do not deny that one can fit a pessimistic story to these facts. Let us reply in two ways; first by "encompassing" these facts within our story— i.e. explaining them away in our own terms. Secondly by suggesting some stray inconsistencies and weaknesses within the pessimistic story itself. The first tactic is defensive, the second is offensive, in intellectual terms.

1) Why did the rate of increase in average earnings rise from 8% to 10%? According to our story this reflected rising inflationary expectations in the monetary context of 1987-1990. It is actually remarkable how little wage settlements reacted to a sharp rise in inflation (from 5% to 10% on the RPI and around 8% on "underlying" measures); we explain this by our view that unemployment was above not below the natural rate. For all this period real wages were growing by substantially less than the 4.7% 1980s average growth in manufacturing (let alone still higher general industrial) productivity.

2) Why did unemployment drop only to 1.6 million and why has it risen to 3 million-plus? Our answer is that owing to our tragic errors in monetary policy we had to hit on the head an economy which otherwise could have remained on a sustained growth path of some 3%. After we had so hit it on the head we joined the ERM proper and continuing raining blows on its prostrate body. The resulting deep recession has produced an unemployment excess, $U - U^*$, of over 2 million. In short it is recession, not the trends of a poorly-performing labour market, that has delivered us this apparent ratchet.

3) Finally why the apparent lack of capacity? We explain the high import penetration partly by reference to the ERM overvaluation; we also note the fairly good export share performance (Graph 13) in spite of this overvaluation, so a further explanation lies in the free trade orientation of the UK economy— we are specialising and dividing labour.

There is also little doubt that the sheer speed of the 1988 expansion overtook available capacity at that time.

Nevertheless a distinction must be made between actual capacity and the potential output (or natural output rate) associated with the natural rate of unemployment. It takes time for the necessary capital to be installed, to exploit the profit opportunities linked with potential output: had growth been steady and controlled in 1988, we would argue that overheating would have been avoided and unemployment would have fallen without the interruption caused by the temporary inflationary pressure and the subsequent squeeze.

As for capacity, the CBI question is qualitative and must be treated with caution. Furthermore capacity, even when "written off", does not thereby cease to exist, it is merely discounted by managers or even sold off; interestingly total private gross fixed investment has fallen only 20% from its peak during this long and severe recession suggesting that apart from "write-off" (i.e. in physical terms) there is large-scale spare capacity.

Turning from encompassing to the offensive, we must stress that the behaviour of expected real wages remained moderate even when unemployment had fallen to 1.6 million; this is inconsistent with a natural rate of 2.5 million and above.

Then we must query the lack of pressure from "outsiders", in the form of long-term unemployed. Those unemployed more than a year had dropped by end 1990 to 0.5 million from 1.3 million in 1987. Furthermore the turnover rate in the labour market has risen to around 0.3 million per month, approximately 14% of the labour force per year (against 9% in 1988). Hence some 50% of the labour force may have "quit" jobs and experienced a spell of unemployment in the last four years; even allowing for double and even more frequent spells among these this high rate of activity suggests a wide experience of unemployment in the labour force. This is not a picture of supine labour market behaviour by the unemployed, not even those with the misfortune to become "long-term" unemployed. Nor would supinity be consistent with other evidence we have on benefits (now exceedingly low relative to the wages of all but the lowest paid), on the greater vigour with which worktesting (plus job- and re-start programmes) is being applied, and finally the weakness of the traditionally militant unions.

A supposed lack of excess capacity is difficult to reconcile with the answers to the CBI's pricing question (virtually no respondents plan price rises), especially given the large rise in imported material costs since exit from ERM. There is clear unwillingness to raise prices and margins, which can only be explained by an extreme desire to raise sales and use of capacity.

Conclusions

This paper brings together the implications of our work at Liverpool for the issue of micro rigidities and macro obstructions in the UK labour market. Our view is that the micro problems have been substantially diminished by the supply-side reforms of the 1980s but that macro policy has been particularly savage during the past four years, as a by-product of the ERM experiment. Looking ahead, we see promising scope therefore for bringing unemployment down sharply without risks of re-igniting inflation. Ironically, we have a government which needs to be persuaded towards greater monetary ease — not a typical democratic experience!

APPENDIX

The Natural Rate Equations

The equations estimated for the quarterly model used FIML, with expectations exogenised but iterated between FIML estimates. In a few cases parameters in the model itself are somewhat different from the final FIML estimates; this arose because the model's parameters were taken from a slightly earlier iteration than the final one shown below. The relevant ones are shown in square brackets.

$$D\log RW = \underset{(0.12)}{0.13} + \underset{(0.31)}{0.37}\ UNR + \underset{(0.07)}{0.20}\ \log(BEN[1 + TAXL])$$

$$-\underset{(0.027)}{0.014}\log(U) - \underset{(0.07)}{0.20}\log(RW[-2]) - \underset{(0.22)}{0.06}\ PUE + \underset{(0.22)}{0.19}\ PUE[-1]$$

$$RXR = -\underset{(0.1)}{0.3} + \underset{(0.55)\ [1.53]}{1.33}\log(RW[1+BOSS+VAT]) + \underset{(-)}{1.0}\log(1+VAT)$$

$$-\underset{0.017)}{0.034}\ TIME$$

$$\log(U) = \underset{(7.8)}{22.7} - \underset{(0.72)\ [2.15]}{2.04}\log(Y) + \underset{(0.55)\ [0.79]}{0.61}\log(RW[1.BOSS+VAT])$$

$$+\underset{(0.0052)}{0.011}\ TIME + \underset{(0.10)}{0.79}\log(U[-1]) + \underset{(0.09)}{0.31}\ ERROR[-1]$$

$$XVOL/0.32\cdot Y^* = \underset{(5.7)}{10.4} + \underset{(0.23)}{0.54}\log(WT) - \underset{(0.62)}{1.2}\log(Y)$$

$$-\underset{(0.24)}{0.44}(0.6\ RXR + 0.4\ RXR^*)$$

The resulting reduced form coefficients, for the natural rate of unemployment, on the major exogenous variables within the current model version are as follows:

$$\log(U^*) = \underset{(7.0)}{11.2}\,UNR + \underset{(4.0)}{5.3}\,\log(1+BOSS) + \underset{(3.9)}{5.0}\,\log(BEN[1+TAXL])$$

$$+\underset{(0.03)}{0.0023}\,TIME + \underset{(4.7)}{7.4}\,\log(1+VAT) - \underset{(2.13)}{2.72}\,\log(WT)$$

+ constant and dummies for productivity shifts (see below) (standard errors bracketed).

---

1. - The Terms Used Are

*	=	equilibriun ("natural")
U	=	unemployment
Y	=	output
RXR	=	real exchange rate (CPI-based)
RW	=	real wage (W/CPI)
BOSS	=	employed tax rate on wages
VAT	=	indirect tax rate
UNR	=	unionisation rate
BEN	=	value (real) of unemployment package
TAXL	=	employee tax rate on wages (incl. national insurance, net of in-work benefit rate)
WT	=	world trade

Productivity Shift Dummies

1) One from 1983 picks up the effect of the rise in union sector productivity and associated wage rises (as poor practices were bought out) — this raises the log of U^* (as union workers are shaken out) by 0.12 in 1983, falling slowly with UNR to 0.10 in 1992.

2) A second from 1987 picks up a further trend in productivity growth raising labour's marginal product generally and also wages — this on balance reduces unemployment, cumulating to a reduction of 0.02 in the log of the natural rate of unemployment.

GRAPH 1

THE OPEN ECONOMY
UNDER IMPERFECT COMPETITION
IN THE LONG RUN

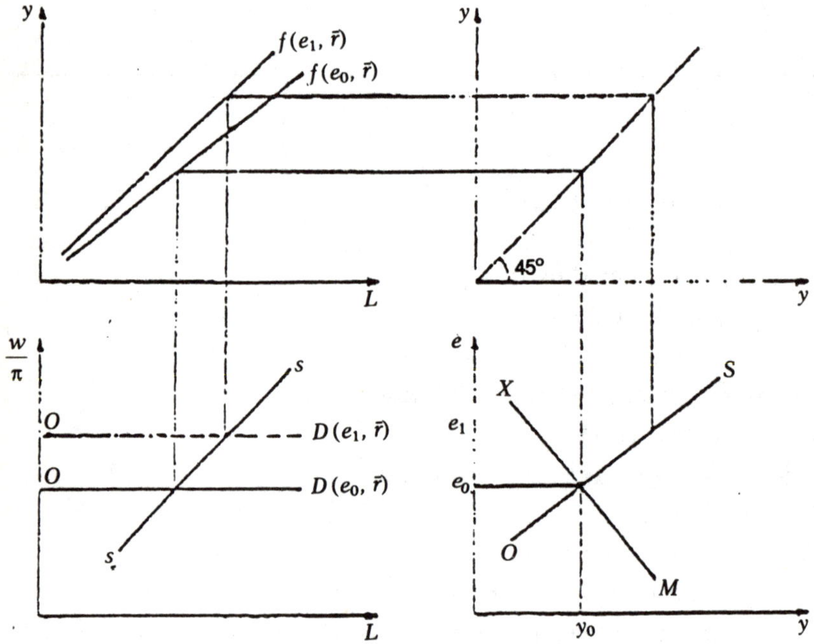

GRAPH 2

ACTUAL AND NATURAL RATE OF UNEMPLOYMENT
(thousands)

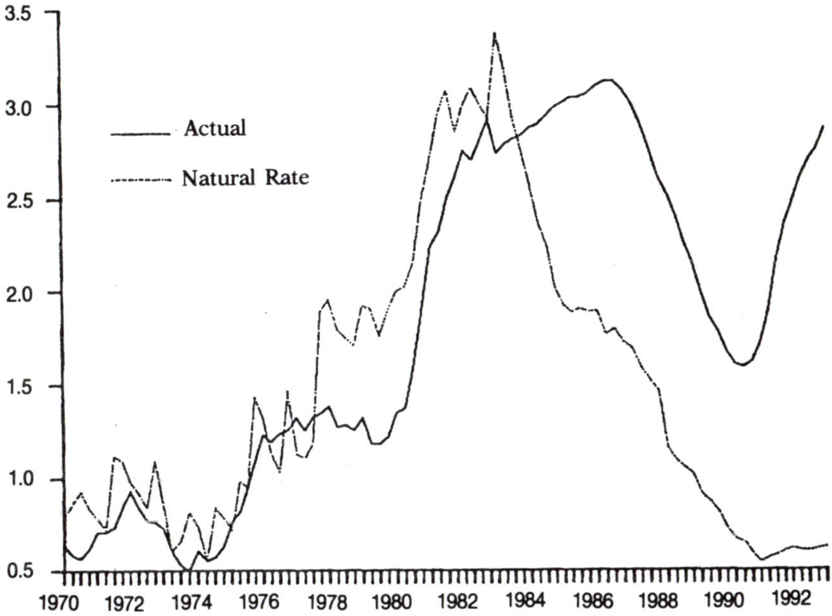

GRAPH 3

EFFECT (ON LOG U^*) OF UNIONISATION

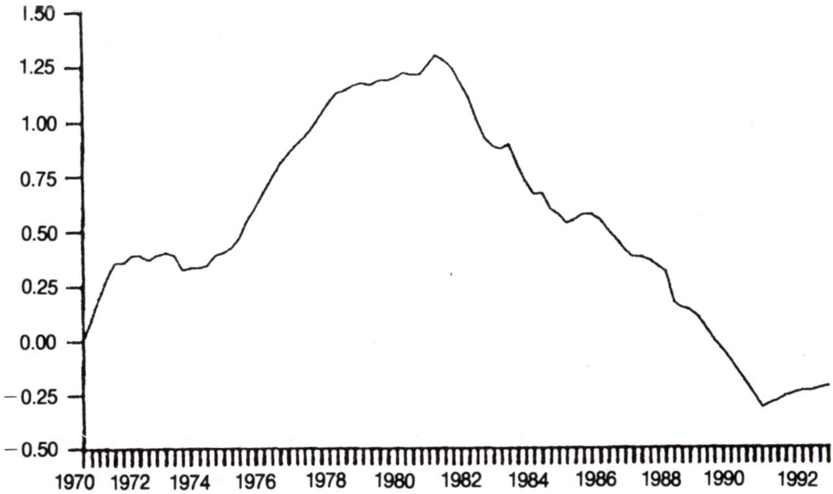

GRAPH 4

EFFECT (ON LOG U^*) OF VAT

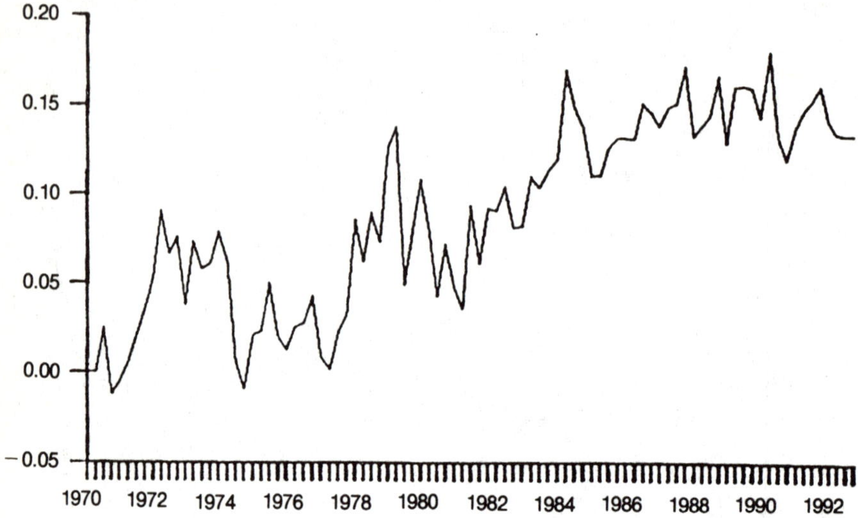

GRAPH 5

EFFECT (ON LOG U^*)
OF EMPLOYERS' LABOUR TAX

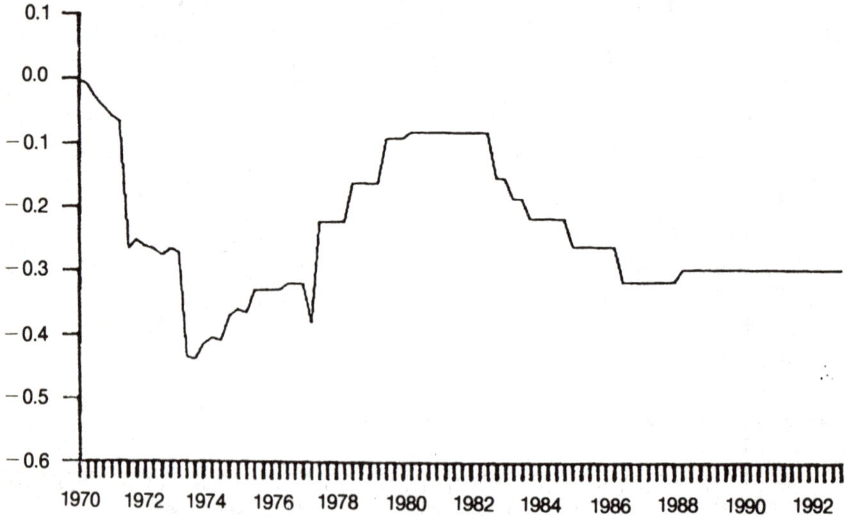

GRAPH 6

EFFECT (ON LOG U^*)
OF EMPLOYEES' LABOUR TAX

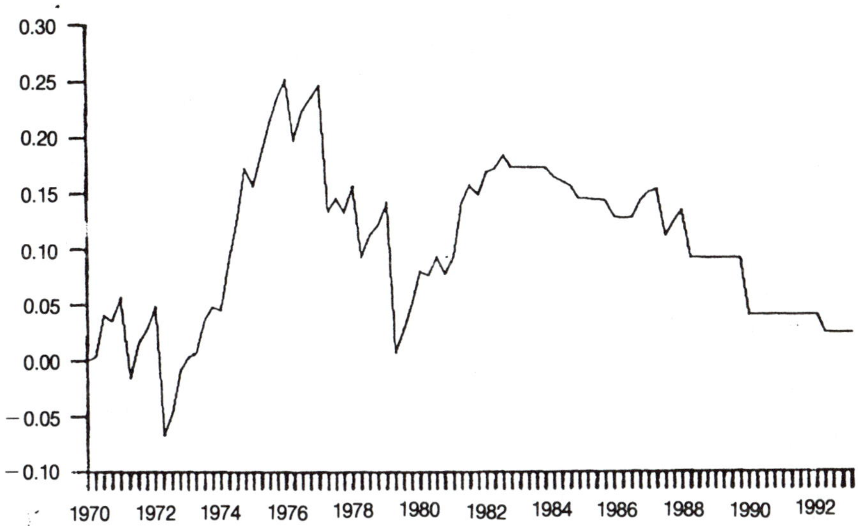

GRAPH 7

EFFECT (ON LOG U^*)
OF UNEMPLOYMENT BENEFIT

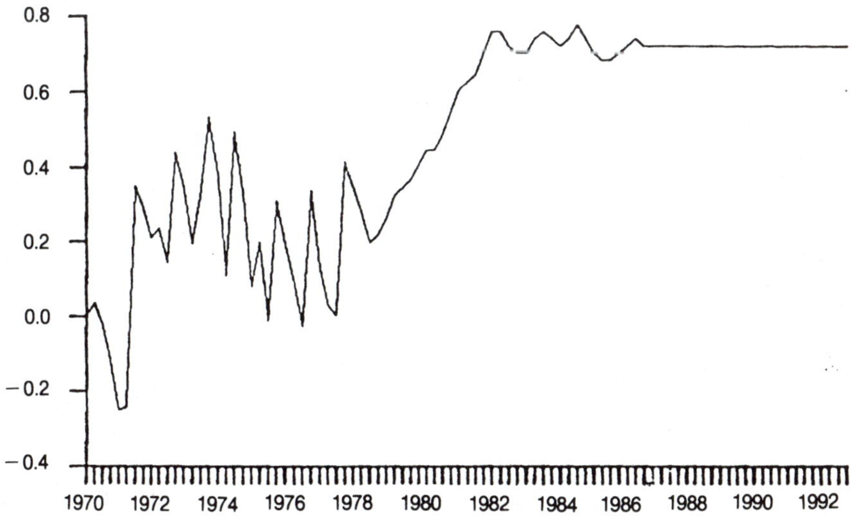

GRAPH 8

EFFECT (ON LOG U^*) OF PRODUCTIVITY AND WORLD TRADE

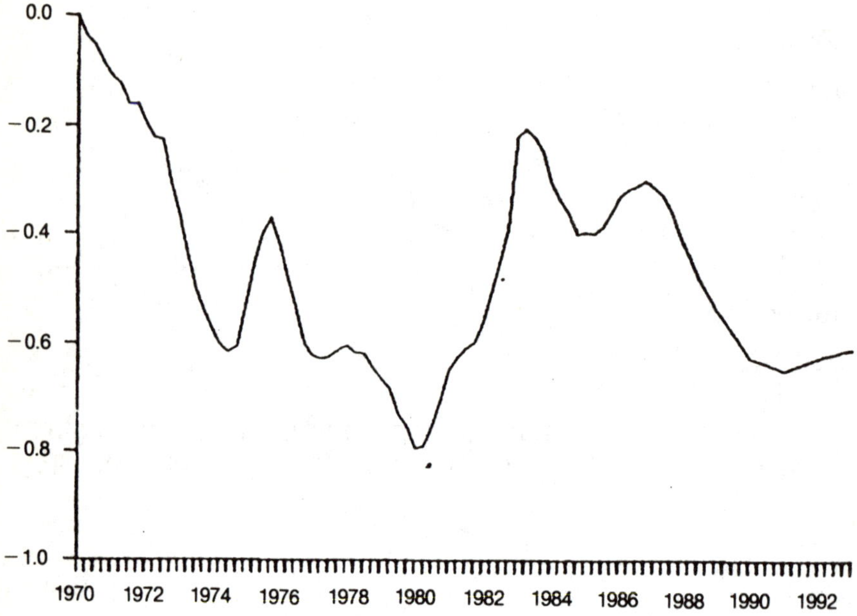

GRAPH 9

EFFECT OF U^* ON $U-U^*$

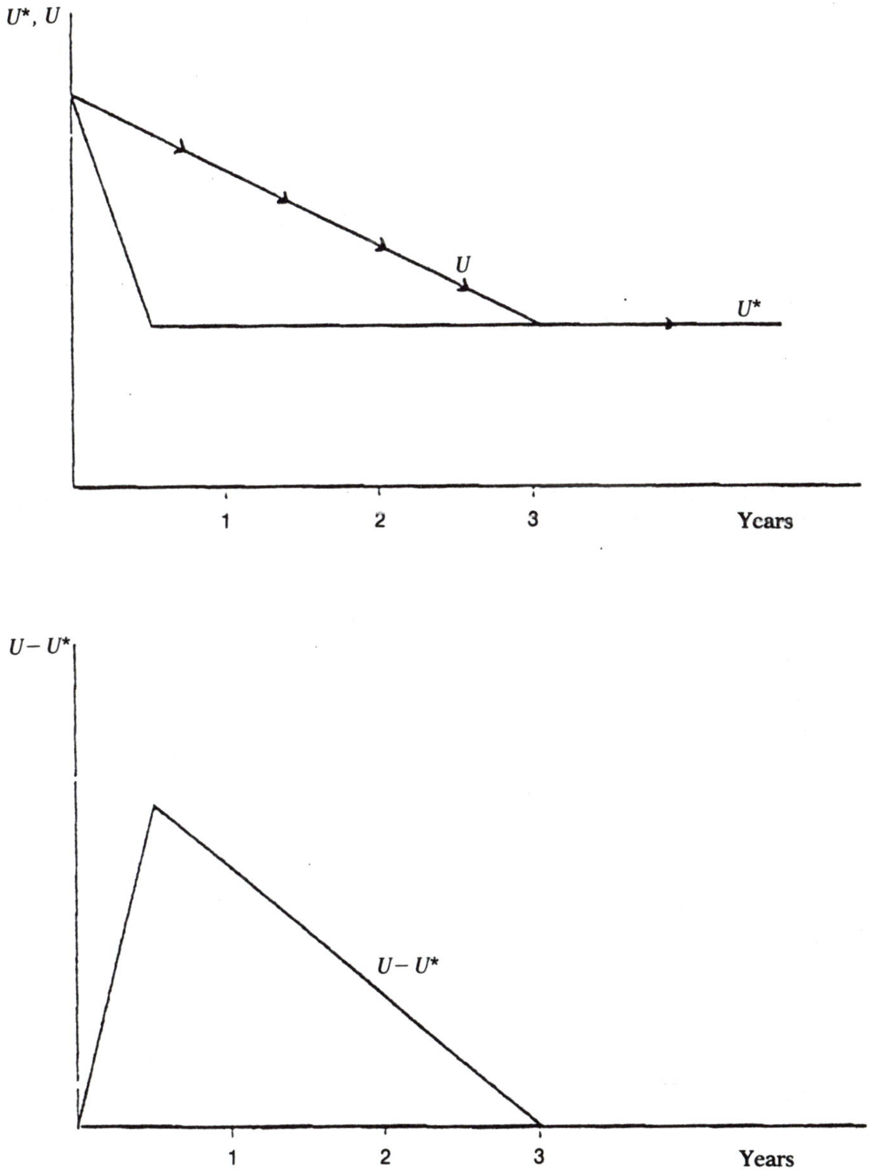

GRAPH 10

EFFECT OF U^* ON $U-U^*$

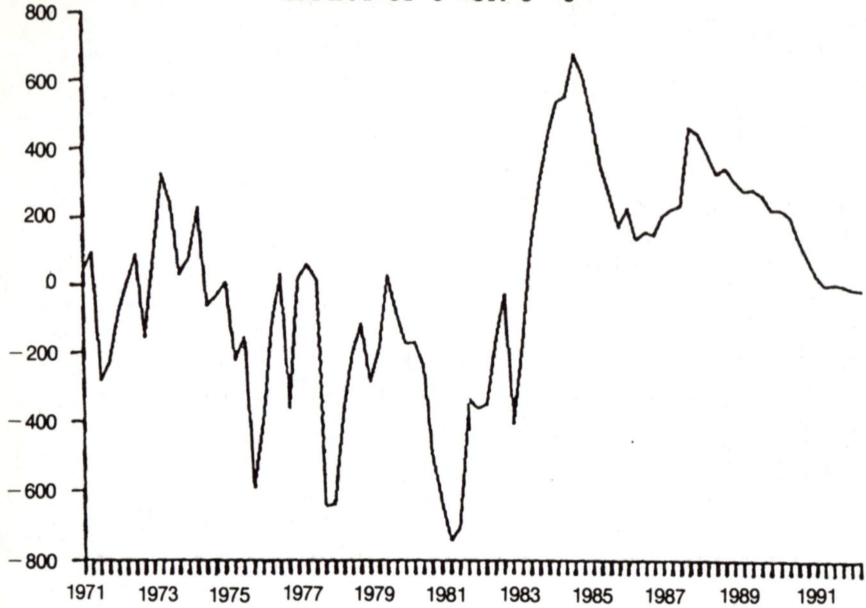

GRAPH 11

EFFECT OF *RL*
(LONG REAL INTEREST RATES) ON $U-U^*$

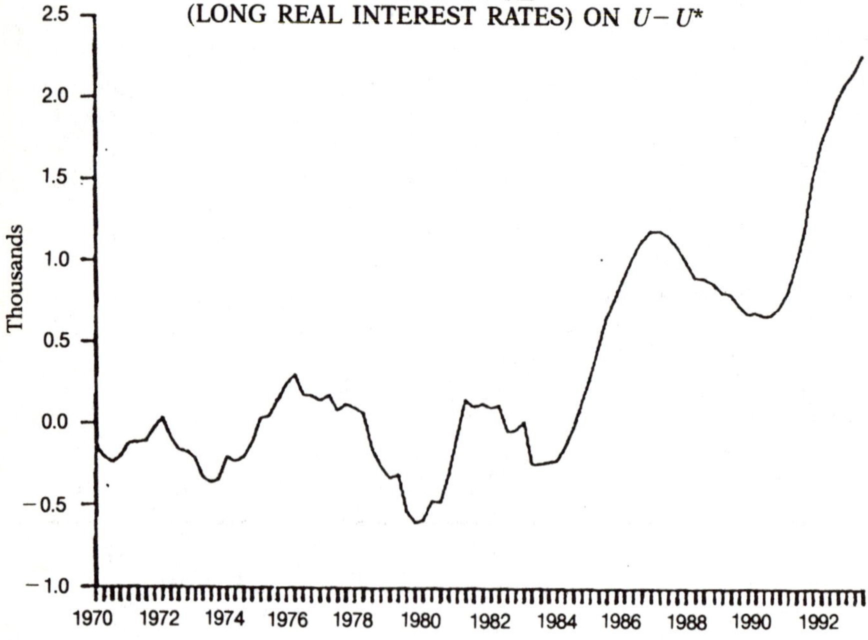

GRAPH 12

CBI SURVEY:
FIRMS REPORTING
BELOW CAPACITY WORKING (%)

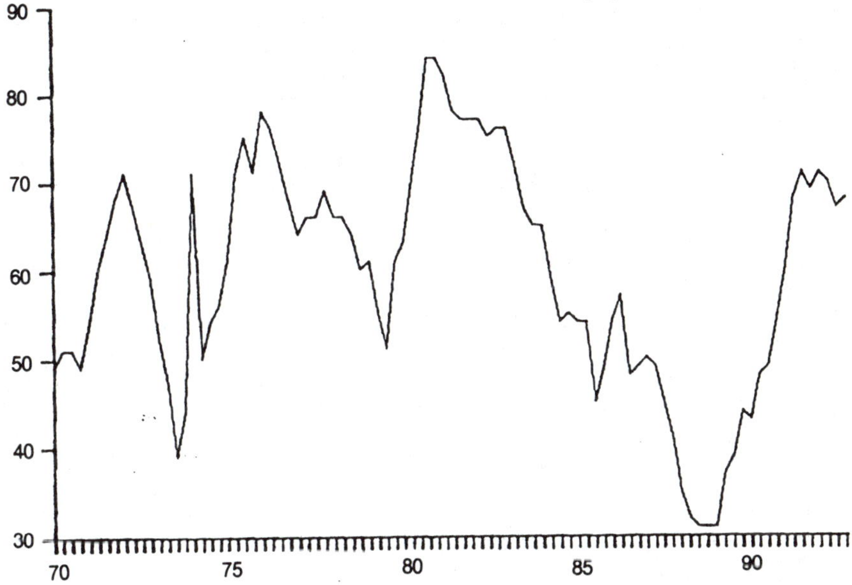

Source: CBI.

GRAPH 13

UK SHARE OF WORLD TRADE
IN MANUFACTURES %

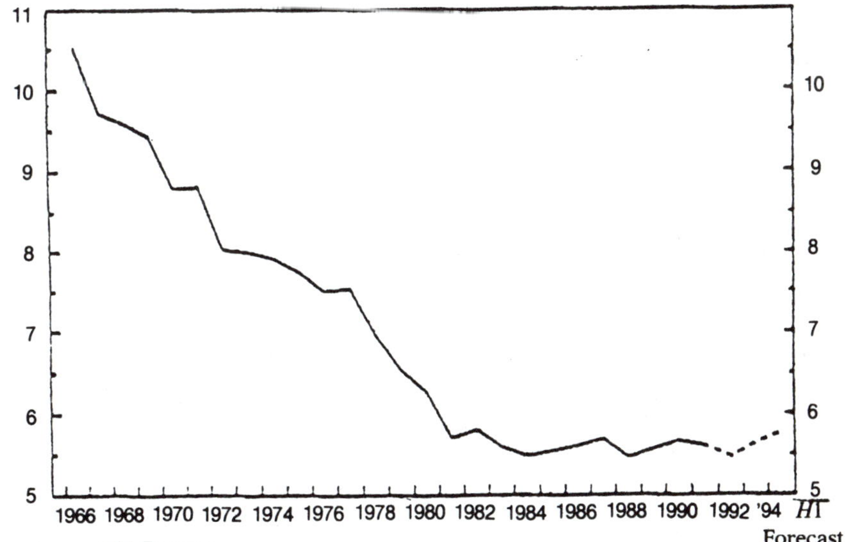

Source: HM TREASURY.

BIBLIOGRAPHY

[1] ANDREWS M. - MINFORD P. - RILEY S., «On Comparing Macroeconomic Models Using non-Nested Tests», Liverpool Research Group in Macroeconomics, University of Liverpool, *Working Paper*, n. 90/03, 1990.

[2] LAYARD R. - NICKELL S., «The Causes of British Unemployment», National Institute, *Economic Review*, n. 111, February 1985.

[3] MANNING A., «Wage Bargaining and the Phillips Curve: the Identification and Specification of Aggregate Wage Equations», *Economic Journal*, n. 103, 1993, pp. 98-118.

[4] MATTHEWS K.G.P. - MINFORD P. - RILEY J., «The Forecasts of Performance of the Liverpool Group: the Record Straightened», Liverpool Research Group in Macroeconomics, *Quarterly Economic Bulletin*, vol. 7, n. 1, 1986.

[5] MATTHEWS K.G.P. - MINFORD P., «Mrs. Thatcher's Economic Policies 1979-86», (The Conservative Revolution: a Special Report), CUP, *Economic Policy*, 1987.

[6] MINFORD P. - SPRAGUE A. - MATTHEWS K.G.P. - MARWAHA S., «The Liverpool Macroeconomic Model of the United Kingdom», *Economic Modelling*, n. 1, January 1984.

[7] MINFORD P. - MATTHEWS K.G.P. - RASTOGI A., «A Quarterly Version of the Liverpool Model of the UK», Liverpool Research Group in Macroeconomics, University of Liverpool, *Working Paper*, n. 90/06, 1990.

[8] MINFORD P., *Rational Expectations Macroeconomics an Introductory Handbook*, Oxford, Basil Blackwell, 1992.

[9] PARKIN M. - BADE R., *Modern Macroeconomics*, Phillip Allan, 1990.

Conclusions

Edmund S. Phelps
MIT, Cambridge (Mass)

I thought at first I might introduce my commentary with the report that this year we reached no consensus and that we would have to abandon the "Conclusions" this year. In fact, there was no agreement I think, on how to apportion the rise of unemployment in the 1990s between the operation of certain shocks through monetary channels, which do not raise the natural rate of interest, on the one hand, and the operation of shocks through non-monetary channels, which do raise the natural rate of unemployment. One of the difficulties in making that apportionment is that often we are talking about the same shock, such as the German unification, which pushed up real rates of interest, which has importance even in non-monetary models. But it also operates through monetary channels, thanks to the EMS or just the everyday functioning of a monetary economy.

But there is another way I think that I could begin this brief set of concluding remarks. We are in rather broad agreement, I think, that, at the end of the 1980s, the equilibrium, or natural, or structural level of unemployment in all, or almost all, of the countries under consideration was very high. For the OECD countries as a whole, the equilibrium unemployment rate must have been, in 1989 and 1990, between 6% and 7%, while I think, most of us would guess that it was in the neighborhood of 3% or 4% in the 1960s. So that is a major increase in the equilibrium rate.

Perhaps there is an emerging consensus, though I'm not sure how far it has gone, that this rise of the natural rate between the 1960s and now is largely because of higher tax rates of certain kinds, not all kinds (payroll tax rates, for example), higher after-tax energy prices to users, higher world real rates of interest, and higher wealth and welfare entitlement.

In my view, which goes a little beyond the econometric estimates we have been able to make so far, much of the underlying problem now is that the 1990s are the decade of China and the rest of East Asia, India, Mexico and Argentina. Maybe Eastern Europe will come along a little later, once its transition is successfully navigated. It's increasingly to those places, I think, that the world's investment will be going in the 1990's. It's already going there to an amazing extent.

As a result, Europe and North America too, will have to suffer from high real interest rates. As a conseguence, not only will we have somewhat slower growth on that account, but we will have higher levels of unemployment, because firms will not be doing all the things they do to grow, most of which support a high level of employment.

It follows from this view that the natural rate is starting from a pretty high plateau in the 1990s. This suggests that, even if the natural rate has not worsened since the late-1980s, it would be a good idea to adopt some structural measures to reduce the natural rate. Whether or not the natural rate has risen a lot in the 1990s relative to the late-1980s, and whatever the mix of shocks through monetary channels, on the one hand, and shocks through non-monetary channels, on the other, it is clear that the natural rate has risen to such a level that some structural remedies would be welcome at this point.

This volume has talked about some structural remedies. Reducing payroll tax burdens would probably be pretty high on most people's list.

This might take the form of outright subsidies for the employment of low-wage labor, although it might be, in some cases, administratively easier just to lower the tax rates on the employment of labor. Energy tax rates are another problem that I think it is worth looking into.

The volume has also talked a lot about training, but I think there is not much agreement on the scope for training. If training is such a great idea, why don't firms voluntarily engage in a lot more of it? More widely, many hold that it would be a rather poor idea to expand the public sector as a way to reduce unemployment. In my view, at least, the reason for that is that doing so would drive up real interest rates. It's a beggar-my-neighbor policy. It crowds out investment in the rest of the world.

At the same time that one holds to the view that the natural rate is worse than it ever was before, and it is really time to do something about it, one can also take the view that, because of the working of the EMS in recent years, in conjunction with the German unification, there has been a demand problem, particularly in Europe, and especially among the countries in the EMS. Therefore, there is some reason to think that a reflation, or a re-ignition of effective demand would be a good idea. Europe would benefict from a very quick and concerted easing of money, but I don't think there has been sufficient discussion of whether or not that is politically possible.

In any case, let me end on the note, which I think it is widely, albeit not unanimously, agreed that it would be a pity if we let a program of monetary reflation distract us from the need to proceed with some of these long over-due structural reforms.

VI - ROUND TABLE: POLICY «RECOMMENDATIONS» ON THE UNEMPLOYMENT PROBLEM

Robert A. Mundell
Columbia University, New York

I have a couple of remarks to make at the beginning to set the tone of the discussion. First, about the problem of unemployment in the OECD area in general. The level of unemployment in the whole OECD area is estimated at something like 30 million people. What are the costs of that unemployment? We are all aware of the many pitfalls in translating the number of unemployed into measures of lost output, but as a crude approximation, it would have to be close to the total production of an economy the size of Britain or Italy. The labor force in Britain, for example, is about 28 million. So, it is as if the whole British or Italian production didn't exist or wasn't being utilized. In round numbers the cost of unemployment in the OECD area amounts to one trillon (one milliard) dollars, the lack of output that results from the absence of those people in the labor force not working in the economy.

In this volume we have heard a lot about the distinction between cyclical and structural unemployment. Cyclical unemployment can be thought of as that correctable by macroeconomic policies, whereas structural unemployment is all the rest. Economists tend to dismiss structural unemployment as "natural" largely because they are not amenable to Keynesian macroeconomic policies. But it still represents lost production, a huge social problem for the unemployed and for the employed who, directly or indirectly, have to support them, and a candidate for more refined study.

There is a category of unemployment that is non-cyclical but is nevertheless induced by microeconomic policy. The more taxes on people who work, and subsidies for those who do not work, the higher the measured unemployment rate will be. The unemployment rate can be raised by unemployment insurance programs, obligatory severance pay, high payroll taxes, and social welfare programs. It is not just that some fraction of the labor force would rather accept unemployment insurance than do an honest day's labor. There is a large borderline area where workers are "choosy" about the jobs they will do, a specificity problem that results from the fact that the job-demand-mix of the economy differs from the job-supply-mix of the labor force.

It is hard to split unemployment exactly into cyclical, structural and micro-policy-induced components. But some start along this road can be found in Llewellyn's paper when he presents the level of unemployment in different OECD countries. He also has a column at the end of his table that estimates the extent to which unemployment is long-term rather than short-term — long-term meaning people who have been unemployed for more than a year.

In looking over this table, I updated its unemployment figures with some estimates for 1993 unemployment from the WEFA *Economic Outlook* for 1993; this is the unemployment rate in the first column on the left-hand side. Then I took the column measuring the fraction of unemployed that was long-term, and assumed that this fraction was stable enough to hold as a rough approximation for 1993. The third column comes from multiplying the first and second columns to get the percentage of the labor force that is unemployed for more than one year. The fourth column gives the ranking according to this long-term unemployment as a percentage of the labor force, starting with the lowest long-term unemployment rate.

Two questions emerge: first, why are unemployment rates much higher in some countries than in others; and second, why is the ratio of long-term to short-term unemployment rates *(LT/ST)* higher in some countries than in others. Two countries with very high unemployment rates — Spain and Ireland — also have a high proportion of long-term to short-term unemployment; the high unemployment in Finland, on the other hand, is mainly short-term, no doubt due to the collapse of Finnish markets in the Soviet Union. Other countries with relatively high *LT/ST* are Italy and Belgium. Countries with very low *LT/ST* ratios include Canada (probably a function of the overvalued Canadian dollar between 1987 and 1991). It is also interesting that the United States and Japan come out about the same for long-term unemployment rates, despite the fact that the total unemployment rate is substantially higher in the United States than in Japan.

A final point. The eight countries with the lowest rankings of long-term unemployment as a fraction of the labor force are all countries *not* in the Economic Community. Could it be that the social welfare policies of the Community have created a problem that would not have existed in the absence of these policies?

With that introduction, we will now focus on policy conclusions or recommendations for the various governments, whether national, European Community or OECD.

TABLE 1

LONG-TERM UNEMPLOYMENT RATES IN OECD COUNTRIES

	(1) U/L	(2) U_{lt}/U	(3)=(1)x(2) U_{lt}/L	(4) Rank
Canada	11.4	7.2	0.82	5
US	6.9	6.3	0.43	2
Japan	2.5	17.9	0.45	3
Australia	10.9	24.9	2.71	11
New Zealand	9.8	21.3	2.09	10
Belgium	9.0	61.6	5.54	18
Denmark	12.5	31.2	3.90	14
France	11.7	38.7	4.53	17
Germany	9.0	45.5	4.1	15
Greece	8.9	47.0	4.18	16
Ireland	16.9	60.3	10.19	20
Italy	13.5	67.1	9.06	19
Netherlands	7.9	43.0	3.40	13
Portugal	5.4	38.3	2.07	9
Spain	22.2	49.1	10.90	21
UK	10.5	28.1	2.95	12
Austria	4.5	15.2	0.68	4
Finland	18.1	9.1	1.65	8
Norway	6.1	20.6	1.26	7
Sveden	8.1	4.4	0.35	1
Svitzerland	4.7	19.8	0.93	6

U = unemployment
L = labor force
U_{lt} = long-term unemployment

Luis Fina Sanglas
EC, Brussels

I shall present the conclusions of the European Council meeting that, as you know, recently took place and the policy recommendations to deal with that problem which is considered the most important one and which merits the highest priority in Community policies and in the policies of the member states.

I would put this in the context of the analysis that is being conducted by the Commission on the characteristics and nature of the present unemployment problem. We recognize that there are both cyclical and structural components which require action both in the short term and in the medium and long term. That was one of the new points stressed by the President of the Commission, Jacques Delors, who insisted on the need to think in the long term and to introduce structural measures to improve the functioning of our economies and of our labor market.

In the short term, particularly in the Community, there are problems which have been discussed at length in this volume: the problem of very high interest rates, changes in the behavior of the economic agents, which have aggravated the situation, and so on. To deal with those short-term problems, the Council recommended a coordinated and rapid reduction of interest rates, a series of measures to stimulate demand reinforcing the measures that had already been put forward in the previous European Council at the end of 1992 in Edinburgh where the Council recommended maintaining the levels of public investment, and reinforcing certain unemployment programs, particularly those combining training with employment.

In the medium term, the problems in the Community can be summarized in three points. First, mass unemployment. In the Community, there are now more than 17 million unemployed, probably 17 and a half million, and a monthly rate of increase of between 100,000, and 150,000, which could lead us, very quickly, to the 20 million mark. This is in a context of low participation rates. If we take these two elements into account, we can look at the unemployment ratio, the relationship between the unemployment levels and the unemployment-age population in the Community which now stands at 60%. In the United States it is 70%; in Japan it is 75%. That means, in our view, that the unemployment rates seriously underestimate the extent of the non-utilization of labour in the Community.

Second, the low rate of employment creation. Growth is not employment intensive enough, and many of the suggested actions go in the direction of trying to find policies and formulae in order to increase the employment intensity of economic growth. I shall not repeat the basic data. You already know it. But there is a sharp contrast between what has happened in the United States, on one hand, and in the Community, on the other. And there is the continuing problem in the European economy of low and decreasing competitivity, a problem that has worsened in the last few years and that needs to be addressed.

To look at those problems, the European Council invited the Commission to produce, for the end of 1993, an analysis and policy prescriptions which are contained in a *White Paper*, that looks at that triad — growth, unemployment and competitiveness — which are the three main problems I mentioned. The Council also broadly decided the themes that should be addressed in that analysis and made specific recommendations. These can be summarized in eight points: 1) to stay on course for monetary and economic union; 2) to speed up the GATT negotiating process in order to increase international trade in a fair environment; 3) to reinforce actions in the field of research and development, on the one hand strenghening cooperation, on the other increasing the resources devoted to these activities; 4) to reinforce all the programs directed at creating networks of transportation and telecommunications infrastructure in Europe; 5) to promote in particular, information infrastructures at Community level; 6) to reinforce education and training to be able to face the new technological challenges of the moment; 7) to reflect on and develop what the Council calls a new development model, which takes into account aspects such as the environment, quality of life, quality of jobs, etc.

and also to look into the different methods of financing the welfare system in the Community; and 8) the final recommendation is to promote a new generation of active labor market policies to increase quality, providing individualized counseling for all young people entering the labor market and for all unemployed people, and also to ensure better targeting and a better mix of the measures that are currently in place in the member States.

Jean-Paul Fitoussi
OFCE, Paris

I have a much shorter list of recommendations. I would like to stress from the outset that the European economy is in a much better shape than some authors of this volume have assessed. It has suffered abnormally high real interest rates for more than a decade but still its growth potential is high. The present recession seems to be policy made, rather than a spontaneous reaction to some exogenous factors, even if German unification did play an important role.

We may offer several hypotheses to explain why interest rates are out of phase with present economic conditions, and why this has been the case for more than a decade. But what is relevant for the present discussion is the notion that the preference function of European governments has dramatically changed since the beginning of the 1980s. First the hierarchy of policy objectives seems to have been inverted, and second even the notion of the existence of a trade-off between these objectives seems to have vanished.

The preference function has become lexicographic i.e., you worry about the second objective only after having reached the first: fight inflation through wage moderation, whatever the cost in terms of unemployment of such a policy could be; only then, if needed will you tackle the problem of employment. Indeed, the common belief was that the policy will deliver the goods and the economy will spontaneously recover, whithout any government intervention.

This, at least was the spirit of the strategy of "competitive disinflation" followed in France. Unfortunately, despite wage moderation, despite a strong increase in competitiveness, despite a recovery of companies' profit margins, the French economy is still trapped in a low growth equilibrium.

The idea that it would be a good idea to return to the neoclassical synthesis has emerged, especially in the paper by Mindford and Reley.

We should also consider demand, and perhaps a good policy should relax some demand constraints. Because fiscal policy seems not to offer much room for manoeuvre, due to high fiscal deficits and high real interest rates, only monetary policy is left.

At this very moment, when inflation does not seem to be a problem any more, monetary policy should be quite expansionary in all European countries. The problem is not the competitiveness of each European country *vis-à-vis* the other, but the competitivenes of Europe taken as a whole *vis-à-vis* the United States and Japan. We should not continue this masochistic process of overvaluing our currencies through high interest rates, and then complaining about our loss of competitivity.

My first recommendation would then be that the European countries try to achieve a coordinated decrease in short term interest rates. Cordinated, because the danger here is to enter a process of competitive devaluation.

My second recommendation is to lower the cost of labour for the unskilled. As has been abundantly documented, the burden of unemployment in almost all countries, falls disproportionately on the unskilled. This may entail unemployment subsidies through a restructing of the social contribution saystem.

My third recommendation is to strive for more coordination between fiscal and monetary authorities: the public debt problem that many countries are confronted with today, is partly, to say the least, the consequence of a too tight monetary policy.

John Llewellyn

OECD, Paris

I have some observations, and nested in them are conclusions. First observation, I was struck by the significant scope being claimed for the existence of room to manoeuvre on the demand side in many of our economies at the moment. This struck me because, firstly, it was more than I had expected, particularly from this group of economists, and secondly, because it is more than you would find at the moment in policy circles, particularly in Europe.

Second observation. There has been relatively little discussion of how actually to get that demand, for the very good reason, of course, that this is more difficult. I would note in this context — I have mentioned it before, but I emphasise it again — that policy makers, especially in Europe, are very concerned today that any demand-led expansion would lead to higher prices, to expectations of higher inflation, and, in turn, to rising long-term real interest rates, however defined and measured. This set of concerns is leading them to be cautious. So, in terms of the analysis of the situation we are facing today, there is quite a schism, in fact, between what several economists have proposed as the starting condition and what I perceive as being taken as the starting position by OECD member governments.

That leads me to some conclusions. One is that I think we should all be very cautious about these estimates, because in making them we are likely to be taken seriously. Second, we should recognise that part of the policy makers' caution is the result of the economists' teachings of the lessons of the last two decades. Policy makers have been taught to be more cautious by the academic writings of these last two decades, based on the experience of them. So, if we are careful about out estimates as we refine them, we must also be very careful about the implications we draw and the way we explain them, because we will be listened to; although what we say enters the policy debate with a lag, and that can be awkward. By the time we are really convincing, the problem may have started to go away!

Third observation. There is a general scepticism about views on the un-employability, on the one hand, of the long-term unemployed and, on the other hand, of the unskilled. This contrasts quite sharply with Phelps; who pointed, with data, to the common tendency for unemployment rates among the unskilled to be higher and, as we also know, for their wages to be relatively lower, or even falling in a whole range of OECD countries. In policy circles, those who are concerned with labour market policies are generally sceptical about the economy's ability to employ the long-term unemployed and the less skilled, at least under present policies.

So, there is a conclusion here, which is an easy one to draw. It is simply the need to understand more. We need to know more about the conditions under which the long-term unemployed do, or do not, get taken back into employment, because this affects the policy design. Labour market policies absorb an enormous amount of resources in some of our countries. So these have to be well spent, and for this we have to know more about the effects of these policies.

Fourth observation. There is much talk about what the French call *délocalisation,* the tendency of firms today to locate abroad. I mention this for two sets of reasons. One is that, if you read the North American press about the NAFTA, if you read the European press about the effects of Central and Eastern Europe, you see that there is a strong belief in many OECD member countries that something very important is going on, namely the movement of capital-intensive plants abroad in search of cheaper, often markedly cheaper, labour.

It is argued that this is partly the result of the new information technologies which make it easier to control such operations abroad, partly that it is easier because of better, and lower relative costs of, transport and because in many cases a lot of countries that previously did not welcome this sort of activity now do. This would furnish one explanation for the declining demand in our countries for unskilled labour that Phelps draw attention to. But some policy discussion goes a lot farther than that, and talks about *délocalisation* being a cause of overall unemployment. And there are policy suggestions about the need to protect OECD countries from this. The discussion gets underway very fast.

I would welcome hearing more about this phenomenon, because it is a subject that all of us collectively, and really rather urgently, need to do more work on, because it could lead very quickly to policy conclusions which are politically popular but might or might not be based on evidence. What we at the OECD, at least, feel is that you cannot simply give a religious answer to this. You cannot simply say, "we know that trade is unequivocally good under any circumstance and cannot cause unemployment". The reason you cannot say that is because it would not be convincing to the man in the street today. We think you have got to go through the mechanisms, try to understand them and, assuming that the conclusion we still find is the conclusion we have always found in the past, then you have got to demonstrate the benefits of free trade by case. So a very important issue has been raised and it warrants looking at very carefully, and rather quickly, by countries and by academics.

As a fifth observation, I would mention Snowers and Karanassou's paper, because I was very taken by their discussion of volatility and persistence. I found it a little bit complicted, as things always are at the beginning when you start out on them. I could not see the immediate implications for policy, because one of the important points was whether what you were analysing was believed to be temporary or permanent, and you don't know that. The authors' reply was that "at least, if it matters, you're better off recognising that it matters" and that is also a fair point.

I use this just to make a general point about policy design: it would be enormously helpful if everyone who does this sort of work would give appropriate thought to how to design policies that are likely to prove robust in the face of quite different shocks which cannot be predicted in advance. I say that because I am now inclined to think that the 1950s and 1960s were not normal but, on the contary, *abnormal*; that the 1970s and the 1980s, with all their shocks, were more the norm than the exception.

In other words, as we entered the 1970s and got hit by all those shocks — oil shocks, exchange rate shocks, and so on — we tended to regard these simply as shocks and say that they had messed up the good functioning of our economies. But we have had a succession of them; we have had shocks for two and a half decades now. That leads me, at least, to conclude that we should regard shocks as normal; and hence we should set policies in such a way as to maximise the chances of our economies being able to cope well rather than badly with them, and put the 1950s and 1960s on one side as being of unprecedented and possibly unrepeatable smoothness.

Last point. I would emphasise again, that when fiscal policy is mentioned, the tone is, «Well yes, it is a problem". But the closer you actually get to the people who are responsible for setting tax rates and controlling expenditures, the more you see that it is a tremendous problem. There is terrific pressure today in all our member countries, without exception, on the public sector budget. So any argument which can enable governments to persuade electorates of the desirability of keeping public expenditures under control, of demonstrating the problems that you get from deficits or, more particularly, from very large debt, is welcome.

It is obviously so welcome that OECD member countries are starting to consider anew the charters that they give to some of their institutions. This discussion about the degree of independence it is appropriate to give a central bank, for example, is a fascinating one. So I would commend Nordhaus in particular, if I might be so bold, for a clear and very simple demonstration which one can make to people, saying: "Look, here is an argument showing why you need to co-operate internally in the setting of policy, because if you do not you can get something which is worse than either of you would have dared think about". The conclusion there is an obvious one, but it is important: it is very useful to explain to policy makers and to the public the benefit of co-operative procedures in policy setting.

So, to summarise the conclusions. We should all be careful about our estimates of spare capacity, particularly that which can be taken up by demand; because, if we are right, we deserve to be listened to, but, if we are going to be listened to, we had better be right. Second, I think we need to know more about the conditions under which the long-term unemployed and the unskilled do or do not get taken into unemployment. I think that is going to be a very big issue for the future. Third conclusion, we have to understand this question of globalisation and *délocalisation* really rather urgently; there is a buring policy question waiting to catch a light there. And, last, I think we can be very helpful to governments if we show to them and to the public useful and convincing arguments, particularly in the fiscal-monetary area, of where co-operative policy setting with institutions that support it can be of help.

Guido Mario Rey

Terza Università, Roma

According to my view, unemployment, at least in Italy, suffers both from structural and cyclical situations, but the real point is that we can't say there is one Italian labor market. There are at least two labor markets, which are quite separate. Northern, and also central, Italy, suffers from a moderate cyclical and, perhaps, also technological unemployment, while the one third of the population that lives in the south suffers from structural unemployment.

If this is the case, and all Italians know that this is the case because the 10% rate of unemployment is an average between 6% in the north and 18% in the south, it is very difficult to give general recommendations. Hence our critical position on the suggestions coming from the Commission, I think that we are not in a position to accept a general policy for fighting unemployment because we have these two situations.

First, there is this market which is segmented. And then there is the second situation, which is not always taken into acount: Italy's labor market is a very peculiar one, because nearly 25% of the labor market consists of independent workers, people who are trying to find a job in the tertiary sector and with low productivity. So we suffer from this situation inside the labor market both from the supply and the demand side.

Now for my recommendations. With this situation, the first recommendation, which I make every time, is that we must give more flexibility to the labor market and favor the possibility of increasing employment in medium and small enterprises, where the larger part of our employment is. So I think that we must give some favored position to this kind of employers. Secondly, according to the situation in the southern part of Italy, I don't believe that an expansionary monetary policy or an expansionary fiscal policy will help this situation very much. We need to have the possibility of developing a really strong policy for the industrialization of this part of our country.

I understand that saying these things in 1993 can seem quite old; but I want to remind my friends that, at the end of the 1970s, we decided that we needed to make the industries of the north more competitive, and we decided to give to the sourthern part of Italy transfers, a social policy and things like that. The result is that, after ten years, we are suffering from structural unemployment in the south, we have a large public debt, and, at this moment, I can say that the policy was wrong because we were not able to ensure self-sustained growth in the south while the north is becoming more selfish as the amount of resources necessary to maintain stable the differences in north-south per-capita income is growing . It has been said that the jury is always out but I think that, in this case, we can make some judgments now.

Patrick Minford
University of Liverpool

I think that the key stylized fact at the moment is the enormously high level of unemployment in Europe and its contrast with that of many non-European countries, particularly if you make appropriate adjustments for definition and so forth. I think the table here makes that point, particularly on long-term unemployment. I would make two sets of recommendations, one on the natural rate side, the other on the demand side.

Let me start with the natural rate. May I say that the jury is out in lots of areas. But I don't think the jury is really out on one important feature of world systems, namely that capitalist systems generally function rather well and socialist systems are generally a failure. And the more you muck about with capitalist systems, the more of a failure they are. I think we have had a lot of evidence from recent and more distant history about that. Therefore, when I make these remarks about the natural rate, it seems to me that the jury is not out on these aspects of how to organize ourselves.

I believe, in fact, that, although in the UK we have a lot of problems, we have nevertheless moved some way in terms of restoring a proper market in the labour market. I have argued already that our unemployment has a very large demand component. So my first set of policy recommendations on the natural rate really is that in Europe there needs to be a complete reassessment of the role of market forces in the labor market. Let me go down a list of things that I would do in Europe.

I would abolish the social charter. This is a complete *cul-de-sac* that will undoubtedly cause endless headaches in Europe if it continues to be taken seriously. To give you just one piece of evidence — I could give you many more — look at Germany today and the comments of leading German industrialists about the problems of investment in Germany and the statement that they are going to relocate their investments in other areas because of high social costs. So the social charter program faces in exactly the wrong direction for Europe and should be scrapped and reversed.

Secondly, the role of unions in Europe is totally out of date. In continental Europe in particular, with the exception of France, you find large unions which create enormous inflexibilities and excess wages and difficulties of adjustment in the labor market. Part of the secret of the low unemployment rates in countries like the United States and Japan is a different type of union and a different type of labor relations related to a modern type of union, more like a company-wide union, which cooperates in a flexible way with the objectives of a given company. That's what we are seeing in the UK, I am glad to say: the growth of company-wide unions which cooperate totally in flexible labor practices. Other things allied to this are the immense degree of regulation of hiring and firing across Europe. This is one part of this whole set of regulatory structures which I would change wholesale, indeed just get rid of.

Then I would turn to the point raised by Professor Rey, which I entirely agree with. Another of the stylized facts of Europe is that regional support of the old sort has been a total failure. In Britain we experimented with this for three decades and got precisely nowhere. From 1979 we virtually abolished the whole concept of regional support with dramatic effects on the divide between our north and our south. Our north is like the Italian south. And the best recipe for the south in Italy's case and the north in our case is to abolish regional support and force them to adjust to market realities. It has dramatic impacts, I can assure you. Look at the resurgence of our north. I mentioned Wales earlier. This is a classic example.

Lastly, I would look, obviously, at the tax rate. You can't have a thriving economy with a high tax rate and part of the European disease is high taxes and high public spending. It's extraordinary. You go through the public accounts in the UK, and I'm sure the same is true in Italy and everywhere else, and you find that there are hundreds of programs all of whose justification is the eradication of unemployment. But unemployment inexorably goes on rising, and the programs rise with it to combat unemployment. Actually, these programs are part of the problem, because they raise taxes, create a fiscal problem which requires taxes to rise, creating an even less well-working labor market.

So my first point, in short, is take the natural rate literature seriously, take free markets seriously, and completely reverse the tone of European comment on these matters, which Mr. Fina graphically illustrates, it seems to me. The European disease is quite obvious in pronouncements by the European Commission. Excuse my aggressiveness.

Secondly, demand. If I may take as my text Mr. Fina's first pronouncement from the Council (he's not responsible, of course; he's just speaking for the Council), that we must keep progress towards EMU. Well, this is totally unrealistic. Our big problems of demand have come from the attempt to achieve EMU grossly prematurely. As Professor Fitoussi notes, we have had extraordinarily and inappropriately high real interest rates in Europe because of the absurd attempts we have made to make currencies come together when they were naturally apart, in a situation of very sharp shocks, particularly in Germany.

So I would say, the first recommendation, if we are going to get a sensible demand policy in Europe, is to have a return to independently managed currencies, each no doubt with the help of an independent central bank (this seems to me to be a quite harmless proposal, with some technical efficiency benefits). Let the central banks talk to each other in Europe, but let their currencies be independent. Let them have a crawling peg.

If you talk about a crawling peg in Europe, this is politically correct; if you talk about floating, which is the same thing, it is politically incorrect. So let me say let us make the ERM a crawling peg arrangement and give our central banks independence; and let us stop talking about the nonsense of EMU, whose time has nowhere near come. That will cure, I think, the demand problems that Professor Fitoussi has rightly referred to. This extraordinary tightness of monetary policy, which has also partly contributed to the enormous problems of fiscal policy, because, of course, if your economy is in massive recession, you don't have any revenues, and you're spending an awful lot to keep people from revolting on the streets.

I believe, finally, after Mr. Llewellyn's comments, that this is an entirely responsible set of recommendations in the spirit of many of his. In fact, economists are constantly being misinterpreted by political policy people. What happens is that the policy people get bitten with a new doctrine, and then there is a thing called "policy overshoot", which is where they misinterpret the policy and, like the convert on the road to Damascus, again go to the opposite extreme. Somehow our role is to keep them somewhere in the middle, where they are sensible.

Index